Management
Control in
Government

Management Control in Government

Alan Walter Steiss
Virginia Polytechnic Institute and
State University

LexingtonBooks
D.C. Heath and Company
Lexington, Massachusetts
Toronto

Library of Congress Cataloging in Publication Data

Steiss, Alan Walter.
  Management control in government.

  Includes bibliographical references and index.
  1. Public administration. 2. Management information systems.
  3. Managerial accounting. 4. Organizational effectiveness. I. Title.
  JF1411.S72   350.007'5   81–48524
  ISBN 0–669–05375–9   AACR2

Published simultaneously in Canada

Printed in the United States of America

International Standard Book Number: 0–669–05375–9

Library of Congress Catalog Card Number: 81–48524

Contents

List of Figures

List of Tables

Acknowledgments

The author would like to express thanks and appreciation to Leo Herbert for his helpful comments on the manuscript, especially the chapters on accounting and audit procedures; to Joseph C. King for his background research on productivity improvement; to Richard E. Zody for some insights into the applications of management by objective; and to Susie Reed and Joy Compton for their patience in typing and retyping the manuscript for this book.

1 Management Control in the Public Sector

Management controls have been applied for as long as formal organizations have existed. Until recently, however, these processes and techniques have not been the subject of systematic analysis or application.[1] The need for more comprehensive procedures to direct and control organizational activities to some purposeful objectives has become a primary concern of management in the private sector in the past fifty years. Systematic application of management-control techniques is an even more recent phenomenon in the public sector.

A number of notable books deal with the subject of management control; however, these books focus primarily on the application of control techniques in business and industry.[2] This book will examine the potential transfer of these important processes to government agencies and public organizations. Increased emphasis on *accountability* in the public sector makes the adoption (and adaptation) of effective management-control techniques all the more imperative.

Definitions of Management Control

Early definitions of management control tend to emphasize the importance of initiating corrective action when errors are discovered or when deviations occur from some predetermined course of events (that is, a plan or program). In one of the better-known definitions, Henri Fayol suggests that: "Control consists of verifying whether everything occurs in conformity with the plan adopted, the instructions issued, and principles established. It has for an object to point out weaknesses and errors in order to rectify and prevent recurrence."[3] Along similar lines, William T. Jerome defines executive control as a "systematic effort to compare current performance to a predetermined plan or objective, presumably to take any immediate action required."[4] Harold Koontz and Cyril O'Donnell emphasize the need to continuously measure performance and to take corrective action "in order to make sure that enterprise objectives and the plans devised to attain them are accomplished."[5]

Positive Action versus Correction

Some authors have closely linked management control, budgeting, and accounting. Overall financial control is the area most often dealt with in management textbooks written for use in the private sector. Robert Anthony has somewhat broadened this traditional definition by suggesting that "management planning is the process by which managers assure that resources are obtained and used effectively and efficiently in the accomplishment of the organization's objectives."[6] In a subsequent book, written with Glenn A. Welsch, Anthony further generalizes this definition by dropping the reference to resources and by placing management control in a hierarchy bounded by *strategic planning*—"the process of deciding on the goals of the organization and the strategies that are to be used in attaining these goals"—and *operational control*—"the process of assuring that specific tasks are carried out effectively and efficiently."[7]

Robert Mockler suggests that greater emphasis should be placed on positive (instead of negative) control action. His definition of management control is:

> a systematic effort to set performance standards consistent with planning objectives, to design information feedback systems, to compare actual performance with these predetermined standards, to determine whether there are any deviations and to measure their significance, and to take any action required to assure that all corporate resources are being used in the most effective and efficient way possible in achieving corporate objectives.[8]

Thus, Mockler asserts that the setting of standards is the most critical aspect of control. The more realistic the standards, the more meaningful are the conclusions drawn from the comparison of actual performance. He also suggests that those individuals within an organization who must apply such evaluative standards should participate in their formulation. "Experience has shown that inaccurate standards are found to be the cause of a deviation almost as often as operating deficiencies."[9]

The emphasis on standards as a frame of reference in the control process is also reflected in Joseph Litterer's definition:

> We are concerned with control in relation to matching performance with necessary or required conditions to obtain a purpose or objective. The essence here is on directivity and integration of effort, required accomplishment of an end. . . . Control is concerned not only with the events directly related to the accomplishment of major purposes, but also with maintaining the organization in a condition in which it can function adequately to achieve these major purposes.[10]

Management controls can provide the tools for determining whether the organization is proceeding toward established objectives. Management control can also alert decision makers when actual performance deviates from planned performance and can help to identify the magnitude of this deviation. This management control system can be represented schematically as shown in figure 1-1.

Four Fundamental Elements of Management Control

As figure 1-1 suggests, management control involves four interrelated activities. First, the organization must establish a set of standards against which any deviations from planned activities can be measured. Second, monitoring devices must be developed to measure the performance of individuals, programs, or the system as a whole. Third, the measurements obtained through various monitoring devices must be compared to determine whether the current state of the system (or some subsystem) approximates the planned state. Finally, action devices must be applied to correct any significant deviation. The corrective action may involve attempts to bring performance in line with plans or to modify plans to more closely reflect performance.

Richard Johnson, Fremont Kast, and James Rosenzweig offer a different but useful set of terms for the four-step control process.[11] They suggest four fundamental elements: (1) a characteristic or condition to be controlled, (2) a sensor—a way to measure the characteristic or condition, (3) a comparator—an individual, unit, or device that compares measurements with the plan or standard, and (4) an activator—an individual, unit, or

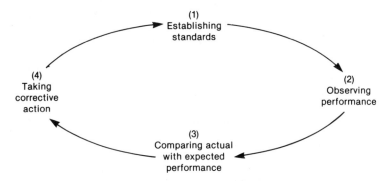

Figure 1-1. Four Elements of Management Control

mechanism that directs action to bring about a change in operating the system.

The terminology of systems theory has found broad application in contemporary discussions of management control.[12] Kast and Rosenzweig, for example, draw analogies to homeostasis and dynamic equilibrium and cite the linkage of the concept of cybernetics to the ancient Greek word for helmsmanship. Robert Albanese discusses the differences between closed-loop and open-loop control processes, suggesting that most control processes of concern to managers are *open loop* in that they require human intervention for maintenance purposes. Gannon contrasts the notion of feedback and feedforward as applied to management control, emphasizing that feedback control is much more common, since feedforward systems are more difficult to establish.

Mockler elaborates on the four steps of the management-control process as follows, suggesting that this process closely parallels the problem-solving/decision-making process.

1. Diagnose the situation in order to define the control problem and the method for dealing with it. This investigation should result in simple statements of:
    a. The specific kind and level of control situation to be dealt with.
    b. The objective and scope of the control effort.
    c. The method to be used in solving the problem.
    d. The organization of the control effort.

2. Examine the control problem and review the facts in order to find the key factors affecting the problem and its solution. The principal areas of investigation include:
    a. Planning factors, such as important premises, goals, objectives, and major policies, implementation plans, and other factors related to planning at all levels within the organization.
    b. The specific characteristics of the operation or decision for which the control tools or systems are being created; this step would include a description of all activities affected by the control problem.
    c. The purpose for which the controls are being developed, including who will be using them and the kinds of decisions which will be made based on the system.
    d. The nature of the controls desired.
    e. The nature of the standards or criteria against which performance will be measured.
    f. Additional factors affecting the exercise of control.

3. Develop and evaluate alternative controls to determine the best tools, techniques, or system, and how they can best be put into operation. This phase might involve: an overall financial management system, cost accounting controls, specific operating controls, a management information system, reporting forms to facilitate information feedback, mathematical and analytical models, etc. Existing controls should be included as one of the alternatives.

4. Exercise the control. This involves comparing actual performance against established standards, determining significant deviations (including checking the accuracy of standards and performance data), and taking action as necessary.[13]

Planning versus Control

It has been said that: "If you don't know where you're going, any road will get you there." There also is truth in the thought: "If you don't know where you're going, no road will get you there." In short, planning is a prerequisite for effective management, whether in the private or public sector.

Planning in the Private Sector

Until the beginning of the twentieth century, most private organizations did not systematically plan their activities. Rather, they merely reacted to more immediate problems as they occurred. The DuPont Company introduced the concept of planning in the private sector around 1900. Although a few major companies followed DuPont's lead, it was not until the end of World War II that many companies began to realize that their success, and even their existence, depended on careful and systematic planning. A number of major companies today have separate planning departments that are larger and more technically competent than the planning agencies in most units of government.

The definitions of planning adopted in the private sector are compatible with the views of public planners. Albanese, for example, suggests that: "Planning is the process or activity of determining in advance specifically what needs to be done in order to achieve particular goals, how it should be done, when and where it should be done, and who should do it."[14] Similarly, Martin Gannon suggests that: "Planning involves two key aspects: developing the *goals* an organization seeks to attain, and deciding on the *means* to achieve them."[15] Gannon further suggests that: "Means to achieve an objective takes two forms: strategies and tactics. *Strategies* are the means to accomplish the overall objective or objectives of the organization. *Tactics* are the means to attain specific objectives that relate directly to the overall objective or objectives."[16] This distinction between strategies and tactics is an important one and has led to a further delineation of levels of planning, including strategic planning, tactical or management planning, and operations planning or programming.

It is interesting to note that writers in the field of business management seldom use the term *comprehensive* in their definitions of planning. Kast and Rosenzweig are an exception; their definition of planning is as follows:

Planning is the process of deciding in advance what is to be done and how. It involves determining overall missions, identifying key results areas, and setting specific objectives as well as developing policies, programs, and procedures for achieving them. Planning provides a framework for integrating complex systems of interrelated future decisions. *Comprehensive planning is an integrative activity that seeks to maximize the total effectiveness of an organization as a system in accordance with its objectives.* [17]

One reason for the absence of the term *comprehensive* is that most authors in the field of business management recognize that there must be more than one plan—that planning must be a dynamic process.

One-Shot Optimizations

The watchword in the field of public planning for many years was: "Make no little plans." Although intended as an admonition against narrow vision and short-range time perspectives, many planners took this dictum quite literally, producing multipage and multicolor documents destined to gather dust on bookshelves, often before the ink was dry. The emphasis of planning evolved from the Master Plan—a guide to the physical development of the city—to the Comprehensive Plan. Comprehensive Plans became elaborate documents, that sought to address a wide range of functions and activities in the public and private sectors that must be considered to implement planning proposals.

Unfortunately, a plan seldom can be all-inclusive in this functional sense. In dealing with the complex set of relationships that must be considered in planning for any dynamic system, it is highly unlikely that all the functional relationships can be handled within a single conceptual framework. To be truly comprehensive, a plan must be more than merely an aggregation of many parts into a whole. The most vital aspect of the comprehensiveness of any plan is its ability to clarify the interactions among selected component parts over time.

All too often, a Comprehensive Plan is formulated as a one-shot effort at the outset of policy development. It has been said, however, that "few plans survive contact with the enemy." And, indeed, rarely are policies and programs executed exactly as initially conceived. Random events, environmental disturbances, competitive tactics, and unforeseen circumstances may all conspire to thwart the smooth implementation of policies, plans, and programs. There is a growing recognition that fixed targets, static plans, and repetitive programs are of relatively little value in a dynamic society.

As G.F. Chadwick has observed, for too long planning education and public planners have been concerned primarily with the contents of plans.

"Planners are not taught to plan—they are stuffed full of bewildering and indigestible facts about the possible contents of plans, as well as many things that are the concern of other professions, but surely, not that of the planner."[18] This focus on contents, in turn, results in one-shot optimizations—plans for some specific future target. Thus, it is common practice to formulate a plan for some date twenty to thirty years in the future. Under such an approach, planning frequently becomes a cumulative activity; that is, all the component parts are added up to determine what the whole might look like. By definition, this cumulative approach is short-range planning over a long period. Problem solving takes precedence over the establishment of effective long-range goals and objectives.

The growing dissatisfaction with the traditional Comprehensive Plan is perhaps best summed up by Constance Perin: "[Comprehensive planning] has patently obsessive characteristics. The 'incompleteness' being masked by endless and diffuse studies may relate closely to the fact that analytic work in . . . planning has yet to make its peace with the tolerable range of error appropriate to each topic it deals with."[19] Thus, Perin concludes that ". . . fear of being found 'wrong' in a recommendation or 'incomplete' in the range of variables studied has led to an abuse of 'open-endedness' and 'flexibility' as important to the planning 'process.' "

The Need to Integrate Planning and Control

The links between planning and control are explicitly recognized in the definitions of several contemporary authors. Kast and Rosenzweig, for example, define organizational control as: "the phase of the managerial process concerned with maintaining organizational activity within allowable limits, as measured from expectations. Organizational control is inextricably intertwined with planning. Plans provide the framework against which the control process works. On the other hand, feedback from the control phase often identifies the need for new plans or at least adjustments to existing ones."[20]

Similarly, Albanese suggests that: ". . . *premises* made when formulating plans influence the process of controlling. Significant changes in any of the major planning premises can cause performance to go 'out of control' . . . . the *characteristics* of plans influence the control process. Long-range plans, for example, require the application of different control techniques than those used in the control of short-range, standing plans. Plans involving more than one subsystem may require more coordination to control than plans limited to one subsystem."[21]

Finally, Gannon suggests that you cannot have one (control) without the other (planning): "*Control* is the monitoring of plans and the pinpointing of significant deviations from them. Hence planning and control are intimately related and, in fact, represent opposite sides of the same coin. Without planning, there can be no control."[22] Most contemporary texts on management and organization theory written for use in the private sector include chapters on both planning and control. More will be said about the relationships between these two management functions in a subsequent section.

Management Information Systems

Effective planning and control of an organization or program require good information systems. Information flow is vital to the decision-making and management processes. Information is the raw material of intelligence that touches off the recognition that decisions need to be made. Information is essential in understanding the circumstances surrounding an issue and in evaluating alternative courses of action. The more pertinent and timely the information, the better the resulting decision is.

Information often is evaluated by its pertinence for decision making. Facts, numbers, and data are processed to provide meaningful information—in this sense, information is incremental knowledge that reduces the degree of uncertainty in a particular situation. Miscellaneous accounting data, for example, provide information when arrayed appropriately in balance sheets and financial statements. However, if the problem is related to an evaluation of the effectiveness of a new program, traditional accounting data, however elaborately processed, may be relatively meaningless. Thus, what constitutes information depends on the problem at hand and the particular frame of reference of the decision maker.

Purpose of a Management Information System

The challenge of an efficient information system is twofold: (1) to provide the proper kinds and quantities of information to each manager, and (2) to present it in an understandable format. The primary objective of a management information system is to aid the manager in making timely and informed decisions. Providing vast amounts of data is not an end in itself, however. In fact, it is quite possible to literally cover up the manager with hoards of data, much of which may be relatively meaningless or useless in making decisions. As Richard Ensign has observed: "Without clear definitions of decision points, their information needs, and the opportunities they present, data processing can drown the managers it is intended to serve."[23] Moreover, data processing is an expense that is hard to justify if it does not improve the decision-making ability of the manager.

Figure 1-2 illustrates the basic components of a management information system. Information is received from both internal and external sources. Relevant information is identified and taken into the decision-making process. Effects of decisions on both the external and the internal environments are then compared against established standards. As necessary, corrective action is then taken at the decision-making stage or at the information-sources stage.

A somewhat more elaborate model of the basic flow of information necessary for the management system is presented by Kast and Rosenzweig in *Organization and Management* (p. 356). Management considers internal and environmental information in the process of establishing objectives (strategic level). Premises regarding governmental relations, political conditions, client needs and desires, internal capabilities, and other factors evolve over time to form a frame of reference for strategic planning. Plans for repetitive and nonrepetitive activities are transmitted to the operating system and are "stored" in the coordination and control systems for later comparisons with operating results (coordinative and operating levels). Detailed orders, instructions, and specifications flow to the operating system.

The output of the system should be examined in terms of quality (effectiveness), quantity (efficiency of service levels), cost, and so on. The operating system should be monitored to maintain *process control,* and an examination of inputs provides feedback at the earliest stage in the operating system. Information flow is an integral part of the control system because it provides the means of comparing results with plans. Feedback data from various phases of the operating system are analyzed, and results are compared with plans. Decisions also are made within the control system itself,

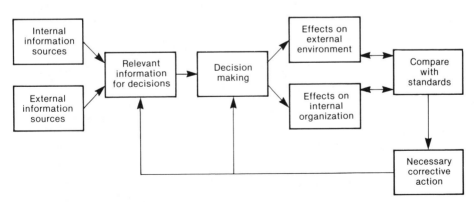

Adapted from Herbert G. Hicks and C. Ray Gullett, *The Management of Organizations* (New York: McGraw-Hill, 1976), p. 527.

Figure 1-2. Basic Components of a Management Information System

because routine adjustments can be preprogrammed in the set of procedures or instructions. A flow of information within the control system triggers changes to the program based on feedback from the operating system. Thus, procedures are changed and files updated simultaneously with routine decision making and adjustments to the operating system.

Summary and exception reports, generated by the control system, become a part of a higher-level process of review and evaluation. This evaluation may lead to adaptation or innovation of goals and objectives. Subsequent planning activities reflect such feedback, and the entire process is repeated. In time, an organization "learns" through the process of planning, implementation, and feedback.[24] Approaches to decision making and the propensity to select certain ends and means change as organizational value systems evolve. This basic model of information flow can be applied to any organization. It shows the necessary flow of information, regardless of the sophistication of the data-processing technology involved.

Anthony Catanese and Alan Steiss offer a variation on this basic theme in their proposed decision-making system.[25] Three specific areas of information provide the data inputs for the formulation of a technical forecast: (1) autointelligence, which provides information about the component elements of the particular system under study; (2) environmental intelligence, which provides information about the broader environment—the "out there"—of which the particular system is a part; and (3) historical data, which are used to bring together and analyze the lessons of past experiences. On these foundations, probablistic forecasts provide the first and fundamental step in rational planning. Such forecasts represent a weighed and balanced analysis, rather than an intuitive impression, of current trends and their possible effect on development in the future.

In view of these predictions, the focus of the search is to determine possible new technical, tactical, and strategic courses of action that will enhance the overall performance of the system. The forecasts outline the probable happenings in the continuance of hypothetical futures. Using various systematic techniques of analysis, the possible directions to be taken can be identified to suggest ways in which the larger environment can be manipulated to the competitive advantages of the system (or organization). Ideas and proposals provided from the forecast-research chain must be matched with the resources available as well as with the overall goals and objectives of the system now and in the foreseeable future. The basic problem of decision makers today, whether in the public or private sectors, is to achieve a balance in the programs and choices made so as to ensure a *systems readiness* in the short-, mid-, and long-range futures. This requires a posture of sufficient flexibility to meet a wide range of possible competitive actions.

Organizational Level and Management-Information Needs

The types and sources of information needed by managers varies by organizational level. John Burch and Felix Strater suggest a three-level classification: strategic, tactical, and technical.[26] At the *strategic* level, long-range plans and policies are very important; external data are of prime significance. Decisions at this level tend to be more intuitive and less subject to predetermined decision rules. The art of management is more important, and the manager relies on the best judgment he or she can muster.

Tactical decisions are those made by middle-level managers. They involve putting into effect the plans of top management and controlling the efforts of first-line supervisors and program managers. The objective of such decisions is to serve as the interface between strategic plans and the operational activities. To perform effectively, middle managers must rely more heavily on information generated within the organization.

Technical decisions are those made by first-line supervisors. Their primary interest is in controlling the day-to-day operations of programs. Internal information is more important to successful decision making at this level, and the process is generally much more structured than at either of the other two levels. This greater degree of structure often allows many of the problems to be stated as mathematical relationships and to be solved in a predetermined manner through the use of standard-operation research techniques.

Much attention has been focused on computerized management information systems. It is important to recognize, however, that managerial decision making typically requires input of much information that cannot be computerized. Thus, overall management information systems should be designed to include explicit attention to nonquantifiable inputs as well as those that result from computerized data-processing applications.[27]

What Can Managers Control?

It has been said that managers manage people rather than things. In other words, by managing people, managers indirectly manage all other types of factors that enter into performance—for example, materials, supplies, equipment, and the financial resources necessary to support these factors. Managers also manage information—an important factor often overlooked in listing the tangible factors of performance. Managers seldom deal directly with a problem situation; rather, they deal almost exclusively with information about the problem. In turn, managers must make decisions that best satisfy not actual conditions but, rather, information about those conditions.

Pareto's Law and Cost Points

There are four aspects of performance that can be controlled: (1) quantity, (2) quality, (3) time, and (4) cost. These four controllable aspects, in turn, can be related to the major functions of an organization. Each of these functions may be very specialized in its use of control techniques. They also are applicable to control sets that might be applied to human and non-human factors of performance. For example, the quality of employee performance might be controlled by written job instructions, policies that assure consistent job behavior, training programs designed to increase skill levels, wage and salary plans that reward quality, and so forth. Inventory-system procedures, on the other hand, provide the control of the quantity of things.

Vilfredo Pareto, a turn-of-the-century Italian economist and sociologist, formulated a "law" that has interesting application in controlling quantity and cost. Pareto's law states that "the significant elements in a specified group usually constitute a relatively small portion of the total items in the group."[28] For example, a university may have over five-hundred sponsored research projects in force at any one time; of these projects, less than 10 percent generate 80 percent of the problems that require the attention of central administration. When Pareto's law applies, the manager should identify the significant elements in the total set and concentrate control efforts on those elements. In effect, this law supports the notion of *management by exception.*

The basic notion of Pareto's law is reflected in Peter Drucker's concept of cost points.[29] A *cost point* is an activity within a manager's area of responsibility that accounts for a significant portion of total cost. There may be several cost points in any one *responsibility* or *cost center.* Drucker suggests that major cost points fall into four major categories: (1) productive costs, which contribute directly to the value of the product or service; (2) support costs, which provide no direct client value but are necessary to support production; (3) policing costs, aimed at preventing things from going wrong; and (4) waste, the cost of efforts that produce no productive, support, or policing results.

A guiding principle in applying controls to any of these cost points is that the marginal cost of the last control expenditure should be equal to the marginal benefit received. The costs and benefits of controlling, however, should not be thought of simply in financial terms. Costs of controlling can take the form of dollars, lost time, negative attitudes, lowered job expectations, dysfunctional job behavior, adverse client relations, and so forth. Benefits can take many forms, such as cost and time savings, improved morale, higher job expectations, improved client and public relations, quality improvements, and so forth.

Most managers and students of management agree with the idea that controls have no value in themselves. As with plans and organization, the value of controls is instrumental to goal achievement. In practice, however, controls often are imbued with some intrinsic value. Long after they serve any useful purpose, controls are retained "for their own value." As with plans that are obsolete and organizations that are unresponsive to the needs of people served, inappropriate controls can hinder goal achievement.

A difficult problem for managers is to determine the most appropriate amounts and kinds of controls to use in their areas of responsibility. Too much control can stifle initiative and encourage behavior designed to "beat the system." Too little control unnecessarily increases the probability that desired results will not be achieved.

Financial versus Nonfinancial Controls

Overall control cannot be maintained without a systematic network of financial controls that extends into every operating area of an organization. These controls help monitor costs, performance effectiveness (profits or benefits achieved), and the use of assets. Such controls are essential to organizational survival. Because this aspect of management control is so important, accounting and finance departments traditionally serve as the locus of the control function in both public and private organizations.

The concept of management control is much broader, however, as suggested by the definitions offered at the outset of this discussion. Management control is a functional process which makes use of a variety of control tools, not just accounting and financial tools. These controls operate in many different situations at all levels of an organization. Operating managers have always found it necessary to develop and maintain a variety of nonfinancial controls.

Nonfinancial controls are those designed to monitor critical activities in programmatic areas of responsibility—activities that affect performance efficiency, economy, and effectiveness. From an operating manager's point of view, such nonfinancial controls may be far more relevant and immediately useful than traditional financial controls. Often these controls must be tailor-made to the particular area of responsibility in which they are to be applied. Many large companies have established systems-development departments to assist in the development of appropriate operating controls. The systems specialist is not trapped by the financial-control mold. He or she is trained to examine total information networks for control, of which financial controls are only one aspect. Therefore, the systems analyst fills the gap in staff-control assistance and provides professional aid to operating managers in developing appropriate networks of controls.

Similar developments can be seen in nascent stages in many government organizations. For example, the recent establishment of a Management Analysis and Systems Development Department (MASD) in the Commonwealth of Virginia represents a significant first step. Enhancing the staff of the Joint Legislative Audit and Review Commission (JLARC) with nonaccountant personnel also strengthens the state's capacity to respond to contemporary management-control needs. Other states and localities have begun to organize similar staffing arrangements.

Types of Controls

Johnson, Kast, and Rosenzweig suggest that controls can be classified as either organizational or operational.[30] Methods of organizational control evaluate the overall performance of the organization or a significant part thereof. Measurement standards in the private sector—such as profitability, ratio of assets to liabilities, and sales growth—provide a broad basis on which to assess the overall performance of an organization. In subsequent discussions, such standards applicable to public-sector activities will be detailed in terms of *measures of effectiveness*. Remedies for failure to meet such control standards often are equally broad based and may include redesigned objectives, reformulated plans, changes in organizational structure, improved internal and external communications, and so forth.

Operational controls measure day-to-day performance by providing comparisons with various standards to determine areas requiring more immediate corrective action. Whereas organizational-control measures may be rather broadly based, operational controls are very specific and situational. Such measures most frequently focus on issues of efficiency and economy. Measures such as productivity ratios, workload measures, unit costs are examples of such *performance measures*. These measures will be discussed in further detail in the section on performance evaluation.

Herbert Hicks and C. Ray Gullett suggest a further classification of controls, based on the time at which they are applied.[31] Many control methods measure results after the fact; they inform management as to how well objectives were met after some time lag or delays. The time lag between the emergence of specific problems and the actual detection may be such that they cannot be corrected; rather, effort is placed on trying to keep the same problems from happening again. Financial and budgetary controls are good examples of such techniques. When financial statements are prepared, they provide a snapshot of how the organization or program has been doing in a preceding time period. Such statements may point out in what areas, if any, future corrective action is needed. It is too late, however, to resolve the specific problems identified.

Concurrent or *real-time controls* measure deviations from standards more or less as they occur. Such controls permit a program to perform within established tolerance as it moves through time. An example of concurrent control techniques in the private sector is the quality-control chart used in production operations. Statistical samples of the product are taken periodically and measured for their adherence to some quality standard. If the samples begin to appear outside the established quality limits, corrective actions can be taken before additional items are produced. Computers have made possible and practical real-time-control devices. A dramatic example of real-time control is the reservation system used by most major airlines. These systems allow airport managers and technical personnel to know exactly and immediately the passenger-load status of any and all airplanes. The inventory-control systems adopted by some retail establishments, such as large department stores or supermarkets, provide another example of real-time controls made possible by computer technology.

Such concurrent control devices are rare in the public sector. Surveys of client satisfaction and other sampling techniques are applicable in the assessment of some public-service-delivery systems. Some public-operated utility systems have adopted such control devices to monitor supply needs in peak-load periods. Experiments have been conducted using concurrent controls in traffic-signal systems.

Whenever a control technique can anticipate and identify a problem before it happens, it is *predictive.* Such controls are related to the planning process and generally involve various forecasting and projection techniques.

Predictive, concurrent, and after-the-fact controls are all valuable to managers. Together they can provide a clearer picture of where the organization or program is and where it should be. A proper balance among these three types of controls can vastly improve the effectiveness of any organization. Historically, however, evaluation in the public sector has relied largely on after-the-fact control measures.

Managers devote a large amount of their time to activities related to controlling. Control is so much a part of managerial work that management and control sometimes are viewed as one and the same activity. They are not identical, however, because goal setting and planning also are essential to effective management. The overwhelming majority of control processes used in organizations are relatively simple, unsophisticated, and noncomputerized. They are not real-time processes, and they more often are open loop than closed loop. Some very effective managerial control is the result of imagination and personal experience rather than formal knowledge about control processes.

The complexity and sophistication of a control system depends on the complexity and the sophistication of the project and the ability of the staff to administer it. A simple project may require a very simple control system, with few indicators to determine whether or not it is progressing on schedule and if it is within the desired cost and performance restrictions. A major project will require an extensive control system. Designing a control system can be an expensive endeavor. Therefore, the anticipated benefits of such a system should exceed the cost.

Basic Conditions of the System

Regardless of the degree of sophistication or complexity of a management control system, all such systems must meet certain basic conditions:

1. The system must be understood by those who use it and obtain data from it. It must be remembered that there are at least four different groups whose needs must be taken into consideration when designing a management-control system.

a. Top-management concerns include policy decisions and the relative effectiveness of particular projects.

b. Planners and analysts are very much concerned with obtaining data on estimating costs and benefits.

c. Operating managers are concerned not only with the strategic effectiveness of the program but with the administrative efficiency as well. They also must determine whether a project or program is on schedule.

d. Outside agencies' concerns include those of members of the legislature and the general public. They too have concerns that must be met through a program-management-control system.

2. The management control system must relate to the project organization, since the organization and the control system are interdependent.

3. The management control system must report deviations from the scheduled plan on a timely basis so that corrective action can be initiated before more serious deviations occur.

4. The system must be sufficiently flexible to remain compatible with the change in organizational environment.

5. It must be economical to be worth the additional maintenance expense.

6. It should indicate the nature of the corrective action required to bring the project or program back into compatibility with the plan.

7. It should reduce to a "language" (words, pictures, graphs or other models) that permits a visual display that is easy to read and comprehend.

8. The management control system should be developed through the active participation of all major executives involved in the project.

Expanded Version of the Corrective Model

The design of a management control system should commence at the very beginning of a project (see figure 1-3). The budgeting for a particular project begins the important function of identifying appropriate *standards*. Standards are based on input measures or the description of resources consumed and include: schedules, performance criteria, outputs, measures, and effectiveness. These standards should be developed as early in the project or program as possible, that is, in the development of the budget estimates and in design of the program schedule, when the resources are identified and an estimate of the anticipated time requirements are made. Based on the budget, a *work-breakdown schedule* (WBS) can be prepared. This schedule shows the physical product, milestones, and technical performance goals or other indicators, as well as the budget estimates required for each task, the starting and completion times for each task, and the assigned responsibilities for the task.

Once the project or program is initiated, management must begin to examine each individual *task*. The tasks for which a formal control process is created and maintained should focus on specific inputs, certain performance criteria, or outputs. After deciding which aspect to focus on, performance and program measures should be developed.

The establishment of a formal control process requires answers to such questions as: (1) What information characteristics are feasible from a technical standpoint? (2) What are the economic costs? (3) What are the expected benefits associated with obtaining information on each characteristic? (4) Does variation in the characteristics make any difference in the performance of the goals or the objectives of the task? Since the design and implementation of a system for program monitoring and control is expensive, it is suggested that managers should be selected for identified program measures.

A management information system includes the means for obtaining measurements of program achievements (that is, performance measures and measures of effectiveness). Such measurement may be through periodic intervention (that is, inquiry) in the ongoing management-information system or through automated reporting procedures (monthly fiscal summaries, for example). Sometimes the measurement may actually be undertaken by the individuals or groups whose performance is to be controlled. Care must be exercised in this approach, however, because self-measurement sometimes results in a loss of meaningful control. There is an inherent tendency

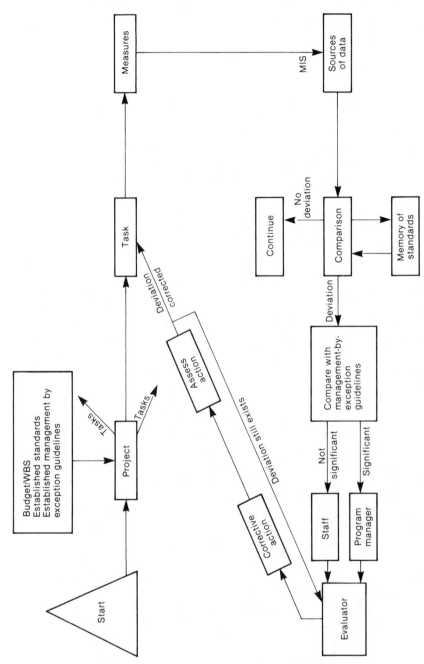

Figure 1–3. A Corrective Model of Management Control

to distort or conceal data that might be used as a basis for sanctions or that might reduce the availability of rewards. To counter this tendency, special organizational units often are created (for instance, internal auditors) to serve as sensors in the evaluation of certain activities or other organizational units.

The best information systems will not keep the manager out of trouble. However, they will help the manager from being surprised when trouble comes along. The acronym GIGO—"garbage in—garbage out"—has become a watchword in computer systems. A management-information system is only as good as its inputs. A good information system should: (1) identify the long-range objectives of projects or programs; (2) analyze available information in terms of its suitability to evaluate the progress of specific programs, projects, and activities (new information techniques should be employed only when a new problem exists or a new approach is being tried); (3) provide for the interfacing of information on specific programs or projects with the overall management information system of the organization (a management information system must be more than a collection of disjointed data designed to meet the unique needs of individual projects and programs); (4) establish a timetable for the development and implementation of additional information; and (5) accomplish this time plan within a framework that meets the needs of management.

The *comparison step* determines whether differences exist between actual activities and results and what should be occurring. That is, the comparator indicates if deviations from the original plan are occurring and, if so, the magnitudes of these deviations. Questions to ask might include: (1) Where does the project stand in relation to cost schedule and expected performance characteristics? (2) What are the interrelationship costs and schedule and performance characteristics such as output and effectiveness? (3) What is the evaluation of progress on the project?

This comparison of actual versus plan is extremely important. Although it provides basic information, not all deviations from the actual plan are of equal seriousness. Therefore, judgements must be made to determine whether the deviation from the plan warrants corrective action.

Evaluation involves the diagnosis or appraisal of the types, amount, and possible causes of deviations reported through the comparison step. The control system detects and reports exceptions, but it must also identify those deviations that, taken together, provide the greatest threat to the successful achievement of program objectives. The manager must evaluate those deviations in actual performance that significantly impact the consumption of scarce resources or the timely completion of scheduled activities. Effective management control is more than merely "putting out brushfires." If each deviation is seen as a crisis, the energies of management can quickly be dissipated, with little or no positive results in bringing the program activities back on track. Managers must decide which events are significant and which deviations must be corrected (or, in some cases, amplified, as they may represent positive as well as negative consequences of program activities).

Unless corrective action is taken when standards are not met, the control process amounts to little more than a historical record-keeping function. As soon as an unfavorable (significant) deviation from established standards is identified, the causes of the problem should be investigated. It may be discovered that the cause of the deviation is an unrealistic plan and may require a revision in the original plan or objectives. All too often plans are assumed to be fixed points rather than dynamic guidelines that may have to be altered to meet changing conditions.

Sometimes the gap between actual performance and the plan reflects a lack of effort; sometimes the gap in performance is the consequence of a simple misunderstanding or a failure to communicate expectations (goals and objectives). Before setting in motion corrective actions directed at the apparent source of the problem, managers should ask themselves: "Have I clearly identified and communicated to the program staff what I expected will be achieved in terms of this program or activity?" At times it must also be recognized that a reduction in productivity may be the result of events outside the immediate control of management.

Finally, management must make a systematic assessment of the effects of corrective action. Did the corrective action actually close the gap between planned and actual performance? If the answer is yes, then the various tasks can continue to be implemented and monitored. However, if the answer is no, then it is necessary to reevaluate the possible causes of the deviation and examine more closely the alternative courses of remedial action.

Notes

1. Chester Barnard's book, *Functions of the Executive* (Cambridge, Mass.: Harvard University Press, 1938) was among the first comprehensive efforts to deal with control and other management processes.

2. A notable exception is Robert N. Anthony and Regina Herzlinger, *Management Control in Nonprofit Organizations* (Homewood, Ill.: Richard D. Irwin, 1975). However, although the Anthony-Herzlinger book includes chapters on programming and budgeting procedures, its primary focus is on the accounting system as a control mechanism.

3. Henri Fayol, *General and Industrial Management* (New York: Pitman Corporation, 1949), p. 107.

4. William Travers Jerome III, *Executive Control—The Catalyst* (New York: John Wiley and Sons, 1961), p. 24.

5. Harold Koontz and Cyril O'Donnell, *Principles of Management: An Analysis of Managerial Functions* (New York: McGraw-Hill, 1968), p. 639.

6. Robert N. Anthony, *Planning and Control Systems: A Framework for Analysis* (Boston: Graduate School of Business Administration, Harvard University, 1965), p. 17.

7. Robert N. Anthony and Glenn A. Welsch, *Fundamentals of Management Accounting* (Homewood, Ill.: Richard D. Irwin, 1977), p. 445.

8. Robert J. Mockler, *The Management Control Process* (New York: Appleton-Century-Crofts, 1972), p. 2.

9. Ibid., p. 2.

10. Joseph A. Litterer, *The Analysis of Organizations* (New York: John Wiley & Sons, 1973), p. 528.3.

11. Richard A. Johnson, Fremont E. Kast, and James E. Rosenzweig, *The Theory and Management of Systems* (New York: McGraw-Hill, 1973), p. 75.

12. For particular applications of such "systems approaches" to management control see: Fremont E. Kast and James E. Rosenzweig, *Organization and Management* (New York: McGraw-Hill, 1979); Robert Albanese, *Management: Toward Accountability for Performance* (Homewood, Ill.: Richard D. Irwin, 1975); and Martin J. Gannon, *Management: An Organizational Perspective* (Boston: Little, Brown, 1977).

13. Mockler, *Management Control Process,* pp. 17–18.

14. Albanese, *Management: Toward Accountability* p. 166.

15. Gannon, *Management: Organizational Perspective,* p. 116.

16. Ibid., p. 117.

17. Kast and Rosenzweig, *Organization and Management,* pp. 416–417.

18. G.F. Chadwick, "A Systems View of Planning," *Journal of the Town Planning Institute* 52 (May 1966):184.

19. Constance Perin, "A Noiseless Secession from the Comprehensive Plan," *Journal of the American Institute of Planners* 33 (September 1967):338.

20. Kast and Rosenzweig, *Organization and Management,* p. 443.

21. Albanese, *Management Toward Accountability,* p. 185.

22. Gannon, *Management: Organizational Perspective,* p. 140.

23. Richard B. Ensign, "Measuring the Flow of Management Information," *Journal of Systems Management* 21 (February 1972):42.

24. Richard M. Cyert and James G. March, *A Behavioral Theory of the Firm* (Englewood Cliffs, N.J.: Prentice-Hall, 1963), p. 123.

25. Anthony J. Catanese and Alan Walter Steiss, *Systemic Planning: Theory and Application* (Lexington, Mass.: D.C. Heath, Lexington Books, 1970), pp. 48–52.

26. John G. Burch and Felix R. Strater, "Tailoring the Information System," *Journal of Systems Management* 22 (February 1973):34–38.

27. John Dearden, "MIS Is a Mirage," *Harvard Business Review* 50 (January–February 1972):90–99.

28. C.J. Slaybough, "Pareto's Law and Modern Management," *Price Waterhouse Review* 2 (Winter 1966):27.

29. Peter F. Drucker, *Managing for Results* (New York: Harper & Row, 1964), pp. 78–84.

30. Johnson, Kast, and Rosenzweig, *Theory and Management,* pp. 82–86.

31. Herbert G. Hicks and C. Ray Gullett, *The Management of Organizations* (New York: McGraw-Hill, 1976), pp. 499–501.

2 Accounting Systems: Traditional Mechanisms of Management Control

As noted in chapter 1, accounting systems traditionally have served as the major mechanisms of management control in many organizations, both private and public. As the American Accounting Association asserts: "Essentially, accounting is an information system. More precisely, it is an application of general theory of information to the problem of efficient economic operations. It also makes up a large part of the general information expressed in quantitative terms. In this context accounting is both a part of the general information system of an operating entity and a part of the basic field bounded by the concept of information."[1] An effective accounting system provides quantitative information for three broad purposes: (1) *external reporting* to various constituencies or client groups (for example, stockholders), elected officials, regulatory bodies, and the general public; (2) *internal reporting* for use in planning and controlling routine operations; and (3) *strategic planning,* that is, assisting in the formulation of overall policies and long-range plans. Traditional accounting procedures have served the first of these broad purposes reasonably well. Accounting records of financial transactions, with some interpretation, have been used successfully in the control of routine operations. However, traditional financial-accounting systems, and especially the procedures of fund accounting used in local and state government, have provided relatively little direct assistance in the activities of strategic planning.

Accounting and Management Information Systems

Accountants, as a matter of course, have furnished decision makers and managers with extensive data in the form of financial statements and reports. There is, however, a subtle but important difference between data and management information. *Data* may be defined as facts and figures from which conclusions may be drawn, whereas *information* is knowledge acquired or derived from facts. In short, information is data that have been analyzed and interpreted. An accounting system appropriate to support the informational needs of management must be expanded beyond traditional definitions, which tend to limit accounting to the processes of keeping books and reporting historical financial data on operating results. As Ross has observed: "The art of management has been defined as the making of irrevocable decisions based on incomplete, inaccurate, and obsolete information. It is probably not too unfair to say that this lack of complete and current information has been due in part to the failure of the accountant to provide it."[2]

Financial Accounting

Accounting serves as an information system to the extent that financial data and events are recorded, classified, summarized, interpreted, and communicated for decision-making purposes. The first three of these functions are closely associated with the control aspects of financial accounting—the process of ensuring efficient progress toward achieving predetermined fiscal objectives. Financial transactions and events are systematically recorded in accounting ledgers and are classified according to some predetermined chart of accounts. Periodically, the data so recorded and classified are summarized through the preparation of financial statements and reports.

Accounting control is not quite the same as management control, however. Management must recognize the need to alter previously established objectives in light of varying circumstances. The recorded, classified and summarized accounting data must be interpreted to reveal and analyze significant changes, trends, and potential developments having impact on policies and programs. The principal emphasis must be placed on the managerial significance of accounting facts, not on the facts themselves. Decision making depends on the effective communication of information for its success and often for its very existence.[3] Unless the interpreted data—the information—are communicated to decision makers and managers in the form that is useful to them, the data are of relatively little value. In short, financial accounting is part of the control function, but it is not synonymous with or the only major component of management control.

The primary purpose of financial accounting is to produce financial statements, as will be discussed further. Financial data must be collected in an acceptable form and with an acceptable degree of accuracy to meet the requirements of outside authorities, whether or not the accountant or the manager regards this information as useful.[4] Financial statements include primarily monetary information, describing the operations of an agency as a whole. Although financial-accounting information often is used as a basis for making future plans (for example, for budget building), the information itself is historical. Entries are made in the accounts only after transactions have occurred. When these financial statements have been prepared, the purpose of financial accounting has been accomplished.

Managerial Accounting

Managerial accounting is that branch of accounting theory and practice concerned with providing information useful in making decisions about the development of resources and the exploitation of programmatic opportunities.[5] Financial accounting focuses on the recording of fiscal transactions. Managerial accounting is involved in the formulation of financial estimates of future performance (the planning and budgeting processes) and, subsequently, in the analysis of actual performance in relation to these estimates (program evaluation and performance auditing).

The objective of managerial accounting is to improve the effectiveness of the planning and control functions. This approach is predicated on two basic assumptions. First, planning should be built on the same information base as the mechanisms of control. What management requires is not a grandiose master plan drawn in the abstract but rather the fundamental ability to know what is being spent where and for what purposes. Planning depends on the same reporting and control mechanisms that make central oversight possible and decentralized management feasible.[6] Building the mechanism of control on one data base (financial accounting) and the planning process on another (program analysis) places too great a stress on the management system as the intermediary. Second, the success of a decentralized management system is dependent on an understanding at the department level of the rules of the game and the incentives and expectations governing planning and budgeting. An important task of managerial accounting, then, is to enlarge the circle of those familiar with the process of planning and budgeting through the communication of pertinent management information as well as financial data.

In this latter connection, managerial accounting often is tied to (or is the product of) the techniques of management by objectives (MBO). MBO, in turn, requires a management-information and program-evaluation system (MIPES) that can anticipate the questions that decision makers must resolve and can focus information so as to facilitate solutions.

The significant features of managerial accounting can be summarized as follows:

1. Greater emphasis is placed on the generation of information for planning and programming purposes, thus seeking to establish a balance with the control function of accounting. Information for planning and programming is supplied through both workload estimates (expected demand levels) and unit-cost data.

2. Performance standards are added to the traditional control mechanisms based on legal compliance and fiscal accountability. Through the use of variance reports, the manager can analyze the extent to which deviations from expected performance (the exceptions) are efficiency variances or a

mixture of controllable and noncontrollable elements such as price changes.

3. Greater experimentation and innovation in the types of information supplied to management at various levels is encouraged.

4. An emphasis on performance standards and unit costs and the identification of cost and responsibility centers generates greater cost-consciousness among operating agencies.

5. The cost approach facilitates the linkage of management-control procedures with performance/program budgeting and performance auditing.

The main focus of managerial accounting is on segments of the total organization, that is, on individual activities, operations, programs, or other responsibility centers. Managerial accounting includes information that represents estimates and plans for the future of these centers, as well as information about the past. Much of the information in managerial accounting reports is nonmonetary. Although these reports contain financial data, they also contain data on number of employees and number of hours worked; quantities of materials used; purpose of travel; and so forth.

Managers need information on a real-time basis (that is, as problems occur and/or opportunities arise). Often they are willing to sacrifice some precision to gain in the currency of data. Thus, in managerial accounting, approximations often are as useful as, or even more useful than, numbers that are calculated to the last penny. Financial accounting cannot be absolutely precise (despite the mystique that often surrounds financial data), so that the difference is one of degree. Approximations used in managerial accounting are greater than those in financial accounting.

Although financial accounting and reporting are required of all public agencies, managerial accounting is an optional activity. No outside authority specifies what must be done in managerial accounting or, in fact, that such an activity must be carried out. There is little point in collecting any data unless the value, as an aide to management, is believed to exceed the cost of data collection.[7]

The informational boundaries of managerial accounting are not rigid. Although differences exist, many of the elements of financial accounting are found also in managerial accounting. Managerial accounting provides a basis for financial interpretations that assist in the formulation of policies and decisions and in the control of current and future operations. Such internal reporting to management may—and often does—require the collection and presentation of financial information in a completely different format than followed for external reporting.[8] In addition, it is necessary to understand management-decision models that have been developed within the field of managerial economics and finance, to supply decision-relevant information.[9] It also is important to understand the communication processes by which this information is transmitted through an organization.

Managerial accounting will not supercede financial accounting. Under an optimal system, however, new processes can be devised for the collection and application of both cost data and statistical data (for example, as to units or performance and services provided). With the adoption of such standards, there also must be recognized sanctions. Some performance and cost configurations will be highly satisfactory, others will be painfully inadequate. Work-unit performance and cost standards must be revised periodically to keep pace with changes in operations and, ultimately, must have the concurrence of those persons impacted by these management expectations.

Cost Accounting

As the name implies, cost accounting is concerned with costs in general and with cost-allocation methods and cost-determination systems. Cost accounting provides a connective link between financial and managerial accounting, encompassing a body of concepts and techniques used in both. Techniques of cost accounting began to find application in the late 1920s and early 1930s as an outgrowth of the scientific-management movement. These techniques were considered a special application of general accounting principles. In more recent applications, cost accounting has become more closely associated with the procedures of managerial accounting, and, in some texts, the two approaches are considered nearly synonymous.

Cost accounting, or adaptations of financial accounting that produce cost figures, and statistical reporting facilitate comparisons between actual expenditure patterns and performance and cost standards. Cost accounting may focus on a determination of costs by either programs, organizational units (agencies or departments), functions, responsibilities (activities), or work units. The stock in trade of the cost accountant includes project budgets, detailed ledger sheets, work schedules, standard costs per work unit, and related performance reports. Cost data generated from such a system may be compared with data of different time periods, with estimated or standard costs, or with alternative costs.

Knowledge of cost-behavior patterns and cost-estimation methods is essential to the development of the techniques of cost accounting. Such cost-allocation methods, at best, are only as good as the cost data used to provide information for inventory valuation or other purposes. Cost data may be collected on a full-costing or a responsibility-costing basis and may involve consideration of both fixed and variable costs or only incremental (variable) costs.

Absorption or *full costing* considers all the costs associated with the particular service in question. Unit costs can be computed by simply dividing current budgetary appropriation for a given activity by the performance unit (for example, yards of sewer pipe installed). This approach, however, has several shortcomings: (1) appropriated funds may not be a good measure of actual performance (for example, encumbrances for items not received or expenditures to cover encumbrances from the preceding fiscal period may be included); (2) current unit costs may be overstated if capital expenditures are included in the appropriation (such expenditures should be amortized over a longer time); (3) existing inventories of materials may be substantial in some cases and should be excluded from cost calculations until actually used; and (4) full costs may be understated if provisions are not made for equipment depreciation.

Responsibility costing limits the costs assigned to any operation to only those that can be directly controlled or at least influenced. This approach avoids the need to include prorated costs arising from auxiliary or support units (personnel departments, accounting departments, central purchasing, general administration) which often are encountered in an absorption or full-costing approach. Similarly, variable or incremental costing (often called "direct costing") provides management information as to the cost of additional units of service and often is helpful in incremental decision making. Fixed costs are eliminated from consideration in this approach, since they represent costs that have to be met regardless of the number of service units provided.

Each of these accounting systems will be discussed in further detail in this chapter (financial accounting) and in the next chapter (managerial and cost accounting). The point to be made here is that each system provides a somewhat different perspective on management information and, therefore, somewhat different capacities for management control.

Financial Accounting and Reporting

As an information system, accounting is concerned with the processes of measuring and communicating financial data to various users. These financial data must be recorded, classified, analyzed, summarized, reported, and interpreted. In this sense, financial accounting is concerned with the historical results of fiscal transactions and the consequent financial position of some organizational *entity*. Activities are carried out and resources committed over an extended period by various entities—businesses, hospitals, universities, governmental agencies, funded programs—with the expectation that certain desirable results will be attained. The accountant has the responsibility of developing and maintaining a system that meets the needs of the entity, whether it be profit or nonprofit oriented. The life of the entity is divided into accounting periods of not more than a year in length so that measurements can be made at relevant intervals (quarterly, monthly, weekly).

A number of standards or principles have evolved that provide the underlying structure for financial accounting. The more important ones relate to the cost, revenue, matching, objectivity, consistency, and exception principles. In general, all fund flows of an entity can be expressed in terms of revenues, receipts, contributions, transfers, costs expenditures, and disbursements. The basic underlying assumptions and principles of financial accounting indicate how these various flows can be measured to provide information.

Funds—Entities of Governmental Accounting

The financial reports of most commercial enterprises are based on the total organizational unit and operations. There is one balance sheet and one income statement for the business or private enterprise. In state and local government, however, an annual financial report can consist of as many as twenty separate sets of financial statements, one set for each fund created to monitor the cash flow of revenues to expenditures. A sound governmental-accounting structure, therefore, must be built around four central components:

1. Funds or groups of funds are accounting entities that embody a whole group of self-balancing accounts (balance sheet and operating-statement accounts) used to denote transactions within state and local government.
2. Major nonfund, self-balancing groups of accounts focus on general fixed assets and general long-term debt of government.
3. Unified records systems consist of a general ledger that contains summary accounts (posted as totals), with the supporting details maintained in subsidiary ledgers.
4. Basic accounting classifications record revenues by fund and by source (and sometimes by collecting agency) and expenditures by fund, organizational unit, function, program, activity, character, and/or object.

A fund is an independent fiscal and accounting entity (and often a legal entity) to which resources are assigned, together with all related liabilities, obligations, reserves, and equities.[10] Transactions are made between funds within a given government (that is, resources are transferred among and charges made against the various established funds). Separate financial statements are prepared for each of the major funds, and combined statements of funds with similar purposes often are distributed.

Further delineation of the standard fund designations of state and local government will be provided in a subsequent section under the discussion of the procedures of fund accounting. The format and purposes of combined statements for financial reporting will also be discussed after the general description of the external financial statement has been provided in the following section.

External Financial Statements

Although financial statements represent the end-products of financial accounting, they provide a good starting point for understanding the accounting process. Financial statements are used to convey to managers and other interested parties information regarding operating results and the financial position of an entity at the selected point of measurement. The three most important financial statements are: (1) the income statement, (2) the balance sheet, and (3) the statement of changes in financial position.

An *income statement* is designed to reflect the profit performance of an entity for some specific period of time—month, quarter, or year. *Revenues* represent an inflow of money and/or other representations of value in return for selling goods or providing some type of service. Sale receipts, rents, dividends, commissions, and fees represent revenue in the private sector; tax assessments, grant receipts, and legislative appropriations represent revenues in the public sector. Generally speaking, revenue should be recognized in the period when the sale is made or the service is rendered, rather than when the cash is received. *Expenses* represent outflows of resources, or the incurring of obligations, for goods and services required to generate revenues. As expenditures and obligations are made, *costs* are incurred by the entity. These costs are recognized as expenses when the value of the cost (utility) has been consumed in generating revenues. Unused utility in costs incurred continues to be recognized as an *asset* until consumed.

For purposes of financial accounting, an expense is recognized when a complete transaction takes place rather than when cash is paid for the goods or service. An item of expense may take many different forms. Present or future expense items are embodied in the cost of equipment and buildings used in operating a business. Such items usually have a high initial cost and are used in operations over an extended period. As they are committed to operations a portion of their usefulness is consumed and a part of the original cost is allocated as an expense. This kind of expense is called *depreciation.*

Net income is simply the excess of revenues over expenses. In the private sector, net income or net loss provides a surrogate for managerial performance, that is, some indication of how well management personnel of the entity have carried out their responsibilities.

A *balance sheet* shows the financial position of an entity at a particular time, that is, the amount of resources available (assets) and liabilities (obligations or debts) outstanding. Assets may be reflected in the form of cash, amounts owed by others to the entity, equipment, or other things of value owned by the entity. Under prevailing accounting practices, assets are recorded on the basis of total cost incurred at the time of their acquisition, since restatement of asset value each period would require frequent and difficult estimates. It must be recognized, therefore, that a balance sheet does not necessarily reflect the fair-market value of assets. Liabilities represent obligations or debts of an entity and include amounts owed for goods and services purchased on credit, accounts or notes payable, salaries owed employees, taxes due, bonds payable, and other forms of debt.

Owner's equity is an important concept in commercial-accounting procedures and is sometimes called net worth, capital, or proprietorship. This equity comes from two sources: (1) earnings retained in the business or commercial entity, and (2) investments made into the entity (for example, through the sale of stock). As will be discussed in the next section, the concept of owner's equity requires further definition when applied to not-for-profit organizations.

The statement of changes in financial position has come into general use in the private sector because of the need for information regarding the financing and investing activities of an entity. This statement is derived from an analysis of the income statement and balance sheet and tracks the inflows and outflows of funds, that is, sources of funds and uses of funds.

Accounting Equation and Financial Reporting

All accounting transactions must balance: the sum of the assets shown on a balance sheet should agree with the equities, that is, liabilities plus owner equity. The equilibrium is known as the basic accounting equation, since the concept of double-entry accounting is derived from it. Regardless of the number or type of transactions for a given entity, the accounting equation is always expected to remain in balance. To be profitable, a business operation must increase the amount of assets and/or reduce its liabilities. The balancing residual is included as an increase in owner equity.

Although many transactions may be classified as balance-sheet entries, few relate completely to income-statement transactions, that is, involve revenue or expenses. Thus the basic accounting equation must be expanded as follows:

Assets = Liabilities + Owner Equity + Revenue − Expense

Thus, an income statement is based on the following basic relationship:

$$\text{Net Income} = \text{Revenues} - \text{Expenses}$$

The goal of profit-seeking entities is to generate revenues in excess of the expenses required to produce the income. Sales of merchandise from a retail store represent revenues; services rendered by a lawyer are revenues to the law firm; interest received by a bank represents revenues. By the same token, taxes billed and fines collected by a city are revenues to the municipal government.

Whereas profit-seeking entities strive to generate net income, not-for-profit organizations (including state and local governments) seek to "break even," that is, to balance revenues and expenses. In the not-for-profit area, revenues are matched against expenditures, not because the expenditures were used to generate revenues but because of the accountability requirements. If a balance sheet is prepared for a governmental entity (program, fund, or agency), it would be based on the equation of assets equal equities. However, the balance sheet would likely reflect only items properly classifiable as current assets and current liabilities, with some type of balancing item (free balance or uncommitted appropriation) used in lieu of owners' equity.

A balance sheet attempts to reflect an entity's financial position at a particular time, based on historical costs. Typically, assets are listed in order of liquidity, with the most liquid shown first; a further breakdown is usually provided between current assets, property and plant, and equipment (fixed assets), and other assets. Liabilities are segregated between current and long-term obligations. A breakdown between contributed capital and retained earnings is provided in the owners' equity section. Balance-sheet data are highly summarized when provided in annual financial reports, with supporting information where needed or required included in footnotes to the financial statements.

Combined and Combining-Funds Statements

In the past, the only financial statements required of state and local governments were those of the individual funds, since each fund is considered an accountable entity. If these statements were shown together, for example in an annual report, no overall total was provided to avoid the impression that the governmental unit could be considered as one accounting entity.

More recently, however, accounting principles for external financial reporting suggest that all funds of a governmental unit should be combined into a single statement, with a separate column for each major fund classification.

Every governmental unit should prepare and publish, as a matter of public record, a *comprehensive annual financial report* (CAFR) that encompasses all funds and account groups. The CAFR should contain both (1) the *general purpose financial statements* (GPFS) by fund type and account group, and (2) combining statements by fund type and individual fund statements. The CAFR is the governmental unit's official annual report and should also contain introductory information, schedules necessary to demonstrate compliance with finance-related legal and contractual provisions, and statistical data.[11]

While a total is provided in the combined statement, it should not be viewed as a consolidation of all funds into an operating total for the entire government. The National Council on Governmental Accounting uses a pyramidal chart to illustrate the various types of financial reporting appropriate to state and local governments.

These financial statements can be considered under two basic headings: (1) combining statements and (2) combined statements. *Combining statements* bring together all the funds of a particular type into one statement and include: (1) the balance sheet, (2) the statement of revenues, expenditures, and changes in fund balance, and (3) a comparison between budget and actual data for revenues, expenditures, and fund-balance changes. No effort is made, however, to provide a grand total for the governmental unit. When all the funds of the unit are combined into a memorandum total, the report is called a *combined-funds statement*. If combining statements are provided, it should be possible to determine individual statements from them.

Although these statements are not consolidated, interfund transfers and similar eliminations may be made in the combining or combined balance sheets or in the combined statement of revenues, expenditures, and changes in fund balances. These interfund eliminations should be disclosed, either in headings or in the notes to the financial statements. Interfund transfers result in double counting of revenues and expenditures and, therefore, would distort the memorandum totals if they were not eliminated from the combined statement.

Perhaps the most significant use of combined statements is a comparison between the budget and actual data on revenues and expenditures for those funds for which an annual budget has been adopted. Unless the budget is adopted on a modified accrual basis, however, a separate schedule must be presented to provide a comparison of fund appropriations with the sum of expenditures for the current fiscal year and encumbrances outstanding at year end.[12] The various bases of accounting—cash, accrual, and modified accrual—will be discussed in a subsequent section of this chapter.

Generally accepted accounting principles require that expenditures in the combined statements not include encumbrances. One approach is to liquidate all encumbrances at the end of the fiscal year and to replace the necessary orders at the beginning of the new fiscal year. This approach, however, results in a carry-over obligation and may "cost" the agency double the amount for the encumbered item if the funds released in the liquidation cannot be expended before the end of the fiscal year. An alternative approach is to segregate encumbrances in the fund balance rather than as expenditures and to carry forward such amounts as are necessary as authorizations to spend in a succeeding fiscal year, that is, to increase appropriations by the amount of last year's encumbrances. Annual expenditures, including expenditures charged against last year's reserve for encumbrances, can then be compared against the current year's appropriation plus last year's reserve for encumbrances. In many localities, however, the current-year appropriations cannot be increased to accommodate a reserve for encumbrances unless another budget ordinance is enacted.

The Accounting Cycle and Recording Process

Transactions provide the basic data for the accounting process, and from recorded transactions, financial statements are prepared for use by various interested parties. A transaction is anything that has an economic impact on an entity, including exchanges of resources between the entity and some external group (sales, purchases, loans, distributions, expenditures, for example) and strictly internal events (equipment depreciation, amortization of prepaid rent and insurance, loss of assets, for example). Most transactions are reflected in *source documents,* such as sales tickets, invoices, purchase orders, checks for salary payments, and so forth. Source documents provide the starting point for developing financial information. An accounting system must ensure that all transactions are identified and recorded, summarized, and reported in order to provide control over the resources of the entity.

Use of Accounts and Ledgers

The so-called double-entry or T-form was developed to provide a standardized method for recording increases and decreases in components of the accounting equation. The standard format of the T-form account is shown in figure 2-1; it has a *debit* (or increase) side and a *credit* (or decrease) side. Since debits must equal credits, the effect on the accounting system is described in terms of double-entry mechanics, as shown in figure 2-2. Increases in revenues are represented by credits and increases in expenses by debits, since they are equity items.

Debit Side (DR)		Credit Side (CR)	
Investment	$90,000	Equipment purchase	$40,000
Revenue	10,000	Lease payments	4,000
		Expenses	8,000

Figure 2-1. T-Form Account

Figure 2-2. Double-Entry Mechanics

Actual accounts may take various forms but for the most part, the double-entry mechanics are maintained. A business may use from a few accounts to more than several hundred to record the transactions of the entity. In manual and some computerized accounting systems, each account may be recorded on a separate page in a ledger. Although it is possible to record each transaction directly into the ledger accounts, it is not the best procedure for at least two reasons. To do so would eliminate a complete record of the transaction (debit and credit) in one place, which is especially important in case of errors. Even more important, the direct recording of each transaction in the ledger accounts is highly inefficient. Rather, journals are used as the original-entry records.

The basic journal—a general journal—provides for a complete record of each transaction. The typical general journal includes information as to the date of the transaction, accounts to be debited and credited, an explanation of the transaction, account numbers, and the financial effect on the accounts involved. A chronological listing provides a basis for tracing entries by the approximate date of the transaction. In actual practice there are numerous variations on the basic journal, but, in all cases they serve the same purpose—to record transactions and to provide a basis for posting to accounts.

Special journals often are established for purposes of separating duties and responsibilities and improving management control. Additional journals are likely first to be developed for cash receipts and disbursements; sales and purchases journals might be established if an entity sold goods on account or made extensive purchases on account. In short, special journals are established for classes of transactions that frequently take place in a given entity.

Transactions and the Accounting Cycle

Before a transaction is recorded, it should be analyzed to determine its debit and credit elements, that is, to determine what asset, liability, and equity items are increased and decreased. The appropriate accounts can then be debited or credited. Often a transaction initiated in one fiscal period will impact one or more succeeding periods. It is important, therefore, to analyze not only the immediate implications of a transaction but also the subsequent consequences. For example, an insurance policy written for a three-year period represents an asset at the time of the initial transaction; however, subsequent charges must be made to expenses as the service potential of the asset is consumed.

Transactions are posted to the account ledgers on a regular basis (usually weekly or monthly), with cross-referencing made between the journals and the ledger accounts. Before using account balances to prepare financial statements, it is considered desirable to prove that the total of accounts with debit balances is equal to the total of accounts with credit balances. This proof of debit- and credit-balance equality is referred to as a *trial balance.*

A trial balance provides proof that the ledger is in balance, but it does not verify that transactions have been correctly analyzed and recorded in the proper accounts. In other words, a trial balance only provides support for the mechanical accuracy of the accounts. By comparing trial balances at the beginning and ending of a fiscal period (for example, each month), it is possible to determine income and expense items that have been incurred during the fiscal period.

After all external transactions have been recorded and verified, various internal adjustments may be required. These include the following classes of transactions:

1. Costs that must be allocated to more than one accounting period, such as the cost of a building or prepaid insurance
2. revenue that must be allocated to more than one period, such as commissions collected in advance of services rendered
3. expenses that have not yet been recorded because of the lack of an external transaction, such as wages earned but not paid because the payroll date comes after the close of the accounting period
4. revenue that has not been recorded because of delays in the accounting process

Once all transactions have been recorded, including the posting of internal adjustments to the proper accounts, the financial statements can be prepared.

This brings the discussion of financial accounting full cycle. The more specific details of generally accepted accounting practices and appropriate illustration of each step in the recording and analysis of the myriad of transactions that serve as the accountant's stock and trade must be left to a qualified textbook on accounting procedures. However, the reader should now have a fuller understanding of the rigor that underlies financial accounting and a better appreciation of why financial accounting has served as a major component of management control for most organizations.

Multiple Accounting Entities in Government

Each accountable unit in the private sector is called an entity. Under normal circumstances, each separate legal business or profit organization is an accountable entity. When a group of entities in the private sector belong to a single corporate structure, the financial statements of all the entities are often consolidated into a single financial report.

In government, however, there are several units with very different functions—the school system, the library, public utilities, authorities, quasi-independent agencies, as well as general government—making it very difficult to have only one accountable entity. Currently, from a standpoint of accounting and financial reporting, no provision exists for considering the entire government unit as an accountable entity. Rather, accounting and control for governmental activities and organizations is carried out through *fund accounting.*

The basic procedures concerning transactions, the accounting cycle, and financial statements, as outlined in the previous sections, also apply to funds as accounting entities. In the private sector, however, external users of financial statements (for example, stockholders) usually exercise some control over the management of entities through comparisons of anticipated earnings with actual earnings. In the public sector, the control of most government funds is through budgeted revenues and expenditures. All revenues in each fund entity usually are expended during the fiscal period, that is, there is no surplus income or earnings. Therefore, external controls must be exercised in relation to some other standards. Revenues are controlled through the appropriation process, and proposed expenditures are controlled through a line-item budget. Expenditures from the fund for any line item—such as salaries, supplies and materials, travel, contractual services, equipment—cannot exceed the dollar amount the legislative body has appropriated in the budget for that particular line item. The control of each line item in a budget, in turn, also prevents the overexpenditure of the appropriation to a given fund entity as a whole. One of the principles of governmental fund accounting is that the financial statements must compare the actual revenues and expenditures with those estimated in the budget.

Fund Accounting

The National Council on Governmental Accounting (NCGA) has defined a fund as:

". . . a fiscal and accounting entity with a self-balancing set of accounts recording cash and other financial resources, together with all related liabilities and residual equities or balances, and changes therein, which are segregated for the purpose of carrying on specific activities or attaining certain objectives in accordance with special regulations, restrictions or limitations."[13] The NCGA recommends eight standard fund designations, as follows:

General fund is used to account for all financial resources, and the activities financed by them, which are not accounted for in some special fund. Among the revenues normally included are general property taxes, licenses, fees, permits, penalties, and fines. Expenditures from this fund are authorized in the general budget. The fund's balance sheet contains statements as to cash assets, income from temporary investments, accounts and taxes receivable, tax liens, and supply inventories on the asset side and statements of all vouchers and judgments payable, matured bonds and interest payable, contracts payable, and statements of all other obligations, including appropriations and any unappropriated surplus, as liabilities.

Special revenue funds are used to account for taxes and other revenues (except special assessments) that are legally restricted for a particular purpose. The purposes may vary widely, as for the benefit of parks, schools, hospitals, streets, and occasionally for such general activities as those carried on by police and fire departments.

Debt service funds account for the financing of the interest and the retirement of principal of general long-term debt. If term bonds have been issued, involving the establishment and maintenance of a sinking fund, a debt service fund accounts for the payments to the sinking fund set up to retire the bonds of maturity.

Capital project funds account for those capital projects that are financed either on a "pay-as-you-go" basis or out of capital reserves, grants-in-aid, or transfers from other funds. This fund is limited to an accounting of receipts and expenditures on capital projects paid out of current revenues. Any bond issues should be serviced and repaid by the establishment of a debt service fund.

Special assessment funds are established to account for special assessments levied to finance improvements or services deemed to benefit properties against which assessments are levied. If improvements are financed through bond issues, the fund must account both for the bond proceeds and for the special-assessment revenue needed to retire such bonds and to pay the interest thereon.

Enterprise funds are established to account for the financing of services rendered primarily to the general public for compensation, such as the operation of water works, sewage disposal plants, electric utilities, and port facilities. The balance sheet should identify as a liability any governmental contributions that must be made from nonutility funds.

Internal service funds (working capital funds) are established to account for the financing of activities or services carried on by one department for other departments of the same governmental unit. Examples of activities financed through such funds are central shops, garages, asphalt plants, central purchasing and central stores, data-processing centers. Internal-service funds include appropriate fixed assets, as well as current assets and liabilities.

Trust and agency funds account for cash and other assets held by a governmental unit as trustee or agent. Expendable trust funds (for example, employee pension funds) are those that may be spent, provided expenditures are in accordance with trust indentures and other governing regulations. Nonexpendable trust funds (for example, loan funds) are those in which the principal (but not necessarily income) must be kept intact. Agency funds consist of money or other assets received by a municipality to be turned over to some other governmental unit, usually without any change in form or nature. The municipality receives no direct benefits from agency funds.

Enterprise funds and internal service funds often are referred to as "proprietary funds" in that they are used to account for operations that are financed and operated in a manner similar to private-business enterprises, where the intent of the governing body is that the costs of providing goods or services on a continuing basis be financed or recovered primarily through user charges. Trust and agency funds are also known as "fiduciary funds" in that the assets are held by a governmental unit in a trustee capacity or as an agent for individuals, private organizations, other governmental units, and/or other funds.

This compartmentalization of resources, transactions, and statements of assets and liabilities is known as *fund accounting* and is one of the dominant characteristics of governmental-accounting systems. Budgetary and accounting requirements tend to vary widely among these funds. These requirements can be summarized by considering four general groupings of funds.

1. Funds concerned with current operations (general funds, special revenue funds, debt service funds, and certain expendable trust funds) emphasize appropriated monies that currently are expendable. Fixed assets and long-term liabilities are excluded from their balance sheets. These funds often use a modified accrual or encumbrance basis of accounting that records the liabilities (expenditures) as they are incurred but does not record most types of revenues until they are received in cash. As a consequence, the result is a rather conservative statement of the balance currently available for approved activities.

2. Capital project funds and special assessment funds are concerned with capital spending. Budgetary restrictions normally are included in the ordinances that create these funds. However, these funds typically are not included in the annual appropriation ordinance.

3. Commercial-type funds record the activities that are expected to earn a profit, or at least recover costs, and include the enterprise funds, internal service funds, and trust funds concerned with invested principal that earns an income. These funds have completed balance sheets that include both fixed assets and long-term liabilities. Revenues and expenditures are recorded on an accrual basis. Budgets for these funds serve as guidelines for operations rather than as legal limits on expenditures.

4. Custodial funds are self-balancing liability accounts that record assets held for others. In some states, for example, certain fines collected by city courts are paid over to the school district. A custodial fund would account for these fines during the interval between collection and their transfer to the school district. Budgetary controls are unnecessary for such funds.

Two self-balancing groups of accounts—dealing with general long-term debt and general fixed assets—constitute a second major component of government accounting. They are not funds because they do not contain resources that can be appropriated. These accounting compartments constitute "holding areas" that accomplish three important purposes: (1) fixed assets and long-term liabilities are segregated from each other, avoiding meaningless data on capital surplus; (2) most funds, therefore, can be operated on the basis of current assets and liabilities only; and (3) each group brings together, in one accounting compartment, related accounts for control purposes.

Accounts showing general fixed assets contain no liabilities, reserves, or surplus data—they serve as an overall inventory, identify responsibility, and provide other control functions. Records of general long-term debt contain no asset or surplus accounts. These records must be kept in great detail so that prompt debt servicing can be accomplished. In short, these accounts serve as intrastructural links to record transactions that are not between established funds.

The use of those nonfund accounts can be illustrated by tracing the transactions that occur when a general obligation bond matures. The bond is recorded initially as part of the general long-term debt account. At maturity, the liability (in terms of a principal payment) becomes a current obligation of a debt service fund. Therefore, it is removed from long-term debt, and the total long-term liability of the municipality is reduced accordingly. When the capital-construction project, financed from the proceeds of a general obligation bond issue, is completed, it is recorded as a capital asset in the general fixed assets account. Should this asset subsequently be sold, the revenues are recorded in the general fund, and the total general fixed assets of the municipality are reduced accordingly.

Unified accounts constitute a third major component in the structure of fund accounting. These records consist of summary accounts, which are also controlling accounts—they contain a total figure for each posting, against which the summation of detailed subsidiary entries must be reconciled. This general ledger provides public officials and managers with an overview of all major transactions.

Basic accounting classifications (or a chart of accounts) provide a uniform basis for cross-referencing both revenues and expenditures. Revenues are classified by fund and by source, and sometimes by collecting agency. Expenditure classifications are more elaborate, often providing details by: fund, organizational unit, function, program, activity, character, and object. Although expenditure data may be recapitulated by individual bases of classification, more frequently one recapitulation will combine several bases in a single report by use of stub and columnar cross-classifications. Standard account classifications, promulgated by the NCGA, have helped to bring about a certain amount of uniformity among state and local governments in the use of terminology and in account titles.

Budgetary Control and the Financial-Accounting Process

The emphasis on budgetary control serves as a major distinction between governmental accounting and profit accounting in the private sector. Budgetary controls are widely used in the private sector within organizations. In the public sector, however, budgetary control has much more significance for the total organization because of the appropriation process. Most governmental units are as concerned with the control of the budget as with any other activity. And the accounting procedures that bring about that control are among the important elements in understanding public management control.

Various types of budgets are found in state and local governments; for example, line-item or object-of-expenditure budgets, performance budgets, program budgets, and zero-base budgets. When concerned with financial reporting, the primary emphasis for the control of governmental activities is through the line-item budget. Other types of budgets will be discussed in the context of management-control objectives in a subsequent chapter. The focus of this chapter's examination of budgetary control is on more traditional budget formats.

Budgetary Accounting

In most cases, actual expenditures should closely coincide with budgetary appropriations—the budget should serve as both a mandate for and a limitation on public spending. During the fiscal year, the accommodation of unforeseen circumstances in the operations of a fund, an agency, or a program should be made in reference to the impacts that such adjustments will have on the budget, as initially approved. Such analyses are facilitated through the application of budgetary-accounting procedures, which also strengthen the fiscal controls attained through fund accounting.

Under budgetary accounting, the adoption of the budget by the governing body at the outset of the fiscal period, in effect, represents the legal authority to spend. Such authorization, however, is viewed as being very specific in terms of the amounts to be spent and items required for each agency's operations during the designated budget period. Therefore, the first accounting entrees for the operating cycle formally record the newly adopted budget—the appropriations—in detail, according to various allocations, that is, subdivisions of appropriations according to agencies, programs, and classes of expenditures, as specified in a chart of accounts. Allocations may be made to specific line items or object codes, with limitations imposed as to the deviations permitted within these expenditure categories.

The basic function of the allocation process is to reserve funds for specific categories of expense. In some cases, specific allocations are encumbered for the outset of the program or project and liquidated on an "as-billed" basis. Examples of such encumbrances include indirect support payments for employee benefits, legal services, or other consultants' fees and major budget items for equipment purchases. The purpose of these encumbrances is to ensure that the monies will be available at the time they are needed, that is, that they will not be spent for other purposes.

Provision may also be made for an allotment system through which allocated appropriations can be further subdivided into time elements, for example, quarterly or monthly allotments for personal services (salaries and wages) or groups of expenditure items in the nonpersonal-services categories. Such an allotment system is particularly appropriate in situations where the expenditure of appropriations is contingent on some future events, such as the availability of grants from other levels of government or the projected opening of a new capital facility (for instance, a branch library or new recreational facility). Under such an approach, the portion of the appropriation in question may be retained in the unallocated, unallotted category until required for actual commitment. Thus, if the facility is not completed on schedule (or if the intergovernmental grant is not forthcoming), funds intended for this purpose are restricted until such time as there is a requirement for their use as originally approved.

Some localities have found it desirable to use allotment procedures to level out expenditure patterns of various agencies and thereby, to promote appropriate fiscal management practices. Such procedures often parallel quarterly or semiannual revenue-collection practices and are undertaken to avoid the need for deficit financing. Allotment procedures that require monthly approvals of the governing body, however, should be avoided. Such procedures often become cumbersome, generate operational uncertainties among public agencies, and result in false economies, as when an agency cannot take advantage of legitimate discounts for prompt payment of bills.

Budget Classification Systems

A budget classification system provides the means for organizing and facilitating comparisons among data on revenues and expenditures. A budget-classification system should serve three basic purposes: program formulation, budget execution and administration, and public accountability. The usefulness of a budget classification system can be judged in relation to: (1) its operational character; (2) its ability to facilitate decision making by bringing important fiscal questions into focus and clarifying and detailing appropriate answers; and (3) its ability to provide information for financial reporting in accordance with generally acceptable accounting principles.

The most widely used budget classification system is based on *objects of expenditure*. Object classifications are used in almost every state government and in the vast majority of local governments. This approach also is used as a supplementary classification by the federal government. Object classifications were introduced as part of the municipal reform movement at the turn of the century and were a direct product of an era when both legislators and the public at large sought to tighten controls on public spending and to limit the discretion of government officials in carrying out approved programs.

The principal objective of an object classification is to control expenditures at the departmental or agency level. Since public agencies, both within any government as well as among governments, tend to buy the same things, it is possible to set up a system of accounts that is uniform throughout the whole of government. Object codes are four-digit numbers (1100 personal services, 1200 contractual services, 1300 supplies and materials, and so forth) which can be further divided into subobject classifications (for example, 1240 travel). The four-digit format provides a large field for additional expenditure categories; the codes can be revised periodically as new areas of expenditure are encountered. There is no detailed object classification for revenues, however—income is accounted for by fund and by source.

A budget built on objects of expenditure frequently is called a line-item budget, since the object codes often are detailed with great specificity, resulting in an array of lines within the budget. Technically, line item refers to the manner in which appropriations are made to agencies within the budget structure. Appropriations may be made on a lump-sum basis, whereby considerable discretion is left to the agency regarding the specific categories of expenditure permitted, or according to specific line item, as described by object codes. Under a line-item/object-of-expenditure budget, agencies often must request legislative approval for any deviations from initially authorized appropriations beyond a predetermined range (for example, plus or minus 10 percent). Even if appropriations are made on a lump-sum basis, agencies may be required to report expenditures according to object and subobject codes.

Line items can be specified at several levels of detail. For example, funds might be appropriated for personal services (salaries and wages) and nonpersonal services (all other operating expenditures), whereby dollars may be shifted from other operating categories to salaries and wages but cannot be shifted from salaries and wages to operations. In effect, appropriations for salaries and wages are encumbered, and any unexpended funds in this line item revert to central appropriations. This approach is used to prevent agencies from holding positions vacant to generate more operating dollars (for example, for "windfall" equipment purchases). Such line itemization can specify appropriations for various personnel categories (for example, professional staff versus technical-support personnel) or for specific object codes (for example, travel or equipment).

A budget and an accounting system based on objects of expenditures are readily understood by legislators and other elected officials. This is one important reason why this approach has survived so long despite its limitations. It is relatively easy to grasp the fiscal significance of a proposed increase of 10 percent in printing or data processing or a salary reclassification for John Jones. Therefore, governing bodies can review the budget and alter the minutiae of proposed expenditures. Larger issues of efficiency and effectiveness that should be examined through the budget process, however, often remain buried in the object detail. Object classifications cannot provide a basis for measuring the performance of an agency or program or the progress made in the implementation of a particular set of activities.

Advantages and Disadvantages of Object Classifications

The object of expenditure format has two distinct advantages not possessed by other types of classifications. The first is accountability—an object classification establishes a pattern of accounts that can be controlled and audited. Under line-item appropriations, funds cannot be obligated except for the objects specified. Each object of expenditure is subject to a separate pattern of documentation. This accounting documentation has been further facilitated by the data-processing capacity of computers. By inserting additional codes in the data field, expenditures can be tracked by appropriation, agency, program or project, and by purpose. Special funding limitations also can be specified.

A second advantage of the object-of-expenditure approach is its use as a mechanism of management control. Deviations above a certain percentage of the appropriated funds must be approved by the governing body. Useful information is provided for personnel management, since there is tight control over the number of positions within an organizational entity. The status of existing personnel and proposed changes in personnel are clearly set forth (often in supplementary schedules). Personnel requirements are closely linked with other budgetary requirements, and, therefore, the control of positions can be used as a level to control the whole budget.

Object classifications have several disadvantages, however. Although data can easily be aggregated by object and subobject codes, these aggregated data afford only limited management insights for purposes of program planning and evaluation. Relatively little direct information is provided to measure performance, and the "big picture"—goals, objectives, policy alternatives, cost-benefit evaluations, and so forth— is buried in detail.

Secondly, since deviations from the detailed breakdowns of appropriations often require legislative approval, agencies may be limited in their ability to innovate and to respond to unforeseen problems and opportunities. The fiscal-watchdog function of this format inhibits the flexibility and responsiveness of program managers.

Finally, building a budget on detailed object codes tends to promote an incremental approach to financial decision making. If X dollars were committed to a given subobject code in the past fiscal period, the tendency is to require X plus 10 percent (or some other inflation factor) for this subobject code in the next fiscal period. Little consideration is given to reasons why X

dollars were spent; to whether these commitments were made in the most economical and efficient way; or to whether these expenditures contribute to the overall effectiveness of the agency's programs.

This problem of incrementalism in budget building and fiscal management is one of the underlying factors leading to the concept of zero-base budgeting. These issues will be discussed further when other budget formats and related classification systems are examined.

Encumbrances—Controlling Proposed Expenditures

Good budgetary accounting includes provision for a system of encumbrances that records the placement of purchase orders or the letting of contracts as an obligation against an appropriation. When the item is delivered and paid for (or the contracted service provided), the expenditure is recorded and the encumbered amount is liquidated. At any time, the account balance shows the original amount budgeted minus actual expenditures and encumbrances. Although the amount originally encumbered need not be exactly equal to the actual expenditure, encumbrances should be estimated as closely as possible.

Why are encumbrances an important part of budgetary controls? By reserving a part of the appropriation as an encumbered expenditure, management is assured that the entity will not overspend the amount of funds available during any fiscal period. As long as encumbrances are not recorded in advance, administrators may be tempted to encourage suppliers to delay tendering their bills until the next fiscal period to appear to stay within their appropriations (allocations and allotments). However, these bills become a burden on the next fiscal period, and thus that period's appropriation may be exhausted prematurely. Payments due on later bills may be delayed again and again, and eventually, the deferred payments may take on the character of a large and not fully recognized floating debt.

Accounting Equation for Governmental Funds

The basic accounting equation developed for profit entities must be altered to reflect the accounting equilibrium of governmental funds. Revenues and expenditures replace income and expenses, and, since there is no owner's equity, the title of the capital section of the equation would be fund balance. Four additional items related to budgetary control also must be added to the equation: estimated revenues, appropriations, encumbrances, and reserves for encumbrances. Thus, the expended equation would be as follows (all elements expressed in positive terms):

Assets + Estimated Revenue + Expenditures + Encumbrances =

Liabilities + Fund Balance + Revenues +

Reserves for Encumbrances + Appropriations

When recording items in accounts, therefore, the following debit and credit conditions would apply:

1. Increases in assets, estimated revenue, expenditures, and encumbrances would always be a debit
2. increases in liabilities, fund balance, revenues, reserve for encumbrances, and appropriations would always be a credit
3. decreases in assets, estimated revenue, expenditures, and encumbrances would always be a credit
4. decreases in liabilities, fund balance, revenues, reserve for encumbrances, and appropriations would always be a credit

In summary, from an accounting standpoint, budgetary transactions that occur in governmental funds are placed in the accounting records: (1) when the budget is adopted; (2) when goods, services, or fixed assets are ordered and the appropriation needs to be encumbered; (3) when goods, services, or fixed assets are received and the encumbrance needs to be released; and (4) when the books are closed at the end of a fiscal period.

Bases for Accounting

One final element of financial accounting requires examination. In discussing combined- and combining-funds statements, it was noted that outstanding encumbrances at the end of a fiscal year present a particular reporting problem unless the accounting system is built on an accrual basis. According to the National Council on Governmental Accounting:

> "Basis of Accounting" refers to *when* revenues, expenditures, expenses, and transfers—and the related assets and liabilities—are recognized in the accounts and reported in the financial statements. Specifically, it relates to the timing of the measurements made, regardless of the nature of the measurement, on either the cash or the accrual method. For example, whether depreciation is recognized depends on whether expenses or expenditures are being measured rather than on whether the cash or accrual basis is used.[14]

There are several bases for accounting. On the revenue side, two bases are possible: the cash basis and the accrued revenue basis. On the commitment (outflow) side, four bases are used: cash, obligation, accrued expenditure, and accrued cost. Various combinations of these bases may be used according to the accounting system adopted by a given organization or governmental unit and the information requirements imposed by auditing procedures.

On a strict cash basis, revenues are recorded only when they are actually received, and expenditures are recorded (as an account debit) when payments are made (a cash disbursement). In other words, this basis of accounting is similar to what an individual does when maintaining a running balance in his or her checkbook. Unfortunately, since tax revenues are collected only on an annual, semiannual, or quarterly basis, the cash-in-hand for a given municipality prior to a tax collection date may be far less than the expenditure demands. As a consequence, payment of bills may have to be postponed (and certain available discounts foregone or penalties incurred).

On a strict accrual basis, revenues are recorded as soon as they are levied, billed, or earned, regardless of the fiscal period in which they are collected. In practice, however, not all revenues can be accrued—accrual of revenue from minor sources may not be feasible because the amounts are not known until actual collections are made (for example, traffic fines) or because such recording may not be worth the time involved.

Expenditures are recorded under this approach when goods are received or services are performed, when a liability is incurred, or when an invoice is received. On an accrued expenditure basis, an account may be debited before the bill is paid (before an actual cash disbursement is made). Or the debiting may occur only when the goods or services are actually used in a program, activity, or project (known as an accrued cost basis). Finally, expenditures can be recorded on an obligation basis, that is, when goods or services are ordered or contracted for, either totally or in combination with one of the other bases for recording expenditures. The obligation basis is a part of budgetary accounting, that is, the system of encumbrances.

Various combined approaches are also possible. A municipality may record revenues on a cash basis but accrue current expenditures and incurred obligations. Under another approach, the revenue side of the ledger resembles the accrual basis in form but remains on a cash basis in substance. For example, property-taxes receivable may be recorded at the time of levy, but then offset by a 95 to 98 percent reserve for uncollected taxes plus a 2 to 5 percent allowance for uncollectable taxes. As taxes are received, the amounts are recorded in the asset account (and the reserve is reduced accordingly). At any time the municipality has what amounts to a credit line in terms of taxes receivable (which might be used, in turn, as collateral for short-term borrowing).

These approaches might be labeled as modified-accrual or modified-cash bases of accounting. Under a modified accrual basis: (1) revenues are recorded as received in cash except for revenues susceptible to accrual, and material revenues that are not received at the normal time of receipt; and (2) expenditures are recorded on an accrual basis except for disbursements for inventory-type items (which may be considered as expenditures at the time of purchase or at the time the items are used), prepaid expenses (which normally are not recorded), interest on long-term debt (which should normally be recorded as an expenditure when due), and the encumbrance method of accounting (which may be adopted as an additional modification).[15]

A modified cash basis often is most practical for relatively small governments, whereby property taxes and other receivables are placed on the books for control purposes but not accounted for as revenue until actually collected. If bills are paid promptly and inventories do not fluctuate very much, the recording of cash disbursements will also produce reasonably satisfactory accounting data in such municipalities.

Accounting becomes more refined as procedures shift in the following sequence: cash basis, modified cash basis, modified accrual basis, accrued expenditure basis, and finally, accrued cost basis. Reliable unit-cost data cannot be developed under a cash basis. Most governments have adopted a system under which obligations are recorded at the time they are incurred (that is, as encumbrances). By accruing both revenues and expenditures, the budget and its execution can be compared and analyzed. Unit-cost data can be at least partially developed (excluding capital assets) using an accrued basis.

Under managerial accounting systems, a cost-based budget often is introduced, and accounting data must be provided on an accrued expenditure and/or an accrued cost basis. All available resources carried over from the previous budgetary period must be taken into account, and accounting controls must be maintained for both new and old (carry-over) resources. On an accrued cost basis, it is recognized that some expenditures may be appropriately postponed from one fiscal period to another. All goods and services used or consumed within a given period are reflected as costs. These costs, in turn, are matched by resources (both new and carry over) that are available to support the intended operations.

To illustrate the sort of problems that may arise if accounts are closed out (and funds revert) at the end of the fiscal year, assume that an agency places a purchase order for a $10,000 piece of equipment near the end of the fiscal year, intending to use funds allocated for that period. The funds are not encumbered, and the equipment is not delivered (or billed) until the next fiscal period. The agency must pay for the equipment out of its new allotment and stands to lose access to the resources in the previous allotment unless an alternative expenditure (likely to be of a lower priority) of the $10,000 is made before the end of the fiscal year. If, because of the uncertainty of the delivery date for the equipment, the agency declines to make an alternative expenditure, in a sense, it must pay for the equipment twice—once out of its new allotment and once because of the lost opportunity to spend the $10,000 from its current allotment. To counter this problem, some governments have adopted early deadlines (for example, two or three months prior to the close of the fiscal year) for the placement of large purchase orders. This practice, however, shortens the effective period for budgeting resources from twelve months to ten or less.

The temptation to overobligate or to overspend to maintain a budget base is removed under the accrued cost basis of accounting. Unspent funds are carried over to the next fiscal period. This approach can supply the manager with the cost information necessary to avoid the all-too-familiar practice of formulating budget requests merely on the basis of the budget level for the previous year. Although a cost-based budget provides management with greater flexibility, it also entails greater responsibility. The accrued-cost basis offers no guarantees of improved management control—if the additional managerial data are not used, or are misused, the cost and potential inconvenience of maintaining such an accounting system may be difficult to justify.

To summarize, four determinants influence the choice of a basis of accounting: (1) the size of the governmental unit; (2) the promptness with which bills are received and paid; (3) the size of inventories and other available resources appropriately carried over fiscal periods; and (4) the desires of management to develop and apply unit-cost data. If the time lag between the placement of an order and the delivery of the goods or services is particularly lengthy, or if the capital-construction period is unusually long (extending the time between the delivery of goods and their use), an accrued cost basis may be most appropriate.

Summary

Chapter 2 has explored the traditional mechanisms of management control provided through financial accounting. Procedures of financial accounting were developed initially for purposes of external reporting—for the preparation of financial statements and reports. Three important financial statements—the income statement, the balance sheet, and the statement of changes in financial position—can be readily developed from financial accounting records. The double-entry accounting equation provides the basis for the recording of financial transactions—the debits and credits of assets, liabilities, and equity items.

A number of modifications must be made in financial accounting procedures, however, when applied in the public sector. Each accountable unit in the private sector—each business or profit organization—is called an entity. From the standpoint of accounting and financial reporting, however, no provision currently exists for considering an entire government unit as an accountable entity. Rather, accounting and control for governmental activities is carried out through fund accounting. Revenues are controlled through the appropriation process, and proposed expenditures generally are controlled through a line-item budget. Basic accounting classifications (or a chart of accounts) provide a uniform basis for cross-referencing both revenues and expenditures. The most widely used classification system is based on objects of expenditure (object and subobject codes).

Budgetary accounting procedures link the budget to actual commitments of appropriated resources made available to agencies through an allocation/allotment process. A system of encumbrances is an integral part of budgetary accounting. The basic accounting equation developed for profit entities must be altered to reflect the accounting equilibrium of governmental funds. Revenues and expenditures replace income and expenses, and the capital section (owner's equity) becomes the fund balance, and four additional items related to budgetary control must be added to the equation: estimated revenues, appropriations, encumbrances, and reserves for encumbrances.

Finally, the various bases for accounting—cash, accrual, modified accrual, and accrued cost—were discussed to illustrate one of the principal bridges between financial accounting and managerial accounting systems. The additional mechanisms of management control that derived from managerial accounting will be discussed in detail in the next chapter. As noted at the outset, managerial accounting will not supercede financial accounting. However, under the optimal system, managerial accounting can coexist with financial accounting, providing much more extensive information to management for purposes of planning and control.

Notes

1. As cited in Joel E. Ross, *Modern Management and Information Systems* (Reston, Virg.: Reston Publishing, 1976), p. 133.

2. Ibid., p. 133.

3. For a further discussion of decision making and the communication process see Alan Walter Steiss, *Public Budgeting and Management* (Lexington, Mass.: Lexington Books, D.C. Heath, 1972), pp. 91–118.

4. Accounting systems, whether in the public or private sectors, must adhere to generally accepted accounting principles (GAAP), defined by the American Institute of Certified Public Accountants as: "a technical accounting term which encompasses the conventions, rules, and procedures

necessary to define accepted accounting practice at a particular time. It includes not only broad guidelines of general application, but also detailed practices and procedures. . . . Those conventions, rules, and procedures provide a standard by which to measure financial presentation." *AICPA Professional Standards,* vol. 1, *Auditing,* New York, July 1980. Many of these accounting principles have been developed for the use of independent auditors as a basis for expressing an opinion on the financial statements of organizations that they audit.

5. Robert G. May, Gerhard G. Muller, and Thomas H. Williams, *A Brief Introduction to the Managerial and Social Uses of Accounting* (Englewood Cliffs, N.J.: Prentice-Hall, 1975), pp. 1–2; Robert J. Mockler, *The Management Control Process* (New York: Appleton-Century-Crofts, 1972), pp. 95–96; Charles T. Horngren, *Introduction to Management Accounting* (Englewood Cliffs, N.J.: Prentice-Hall, 1978), p. 4; Robert N. Anthony, *Management Accounting Principles* (Homewood, Ill.: Richard D. Irwin, 1965), pp. 185–187, 243–245.

6. Robert Zemsky, Randall Porter, and Laura P. Oedel, "Decentralized Planning: To Share Responsibilty," *Educational Record* 59 (Summer 1978):244.

7. Robert N. Anthony and James S. Reese, *Management Accounting: Text and Cases* (Homewood, Ill.: Richard D. Irwin, 1975), p. 422.

8. James H. Rossell and William W. Frasure, *Managerial Accounting* (Columbus, Ohio: Charles E. Merrill, 1972), p. 4.

9. May, Muller, and Williams, *Brief Introduction,* pp. 1–2.

10. National Committee on Governmental Accounting, *Governmental Accounting, Auditing, and Financial Reporting* (Chicago: Municipal Finance Officers Association, 1968), pp. 6–7.

11. *Statement 1. Governmental Accounting and Financial Reporting Principles* (Chicago: Municipal Finance Officers Association of the United States and Canada, 1979), p. 19.

12. Ibid., pp. 23–24.

13. Ibid., pp. 5–6.

14. Ibid., p. 11.

15. American Institute of Certified Public Accountants, Inc., *Audits of State and Local Governmental Units* (New York, 1979), p. 16.

3 Managerial-Cost Accounting

Financial accounting emphasizes the preparation of reports on an organization's fiscal affairs for external users. Managerial accounting focuses on the development of information for internal users. Financial accounting is concerned with the accurate and objective recording of past events. A major feature of managerial accounting is its emphasis on the future. Budgets provide a primary mechanism for disciplining future decisions. The content, format, timing, and distribution of these reports have a significant impact on the overall capacity for management control. The same basic accounting system can be used to compile data for both financial and managerial accounting. However, an organization often must accommodate to an accounting system developed in response to externally imposed, legal requirements rather than to its own management needs. There are no generally accepted principles to inhibit any particular measurement in managerial accounting. Instead, from a management point of view, any accounting system or method is desirable as long as it produces incremental benefits in excess of its incremental costs.

Functions of Managerial Accounting

Managerial accounting is concerned primarily with four basic functions: planning, cost determination, cost control, and performance evaluation. *Planning* involves the formulation of strategic decisions regarding the basic goals and objectives for an organization and its programs. It also involves the establishment of operational guidelines within the limitations imposed by technology and the environment. Before decisions can be made regarding the commitment of scarce resources in support of any particular objective or program, it is necessary to *determine the component costs,* both in the more immediate future and in the long run, and to weigh these costs against anticipated benefits. Once commitments are made, it is essential that costs *be monitored* in some effective fashion to ensure that these costs are appropriate and reasonable for the activities performed. And finally, the overall *performance* of a program, subunit, or activity must be evaluated to improve future decisions. In the private sector, a budget represents a financial summary of a company's plans for operation. Through management control, utilizing managerial-cost accounting, and performance-evaluation techniques, decisions can be made consistent with these plans. Although a budget often is more rigid in government, similar techniques can be used to provide a basis for more effective planning and control.

The planning hierarchy—strategic, management, and operations planning—and its relevance to management control will be examined in further detail in a subsequent chapter. A separate chapter will also be devoted to the techniques and procedures of performance evaluation. The primary focus of chapter 3, therefore, will be the functions of cost determination and cost control.

Basic Concepts of Cost

Cost can be defined as a release of value required to accomplish some goal, objective, or purpose.[1] Costs should be incurred only if they can be expected to lead to the accomplishment of some predetermined end or serve as a means to an end. Certain entities might incur costs for the purpose of generating revenues in excess of the resources consumed (for example, a public utility). This profit measure is not applicable, however, for most activities in the public sector. Rather, costs are incurred in the provision of some required public service. The test as to whether the cost is appropriate and reasonable is still the same: Did the commitment of resources advance the program or agency toward some agreed-upon goal or objective?

Cost is not a unidimensional concept, however. One of the primary objectives of managerial-cost accounting is to further define and categorize the basic components of cost that must be incurred in the implementation of programs and plans.

Costs can be defined by how they change in relation to fluctuations in the quantity of some selected activity; for example, number of hours of labor required to complete some task, the dollar volume of sales, the number of orders processed, or some other index of volume. Some costs are uniform per unit, but their total fluctuates in direct proportion to the total of the related activity or volume. These are known as *variable costs*. The cost of more materials, parts, supplies, commissions, and many types of labor are variable. Other costs do not change in total but become progressively smaller on a per-unit basis as volume increases. These are known as *fixed costs*. Note that the variable or fixed characteristic of a cost relates to its total dollar amount and not to its per-unit amount.

Costs may also be semifixed, described as a step-function, or semivariable, whereby both fixed and variable components are included in the related costs. Supervisory salaries might be described as a semifixed cost; at some level of increased activity, additional supervisory personnel may be required. Maintenance costs often exhibit the characteristic of semivariable costs, that is, a fixed level of cost is required initially, after which maintenance costs increase with the level of activity. Since costs usually are classified as either fixed or variable, the incremental character of these mixed categories often is a determining factor—if the increments between levels of change are large, the costs are identified as fixed; if the increments are relatively small, the costs are usually defined as variable.

Five basic cost components are involved in any activity, operations, project, or program: (1) labor or personal services (that is, salaries and wages and various employee benefits), (2) materials and supplies (or consumables), (3) equipment expenses (sometimes categorized as part of fixed-asset expenses), (4) contractual services (that is, "packages" of services purchased from outside sources), and (5) overhead. Overhead has a fairly specific meaning when applied in the private sector, usually defined as all costs other than direct labor or material that are associated with the production process. Used in this context, overhead may involve variable costs (for instance, power, supplies, contractual services, and most indirect labor) or fixed costs (for instance, supervisory salaries, property taxes, rent, insurance, and depreciation). In the jargon of cost accounting, various direct-cost components, such as direct labor and direct materials, are reclassified as *prime costs,* whereas direct labor and overhead are reclassified as *conversion costs.*

In cost accounting, decisions must be made as to the distribution of direct and indirect costs. A *direct cost* represents a cost incurred for a specific purpose which is uniquely associated with that purpose. The salary of a day-care-center manager, for example, would be considered a direct cost of the center. If the center were divided into departments according to different age groups of children, with a part of the manager's salary allocated to each department, then the salary would be an indirect cost of each department. *Indirect cost* is a cost associated with more than one activity or program that cannot be traced directly to any of the individual activities. In the public sector, the terms indirect cost and overhead often are used interchangeably.

In theory, all costs are controllable by someone within an organization, given a long enough time. For purposes of managerial-cost accounting, however, *controllable costs* are defined as those costs that are subject to the influence of a given manager of a given department, agency, or program for a given time. The supervisor of an emergency room in a hospital, for example, might exercise significant control of the cost of supplies, maintenance, assigned nursing staff, and so forth but may have little or no control over the cost of doctors working in the emergency room or insurance costs allocated to this aspect of the hospital's operations. *Noncontrollable costs* include all costs that do not meet this test of "significant influence" by a given manager; thus, costs assigned to the manager of any department may contain both controllable and noncontrollable elements. Although clear distinctions between controllable and noncontrollable costs often are difficult to make, every effort must be made to separate these cost components for purposes of performance evaluation.

Other cost categories often encountered in managerial-cost accounting are outlined below.

1. Engineered costs are costs that can be predicted with a reasonable degree of accuracy, given some level of activity.
2. Discretionary costs are usually established for some short period of time, based on the judgment of management and are subject to variation at the discretion of the managar (also called managed costs).
3. Committed costs typically result from long-term decisions relating to activities or programs (depreciation, for example).
4. Product costs initially are identified as part of the inventory on hand and become expenses only when the inventory is sold.
5. Period costs are deducted as expenses during a given fiscal period without having been previously classified as product costs (for example, administrative expenses).
6. Out-of-pocket costs involve current or upcoming outlays of funds for some decision that has been made.
7. Sunk costs are costs that have already been incurred and therefore, are irrelevant to the current decision-making process (also called historical cost); allocation of cost expirations based on depreciation and amortization schedules are examples of sunk cost.
8. Marginal costs represent the cost of providing one additional unit of service (or product) over the previous level of activity.
9. Differential costs represent the difference in total costs between alternative approaches to providing some service or product.
10. Opportunity costs involve the maximum return that might have been expected if a resource had been committed to an alternative, that is, the effect of having to give up one opportunity to select another.
11. Associated costs are any cost involved in utilizing project services in the process of converting them into a form suitable for use or sale at the stage when benefits are evaluated; associated costs are incurred by the beneficiaries of public programs and service.
12. Investment costs vary primarily with the size of a particular program or project but not with its duration.
13. Recurring costs are those operating and maintenance costs that vary with both the size and the duration of the program; recurring costs may include salaries and wages, equipment maintenance and repair, materials and supplies, transfer payments.
14. Life-cycle costs are costs incurred over the useful life of a facility or

duration of a program, including investment costs, research and development costs, operating costs, and maintenance and repair costs.

It may be noted that many of these cost categories operate in pairs, for example, product and period costs, investment and recurring costs, out-of-pocket and sunk costs, and so forth.

Cost Approximation Methods

The first step in the classification and control of costs is to determine how the costs in question function under various applicable conditions. This process frequently is called *cost approximation* or *cost estimation* and involves an attempt to find predictable relationships between a dependent variable (cost) and an independent variable (some relevant activity), so that costs can be estimated based on the behavior of the independent variable over time. This cost function often is represented by the basic formula $y = a + bx$, where y is the dependent variable (cost), x is the independent variable, and a and b are approximations of true (but unknown) parameters. In practice, such cost approximations typically are based on two major assumptions: (1) Linear cost functions can be used to approximate nonlinear situations, and all costs can be categorized as either fixed or variable within a relevant range; and (2) the true cost behavior can be sufficiently explained by one independent variable instead of more than one variable. Problems of changing price levels, productivity, and technological changes also are assumed away under this approach.

The analytical task in choosing among possible cost functions is to approximate an appropriate slope coefficient (b)—defined as the amount of increase in y for each unit increase in x—and a constant or intercept (a)—defined as the value of y when x is 0. The analyst may use goodness-of-fit tests, ranging from simple scatter diagrams to full-fledged regression analysis, to ensure that the cost function is plausible and that the relationship is credible. Physical observation, when possible, probably provides the best evidence of a credible relationship.

Four major types of cost functions are suggested by this discussion of fixed and variable costs:

1. A fixed cost does not fluctuate in total as x changes within the relevant range, that is, $y = a$, because $b = 0$.
2. A proportionately variable cost fluctuates in direct proportion to changes in x, that is, $y = bx$, because $a = 0$.
3. A step-function (or semifixed) cost is nonlinear because of breaks in its behavior pattern, that is, $y_1 = a_1, y_2 = a_2, y_3 = a_3$, and so forth.

4. A mixed or semivariable cost is a combination of variable and fixed elements, that is, its total fluctuates as x changes within the relevant range, but not in direct proportion, that is, $y = a + bx$.

The first three of these cost functions are relatively straightforward and simple to resolve. The mixed-cost situation is the more common, however, and more problematic.

Figure 3–1 provides a graphic interpretation of a mixed cost. The fixed portion typically is the result of providing some capacity, whereas the variable portion is the result of using the capacity, given its availability. A photocopying machine, for example, often has a fixed monthly rental cost plus a variable cost based on the number of copies produced. Ideally, there should be no accounts for mixed costs—all such costs should be subdivided into two accounts, one for the variable portion and the other for the fixed portion. In practice, however, such distinctions seldom are made because of the difficulty of analyzing day-to-day cost data into variable and fixed sections. Even if such distinctions were possible, the advantages might not be worth the additional clerical effort and costs.

There are several basic methods for approximating cost functions. These methods are not mutually exclusive and frequently are used in tandem to provide cross-checks on assumptions. The five most commonly used methods include the following:

1. Analytic or industrial-engineering method entails a systematic examination of labor, materials, supplies, support services, and facilities, sometimes using time-and-motion studies, to determine physically observable input-output relationships.
2. Account analysis involves a classification of all relevant accounts into variable- or fixed-cost categories by observing how total costs behave over several fiscal periods.
3. High-low method calls for estimations of total costs at two different activity levels, usually at a low point and a high point within the relevant range; the difference of the dependent variable is divided by the difference of the independent variable to estimate the slope of the line represented by b.
4. Visual-fit method applied by drawing a straight line through the cost points on a scatter diagram, which consists of a plot of various costs experienced at various levels of activity.
5. Regression methods refer to the measurement of the average amount of change in one variable that is associated with unit increases in the amounts of one or more other variables.

The high-low method often is used when there are a limited number of data points. This approach can be illustrated by the following example.

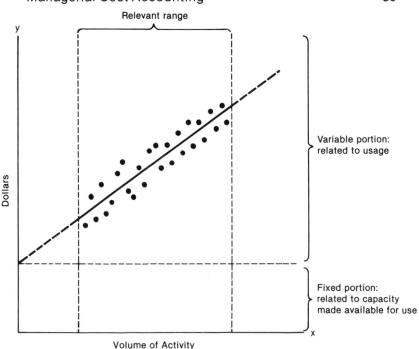

Figure 3–1. Graphic Illustration of Mixed Cost

Several municipal golf courses operated by the City of Rurbania require varying levels of maintenance, depending on the season of the year. Over the past twelve months, repair costs for the various types of power equipment used in this maintenance program have ranged from a high of $3,000 during the month of September to a low of $1,900 during the month of February. The hours of labor required by the groundskeepers also varied considerably during this twelve-month period, from a high of 2,300 hours in September to a low of only 700 hours in February. Using the high-low method, the following cost function can be derived:

	Labor Hours (x)	*Repair Expense (y)*
High (*h*)	2,300	$3,000
Low (*l*)	700	$1,900
Difference (*d*)	1,600	$1,100

$$\text{variable rate } (b) = \frac{d_y}{d_x} = \frac{\$1,100}{1,600} = \$0.6875 \text{ per labor hour}$$

fixed component = total mixed cost less variable component

$$\text{At } x_h = \$3,000 - \$0.6875(2,300)$$
$$= \$3,000 - \$1,581 = \$1,419$$
$$\text{At } x_l = \$1,900 - \$0.6875(700)$$
$$= \$1,900 - \$481 = \$1,419$$

Therefore, the mixed-cost formula is $1,419 per month plus $0.6875 per labor hour. In budgeting for equipment-repair costs, these calculations would suggest that an annual fixed cost of $17,028 (12 × $1,419) plus a variable cost of $0.6875 per labor hour should be provided. Assuming that 18,000 labor hours are required annually, the total equipment-repair budget for the municipal golf courses in Rurbania would be 18,000 × $0.6875 + $17,028, or $29,403.

The high-low method becomes statistically less reliable as the number of available data points increases. In the previous example, the high-low method used only two out of twelve available data points. Since there is a danger in relying on extreme points, which may not be representative of normal cost situations, the high-low method may have limited application in cost approximations.

Regression analysis (or the least-squares method) seeks to determine the best fit of a straight line drawn between the plots on a scatter diagram. Regression analysis seeks to identify the average amount of change in a dependent variable that is associated with changes in one or more measurable independent variables. When only two variables are studied (for example, shipping costs in relation to the number of units shipped), the analysis is called simple regression; when more than two variables are analyzed (for instance, shipping costs in relation to units shipped, weight of those units shipped, and shipping distance), it is called multiple regression.[2] Although the subject of regression analysis is too extensive to deal with at this point, it may be helpful to provide a basic example using data from the previous cost analysis.

The data and calculations required to solve the simple-regression equations for the twelve months of equipment-repair expenses for the maintenance of the Rurbania municipal golf courses are shown in table 3-1. Note that the fixed-cost component (a) is somewhat higher —approximately $1,447 per month—than when only the two extreme data points were considered, and the variable-cost component (b) is lower—$0.62707 per labor hour. Thus, if 18,000 labor hours were to be budgeted on the basis of this analysis, the total equipment-repair budget would be 12 × $1,447 + 18,000 × $0.62707 or $28,651. This analysis might be repeated using data over several years (thus increasing the data points) if the equipment-repair operation has been fairly stable (for example, if no new major items of

Table 3-1
Simple Regression Analysis

Month	Labor Hours (x)	Repair Expense (y)	x^2	y^2	xy
August	2,200	$2,800	4,840,000	7,840,000	6,160,000
September	2,300	3,000	5,290,000	9,000,000	6,900,000
October	1,900	2,500	3,610,000	6,250,000	4,750,000
November	1,200	2,500	1,440,000	6,250,000	3,000,000
December	1,200	2,400	1,440,000	5,760,000	2,880,000
January	900	2,000	810,000	4,000,000	1,800,000
February	700	1,900	490,000	3,610,000	1,330,000
March	1,100	1,900	1,210,000	3,610,000	2,090,000
April	1,400	2,100	1,960,000	4,410,000	2,940,000
May	2,000	2,600	4,000,000	6,760,000	5,200,000
June	2,100	2,800	4,410,000	7,840,000	5,880,000
July	2,200	2,900	4,840,000	8,410,000	6,380,000
Totals	19,200	$29,400	34,340,000	73,740,000	49,310,000

Regression Equations

$$y = na + b\Sigma x$$
$$xy = a\Sigma x + b\Sigma x^2$$

Solving simultaneously:

$$29,400 = 12a + 19,200b$$
$$49,310,000 = 19,200a + 34,340,000b$$
$$47,040,000 = 19,200a + 30,720,000b$$
$$49,310,000 = 19,200a + 34,340,000b$$
$$-2,270,000 =$$
$$b = 0.62707$$
$$a = 1,446.69$$

equipment have been added that have different repair requirements). Alternately, the equipment-repair budget might be developed to support two semi-annual allotments to reflect the different cost requirements during the heavy-use months (May through October) and the lighter-use months (when some major overhauls of equipment might be undertaken). Under this approach, two separate regression analyses might be prepared.

Whatever method is used to formulate cost approximations, it is important in managerial cost accounting to have reasonably accurate and reliable predictions of costs. Such cost estimates usually have an important bearing on a number of operational decisions and can be used for planning, budgeting, and control purposes. The division of costs into fixed and variable components (and into engineered, discretionary, and committed categories) highlights major factors that influence cost incurrence. Although cost functions usually represent simplifications of underlying true relationships, the use of these methods depends on how sensitive the manager's decisions are to the errors that may be introduced by these simplifications. In some situations, additional accuracy may make little difference in the decision; in others, it may be very significant. Selection of a cost function often is a decision concerning the cost and value of information.[3]

Sensitivity and Contingency Analyses

Many decision situations involve conditions of *uncertainty;* therefore, cost analysis often must provide for explicit treatment of uncertainty. Uncertainty about the future—typically present in most long-range decision situations—is difficult to account for in the analysis of costs. Several techniques, applicable under varying circumstances, have been developed for dealing with such uncertainty. Two of these techniques—sensitivity and contingency analyses—are particularly applicable to the problems of cost determination discussed to this point.

Sensitivity analysis measures (often rather crudely) the possible effects on alternatives under analysis resulting from variations in uncertain elements. In most problems, there are a few key parameters about which there is a good deal of uncertainty. Analysts faced with this situation must first attempt to determine a set of "expected values" for these parameters, as well as for all other parameters. Recognizing that the expected values for uncertain-cost components, at best may be only "guesstimates," the analyst might use several values (optimistic, most likely, and pessimistic) to determine how sensitive the results might be (for example, the relative ranking of the alternatives under consideration) in light of variations in the uncertain parameters. In short, sensitivity analysis is a "what-if" technique that attempts to measure how the expected values in a decision situation will be affected by changes in the data.

The data in table 3-2 might serve to illustrate how sensitivity analysis can be applied to disclose the variations in rankings among alternatives based on anticipated costs. Two related points concerning uncertainties are illustrated in this table. First, it points up that the range of uncertainty may vary from alternative to alternative. Second, it underlines the fact that uncertain costs may not always be the critical factor in determining the best solution; although uncertain costs are lowest in the case of alternative C, it still ranks third except under conditions of high, or pessimistic, uncertain costs.

Table 3–2
Sensitivity Analysis under Various Uncertain-Cost Levels

Cost Levels	A	B	C
Expected value of certain costs	$ 9,150	$ 8,560	$ 9,875
Medium expected value of uncertain costs	$ 6,550	$ 6,775	$ 6,450
Expected value of all costs	$15,700	$15,335	$16,325
Ranking of alternatives	2	1	3
High expected value of uncertain costs	$ 8,120	$ 8,880	$ 7,530
Expected value of all costs	$17,270	$17,440	$17,405
Ranking of alternatives	1	3	2
Low expected value of uncertain costs	$ 5,400	$ 5,600	$ 5,200
Expected value of all costs	$14,550	$14,160	$15,075
Ranking of alternatives	2	1	3

Contingency analysis examines the effects on alternatives under consideration when a relevant change is postulated in the criteria for evaluation. This approach can also determine the effects of a major change in the general environment of the problem situation. In short, it is a form of "with-and-without" analysis. In the field of public health, for example, various approaches to a state agency's responsibility for environmental-health programs might be evaluated with and without a major new program of health-code enforcement. In a local context, various possible park sites might be evaluated under conditions of existing population distribution and the configuration of present access routes. Additional evaluation then might be made, assuming different population distributions and under various route configurations.

Although these techniques for dealing with uncertainty may be useful in a direct analytical sense, they also may contribute indirectly to the resolution of problem situations. Through sensitivity and contingency analysis, it may be possible to gain a better understanding of the really critical uncertainties of a given problem. With this knowledge, a newly designed alternative might be formulated that would provide a reasonably good hedge against a range of the more significant uncertainties.

Cost-Accounting Procedures

The importance of developing accurate cost measures for fiscal planning and control has led to the establishment of cost accounting as a major tool of management. Cost accounting is the process of assembling and recording all the elements of expense incurred to attain a purpose, to carry out an activity, operation, or program, to complete a unit of work or project, or to do a specific job. Decisions must be made as to the distribution of direct and indirect costs in the operation of any class of cost accounts to arrive at an accurate estimate of total cost. The expense of obtaining the cost data, however, must be maintained at a reasonable level, and the distribution should not go beyond the point of practical use.

Classes of Cost Accounts

Several classes of cost accounts may be relevant in measuring the cost of public programs. *Absorption* or *full costing* considers all the fixed and variable costs associated with the goods or services in question. Unless an accrual accounting system has been installed, however, this approach may encounter several problems. Budgetary appropriations may not be a good measure of current expenses, since encumbrances for items not yet received may be included, or expenditures to cover outstanding encumbrances from the preceding fiscal period may be excluded. Therefore, a common approach to determining unit costs by simply dividing the performance unit (for example, number of streetlights maintained) into the current budget allocation for the activity may produce rather misleading results. Even if the costs are limited to expenditures, current unit costs may be overstated if new capital equipment is included in the expenditures or if there is a large increase in inventories. On the other hand, unit costs may be understated in most municipal accounting systems because of a failure to account for the drawing down of inventories or for depreciation (or user costs) of equipment.

The method of assigning overhead or indirect costs to operating departments is one of the more controversial aspects of the full-costing approach. *Overhead* includes the cost of various items that cannot be conveniently charged directly to the jobs or operations that are benefited, including general administrative expenses. It can be argued, for example, that the public-works department should be assigned part of the costs of the personnel department, the accounting department, and other service or auxiliary agencies. These indirect costs often are distributed to operating departments or projects on a formula basis, as determined by labor hours, labor costs, or total direct costs of each job or operation.

Many of these indirect costs, however, are clearly beyond the control of the managers of operating departments. *Responsibility costing* assigns to an agency only those costs that its managers can control or at least influence. Many argue that this approach is the only proper measure of an agency's financial stewardship. Responsibility costing will be discussed further in a subsequent section of this chapter.

A useful approach to cost accounting is to consider only the variable or incremental costs of a particular operation. For example, the city manager might want to know how much extra it would cost to keep the public swimming pools open evenings, or how much increasing the frequency of trash collection from two to three times a week would cost. This approach, called *direct costing,* is relatively easy to associate with the budget and is very helpful for incremental decision making.

Two approaches to cost accounting frequently used in the private sector are job-order costing and process costing. *Job-order costing,* as the name implies, is used by companies whose products are readily identified by individual units or batches, each of which receives measurable attention and effort. Industries that commonly use the job-order method include construction, printing, furniture, machinery manufacturing, aircraft, and so forth. The essential feature of the job-cost method is the attempt to apply costs to specific jobs, which may consist of a single physical unit (for example, a custom sofa) or a few like units in a distinct batch or job lot (for example, twelve end tables).

Process costing is most often found in such industries as chemicals, oil refining, textiles, plastics, food processing, meat packing, mining, glass, cement. These industries are characterized by the mass production of like units, which usually pass in continuous fashion through a series of uniform production steps called operations or processes. Costs are accumulated by departments (often identified by operations or processes) with attention focused on the total department costs for a given period in relation to the units processed. *Average unit costs* are determined by dividing accumulated department costs by the quantities produced during the period. Unit costs for various operations can then be multiplied by the number of units transferred to obtain total costs applicable to those units. Cost differences in individual products cannot be determined using this method.

Process costing creates relatively few accounting problems when applied in the public sector. Unit costs can be calculated for many activities by simply dividing total program costs for a given period by the number of persons served, miles of roads patrolled, number of inspections made, tons of trash collected, or some other applicable measure of activity volume during the same period. When it is important to determine costs in greater detail by individual projects or tasks, a job-order-costing approach is needed just as it is in the private sector.

Cost Allocation

Cost allocation (sometimes called "cost absorption") is necessary whenever the full cost of a service or product must be determined. Examples of this requirement in the public sector include the costing of governmental grants and contracts, the establishment of equitable public-utility rates, the setting of user rates for internal services that are expected to operate on a breakeven basis (that is, recover full costs), and the determination of fees (for inspections, for example). The costs that must be considered in cost allocation include the variable, fixed, direct, and indirect components.

Variable costs that can be directly associated with a given service or activity do not represent an allocation problem. Such costs usually can be measured directly, using methods outlined in the previous section.

A given department may also experience direct, fixed costs, which should be allocated to specific services or projects. These direct costs, however, do not vary with the activities being measured. Such costs might be allocated by assuming some level of operation (number of persons to be served, for instance), and dividing the total annual cost by the estimated level of activity to arrive at a unit rate. Other direct, fixed costs may have to be allocated on the basis of some arbitrary physical measure, such as floor space occupied. In either case, it is important that full accrued costs are allocated to avoid the problem of encumbrances previously alluded to.

Costs identified as direct to the total agency or organization that must be allocated to various departments or programs for purposes of determining full unit costs represent a major allocation problem. The salaries of various administrative and support personnel in a hospital, for example, are direct costs of the hospital as a whole. When allocated to various separate departments or service functions—such as the intensive-care unit, nursery, surgery, cafeteria, laboratories, and other components of the hospital— these salaries become indirect costs to these units. The basis for such allocations, although often arbitrary, should be reasonable and should be based on services provided to these related units.

As previously noted, some overhead items can be identified directly with specific departments or programs (that is, they are direct costs of these departments); others have to be arbitrarily allocated because they cannot be traced directly to the individual departments (they are indirect costs). Therefore, overhead often is separated into two categories. Actual overhead costs incurred typically are recorded by means of an overhead-clearing account and some type of subsidiary record, such as a departmental-expense analysis or overhead-cost sheets. Allocated or applied overhead (indirect costs) is distributed through the use of predetermined rates.

One approach to the allocation of overhead as an indirect cost involves the identification of a number of indirect-cost pools. Each pool represents the full costs associated with some specific administrative or support function (which cannot be allocated directly to individual projects or activities)—such as the operation and maintenance of the physical plant (including utility costs), central stores, motor pool, computing center, or other internal-service units, general building and equipment usage, central administration. These cost pools are then arrayed from the most general to the most specific with regards to the particular programs or activities for which the overhead rates are to be established. Costs from the more general pools are allocated (or stepped down) to the more specific pools and finally, to the primary functions or activities. The overhead rate (or indirect-cost rate) is then determined by dividing the total direct costs associated with the activity or program into the total indirect costs allocated to that function. Through this approach, it is possible to determine the impacts on the full costs of individual programs, projects, or activities arising from changes in these indirect costs.

Under- or overapplication of overhead may develop when predetermined rates are used, and significant differences might arise from month to month. However, if the cost-approximation methods have produced reliable estimates, these accumulated differences should become relatively insignificant by the end of the fiscal year.

Accounting for Cost Flows

The procedural steps for summarizing and posting data to cost accounts are shown in figure 3-2. Various accounting mechanisms must be maintained to ensure the proper recording of cost flows in the transformation from basic cost data to work-and-cost statements. These mechanisms are identified in the following discussion.

The primary record of work performed and expenses incurred—the basic data for cost accounting—often is provided by field reports or job tickets. Each worker may be assigned to a number of jobs or projects, or may work in several different departments or programs during a given period. This distribution of effort should be supported by some record that can be used to identify the amount and kinds of labor expended on each activity, program, or project. A project supervisor or crew foreman may prepare these reports, or it may be desirable to have each individual employee prepare a daily or weekly time sheet or time-and-effort report, indicating work assignments and time spent on each activity. Field reports should be summarized at the end of each payroll period before posting to job-cost sheets or work-and-cost ledgers.

Information from these records can also be used to prepare the payroll register, checks, and journal entries. The journal entries serve as the basis for entries into control accounts and subsidiary records. Hours that cannot be charged directly to a specific project or activity might be indicated as indirect labor.

Daily (or weekly) reports of equipment operators provide summaries of

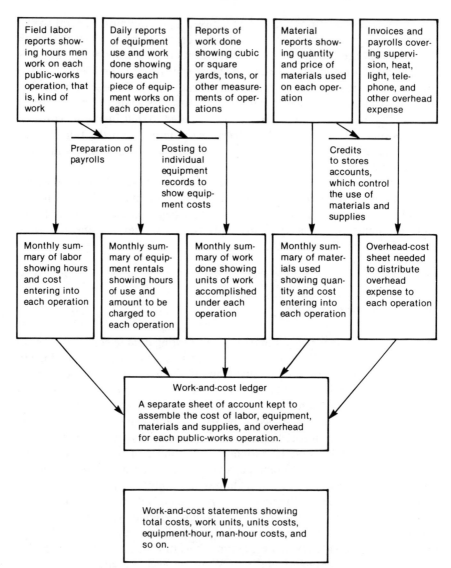

Figure 3–2. Posting Data to Cost Accounts

equipment-use charges (or rental charges) to be distributed to the jobs on the cost ledger. These reports also can be used to post individual-equipment records (showing for each piece of equipment the expenses for labor, gasoline and oil, other supplies, repair costs, overhead, and depreciation). Supervisory personnel may have to provide a separate bill of materials and a statement of the equipment service rendered to each job or operation. Materials and supplies reports indicate withdrawal of stores from stockrooms (inventory), providing credit to stores accounts as well as charges to operating-cost accounts.

Minimal accounting procedures and records are needed if physical-inventory counts are used to periodically update inventory balances. Charges are made to the accounts directly from approved invoices. A subsidiary stores ledger may be established to provide an up-to-date record of the various items on hand. The individual stores records should be debited for amounts received in addition to debiting the control account in the general ledger for purchases. Items removed from stores should be posted to both the general ledger and stores ledger (from copies of the store's requisitions) to provide an up-to-date record.

In smaller municipalities, an inventory of supplies might be accounted for through the general fund by means of periodic physical inventories. Materials and supplies purchased initially would be charged to expenditures, as invoices are approved for payment. A year-end count would be made of the items on hand, and the inventory recorded with an off-setting credit to expenditures. In larger municipalities, the inventory of supplies might be accounted for by means of internal service fund, with a perpetual-inventory system of the type briefly described.

Many indirect costs are reported in substantially the same manner as direct costs (from time reports, stores records, and so on). Certain indirect costs also may be determined from invoices for such terms as utility services, travel expenses, and general office expenses. These indirect costs are posted initially to an overhead clearing account and then are allocated to jobs or activities on a predetermined basis (using indirect cost rates).

The work-and-cost ledger is the final assemblage of the information with respect to all work performed and all costs incurred. Accounts in the work-and-cost ledger generally are posted monthly and are closed on completion of a specific job or project, or at the end of the regular accounting period when unit costs on an activity or program are recorded.

The manager will find cost accounting useful as a basis for decision and action only to the extent that significant information is properly presented. Work-and-cost statements are the essential link between cost records and the manager's use of this information. Monthly summary statements of work completed, expenses, unit costs, and labor-hour production are desirable. Such statements may be readily compiled from information that appears on the work-and-cost ledger. Other statements may be prepared periodically, according to management needs, on such subjects as total labor costs, employee productivity, equipment-rental recoveries, noneffective time and idle equipment, and losses of supplies due to waste or spoilage.

All such statements and reports should be prepared promptly and should be accurate, easy to understand, and classified according to organizational lines of responsibility. Special tables, charts, and graphs enable the essential items to be readily visualized. These visuals may be supplemented by brief written summaries to highlight significant developments and problems. Comparative statements may be prepared in which actual costs of the period under consideration are compared with standard costs or with costs of some prior period. Standard costs will be discussed further in a subsequent section.

Clearing Accounts

Clearing accounts, introduced in the previous section, merit further discussion. Although general accounts usually carry charges for materials, supplies, and equipment at the time these items are purchased, cost accounts recognize these charges only as articles are consumed. This difference between general-accounting and cost-accounting practices necessitates the use of clearing or control accounts. If clearing accounts are established on both ledgers, the total of all basic elements of expense appearing on the work-and-cost ledger should agree with the total expenditures on the appropriation ledger for a given department or agency.

Since personal services are charged to the proper cost accounts on the basis of the same records as used in preparing the payroll, these charges are exactly the same in amount—that is, a clearing account is not necessary. However, noneffective time, such as vacations and sick leave, are chargeable against overhead expense (and subsequently must be prorated back to the direct-cost account). A salary clearing account may be used by universities that pay their academic-year faculty on a twelve-month basis. One-ninth of the faculty member's salary is placed into the clearing account each month (on an as-earned basis), and one-twelfth of the earned salary is paid to the faculty member each month from the clearing account.

Materials and supplies may be purchased and stored for some time before they are actually used. Charges for these goods should be entered into the appropriate cost accounts only when they are consumed in the performance of work. To allow for this time lag, a stores (or inventory) clearing account should be maintained. Purchases of materials are made from this account, and as goods are issued for use, the stores account is credited and the proper appropriation/expenditure and cost accounts are charged.

Equipment costs consist of two elements: acquisition and maintenance. From a cost accounting standpoint, it is desirable to spread the acquisition cost over the active life of the equipment, thereby assigning an appropriate share of the original cost to the activities and jobs on which the equipment is used. Certain maintenance expenditures, especially for motor vehicles and other machinery, are not uniform from day to day. Therefore, it is usually impractical to charge such costs directly to jobs on which the equipment is used. Rental rates or user charges solve the problem of properly allocating both the acquisition on costs and the expenses of upkeep and operation. Such rates are established periodically for various types and pieces of equipment, reflecting the actual cost of operation. All equipment costs are charged initially to an equipment clearing account. As the equipment is used, the proper cost accounts are charged with equipment rental or user charges, and the equipment clearing account is credited. Rentals paid for privately owned equipment leased by the municipality are charged directly to the appropriation/expenditure and cost accounts in the same manner as payrolls. These procedures bring agreement between cost and general accounts.

As noted, overhead or indirect costs may be accumulated in a separate clearing account and then allocated to the job or activity accounts on some equitable basis. These allocations may be made weekly or monthly, or may be made at the end of a fiscal period (quarterly or annually).

A final procedure is necessary if the appropriation accounts are to control the cost accounts in connection with work done by one department for another within the same government. Such interagency services should appear as an expense in the cost accounts. To bring the appropriation/expenditure account into agreement, interagency bills for cost transfers should be prepared based on actual work records, charging one department and crediting the other for the work done. The appropriation/expenditure account of the department doing the work should be credited to increase the total available funds rather than to reduce the expenditures of that department by subtracting the amount from the expenditures previously shown.

Standard Costs and Variance Analysis

Standard costs relate the cost of production to some predetermined indices of operational efficiency. If actual production costs vary from these standards, management must determine the reasons for the deviation and whether it is controllable or noncontrollable with respect to the responsible unit. Misdirected efforts, inadequate equipment, defective materials, or any one of a number of other factors can be identified and eliminated through a standard-cost system. In short, standard costs provide a means of cost control through the application of variance analysis.

Standard-cost systems have received broad application in the private sector. Their use in government and in the not-for-profit area has been very limited, although such standards have potential application in a number of public-sector environments.

In setting up standards, optimal or desired (planned) unit costs and related workload measures (for example, measures of time-and-effort, number of persons served, yards of dirt moved, or some other measure of activity volume) are established for each job or activity. Total variances are determined by comparing actual results with planned performance. Then price, rate, or spending variances should be determined for differences between standard and actual costs. Quantity or efficiency variances can be developed for differences between actual and standard usage. Knowledge of cost (price) and usage (efficiency) differences enables the manager to identify more clearly the cause and responsibility for significant deviations from planned performance.

Although there are no hard-and-fast methods for establishing standard costs in the public sector, workload and unit-cost data from previous years serve as a logical starting point. More detailed studies may be required to determine the quantity and cost of personal services, materials, equipment, and overhead associated with particular kinds of work or volume of activity. For each of these cost elements, unit costs can be estimated by adjusting trend data for expected changes during the next fiscal period. Standards should be established for each of the cost elements entering into a given job or operation. These standards can then be combined to establish a unit-cost standard for the particular type of work, activity category, or program element.[4]

Standard costs should be systematically reviewed and revised when they are found to be out-of-line with prevailing cost conditions. Changes in these standards may be required when new methods are introduced, policies are changed, wage rates or material costs increase, or there are significant changes in efficiency of operation. Furthermore, standard costs are local in their application—such standards often will differ from city to city, reflecting different labor conditions, wage rates, service-delivery problems, and operation methods.

Responsibility Accounting and Performance Evaluation

The overall performance of an organization can be evaluated from the aggregate information provided through a financial-accounting and reporting system. A key to effective management control, however, is the design of an information system that can provide periodic reports on the performance of individual departments, programs, and managers responsible for various activities, so that, where necessary, corrective action can be taken on a timely basis. Ideally, the design of an organizational structure and a management control system should be interdependent. In practice, however, the organizational structure usually is in place and taken as a given when control systems are developed or modified. The concept of responsibility accounting has emerged to accommodate the need for management information within an organization at a more specific level of detail than can be provided by procedures of financial accounting. Responsibility accounting is a system of accounting that recognizes various responsibility centers within an organization, reflecting the plans and action of these centers by assigning pertinent costs and revenues to them.[5]

Responsibility Centers and Cost Centers

Responsibility accounting attempts to report results (actual performance) so that: (1) significant variances from planned performance can be identified; (2) reasons for the variances can be determined; (3) responsibility can be fixed; and (4) timely action can be taken to correct problems. This information is reported to managers directly responsible for an activity or operation as well as to the next higher level in the management hierarchy. Under this approach, departments, programs, and functions are referred to as responsibility centers. In municipal government, for example, the cost of operations of the traffic-control division, the vice squad, the detective division, the forensic laboratory, and so forth might be reported separately so that the police commissioner could hold each unit accountable for their respective areas of responsibility.

In the private sector, responsibility centers may take several forms: (1) a *cost center* is the smallest segment of activity or area of responsibility for which costs are accumulated; (2) a *profit center* is a segment of a business, often called a division, that is responsible for both revenue and expenses, and (3) an *investment center,* like a profit center, is responsible both for revenue and expenses but also for related investments of capital. Since relatively few public agencies generate sufficient revenues to be self-supporting (an exception being some forms of public utilities), but instead rely on appropriations from the general fund, the cost center is the most common building block for responsibility accounting. In fact, the terms cost center and responsibility center often are used interchangeably in public-sector applications.

Costs charged to responsibility centers should be separated between direct and indirect costs. Since not all direct costs are controllable at the responsibility-center level, direct expenses should be further broken down between controllable and responsibility center to estimate the full cost of operations at that level. A distinction is sometimes made between a cost center, as one that is fully burdened with indirect costs, and a service center, which may be assigned only the direct portion of overhead.

Controllability is a matter of degree. A controllable cost has been defined as any cost that is subject to the influence of a given manager of a given responsibility center for a given period. Responsibility accounting focuses on human responsibility, placing emphasis on the work of specific managers in relation to well-defined areas of responsibility. Managers often inherit the effects of their predecessors' decisions. The long-term effects of costs such as depreciation, long-term lease agreements, and the like seldom qualify as a controllable cost on the performance report of a specific responsibility-center manager. To illustrate this point, consider the costs of nursing services in a hospital. The extent to which these costs are controllable at the responsibility or cost-center level depends on the policies of top management regarding intensive care, the lead time available for planning the number of nurses in relation to patient loads, the availability of short-term or part-time help, and so on. Some nursing managers may have relatively little control over such cost-influencing factors. These factors must be taken into account when judging performance. Clearly, an item such as depreciation on the hospital building is outside the realm of controllable costs at the responsibility-center level.

Performance Reports

Most performance measurement models in the private sector are tied to profits; for example, profit percentage (profit divided by sales), return on investment (profit divided by initial investment); and residual income (profit minus deduction for capital costs). At the cost-center level, however, profits are not a viable measure; rather, performance measurement most often is provided by comparing actual costs against a budget. Thus a variance can be defined as the difference between the amount budgeted for a particular activity (during a given period) and the actual cost of carrying out that activity. Variances may be positive (under budget) or negative (over budget).

Performance reports usually are aggregated "from the bottom-up." An array of detailed expenditure categories may be monitored within a given cost center (for example, various objects of expenditure or line items). These categories may be aggregated (and reported to the next level in the management hierarchy) into a single comparison in terms of the actual costs of personal services (salaries, wages, and employee benefits) and of operations (all other direct costs) versus the amounts budgeted for these broad categories. Specific items might be broken out from operations (for example, travel, computing, rental charges), depending on the nature of the cost center's activities (and the needs of management). This aggregation/selective reporting supports the concept of management by exception—the manager's attention at each level in the management hierarchy can be concentrated on the variance from the budget deemed to be most important.

An alternate reporting format would be to group according to predetermined program elements (this approach is particularly applicable where a program-budget format has been adopted). The aggregation of data would then proceed by subprogram and programs. Yet another approach is to report costs by levels of service (particularly applicable where a zero-base-budget format has been adopted). The costs associated with providing a minimum level of service during a given period and with increments of service above this minimum can provide important management insights for future planning.

Performance reporting can be undertaken without a full-blown responsibility-accounting system supported by designated cost centers. Performance data can be developed for management purposes independent of the budget and control accounts. In fact, this kind of performance reporting has been used in governmental operations for some time, particularly in the justification of budget requests. It also has been used as a management-control mechanism for assessing cost and work progress where activities are fairly routine and repetitive.

Under this approach, units of work are identified and changes in the quantity (and on occasion, quality) of such units are measured as a basis for analyzing financial requirements. The impacts of various levels of service can be tested, and an assessment can be made of changes in the size of the client group to be served. This approach is built on the assumption that certain fixed costs remain fairly constant regardless of the level of service provided and that certain variable costs change with the level of service or the size of the group served. Marginal costs for each additional increment of service provided can be determined through such an approach. With the application of appropriate budgetary heuristics, these costs then can be converted into total-cost estimates.

A number of attempts have been made to formulate more specific productivity measures applicable to the public sector (the concept of public productivity improvement will be discussed in further detail in a subsequent chapter). In general, these efforts have been limited because of the inability of management to identify appropriate, valid, output relationships. Limitations in this area are one of the major weaknesses of management control in the public sector. Therefore, efforts must continue to improve techniques available to public managers for performance measurement and evaluation. Responsibility-accounting procedures can provide important inputs to these efforts.

Responsibility Accounting and Management
by Objective (MBO)

The emphasis on controllable costs and budgeted results in responsibility accounting makes it a good supporting companion to MBO procedures. MBO involves the joint formulation by a manager and his or her superior of a set of goals and objectives and of plans for achieving them in a forth-coming period.[6] MBO plans often take a form that is amenable to respon-sibility accounting in that they include a budget with supplementary objec-tives, such as levels of safety, management training, and so on, that may not be incorporated in the budget. The performance of the manager is then evaluated through these budgeted objectives. An MBO budget is negotiated between a particular manager and his or her superiors for a particular period with a particular set of expected internal and external influences in mind. Thus, managers are not held responsible for costs that are beyond their control and, consequently, may be willing to accept assignments that evidence more than the usual management challenges.

Responsibility versus Blame

Variances, budgeted results, and other techniques of responsibility account-ing are neutral devices. When viewed positively, they can provide managers with significant means for improving future decisions. They also can assist in the delegation of decision-making responsibility to lower levels within an organization. These techniques, however, frequently are misused as negative management tools—as means of finding fault or placing blame. This negative use stems, in large part, from a misunderstanding of the ra-tionale of responsibility accounting.

Responsibility accounting seeks to assign accountability to those indi-viduals who have the greatest potential influence, on a day-to-day basis, over the costs in question. It seeks to determine which individuals in an organization are in the best position to explain why a specific outcome has occurred. It is the reporting responsibility of these individuals to explain the outcome regardless of the degree of their control or influence over the results.[7]

It is easy to criticize the concept of controllability; nearly every cost is affected by more than one factor. Energy prices, for example, are influ-enced by various external forces, and energy usage is influenced by more than one manager within an organization. By the same token, a purchasing manager may have some influence over unit prices but relatively little influ-ence over the use of materials purchased. In some cases, however, the pur-chasing manager may influence the results of material usage, particularly if he purchased inferior-quality materials or was "locked into" a bidding pro-cess that resulted in the acquisition of materials that only met minimum specification.

Passing the buck is an all-too-pervasive tendency in any large organiza-tion. When responsibility is firmly fixed, however, this tendency is sup-posedly minimized. Nevertheless, a careful balance must be maintained between the careful delineation of responsibility on the one hand and a too-rigid separation of responsibility on the other. When responsibility is overly prescribed, many activities may fall between the cracks. This problem is particularly evident when two or more activities are interdependent. Under such circumstances, responsibility cannot be delegated too low in the organization but must be maintained at a level that will ensure cooperation among the units that must interact if the activities are to be carried out successfully.

Introducing Managerial-Cost Accounting in Government

If the objective of a governmental unit is to control cost as well as to control expenditures against the budget appropriation, then total costs as well as expenditures must be accounted for in the financial activities of that unit. The requirements for full costing, in terms of accrual accounting, may be more than many governments are prepared to undertake. A shift to accrual accounting initially may be difficult and costly, involving a level of sophistication seldom found in local-government accounting. Most governments will not undertake this conversion unless there is a clear demonstration that better management (in terms of economies and efficiencies) will be attained.

Adopting a Modified Accrual Basis

In those governments that have adopted detailed encumbrance procedures in conjunction with cash-obligation accounting, it often has been found that a shift to a modified accrual basis, accompanied by simplifications in allotment procedures, does not increase overall administrative costs. And, in some cases, this shift can result in measurable savings. The changeover involves making adjustments for inventories, depreciation of fixed assets, the use of clearing accounts for various cost components, and a clear delineation and allocation of direct- and indirect-overhead costs. Many of the exceptions from a full-accrual basis can be accommodated in the accounting system through entries in worksheets rather than in the general ledger. That is, the accrual data can be developed as an adjustment by worksheet rather than as an adjustment in the accounting records.

Matching the cost of various programs and activities against anticipated results (in terms of direct benefits and/or program effectiveness in achieving some identified objective) is a key component in program budgeting. However, without full costing (and life-cycle costing in the case of major projects that extend over time), assessments of costs and benefits may be incomplete and inappropriately applied as a decision-making mechanism.

Computing unit costs at the departmental or agency level can provide an important means of monitoring and controlling repetitive operating costs. These unit costs can be compared with: the cost of earlier fiscal periods, the cost of other departments carrying out similar operations, or standard costs.

Although cost recovery is a standard fixture of commercial-type funds, the problem also exists, albeit to a lesser extent, in some governmental operating funds as well. For example, the public-works department may be expected to repair a street torn up in installing lines for a private-utility company. These repairs should be made on a cost-reimbursement basis. The charge for this service should include a fair share of equipment costs (often overlooked without an accrual accounting system or equivalent data). Costs of long-term municipal resources also often can be applied as part of a city's contribution to a state or federal grant program if these costs can be clearly documented.

Accounting for Fund or Program Responsibility Centers

Figure 3-3 illustrates how line-item expenditures can be compared to appropriations under the modified accrual basis of accounting. Current budgetary procedures suggest that expenditures also be classified by function or program, activity, and character. Expenditure records are a poor means for making comparisons on a periodic basis, with other operating units, or for other analytical reasons. If the city illustrated in figure 3-3 is interested in unit costs, departmental costs (or cost-center costs), or program costs, modified accrual expenditures must be converted into costs. Using the data in figure 3-3, the data in table 3-3 can be assumed to illustrate this conversion. These changes between expenditures and costs can be reflected in accounts, or they can be shown as items on a worksheet (see table 3-4).

These costs can now be shown by department and by type of cost. With these adjustments, the departments now become cost centers. Cost centers other than departments may be used to determine costs for a particular activity, for example, costs for a particular police service rather than for the total department. By comparing table 3-5 with figure 3-3, the various difference between costs and expenditures by department and object code can be seen. Another important distribution of costs would be to programs instead of cost centers. This distribution will be discussed in a later chapter.

Summary

Chapter 3 has focused on two basic functions of managerial accounting— cost determination and cost control—and on the more specific techniques

Dept	775	410	100	25	140	100
Total	755	400	100	25	130	100
A	315	154	45	5	61	50
	308	150	45	5	58	50
B	110	75	15	5	10	5
	110	75	15	5	10	5
C	95	62	15	5	9	4
	92	60	15	5	8	4
D	140	46	10	5	44	35
	136	45	10	5	41	35
E	115	73	15	5	16	6
	109	70	15	5	13	6
	Total	Personal Services	Supplies	Travel	Capital Outlay	Debt Service

Appropriation
Actual

Figure 3-3. Actual Expenditures (Including Encumbrances) Compared to Appropriations, by Department and Object

of cost accounting and responsibility accounting, which support these basic functions. Two additional concerns of managerial accounting—planning and performance evaluation—are explored in further detail in subsequent chapters. A basic tenet of managerial accounting is that costs should be incurred only if they can be expected to lead to the accomplishment of predetermined goals and objectives. Thus, although financial accounting is concerned primarily with the accurate and objective recording of past

Table 3–3
Modified Accrual Expenditures Converted to Costs
(dollars)

Personal services		
Accruals of Salary Costs at beginning of year	− 3,000	
at end of year	+ 13,000	
Increase in Salary Costs for period		+ 10,000
Supplies		
Inventory at beginning of year	+ 15,000	
Inventory at end of year	− 10,000	
Change in inventory		+ 5,000
Travel accrual at end of year		+ 2,000
Capital outlay		
All capital expenditures would be eliminated		− 130,000
Debt service (only interest considered at cost)		− 70,000
Capital costs (depreciation of all long-term assets)		+ 225,000

Table 3–4
Costs versus Expenditures
(dollars)

Account	Total Expenditures	Additions	Subtractions	Total Costs
Personal services	400	13	3	410
Supplies	100	15	10	105
Travel	25	2		27
Capital outlays	130		130	
Debt service	100		70	30
Capital costs		225		225
Total	755	255	213	410

events (financial transactions), managerial accounting seeks to provide management information for improved decisions in the future.

Various perspectives of cost were discussed, including fixed and variable costs; direct and indirect costs; controllable and noncontrollable costs; prime and conversion costs; engineered, discretionary, and committed costs; production and period costs; out-of-pocket and sunk costs; marginal and differential costs; opportunity costs; associated costs; and

Table 3–5
Type of Cost by Departmental Cost Center

Cost Center	Total	Personal Services	Supplies	Travel	Capital Outlay	Debt Service
Total	797	410	105	27	225	30
A	330	155	43	7	110	15
B	115	76	17	5	15	2
C	96	61	14	5	15	1
D	141	46	15	5	65	10
E	115	72	16	5	20	2

investment, recurring, and life-cycle costs. An understanding of these basic cost concepts is essential to the application of managerial-cost-accounting procedures.

An initial step in the control of costs is to determine how costs function under various conditions. This process, called cost approximation or cost estimation, involves an attempt to find predictable relationships (cost functions) between a dependent variable (cost) and one or more independent variables (organizational activities). Of the several methods for approximating cost functions discussed in this chapter, the regression methods are generally most reliable.

Cost accounting is the process of assembling and recording all of the elements of expense incurred (cost) to attain a purpose or to carry out an activity, operation, or program. Costs must be allocated according to their variable, fixed, direct, and indirect components whenever the full cost of a service or product must be determined. Various accounting mechanisms must be maintained to ensure the proper recording of cost flow. In particular, provision must be made in cost accounting for the balancing of inventories, depreciation of fixed assets, the use of clearing accounts for various cost components, and a clear allocation of direct and indirect overhead costs.

Standard costs relate the actual costs to some predetermined indices of operational efficiency. Optimal or desired (planned) unit costs and related workload measures are established for each job or activity, and actual results are then compared with planned performance.

Responsibility accounting seeks to assign accountability to those individuals who have the greatest potential day-to-day influence over the costs in question. Responsibility accounting recognizes various cost centers within an organization and reflects the plans and actions of those centers by assigning pertinent costs and revenues to them. The concept of controllable costs, defined as any cost that is subject to the influence of a given cost-center manager for a given period, is a key to responsibility accounting. A variance can be defined as the difference between the amount budgeted for a particular activity and the actual cost of carrying out that activity during a given period. The emphasis on controllable costs and budgeted results in responsibility accounting makes it a good supporting companion to management by objectives.

The chapter concluded with a brief examination of the procedures required to introduce managerial-cost accounting in government. Adoption of certain modified accrual accounting practices is an important first step to accomplish this conversion. Once in place, these procedures can provide the public manager with critical information with which to achieve more effective management control.

Notes

1. Leo Herbert, Larry N. Killough, and Alan Walter Steiss, *Accounting, Budgeting, and Control for Governmental Organizations* (Blacksburg, Virg.: VPI & SU, 1981)p. 11 (chp. 13).

2. For further discussion of this analytical approach, see George J. Benston, "Multiple Regression Analysis of Cost Behavior," in *Contemporary Cost Accounting and Control* (Belmont, Calif.: Dickenson Publishing, 1970), pp. 657–672.

3. Charles T. Horngren, *Introduction to Management Accounting* (Englewood Cliffs, N.J.: Prentice—Hall, 1978), p. 225.

4. A more advanced forecasting model is presented in Claudia DeVita Scott's *Forecasting Local Government Spending* (Washington, D.C.: Urban Institute, 1972). Under this approach, developed initially for the City of New Haven, each particular class of expenditure is projected according to various explicit assumptions regarding the demand for and supply of service, including demographic projections. Since each service is treated independently, it is possible to examine the impact of a decision to expand or contract particular services in some given period.

5. Horngren, *Introduction to Management Accounting,* p. 246.

6. R. Brady, "MBO Goes to Work in the Public Sector," *Harvard Business Review* (March–April 1973):65–74.

7. Horngren, *Introduction to Management Accounting,* p. 252.

4 Further Cost Considerations

In chapter 3, cost was defined as a release of value required to accomplish some goal, objective or purpose. It is important to recognize that program costs (value) change over time. Therefore, the factors that influence *future costs* must be examined as part of a planning process as well as reflected in a system of management control. Many government officials tend to think of costs strictly in terms of inputs—the financial resources required to support personnel, equipment, materials, and so forth. Costs that cannot be conveniently measured in dollar terms often are dismissed as noncost considerations. Such manipulations, however, do not eliminate the fact that there are important differences between *monetary costs* and *economic costs*. Future costs may have economic implications beyond their more measurable monetary value. When estimating future costs, it is also important to bear in mind that the concept of value often is viewed differently by different people. It is important to ask: "Who will benefit from this expenditure, when, and by how much?" It also is important to extend the question of "How much will the program cost?" by asking "To whom?" These important considerations regarding the commitment of scarce resources must be reflected in any management-control system, particularly one that is developed for the public sector.

Factors Influencing Future Program Costs

No programmatic decision is free of cost, whether or not the decision leads to the actual expenditure of money. And certainly, the choices among alternative strategies for the accomplishment of program goals and objectives may involve many costs. Such choices include not only the expenditure of money but also the consumption of physical resources, the employment of human resources, and the use of time—all critical commodities in government.

In organizing resources to achieve program objectives, the manager must be cognizant of the following factors that influence future costs:

1. Scope and quality of services to be delivered
2. volume of activity required to deliver services

3. methods, facilities, and organization for performing these activities
4. qualities and types of labor, materials, equipment, and elements required by public programs
5. price levels of the various cost elements

These cost-conditioning factors must be analyzed as they relate to each program, activity, and operation to be performed. This analysis should be a continuous process—cost factors should be considered: (1) in developing plans and programs; (2) in preparing budget requests; and (3) after commitments have been authorized and a program or project enters the implementation phase.

Scope, Quality, and Volume

Decisions on standards of service must be made regardless of the accounting system or budget format adopted. Present service standards may be based on past practices that are no longer applicable to current client needs. Therefore, although an inventory of public activities can provide a picture of the present levels of service and methods of delivery, it provides no automatic formulae for determining appropriate service standards for the future. Comparisons with model standards may be helpful. Such models, however, often represent arbitrary goals designed to fit ideal situations. Comparisons of service levels with those of other government agencies should never be taken as conclusive, because of local variations. Such comparisons frequently raise important questions, however, and thereby bring to light instances where service standards may be too low or too high.

Once the desired standards of quality have been formulated and agreed on, the next step is to determine the *volume of work* that will be involved, using the existing organization and established work methods. Many services can be measured by *units of production* (workload measures). Departmental record and reporting systems, if accurately maintained, can provide valuable data on workloads. In other cases, it may be necessary to undertake descriptive analyses of the nature and scope of the activity, including an identification of the required facilities, schedules for performing appropriate activities, and other conditions that might provide some clues as to the volume of work required. Further refinements are possible where procedures have been established for converting volume standards to standard units of personnel and materials or where cost accounting systems have been installed.

Components of Service Delivery

The components of service delivery—the methods, facilities, and organization for performing the work—represent a third set of factors in determining expenditure requirements. Having established the volume of work required to perform certain activities under existing organization and methods, it may be appropriate to examine alternative approaches to determine if greater efficiency and effectiveness can be attained. The development of alternatives should both precede the formulation of budget requests (that is, in the identification of program strategies) and follow the actual allocation of resources (to ensure that the adopted approach fits the resources available).

The program staff should analyze work methods to establish the appropriate mix of personnel, equipment, supplies, and other operating aids to do the job with the least effort and at the least cost. Particular attention should be given to possible increases in productivity through simplified procedures and the use of labor-saving equipment. Department heads and key supervisory personnel should be involved in an analysis of the organization structure to determine the most effective way to coordinate, direct, and control the personnel and equipment used. Information should be available as to what part each organizational unit plays in carrying out each activity and what the limits of responsibility are in each such assignment.

Data on the volume of work, when combined with analyses of methods, facilities, and organization, should provide a basis for determining the quality, quantity, and type of labor, material, equipment, and other cost elements required to carry out each activity at some predetermined level of service. The kind of standards to be applied will vary according to the operation and the available data. If an activity has been subjected to a thorough analysis of life-cycle costs, it may be possible to establish definitive quantity of standards for many of the important cost elements.

For most operations, personnel (labor) is the most critical cost element. Therefore, performance measures that interpret the volume of work in terms of the man-hours (man-days, man-weeks, and so on) required to carry out an activity or program are most useful to a program manager. In addition, it may be possible to establish unit-cost standards for those activities of a type and importance to justify cost-accounting procedures. For nonrepetitive (nonroutine) activities, however, workload and unit-cost measures may not provide the necessary keys to determine the quantities of various cost elements required. In such cases, the manager may have to rely on more subjective measures to provide an adequate basis for programmatic decisions.

Price Levels

The final factor influencing future program costs is the price level of the various cost elements. Personnel represents the most important cost element in most public programs and is subject to management control in two important related areas: job classifications and salary rates. Periodic reviews should be conducted to see that each employee has the proper work assignment in view of his or her pay rate. All too often, skilled employees with higher pay classifications are assigned to tasks that lower-rated persons should perform. Eliminating positions at the lower end of the pay scale may result in false economies if higher-paid personnel eventually have to do the work.

Changes in the salary plan for a given agency should be made only after a thorough study of such factors as: (1) trends in the cost of living, (2) rates paid by comparable public agencies, (3) prevailing rates in the private sector for equivalent job skills, and (4) evaluation of fringe benefits, including sick leave, vacations, extra holidays, and security of tenure. Often improved fringe benefits can provide a bigger "payoff" to employees than increases in the salary and wage scale, which are subject to a larger "tax bite." Sound personnel and pay policies will prove to be a long-run economy.

Prices for materials and equipment are subject to management control only to the extent that the scheduling of these requirements may enable purchases to be made at the lowest price, consistent with necessary quality. Continuous analysis should be made of price trends of frequently used commodities to determine what levels can be anticipated in preparing cost estimates, and appropriate inventories should be maintained of items that are subject to price fluctuations (that is, by purchasing such items in appropriate quantities when they are at a low point in the price cycle). The cost of maintaining an inventory (space requirements, shelf-life of various items, anticipated price changes, and so forth) must also be considered.

Monetary Costs versus Economic Costs

Monetary costs or project outlays may involve research and development costs, investment costs, as well as the cost of operations, maintenance, and replacement. These are the costs that are commonly reflected in financial accounts. Economists often look beyond these concepts of cost to include opportunity costs, associated costs, and social costs. These additional cost perspectives should also be reflected in management planning and control systems.

Monetary Costs

Research and development costs are "front-end" costs that may or may not figure into the actual expenses of a given project or program. R&D costs incurred explicitly for a given project should be included as a project expense. However, general R&D costs that produce advances eventually used to the benefit of more than one project or program must be considered as *sunk costs* and should not be included in the direct-cost estimate for a specific project or program.

Investment costs—expenses incurred to obtain benefits in future periods—may also result in sunk costs or in actual project outlays, depending on the timing of these investments. Consider the decision to build a public-health clinic on land that was purchased some years ago for the purposes of constructing some other public facility (which was never built). Only those additional investment costs required to prepare the site for the clinic should be considered as project outlays and not the previous investment for the purchase of the land, which is a sunk cost.

The decision to build the clinic on this site, as opposed to some other location that would require further investment in land, should be conditioned by whether or not the property owned by the government represents an *inheritable asset.* Sunk costs can become inheritable assets if previous investments can be used to the particular advantage of one alternative over another. The decision to use the property owned by the government for the clinic site should not be based on the past investment if placing the clinic in that location would be an inferior alternative because of identifiable client needs. This decision would simply result in throwing good money after bad.

It is important to distinguish between investment costs and *recurring costs.* Investment costs include those expenditures that vary primarily with the size of a particular program or project but not with its duration. Recurring costs include those operating and maintenance costs that may vary with both the size and duration of the program. Such recurring costs include: salaries and wages, employee benefits, maintenance and repair of equipment, miscellaneous materials and supplies, transfer payments, insurance, and direct overhead costs. These recurring or operating costs do not add to the stock of capital but rather are incurred to maintain, as far as possible, the value of the existing stock. In preparing cost estimates, it is important that these recurring costs be considered over the life cycle of the project or program and not just the costs that might be incurred in the initial budget year.

As these distinctions suggest, some program costs are fixed, that is, are the same regardless of the size of the program or its duration, and other costs are variable. Variable costs may change significantly as the scope of the project or program is increased. Often there is some uncertainty regarding these costs, particularly if the project has a relatively long duration. It is important, therefore, to consider the *marginal* or *incremental* cost of increasing the size or scope of a program or project.

For example, suppose that a county health department is faced with the decision to build one or two health clinics in a given section of the county. The marginal cost of the second clinic is how much more it would cost to build two clinics than it cost to build one. It might be possible, for example, to get quantity discounts on materials and equipment that would reduce the cost of a second clinic. If it is possible to build one clinic for, say, $200,000 and two clinics for $350,000, then the cost of the second clinic that should be considered is the marginal cost of $150,000 and not the average cost of $175,000.

Costs should be considered regardless of where they are carried on the accounts, what organizational units they are connected with, or where the money will come from. Once these costs have been identified, however, it may be important in the final decision to determine whether these costs are to be borne, in part, by another agency or by another level of government.

Opportunity, Associated, and Social Costs

This leads to the concept of *opportunity costs*. If resources are committed to one program, the opportunity to use these resources elsewhere has been preempted. The concept of opportunity costs can be illustrated by returning to the health-clinic example. Having determined the monetary costs required for the proposed facility—the land, materials, labor, staff, capital equipment, and so forth—it may be appropriate to describe some of the alternative uses for these resources. For example, what else could be done with the land? What else could the money to be committed for staff be used for? If bonds are to be issued to finance the capital construction, what other uses might be made of the funds required to meet interest and principal payments (and what is the impact on the community's debt margin)? If these alternate uses are deemed important enough, attempts should be made to estimate the value of such alternatives, that is, to evaluate the benefits that must be given up if the decision is made to go ahead with the proposed clinic. Keep in mind that a basic purpose of cost analysis is to estimate the value of alternatives forgone. Opportunity costs may be extremely important in making decisions among alternative program strategies.

Public spending may preempt other public spending, private investment, or consumption. Which of these sectors is impacted depends on how the project or program is financed. The preemption of other public spending is the most commonly recognized form of opportunity cost—the funding of project A may displace the funding of project B. However, opportunity costs may exist in other areas as well. For example, if the public project is financed by taxation, those who pay taxes lose opportunities to consume or invest the equivalent resources. If the project is financed by issuing bonds that are sold to the public, investment opportunities may be lost in the private sector. Public projects may have opportunity costs because they preempt funds—such projects may also preempt physical opportunities. The siting of a public recreational facility may consume choice lands that could provide desirable sites for residential developments.

Associated costs are "any costs involved in utilizing project services in the process of converting them into a form suitable for use or sale at the stage benefits are evaluated."[1] Associated costs are incurred by the beneficiaries of public programs and services. The incremental costs of travel, food, lodging, and so forth represent the associated costs that must be borne by the users of a public recreational facility. If access to the facility is improved, so that the users' travel costs are reduced, these savings in associated costs might be attributable as benefits arising from improved access.

Associated costs often are an important consideration in the siting of public facilities. Evening classes held by the extension division of a major university at some distance from the population these classes are intended to serve may generate considerable associated costs for the students (especially in these times of high gasoline prices). Moving the classes closer to the target population may increase the direct cost to the program (for instance, in higher rental costs for facilities) but may substantially reduce the associated costs.

Social costs may be defined as the subsidies that would have to be paid to every person who is adversely affected by a public project to compensate them for their "suffering" or disbenefits. Rarely is such compensation actually made (except perhaps when affected individuals enter into litigation and are awarded damages). Therefore, social costs represent an analytical concept.

Social costs can be handled two ways in making a cost analysis.[2] They may be treated as external costs and subtracted from the market value of the output of the project to obtain a net social value. Or they may be treated as opportunity costs, whereby the resources dedicated to the project are examined in terms of potential benefits to those who are adversely affected if these same resources were spent on some alternative program. For example, the development of a sewage-treatment facility may result in reduced property values in adjacent residential areas. These losses may be treated as "negative benefits" and subtracted from the overall benefits of the project to the larger community. Alternatively, the benefits accruing to these property owners from an alternate use of project funds (for example, for the development of a park site) might be calculated, and the project with the larger "yield" would represent the better use of these resources.

Unfortunately, social costs, if included at all in a cost analysis, seldom are treated fairly. Such cost considerations are either underplayed by proponents of the project or overplayed by the opponents of the project. Social costs often carry significant emotional overtones and, therefore, may be difficult to evaluate. Nevertheless, such an evaluation may be a very important part of the overall project/program analysis.

Discounting Future Costs and Benefits

Time is a valuable resource in any public program or project. And yet the value of time often is overlooked, particularly when dollar expenditures this year are compared with those of last year and next year. In developing a cost analysis, however, it is important to recognize that dollar values are not equal over time. Resources on hand today are usually worth more than identical resources delivered at some time in the future. That is, achieving the same results will cost more in the future than they do today because of the impacts of inflation. Therefore, it is important for a program manager to determine what the equivalent value of future costs is in today's terms. This equivalent value often is calculated through the process of *discounting*.

It is generally recognized that the discount rate is a critical factor in the evaluation of any proposed government project that has a life span of greater than one year. The choice of the discount rate may make the difference between the acceptance and rejection of a project. Unfortunately, there are no simple guidelines for determining an appropriate discount rate for public investments.

In theory, the proper criterion on which to judge the desirability of a governmental project, from the viewpoint of the general welfare, is the value of the opportunities bypassed in the private sector when the resources are withdrawn from that sector. It follows from this construct that the appropriate discount rate for the evaluation of a public project is the rate of return that the resources would otherwise provide if utilized in the private sector. In other words, if the same dollars were invested in the private sector, what would be the likely rate of return on this investment?

For several reasons, however, this theoretical approach to the determination of a discount rate fails to yield a fair figure. Private-sector investments seldom have the life span of project commitments in the public sector—the rate of return on a five-year investment seldom provides an equitable basis on which to judge a twenty-year public-debt commitment. Public funds frequently must be invested in facilities and services for which there are no private-sector incentives for investment. Private developers who became involved in the federally promoted "new-town" program in the early seventies anticipated a 15- to 20-percent return on their investment within the first few years. They quickly found that the infrastructure costs of such communities (costs that are borne by the public sector in more conventional urban developments) "ate up their profits," resulting in a 5- to 6-percent return on investment over a relatively long (in private-sector terms) time span. In lieu of these theoretical constructs, various standard-discount rates have been established for the evaluation of public-sector investments. Many economists argue, however, that these rates are too low to provide a fair evaluation.

An alternative approach that reflects both local conditions and the marketplace for investments is to determine: (1) the rate of return that could be achieved if an equivalent amount were to be invested for the same period of time, or (2) the cost of borrowing the capital necessary to finance the project or program. Thus, if an allowable investment of public funds would yield 8 percent, or if the project could be financed through the issuance of bonds carrying a 7.5-percent interest rate, these percentages might be appropriately applied for the purposes of discounting future costs and benefits.

Although the choice of the particular discount rate may be difficult to justify, the procedures for discounting are quite simple. Once you choose an appropriate rate, a table of discount factors can be consulted to determine the appropriate figure to apply to each year in the stream of costs and benefits. However, as the data in table 4-1 illustrate, the selection of the discount rate can significantly affect the final decision.

Uncertainty and Cost Sensitivity

The second special problem in cost analysis is the need to provide some indication as to the effects of *uncertainty* on cost estimates. Seldom will estimates of program costs be precise, especially those costs that are estimated for a few years beyond the next budget. The existence of uncertainties may have an important impact on final program decisions. The effect of this uncertainty should be assessed as fully as possible.

Particular attention should be given to those cost components that are substantial and that would seem likely to vary significantly as alternatives are considered. It may be appropriate to perform some form of *sensitivity analysis* to determine what effect uncertainty has on the cost of these components. Sensitivity analysis tests the effects of possible variations in a specific cost component on a decision or choice among alternatives. If, for example, a slight change in the actual cost of one cost component would change the decision, it can be said that the decision is sensitive to the cost of that component.

Table 4–1
Discounting $1,000 over Ten Years

Year	Discount Factor @ 4 percent	Value	Discount Factor @ 5 percent	Value	Discount Factor @ 6 percent	Value
1	0.961538	$ 961.54	0.952381	$ 952.38	0.943396	$ 943.40
1	0.924556	924.56	0.907029	907.03	0.889996	890.00
3	0.888996	889.00	0.863847	863.85	0.839619	839.62
4	0.854804	854.80	0.822702	822.70	0.792093	792.09
5	0.821927	821.93	0.783526	783.53	0.747258	747.26
6	0.790314	790.31	0.746215	746.22	0.704960	704.96
7	0.759917	759.92	0.710681	710.68	0.665057	665.06
8	0.730690	730.69	0.676839	676.84	0.627412	627.41
9	0.702586	702.59	0.644608	644.61	0.591898	591.90
10	0.675564	675.56	0.613913	613.91	0.558394	558.39
Total		$8,110.90		$7,721.75		$7,360.09

Source: Alan Walter Steiss, *Local Government Finance* (Lexington, Mass.: Lexington Books, D.C. Heath and Company, Copyright 1975, D.C. Heath and Company), p. 213. Reprinted by permission of the publisher.

A classic example might be the decision between two alternative ways of cleaning and maintaining a health clinic or other public facility. One alternative might be labor intensive, that is, heavily dependent on custodial workers, and the other might be capital or machine intensive. Assume that over a ten-year period both alternatives provide the same degree of effectiveness. Suppose it is determined that over the same period the cost of labor-intensive alternative is less expensive than the capital-intensive approach. Obviously, estimates have been made as to the amount of pay raises that each individual would obtain over the ten-year period. If it is estimated that employees will get a 5-percent increase annually, but instead they actually receive a 7-percent increase, would the decision to recommend the labor-intensive alternative still be valid? It is very important to examine cost elements and the sensitivity of decisions to those estimates.

Cost-Benefit Analysis

In theory, the solution to the resource-allocation problem is relatively simple; it is only difficult in practice. In theory, the solution involves the application of available means (limited resources) to achieve the greatest possible value of identified wants (maximize benefits). In modern society, the means often become public budgets. Therefore, the resource-allocation problem is one of (1) maximizing benefits for an established level of cost or a predetermined budget allocation—the so-called fixed-cost or fixed-budget approach; or (2) ascertaining the minimum level of expenditure necessary to achieve some specified level of benefits—the fixed-benefit approach. Either (or both) of these approaches may be used, depending on the context of the allocation problem. In either case, the objective is to facilitate comparisons among alternatives, and, for this purpose, it generally is necessary to hold something constant. The fixed level of benefits or budget may be specified by someone outside the analysis, that is, it may be a given and may be treated as such by the analyst. Very often, however, a major part of the analysis must focus on such a determination.

Statement of the Problem

The crux of cost-benefit analysis lies in a statement of the problem, for explicit knowledge of the problem provides the basis for its solution. As Anatol Rapoport has observed: "The success with which any problem is solved depends to a great extent on the clarity with which it is stated. In fact, the solution of the problem is, in a sense, a clarification (or concretization) of the objectives."[3] Vague problem statements lead to vague methods, where success is doubtful or, at best, erratic. The more a given situation is clarified, the better the classification of the problem and the greater the promise of a successful solution.

A common error in resource-allocation decisions, however, arises from an emphasis on finding the right answer rather than on asking the right question. As Peter Drucker has observed: ". . . there are few things as useless—if not as dangerous—as the right answer to the wrong question."[4]

Cost-benefit analysis is a logical extension of other management-science methodologies, such as systems analysis and operations research. In evaluative scope, however, cost-benefit techniques are more ambitious than most other analytical approaches and, therefore, are more vulnerable to criticism at certain (well-recognized) points. As A.R. Prest and R. Turvey have noted: "One can view cost-benefit analysis as anything from an infallible means of reaching the new Utopia to a waste of resources in attempting to measure the unmeasurable."[5] Some of the criticisms of cost-benefit analysis are based on misconceptions; others are perfectly valid. Many of the valid criticisms, however, are equally applicable to other techniques of analysis. All too often, arguments as to the need to replace relatively poor analysis with better approaches tend to degenerate to assertions that, since analysis is difficult, relatively costly, and often politically troublesome, it should be abandoned in favor of the intuitive approaches. Like the man says: "Don't confuse me with the facts, my mind is made up."

Unfortunately, the techniques of cost-benefit analysis often are misunderstood by public officials and misapplied by unscrupulous analysts. The objective of these analytical techniques is not to make decisions, nor to justify previous decisions, nor to delay matters so that some prior course action or commitment of resources has a greater chance of acceptance or continuance. Rather, two of the primary objectives of cost-benefit analysis are to reduce uncertainty and to bring risk into some range of tolerance by providing more information concerning the consequences of various courses of action in the solution of a problem.

Objective Function, Constraints, and Externalities

In the traditional formulation of the cost-benefit approach, as first outlined by Otto Eckstein, the allocation problem is clarified through the identification of: (1) an objective function, (2) constraints, (3) externalities, (4) a time dimension, and (5) risk and uncertainty.[6] Cost-benefit analysis seeks to rank alternative uses of resources. In the usual situation, several projects or programs are competing for the same scarce resource—each project can be pursued at one or more levels of effort. The problem may be to choose which of several alternatives to adopt and then to choose its optimal scale from several available.

The first step in cost-benefit analysis, therefore, is to select an *objective function*—a measure of the benefits and/or costs associated with each alternative under consideration (quantified in dollar terms to the extent possible). Conceptually, an objective function should represent an indicator of "success"—a benefit measure—that is to be maximized. At times, the resource-allocation problem can be dealt with more effectively by minimizing something, for example, costs. In practice, public managers often are instructed to minimize costs in carrying out their program responsibilities. As a consequence, cost-benefit analysis may be reduced to a cost-efficiency analysis—to obtain the maximum level of output or performance for some fixed level of cost (often inadequate to achieve true program effectiveness).

Frequently, the objective of cost-benefit analysis is stated as the maximization of benefits and the minimization of costs; in reality, however, both cannot be done simultaneously.[7] Costs can be minimized by spending nothing and doing nothing, but in that case no benefits result. Benefits can be maximized within a particular project by spending until marginal returns are zero, but such action may require more funds than are available. Therefore, some composite criterion is needed.

The first cost-benefit criterion to be used was the benefit-cost ratio introduced by the Flood Control Act of 1936.[8] This act established the requirement that water-resource-development projects could be initiated only if an evaluation showed that expected "benefits to whomsoever they may accrue (are) in excess of the estimated costs." A second criterion, well established in the business world and reflecting a legacy of prominent economists such as John Maynard Keynes and Kenneth Boulding, is the *internal rate of return.* A third, and more recently developed indicator is *net benefits,* that is benefits minus costs. This latter criterion purports to summarize all relevant factors and, therefore, is intuitively appealing.

Constraints specify the "rules of the game," that is, the limitations within which solutions must be sought. Frequently, solutions that are otherwise optimal must be discarded because they do not meet these imposed rules. Constraints often are incorporated into mathematical models as parameters or boundary conditions. On a more fundamental level, a fixed budget (or any other imposed resource limitation) is a constraint that limits the level of benefits to be attained (as well as the range of applicable alternatives).

Externalities are those factors—inputs (costs), outputs (benefits), and constraints—that initially are excluded from the problem statement to make it more manageable. The long-range effects of these factors, however, ultimately must be considered. This step usually is undertaken after the objective function or model has been carefully tested and the range of feasible and acceptable alternatives has been narrowed.

In examining the *time dimension* or various alternatives, it is necessary to delineate life-cycle costs and benefits. Life-cycle costing stems from the concept that the funds necessary initially to undertake a program or project should not be the primary consideration, nor should the funding requirements of any particular period dominate the decision. Rather, the decision to undertake a particular course of action should take into account the total-cost impact over time.

Benefits also may vary widely over the life of a program or project. A time lag may be experienced between the initiation of a project and the realization of the first increment of benefits. Benefits may accumulate rapidly or may build gradually; they may reach a peak and decline rapidly or may taper off slowly. Benefits may come in fairly uniform increments or in large blocks. In short, the timing of costs and benefits cannot be ignored. It is not sufficient to merely add the total benefits and subtract the total costs estimated for a given program alternative. Rather, it is necessary to consider the "stream" or pattern of benefits and costs over time and to calculate a measure that can reflect the impact of deferred benefits or future costs.

Benefits that accrue in the present often are "worth" more to their recipients than benefits that accrue sometime in the future—in common parlance, this is the "bird-in-the-hand" phenomenon. Similarly, funds that must be invested today "cost more" than funds that must be invested in the future, since presumably one alternative use of such funds would be to invest them at some rate of return that would increase their value. Therefore, it is necessary to calculate the *present value* of both costs and benefits by multiplying each stream by an appropriate discount factor.

If the alternative is to invest available funds at some interest rate (i), then an appropriate discount factor can be expressed as:

$$\frac{1}{(1 + i)^n} \text{ or } (1 + i)^{-n}$$

where (n) is the number of periods (years) into the future that the benefits or costs will accrue. A high discount rate means that the present is valued considerably over the future, that is, there is a considerable time preference, a higher regard for present costs than for equal future costs, and/or a willingness to trade some future benefits for current benefits. Two reasons exist for discounting public projects: (1) to reflect opportunity costs of public investments, for example, the cost of investing in project A now over investing in project B at sometime in the future; and (2) to reflect a social preference for earlier over later benefits.[9]

In evaluating future costs and benefits, the analyst encounters the problems of risk and uncertainty. Uncertainty is associated with those situations in which one or more courses of action may result in a set of possible specific outcomes but where the *probabilities* of the outcome are neither known or meaningful. If an administrator or public official is willing to assign objective or subjective probabilities to the outcome of uncertain events, such events may be said to involve risk. Risk is associated with situations in which probability distributions can be assigned to the various outcomes, that is, all possible outcomes can be enumerated or described and a likelihood of occurrence can be assigned to each outcome. In short, risk is reassurable uncertainty. Most individuals have a certain tolerance for risk, that is, a willingness "to take a chance" if there is a reasonable possibility for a fair payoff and the cost is not too high. Establishing a probability function can bring problems within more manageable bounds by reducing uncertainty to some level of risk that may be tolerated, depending on an individual's risk threshold. Probabilities can be established either by empirical measurement (by induction) or by statistical inference (by deduction).

Benefit-Cost Ratio

The benefit-cost ratio can be expressed mathematically as follows:

$$R = \frac{\sum\limits_{n=0}^{N} B_n (1 + i)^{-n}}{\sum\limits_{n=0}^{N} C_n (1 + i)^{-n}} = \frac{B}{C}$$

Thus, if the discounted stream of benefits (B) over the life of the project equals \$600,000 and the discounted stream of costs (C) is \$480,000, then the benefit-cost ratio would be 1.25.

A variation on the basic benefit-cost ratio emphasizes the return on invested capital by subtracting costs from both sides of the ratio. In the previous example, assume that the present value of operating costs represents \$160,000 of the total stream of costs. Subtracting operating costs from both benefits and total costs results in the following net benefit-cost ratio:

$$\frac{\$600,000 - \$160,000}{\$480,000 - \$160,000} = 1.375$$

The net benefit-cost ratio becomes larger as operating costs account for an increasingly larger portion of total costs (discounted to present value). In the previous example, for instance, if operating costs accounted for half of the discounted total costs (or $240,000), the net benefit-cost ratio would be 1.5.

Net benefit-cost ratios may be preferable for private enterprise, in which capital is more constraining than operating expenses, especially when taxes are considered. A number of economists argue for the use of gross ratios in the public sector, however, on the basis that legislative bodies should consider operating costs as well as capital costs, giving agencies credit for saving on operating costs by permitting them to spend more on capital costs.

Internal Rate of Return

Since the costs associated with any investment decision usually accrue first, the undiscounted sum of benefits must be considerably larger to yield a favorable project. This characteristic of long-term investments is recognized implicitly by the analytical technique of internal rate of return, which is defined by the following equation:

$$r = \sum_{n=0}^{N} \frac{B_n}{(1 + r)^n} = \sum_{n=0}^{N} \frac{C_n}{(1 + r)^n}$$

It should be noted that the internal rate of return is not set equal to anything. The right side of the equation is the present value of costs and the left side is the present value of benefits. The internal rate of return is that interest rate (r) that brings the two sides of the equation into equilibrium, that is, the return on investment (discounted benefits) that equal the cost of capital.

To illustrate the applicaton of this criterion, assume that a firm is confronted with an investment decision on a new product line. A first-year investment (start-up costs) of $200,000 is required, with estimated annual operating costs of $80,000 and a shut-down cost of $150,000 in the fifth year of operation (when major modifications in the product line would dictate a new investment decision). It is estimated that the firm will have three years of operational returns on this product line, during which time gross profits will average $210,000 annually. In short, for an investment of $590,000 over five years, the firm will obtain a return of $630,000. The question is: At what anticipated rate of return (or cost of capital) would this be a worthwhile investment?

The costs and benefits of this project are shown in table 4–2. An internal rate of return of approximately 20 percent provides one solution to the equation. In other words, if capital costs were less than 20 percent in terms

Table 4–2
Internal-Rate-of-Return Calculations on Five-Year Project

| | | | | Present Value | |
Year	Benefits	Costs	Discount Rate @ 20 percent	Benefits	Costs
1	0	$200,000	0.83333	0	$166,000
2	$210,000	80,000	0.69444	$145,832	55,555
3	$210,000	80,000	0.57870	121,527	46,296
4	$210,000	80,000	0.48225	101,273	38,580
5	0	150,000	0.40188	0	60,282
Total	$630,000	$590,000		$368,632	$367,379

of the interest rate in the current market, the proposed project would be desirable. In practice, the firm would likely examine several alternative investments and select that alternative that exhibits the best internal rate of return. The impact of a modest shift in benefits can be illustrated by the fact that, if the project could be extended by one year, that is, if an additional $210,000 could be earned for an additional $80,000 in operating costs, the internal rate of return would more than double (that is, would be over 40 percent).

Net Benefits

Net benefits is the criterion recommended, if not used, most frequently in contemporary cost-benefit analysis. The formula for calculating the present value of net benefits is:

$$N = -C_0 + \frac{(B_1 - C_1)}{(1 + i)} + \frac{(B_2 - C_2)}{(1 + i)^2} + \ldots + \frac{(B_n - C_n)}{(1 + i)^n}$$

Two projects of equal net benefits might not be regarded indifferently, however. Suppose two projects offered net benefits of $1,000—one involving a present value of benefits of $2 million and a present value of costs of $1.999 million, and the other project with a present value of benefits of $10,000 and a present value of costs of $9,000. Suppose that something went wrong—perhaps the calculations of costs and benefits were off by 10 percent. The first project might have negative net benefits of as much as $200,000, whereas the second would do no worse than break even.

It is sometimes incorrectly assumed that an alternative that ranks first in net benefits will also rank first in its benefit-cost ratio—that these techniques are readily interchangeable. Net present value (net benefits) calculations measure difference, whereas benefit-cost calculations produce a ratio. To illustrate this point, suppose the benefits in alternative A have a present value of $300,000 and costs have a present value of $100,000. The net present value of this alternative would be $200,000 and the benefit-cost ratio would be 3.0. If the present value of benefits in alternative B were $200,000 and that of costs, $40,000, alternative B would have a smaller net present value ($160,000) but a higher benefit-cost ratio (5.0). Knowing the benefit-cost ratio for a given project is not sufficient; it also is necessary to know the size of the project before as much information is available as is given in the present value of net benefits.

Cost Savings as Benefits

A major problem in cost-benefit analysis is the treatment of items that may be considered either as benefits or as cost savings. In dealing with this question, the net-benefits criterion is superior to the benefit-cost ratio method.

To illustrate this point, suppose that a public project is estimated to cost $2 million and to have measurable benefits of $2.4 million (all figures in present-value terms). In addition, it is estimated that this project will increase land values in some parts of the community by an aggregate $600,000 while decreasing other land values by $200,000 (the project might involve the construction of a sewage-treatment plant, the increased service of which would increase some land values while proximity to the facility might lead to the decrease of other land values). If it could be determined that these changes in land values were not simply capitalization of otherwise measured benefits and costs (so that including them would result in double counting), it would be appropriate to incorporate them in the cost-benefit analysis.

How to treat these additional factors, however, remains a problem. Land-value increases could be included as benefits, and decreases in land values could be considered as a cost, resulting in a benefit-cost ratio of 1.364. Or the net change in land value (that is, $600,000 minus $200,000) could be included as benefits, resulting in a ratio of 1.4. Or the net change could be considered a cost savings, yielding a ratio of 1.5 (that is, $2.4 million divided by $1.6 million). In considering several alternative investments, extensive accounting rules and procedures must be devised to keep the analysis comparable. Such ambiguity does not exist in the application of the net-benefits criterion as long as the algebraic sign and the period in which benefits and costs accrue are known.

Monetary Surrogates

In the ideal cost-benefit analysis, all inputs and outputs are evaluated in monetary terms, although in principle any common unit will serve equally well. It is difficult, however, to identify precisely the outputs from many public activities—such as hospitals, libraries, and recreational facilities,—in direct-dollar terms. Therefore, such outputs often are approximated through the use of crude surrogates, that is, indirect measures that purport to gauge benefits in monetary terms. For example, the projected travel-time savings associated with various highway-improvement alternatives often are used as surrogates for a segment of benefits and are translated into monetary values by multiplying some dollar index by the anticipated number of users.

Various indices, sometimes called "proximate criteria," may be used to develop information as to how participants (that is, individuals or groups who are to receive program benefits) view the mission of a program. As with surrogates, attempts often are made to translate these indices into monetary terms. These indices (which, hopefully, are empirically measurable) are then used to identify the desired level of performance of a program. Using this approach, it may be possible to describe different levels of output (performance) in terms of the participants' expectations.

The problem of measuring benefits in monetary terms has led some analysts to return to the more fundamental criterion of average cost. In a benefit-cost ratio, the value of outputs (or benefits) is in the numerator and costs are in the denominator. In the average-cost criterion, costs are in the numerator and output in some physical term is in the denominator. For example, assume the following analysis of two programs designed to encourage students to remain in high school (prevent dropouts) by stimulating their interests in vocational opportunities. Program A is estimated to cost $1.2 million and is designed to reach 320 students, for an average cost of $3,750 per "dropout prevented." Program B, designed to accommodate 400 students, is estimated to $1.8 million, for an average cost of $4,500 per "dropout prevented." On an average-cost basis, program A appears to be the better investment. If it is assumed that the completion of vocational training will add some $15,000 to the life-time earning capacity of each student (a rough surrogate of benefits), then the benefit-cost ratio of program A is 4.0, whereas the benefit-cost ratio of B is 3.33. However, the net benefits of A would equal $3.6 million ($4.8 million minus $1.2 million), and the net benefits of B would be $4.2 million ($6 million minus $1.8 million). Therefore, which program is more effective relative to its costs?

If the capacity of program A could be increased by 80 students at a 25 percent increase in estimated costs, bringing the total cost to $1.5 million, then it obviously is the superior alternative. The expanded version of A would have net benefits of $4.5 million and a benefit-cost ratio of 4.0. But what if the fixed costs of program A were $400,000, so that any expansion beyond the 320 students would require this minimum fixed-cost investment? Under this assumption, the cost of program A to serve 400 students would be the same as program B (that is, $1,200,000 + $400,000 + .25 ($800,000) = $1,800,000), and all criteria would be the same between the two alternatives. As this brief example illustrates, cost-benefit analysis involves more than merely comparing benefit-cost ratios.

Cost-Benefit Analysis and Capital Budgeting

The application of cost-benefit techniques often can assist in the analysis of capital projects. Such projects usually involve long-term funding commitments and accumulate a stream of benefits over a long period. Typically, the costs and benefits of each alternative under consideration accrue in different periods. Special problems may arise when differences exist in the timing of benefits.

To illustrate the use of cost-benefit analysis in capital budgeting, consider the following example. The City of Rurbania is contemplating an investment in new street-cleaning equipment which it is estimated would yield an annual savings of $25,000 in operating costs. The new equipment will cost $120,000, while the existing equipment can be sold for $20,000, resulting in a net investment cost of $100,000. Three different methods might be used to evaluate this capital investment.

The payback method, frequently used in the private sector, is perhaps best described as a risk-aversion model. This approach considers the length of time required for the benefits generated by an investment to equal the original expenditure of funds without regard to the timing of the flows. In the example, the net expected investment cost is $100,000, and the expected annual benefits are $25,000; therefore, the payback period is four years. A short payback period is considered desirable because the risk of economic changes altering the value of the project is reduced and because recovered funds can be put to other uses. A major deficiency in this method is its failure to equate the value of funds to different time periods.

Discounted-cash-flow techniques were developed to overcome this deficiency in the payback method. As with the internal rate of return, this method identifies an interest rate that will equate the current value of projected benefits with the value of the initial investment. This rate is then compared with the cost of capital to determine if the project should be pursued. The basic equation for this approach is:

$$\text{Present Value} = \frac{S[1 - (1 + i)^{-n}]}{i}$$

where S is the future value of benefits, i is the interest rate, and n is the expected life. Assuming that the expected life of the equipment in the example is six years, the equating rate would be as follows:

$$\$100,000 = \$24,000 \frac{[1 - (1 + i)^{-6}]}{i}$$

Using a present-value table, i can be determined to be 0.1298 or 12.98 percent. Before a determination can be made as to the appropriateness of the project, it is necessary to estimate the cost of funds for the City of Rurbania. If the cost is less than 12.98 percent, the investment in new equipment would appear to be reasonable.

Until recently, discounted-cash-flow techniques have received only limited application in the public sector. Public agencies either did not discount fund flows or used some relatively low rate, such as the interest rate of government bonds. Some agencies assume that the rate should approximate the average rates used by profit-oriented firms. These rates, however, tend to be much higher than would be applicable in the public sector because of the higher cost of borrowing and the higher risk threshold of many private investors (that is, their desired rate of return on investments). Although there is no single, correct rate applicable to all public investments, the cost of funds must be recognized and an attempt made to approximate this rate for the purposes of cost-benefit analysis.

Extending the previous example and assuming a discount rate of 10 percent, the net benefits of the new-equipment acquisition could be determined by using the net-present-value method of discounting cash flows, as follows:

$$\text{Net Benefits} = \frac{S[1 = (1 + i)^{-n}]}{i} - \text{present value of costs}$$

$$= \frac{\$25,000 [1 - (1.10)^{-6}]}{.10} - \$100,000$$

$$= \$108,881 - \$100,000 = \$8,881$$

Since net benefits exceed the cost of the new equipment by \$8,881, it is likely that the City of Rurbania should proceed with the new-equipment acquisition.

Public-Sector Applications of Cost-Benefit Analysis

Cost-benefit analysis is most applicable in the selection among alternative means of accomplishing rather specific objectives, particularly where costs and benefits can be quantified on some reasonably reliable basis. Problems associated with the measurement of benefits and the uncertainties often encountered in many public programs makes such quantification a difficult task. Cost-benefit analysis is of limited usefulness in evaluating programs of relatively broad scope or in comparing programs with widely differing objectives. Many public programs have redistributive effects, whereby some individuals or groups benefit at the expense of others. Cost-benefit analysis can contribute relatively little toward establishing a social-welfare function that might resolve the relative merits of various patterns of income distribution.

Notwithstanding these limitations, a more systematic comparison of costs and benefits, coupled with consideration of time-preference and marginal productivity of capital investments, can contribute significantly to a more rational basis for public decisions, particularly when contrasted with the uncoordinated and intuitive methods of many more traditional approaches. Examining expenditures by objectives and programs instead of merely by spending agencies, considering total benefits for alternative programs alongside of total costs of inputs, emphasizing quantification whenever possible, making implicit judgments more explicit, and minimizing the influence of prejudgments and biases, are all important contributions of cost-benefit techniques.

Cost-Effectiveness Analysis

Many analytical mechanisms (including cost-benefit analysis in many applications) are designed to pursue efficiency, often at the expense of effectiveness. This characteristic of decision making can be observed in the continual emphasis on the achievement of economies without decreasing service, that is, the focus on the elimination of waste: with fixed resources, to produce more of A without decreasing the production of B. Questions of efficiency generally are defined and answered strictly in economic terms, with minimum consideration given to priorities and/or relative worth of the programs pursued.

Many (if not most) governmental programs, however, must produce and be responsive to noneconomic returns. By adopting technical analyses that focus on efficiency, public decision makers often lose the very information necessary to determine effectiveness. It is possible for example, to have an efficient transportation link that moves traffic from point A to point B with relatively little waste. Such a link, however, is irrelevant if the real need is to go to point C. Effectiveness considers the relative worth of point B versus point C with reference to specific values (goals and objectives) and variables (fiscal and policy constraints). Consideration of this relative worth—the actual impact of resource commitments in terms of program performance—represents effectiveness.

Output-Oriented Analysis

Under cost-effectiveness analysis, a distinction is made between efficiency and effectiveness in an attempt to set aside strictly financial controls in favor of nonmonetary accounting techniques to measure the output of public programs. This output or performance orientation of cost-effectiveness analysis is its most notable attribute. Under this approach, the effectiveness of an alternative is measured by the extent to which, if implemented, it will attain some desired goal or set of objectives. In this context, *goals* may be defined as codifications of desired patterns or levels of achievement—goals describe the desired state of any system. Goals are established by: (1) identifying current levels and types of performance (achievement) in each discrete program category; (2) estimating the current impacts of public resources on that achievement; and (3) defining the desired levels and types of achievement. The processes of public planning and decision making must have the capacity to manipulate and control certain variables to achieve (or move toward) some agreed-on goals. The decision-making process is complicated by the fact that goals are not mutually exclusive. A single set of variables may be common to a number of goals. The primary variables of a low-priority goal may be secondary variables of a high-priority goal.

Cost-effectiveness analysis is based on the concept of *marginal change* from the current state of affairs.[10] Normative statements of performance—goals—can be defined as positive changes from the current level of operations. Effectiveness measures—indicators that measure the direct and indirect impacts of resource allocations—determine the state of a given system at any point in time. The formulation of effectiveness measures and related operational criteria facilitates the evaluation of alternative methods of resource allocation and serves as the basis for a planning and management-control framework that permits reevaluation and modification of criteria and measures, as well as program structures, as activities are implemented.

Effectiveness Measures and Cost Curves

There usually is more than one way of achieving a goal or set of objectives. The purpose of cost-effectiveness analysis, therefore, is to determine the most effective program (from among several alternatives) at each level of goal achievement (or output). The preferred alternative usually is taken to be the one that produces either the desired level of effectiveness for the minimum cost or the maximum level of effectiveness for a given level of cost. Although costs can ordinarily be represented in monetary terms, levels of achievement usually are expressed by nonmonetary indices (effectiveness measures). Such measures often are expressed in relative terms, for example, percentage reduction in unemployment; percentage reduction in the incidence of a disease; percentage increase in some measure of educational attainment. Effectiveness measures can be arrayed along an effectiveness scale to indicate the degree of goal achievement evidenced by each alternative.[11]

A cost curve is developed for each alternative, representing the sensitivity of costs (inputs) to changes in the desired level of effectiveness (outputs). Costs may change more or less proportionately to the level of achievement, that is, each additional increment of effectiveness desired requires approximately the same units of expenditure. However, if effectiveness increases more rapidly than costs, then the particular alternative is operating at a level of increasing returns (represented by a positively sloped curve accelerating at an accelerating rate, as illustrated by the initial segment of cost curve A in figure 4-1). If costs increase more rapidly than effectiveness, the alternative is operating in an area of diminishing returns.

Increasing returns do not mean that an alternative should be automatically adopted (or if an ongoing program, expanded). Conversely, diminishing returns should not automatically disqualify a program alternative. It is useful to know, however, that an additional commitment of, for example, $200,000 to one alternative will carry it 20 percent closer toward an estab-

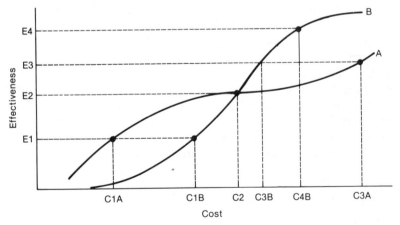

Figure 4-1. Cost-Effectiveness Comparison

lished goal, whereas the same resources added to another alternative will carry it only 10 percent closer.

Cost-effectiveness analysis relates incremental costs to increments of effectiveness. For some types of problems, practical models of these relationships can be developed with relative ease; for other problems, cost curves can be approximated from historical data. Construction of cost curves and effectiveness scales should become increasingly more sophisticated as the input-output relationships associated with various alternatives are better understood.

The Optimum Envelope

Assuming that the cost and effectiveness of each alternative can be determined for different levels of input-output relationships, the problem still is how to choose among these alternatives. In principle, the criterion should be to select that alternative that yields the greatest excess of positive impacts (attainment of objectives) over negative impacts (resources used, or costs and externalities that reduce effectiveness). In practice, however, this ideal criterion seldom is applied, since there is no practical way of subtracting dollars spent from the nonmonetary measures used to identify effectiveness.

Therefore, a cost-effectiveness comparison of alternatives must be made, as shown graphically in figure 4-1. Alternative A achieves the first level of effectiveness (E1) with a relatively modest level of cost (C1A), whereas twice the level of resources (C1B) would be required to achieve the same level of effectiveness under alternative B. Both alternatives achieve the second level of effectiveness (E2) at the same level of cost (C2). Alternative B requires less resources (C3B) to achieve the third level of effectiveness. And only alternative B achieves a fourth level of effectiveness; the cost curve of alternative A is not projected to reach this level.

To determine which of these alternatives is more desirable, it is necessary to define the *optimum envelope* formed by these two cost curves. If resources in excess of C2 are available, alternative B clearly provides the better choice; however, if resources less than C2 are available, alternative A provides the greater effectiveness for the dollars expended. In general, the choice between two alternatives cannot be made just on the basis of cost and effectiveness (unless one alternative dominates at all levels of effectiveness). Either a cost limit must be specified and effectiveness maximized for that allocation of resources or a desired level of effectiveness must be specified and costs then minimized for that level.

Public programs often do not represent the most effective alternatives that are technically available. Legislative constraints, intergovernmental relations/expectations, union rules, employer rights, community attitudes, and so forth are among the more obvious constraints to full optimization. Cost-constraint analysis examines the impacts of these limitations by comparing the cost of the program that could be adopted if no constraints existed to the cost of the constrained program. Once this cost differential is determined, decisions can be made as to the feasibility of attempting to eliminate the constraints. On the basis of this analysis, decision makers can be provided with information on how much the relaxation of a given constraint would save the program (or how much greater effectiveness could be achieved). The cost of the constraint also is indicative of the amount of resources that might be committed to overcome the constraint, if such effort were acceptable. In some cases, maintaining a constraint might be more important for social or political reasons than a more effective program.

An Application of Cost-Effectiveness Analysis

The use of cost-effectiveness analysis can be illustrated by returning to a previous case study involving the two programs designed to encourage students to remain in high school by stimulating their interests in vocational opportunities. Assume that program A has a fixed cost of $50,000 for each 40 students and that program B has a fixed cost of $40,000 for each 40 students. Further, assume that while the variable costs under program A decrease as the number of students increase, the variable costs under program B increase with increased participants. These cost assumptions are summarized in table 4–3 by student units of 40 each. From this table it can be seen that up to 200 participants, program B is more cost-effective, but beyond 200 participants, program A is more cost-effective. Conversely, if the funds for this project are limited to $775,000 or less, program B would be the preferred alternative; for funding in excess of $775,000, program A would be the better choice.

The techniques of cost-effectiveness analysis are relatively new and, consequently, have not reached full maturity. Initially, this approach was developed for application when benefits could not be measured in units commensurable with costs. In these early applications, the output or level of effectiveness was usually taken as a given, and several alternatives were examined in the hope that one would have lower costs than the others. These initial cost-effectiveness analyses revealed a number of important aspects of public decisions regarding the allocation of scarce resources.

In contemporary applications, cost-effectiveness analysis provides an explicit output orientation for the evaluation of program alternatives. It places particular emphasis on goals (the fixed-benefits approach) and the application of effectiveness measures to monitor progress toward these goals. The extended time horizon adopted in cost-effectiveness analysis

Table 4-3
Cost-Effectiveness Comparison of Two Dropout-Prevention Programs

Student Units	Program A				Program B			
	Fixed Costs	Variable Costs	Total Costs	Cumulative Costs	Fixed Costs	Variable Costs	Total Costs	Cumulative Costs
First 40	50,000	114,000	164,000	164,000	40,000	95,000	135,000	135,000
Next 40	50,000	110,000	160,000	324,000	40,000	105,000	145,000	280,000
Next 40	50,000	106,000	156,000	480,000	40,000	115,000	155,000	435,000
Next 40	50,000	102,000	152,000	632,000	40,000	125,000	165,000	600,000
Next 40	50,000	98,000	148,000	780,000	40,000	135,000	175,000	775,000
Next 40	50,000	94,000	144,000	924,000	40,000	145,000	185,000	960,000
Next 40	50,000	90,000	140,000	1,064,000	40,000	155,000	195,000	1,155,000
Next 40	50,000	86,000	136,000	1,200,000	40,000	165,000	205,000	1,360,000
Total	400,000	800,000	1,200,000		320,000	1,040,000	1,360,000	

leads to a fuller recognition of the need for life-cycle costing and marginal analysis and the importance of incremental costs.

As with other analytical techniques, the cost-effectiveness model need not be adopted "whole cloth." A number of subroutines of this approach may be introduced into ongoing procedures of budget analysis. Of particular importance would be considerations developed through the technique of cost-effectiveness-curve analysis. As the complexity of the resource allocation problem becomes more evident, other subroutines then may be adopted, depending on the availability of data and the needs and capabilities of the analysts.

Notes

1. U.S., Congress, House Subcommittee on Evaluation Standards, Report to the Interagency Committee on Water Resources, *Proposed Practices for Economic Analysis of River Basin Projects* (Washington, D.C., May 1958), p. 9.

2. Ronald H. Coase, "The Problem of Social Cost," *Journal of Law and Economics* (October 1960):1–44.

3. Anatol Rapoport, "What is Information?" *ETC: A Review of General Semantics* 10 (Summer 1953):252.

4. Peter F. Drucker, "The Effective Decision," *Harvard Business Review* 45 (January–February 1967):95.

5. A.R. Prest and R. Turvey, "Cost Benefit Analysis: A Survey," *The Economic Journal* 75 (1965):583.

6. Otto Eckstein, *Water Resource Development* (Cambridge, Mass.: Harvard University Press, 1958).

7. For further discussion of this point, see Leonard Merewitz and Stephen H. Sosnick, *The Budget's New Clothes* (Chicago: Markham, 1971), pp. 85–86.

8. In 1844, the Frenchman, Jules Depuit, devised one of the earliest and still one of the more sophisticated methods of quantitative evaluation [reprinted as "On the Measurement of the Utility of Public Works," in *Readings in Welfare Economics,* ed. Kenneth Arrow and Tibor Scitovsky (Homewood, Ill.: Richard D. Irwin, 1969), pp. 225–283]. It was several decades before practical applications of these methods were developed.

9. For a further discussion of discounting in the public sector, see Alan Walter Steiss, *Local Government Finance: Capital Facilities Planning and Debt Administration* (Lexington, Mass.: Lexington Books, D.C. Heath, 1975), chap. 10.

10. Charles Kepner and Benjamin B. Tregoe, *The Rational Manager* (Princeton, N.J.: Princeton University Press, 1965).

11. E.S. Quade, *Analysis for Public Decisions* (New York: American Elsevier, 1975), p. 92.

5 Management Information Systems

The effective planning and control of any organization, project, or program requires relevant management information. Information flow (communications) is vital to the decision-making and management processes. Information is the raw material of intelligence that triggers the recognition that decisions need to be made. Timely information is essential in understanding the circumstances surrounding any issue and in evaluating alternative courses of action to resolve any problem. In this sense, information is incremental knowledge that reduces the degree of uncertainty in a particular situation. Although vast amounts of facts, numbers, and other data may be processed in any organization, what constitutes management information depends on the problem at hand and the particular frame of reference of the manager. Miscellaneous accounting data, for example, can provide information when arrayed appropriately in balance sheets and financial statements. Traditional accounting data, however elaborately processed, may be relatively meaningless if the problem is related to an evaluation of the effectiveness of a new program. Thus, to achieve better decisions, the information available to management must be both timely and pertinent.

Conceptual Framework of a Management Information System (MIS)

In a time when many words frequently are used with no real attempt to define their explicit meaning, it should not be surprising to find that many people are puzzled by the term *management information system*. As a concept, MIS often is vaguely described and broadly misunderstood. Some people confuse MIS with an electronic data-processing system, thinking that the all-knowing computer will provide the answers to complex problems if and when the manager simply learns to press the right buttons. Many management information systems make effective use of modern data- and word-processing equipment. However, an MIS is much more than an electronic marvel—a "black box" to direct and control the destiny of complex organizations. An MIS is first and foremost a process by which information is organized and communicated in a timely fashion to resolve management problems.

A System of Information for Management

The concept of MIS can best be understood by examining separately the three words: management, information, and system. This undertaking may be enhanced by taking these words in reverse order.

A *system* is fundamentally a set of two or more elements joined together to attain a common objective. As one critic of systems has suggested, the term has begun to appear in common parlance with about the same frequency as the term *et cetera*—and often with about as much real meaning. If a particular system is identified, it often is found to be made up of a number of smaller systems or *subsystems.* Usually it is necessary to continue down the hierarchy of subsystems until the basic *elements* that define the total system are reached. Failure to penetrate beyond the surface is one reason why systems are so often misunderstood.

A properly functioning system is characterized by synergy. That is, all elements and subsystems work more effectively together in the system than if they were operating independently. The output of an integrated system properly may be expected to be far greater than the sum of the outputs of its component subsystems. To understand these output relationships, however, it is first necessary to identify and understand the subsystems and elements that serve as the components of the larger system.

Information is different from data, and this distinction is very important. Data are facts and figures that are not currently being used in a decision process. Files, records, and reports not under immediate consideration are examples of data. By contrast, information consists of classified and interpreted data that are being used for decision making. Thus, the memory of an MIS system is a repository for information by which "right" decisions can be tested for acceptability, as well as for raw data.

Organizational *memory,* like human memory, is characterized by a selective process—those items are retained that may have some future application. And since the future is uncertain, organizations tend to retain more data than can possibly be used as information, thus complicating the retrieval process. Organizational memory also is dissociative and combinatorial—stored information can be reassembled into new patterns that meet the overall needs of an organization (and particular decision situations) more effectively.

Finally, for purposes of an MIS, *management* consists of the activities carried out by managers. Managers must *plan, organize, implement,* and *control* those operations within their realm of organizational responsibility. Managers must continually develop, adapt, and implement strategic, tactical, and technical innovations to enhance the capacity of the organization to meet the demands and expectations that impinge on it. Since decision making is a major requirement for each of these managerial functions, an MIS becomes a facilitating system for developing decisions in planning, organizing, implementing, and controlling. This is what gives purpose to an MIS. The specific objective to an MIS is to communicate information for decision making in a synergistic fashion—where the whole becomes greater than the sum of the individual parts.

MIS and Computers

Although many management information systems are built on the data-handling capacity of modern computers, all computers are not management information systems. It is possible to have a successful MIS without heavy reliance on high-speed data-processing hardware. It is important to recognize that managerial decisions often require information inputs that cannot be computerized. Thus, overall management information systems must be designed to include explicit attention to nonquantifiable inputs as well as to those that result from computerized data-processing applications.[1]

To be sure, computers have made possible the collection and dissemination of greater quantities of information more quickly and economically. Computers can help to achieve better management information if used to process properly designed information flows. However, computers are not the automatic answer to the need for better information. As a matter of fact, undue preoccupation with how data will be processed and the characteristics of the hardware can result in a major setback for the design of an effective MIS.

Hardware should be the last matter to be considered when thinking about an MIS. It is first necessary to decide what kind of information is needed—how soon, how much, and how often. The kind of equipment that will best serve these needs is a secondary, although important, consideration. Many wrong notions about data processing can be dispelled by concentrating first on the information and communication requirements and by consequently shrinking to more realistic size the plans for the computer hardware.

Furthermore, large centralized data-processing centers are not a prerequisite to or concomitant of an MIS. The desirability of such large "figure factories" or "number crunchers" depends more on the size and nature of the organization than on the purposes of an MIS. Many excellent management information systems are serviced by relatively simple, local data-processing operations, tailored to the particular needs of the users. In the late 1960s and early 1970s, many governmental organizations were sold on the notion that bigger is better, only to find that, with the rapid changes in computer technology, they were saddled with a "dinosaur" that consumed vast quantities of resources but could not serve the expanding needs of particular users.

Information and Communication

The effective communication of information is the warp and woof of management processes. The importance of communication to the overall operation of an organization and, in particular, to decision making has been discussed in some detail by Herbert Simon and others.[2] As Alex Bavelas and Dermot Barrett have observed: "The goals an organization selects, the methods it applies, the effectiveness with which it improves its own procedures—all of these hinge upon the quality and availability of the information in the system."[3] An organization can be conceptualized as a configuration of communication patterns through which individuals and groups are connected in varying degrees of stability and cohesiveness. Before the basis for an MIS can be discussed, therefore, it is important to more fully understand the role of communications in modern organizations.

Communication Networks

Organizational communications: (1) make possible the circulation of orders and directives and the flow of data and information within the organization; (2) initiate particular patterns of activity before, during, and after decision-making situations; (3) serve as a vehicle for the exercise of influence—both informal influence (as in persuasion) and more formal influence (as in authority); and (4) provide support and confirmation of the formal structure of authority and control. In addition to providing the matrix that links organizational members in these various ways, the communication system serves as the instrument by which an organization is embedded in its broader environment—the "outer world." The communication system also makes possible more uniform definitions of problems and issues requiring managerial decisions.

As E. Colin Cherry has pointed out, organizational communications consist of "a number of networks superimposed."[4] Often the various networks can be separated for empirical analysis, even though they are superimposed. At other times, one set of channels carries messages that have multiple levels of meaning. In such instances, communication networks may be little more than analytic constructs. The sorting of messages into different networks often lacks refinement because of the tendency for individuals to use rewarding channels again and again, even though such use goes beyond the original intent for which the channel was established. It may be useful, however, to describe some of the different types of communication networks to be found in an organization, especially since the characteristics of each network may lead to different management-control consequences.

The Authority Network. Traditionally, primary attention has been given to organizational communications involved in the exercise of authority relations. Channels in this network are defined by the legitimacy that one individual or group has vis-a-vis others with respect to the issuance of directives, commands, and decisions. A prevailing feature of such networks is their directionality; orders usually flow vertically within an organization, from a relatively few individuals at the top to the many in the lower regions of the authority structure.

The Information-Exchange Network. The information-exchange networks is sometimes thought of as an inversion of the authority-communication flow. Its messages usually are concerned with the internal operations of the organization and with the broader external environment. Although its directionality often is assumed to be the opposite of that involved in authority communication, this network frequently is used by those above to supply information for decisions to lower echelons in the organization.

Task-Expertise Communication Networks. As Victor Thompson has commented, as the technical base for organizational activities becomes increasingly salient, problem-solving communication seems to develop its own channels.[5] The task-expertise network provides a vehicle whereby technical know-how can be brought to bear on the performance of organizational activities. An important feature of this network is its fragmentation; relatively unrelated islands of expertise are created throughout the organization. Occupational groups and professions use specialized jargons in handling the tools and techniques of their trades. Such groups also provide norms concerning work standards and levels of performance.

There is undoubtedly considerable overlap in communication structures involved in the transmission of messages concerning authority, information, and expertise. All three networks tend to be involved in task specialization. However, quite different characteristics may be associated with each. For example, in the task-expertise network, the flow of messages seems to be two-way and predominately lateral, whereas the direction of flow in the authority and information-exchange networks tends to be more one-way and vertical.

Informal Lateral Networks. In his empirical studies of British industries, T. Burns concluded that: "The 'vertical' system (of communication) would be virtually unworkable without the considerable flow of information laterally."[6] Burns also found that communication circuits were maintained "among groups of equivalent status which crossed departmental boundaries; communication 'leaked' from level to level through contact individuals (not necessarily in the direct executive line concerned) and the ground at a lower level was prepared for likely action."[7] Thus, new, highly specialized information channels sometimes develop when regularized channels fail to function adequately. Unlike formal channels, the informal portion of the communication system is not directly subject to management control. It frequently is the result of natural social groupings.

This informal communication network often called the "grapevine," can reinforce formal information flows or can work contrary to these channels. K. Davis has presented findings that tend to contradict the common assertion that the grapevine "thrives when other channels of information are closed."[8] He concludes that: "Formal and informal communication systems tend to be jointly active, or jointly inactive. Where formal communication was inactive, . . . the grapevine did not rush to fill the void . . . instead, there simply was lack of communication."[9] Regardless of which of these assertions is correct, it is in management's best interest to understand completely the informal networks with the objective of influencing these lines of communication in constructive directions.

Status Networks. Networks carrying messages about status may be less well defined. Rather than having directionality, they have many connections that are occasional and fleeting and cut across almost all other networks. Not only is information about status carried over networks, but also status often is attached to nodes within a network, as well as the network itself. Perceptions of one's own position within the status sysem also influences the extent to which certain communication channels are utilized. Thus, D.C. Barnlund and C. Harland, summarizing their experimental work in small-group communication, suggest that ". . . the larger the status differential, the more restricted the channels of communication, the greater the tendency for information to flow from low to high status persons, and the more distorted the content of the messages."[10]

When networks are highly differentiated, isolation may be very costly; duplicate channels must be maintained for certain communication functions, and message content may be lost because of high friction of transmission between channels. Such conditions frequently occur in decision situations that require inputs from both the structure of government and the broader public. Interest groups may develop their own communication networks and gain access to the parallel networks of government at a variety of points. Informal points of contact may supersede formal channels, with the result that the more normative patterns of decision making are circumvented or blurred. A parallel problem is that the demands of various interest groups run the risk of becoming distorted in transmittal through the groups' communication channel and may be further distorted when transmitted from one system to another.

When communication networks are undifferentiated and overlap extensively, one set of messages may be submerged by another. Perhaps the most evident situation arises from an overlap of the networks of authority and friendship. In such cases, orders and commands may not carry sufficient force to be implemented effectively. By the same token, an undue overlap between the status and information-exchange networks may result in an information input receiving greater weight than it merits in a decision, simply because of the status enjoyed by the source.

Basic Types of Communication Flows

Five basic types of communication flows involved in management control may be suggested from the foregoing discussion.

1. Expressive communication is largely directed to an external audience and consists of annual reports, press releases, progress reports, and other materials designed to "educate and inform" persons outside the organization.
2. Eductive communication includes messages designed to draw forth or elicit information, generally transmitted in the form of questions directed at specific individuals within the organization.
3. Informative communication is restricted, for the most part, to the transmission of data and information at various levels of interpretation and analysis, short of specific proposals or recommendations.
4. Influential communication includes advice, suggestions, recommendations, proposals, responses to eductive messages, and so forth; often supported by informative communication.
5. Authoritative communication includes orders, commands, directives; in general, communication designed to initiate action on the part of others.

Of the five basic types of communication flows, the two most pertinent to management control are informative and influential communication. There are four conditions which must be met to make a communication, or any portion of it, informative:

1. The information being transmitted must have been previously unknown to the receiver. A communication is informative to the extent that the receiver learns something from it—an idea, concept, a point of view, or a relationship among these.

2. The information offered must be acceptable to the receiver as information according to his or her own ideas, beliefs, needs, and attitudes. People are most likely to accept information that: (a) they are looking for, (b) they can use in some way (including psychologically) at once, (c) they can see some possible use for in the immediate future, or (d) they fancy because of the physical or contextual conditions under which it occurs. If receivers

perceive that their beliefs are likely to be challenged or their foundations questioned, they will probably ignore or at least misunderstand the content or intent of the communication.[11]

3. The content of the communication must be clear to the receiver. If the message, or any portion of it, seems ambiguous to the receiver, to that extent it will be either noninformative or misinformative.

4. The message must be meaningful to the receiver. To be meaningful, the message content must be such that it can be readily assigned to any appropriate place in the receiver's knowledge of the subject and the relationship between ideas as the receiver sees them.

With the possible exception of the first, these conditions also apply to influential communication. Recommendations or proposals can influence the decisions of others only if they are meaningful and useful, unambiguous, and acceptable to the receiver's system of values and attitudes.

Storage of Communication—The Function of the Memory Bank

For many problem-solving tasks, the individual has stored knowledge that he or she brings to bear in the decision-making process. This knowledge or experience may be sufficient (at least as the individual sees it) to deal with the problem. On the other hand, he or she may seek additional information and hence require inputs from formal and informal communication networks. Pieces of information may be stored in the minds of different group members as well as in material records. Items from all sources may be selectively recalled, combined with new incoming information, and communicated during the deliberation and decision process of the group. In this sense, groups act like individuals; however, in the process of drawing on a range of memories, decisions are produced that differ from those of any one of the individual members.

Information is not subject to the laws of conservation of matter and energy. Information can be both created and wiped out—although it cannot be created from nothing nor completely destroyed. Since information has physical reality, its storage—memory—is a physical process that can be represented in seven distinct stages[12]:

1. Abstraction or coding of incoming information into appropriate symbols
2. storage of these symbols by means of some appropriate recording device—distribution of written symbols on paper, activity patterns of cells in nervous tissues, or patterns of electric charges in electronic devices

3. dissociation of some of this information from the rest
4. recall of some of the dissociated items, as well as the combination of items into larger assemblies
5. recombinations of some of the recalled items into new patterns that were not among the inputs into the system
6. new abstractions from the recombined items, preserving their new pattern, but obliterating its combinatorial origin
7. transmission of the new items to storage or to applications to action

The memory bank of an information system contains information concerning past experiences, programmed decisions, information to test the feasibility and acceptability of decisions, and so forth.

Only part of past experience is selected for storage. In human memory, a selection of what we would like to remember is combined with a selection of what our subconscious mind chooses to emphasize.[13] In addition to being selective, memory is dissociative and combinatorial. Information and experience can be broken down into their component parts for storage and then reassembled into new patterns quite different from the intake from the outside world. If improbable combinations and associations turn out to be highly relevant to a particular situation and lead to significant actions, they may be called strokes of genius, flashes of insight, or innovations. Putting information together and estimating that a particular combination is worth pursuing is one of the fundamental activities of management. It results in outputs that better meet the needs of the situation.

Memory serves a number of important functions in the management control process. It is a major component in the screening and selection process by which inputs are sorted out and converted into intakes. Selected information is transmitted to memory and stored for possible recall at later stages in the process. In defining a problem, selective recall serves to classify the general nature of the problem and to identify the constraints and boundary conditions of possible solutions. Combined information may be recalled from the system's memory bank, and further input is generated and stored for future recall.

Once a preliminary decision is reached as to the appropriate control mechanisms to be applied, selective-information combinations are recalled and applied to modify the decision in light of what is judged acceptable and feasible. In this process, the normative decision (what ought to be done) is measured against past experiences (drawn from memory) as to what might be the limits of appropriate action. This process of combining selected data and memories with the "right" decision to achieve an acceptable decision might be thought of as a second screening process. The screen is continuously modified by the system's output, that is, the result of decisions that are translated into action.

Expectations and Communication

Expectations play an important role in organizational communication. When messages are systematically sent and received, patterns of interaction develop among the communication nodes. Habitual usage of particular channels, over time, generate expectations that have the force of custom. Messages often are carefully worded according to a certain set of expectations shared by the receivers. As Jay Jackson has postulated, shared expectations within an organization become sanctions that normatively regulate behavior.[14] Any message that does not conform to such shared expectations is likely to be ignored or to produce negative responses on the part of the receivers. John Dorsey has suggested that when we are about to receive a message, we often have more or less definite expectations as to the probable form, mode, or tenor, if not the content, of such communications.[15]

By the same token, communications directed toward human beings are accompanied by the implicit expectation that, if the meaning is apprehended (and within the set of expectations of the receiver), responses will be forthcoming within a given range of possibilities. If an appropriate response is not produced, the communicator has three possible courses of action: (1) to ignore (or fail to notice) the discrepancy between expectations and responses and proceed as if there were no discrepancy; (2) to take note of the discrepancy and try again, perhaps by modifying the mode or content of the communication; or to take note of the discrepancy and revise his or her expectations to conform to the responses observed. As a rule, either (2) or (3), or a combination of these, is the usual outcomes of such situations. And these operations, in which the communicator modifies her or his behavior (either "internally" or "externally") on the basis of observation, are examples of feedback in human action.

Expectations and the systems that they constitute are built up, reinforced, or modified by the operation of feedback as a person experiences his or her environment, both internal and external. It is the interaction of expectations and the resulting feedback that make communication possible. Expectations act as standards by which each participant can gauge the extent to which he or she understands the other and, in turn, is understood. Feedback permits self-correction or adjustment in behavior in the light of comparisons between responses and expectations.

In most decision-making situations, expectations are more complex than the expectations of each person concerning the probable overt behavior of others in response to communications. A set of expectations exist within the system against which decisions must be tested. In other words, the initiator of a decision also has expectations about what he or she thinks are the expectations of the system. This perception, in turn, will influence his or her behavior in presenting a decision. By the same token, those in the system to whom the decision is presented will try to interpret the initiator's expectations, which in turn will influence their behavior. Thus the relationship between the expectations of both the initiator and the respondents in an ongoing decision-making system are reciprocal, or complementary. Interaction takes place within the framework of these complementary expectations and both influences and is influenced by them.

Selective Filtering—Omissions and Distortions

As messages are transmitted within an organization, the omission of detail may provide one means of reducing communication overload. When such omissions are systematic with respect to certain categories of information, the process may be labeled "selective filtering." Such selective filtering often is crucial to effective communication in complex situations.

Communication systems become more effective when languages are employed that carry larger amounts of meaning with relatively fewer symbols. Organizations find such communication devices as charts, diagrams, and other graphics, coding and classification systems, occupational jargons, and so forth helpful in increasing the efficiency of communication. The degree to which knowledge relevant to a given problem may be transmitted within an organization depends on the extent to which details may be summarized and condensed in an efficient shared language. Very often, however, technical jargon loses its meaning as it is transmitted upward in the organization.

The omission of detail may take place at any point in the communication system. With more complicated data and information, however, a series of summarizations may occur, beginning early in the communication process. As Herbert Simon and James March have suggested: "The more complex the data that are perceived, and the less adequate the organization's language, the closer to the source of information will the uncertainty absorption take place, and the greater will be the amount of summarization at each step of transmission."[16]

Selective filtering and other mechanisms of adjustment, however, may lead to the deletion of important aspects of communications or the introduction of message distortions. Since it is often difficult to provide meaningful information about intangible and nonstandard objects or concepts, message distortion is a common problem in organizational communication. Therefore, conscious efforts must be made in organizations to develop means by which less objective communication contents can be handled more effectively. As Richard Cyert and James March have observed: "Any decision-making system develops codes for communication about the environment. Such a code partitions all possible states of the world into a relatively small number of classes of states. . . . Thus, if a decision rule is designed to choose between two alternatives, the information code will tend to reduce all possible states of the world to two classes."[17] Such rules for the codification of information inputs, however, frequently introduce additional distortions.

Taking a broader perspective, systematic biasing of message content may not always be dysfunctional. Gordon Allport and L. Postman found, in experimental situations, that transmitted messages "tended to grow shorter, more concise, and more easily grasped and told," and that there were "selective perceptions, retention, and reporting of a limited number of details from a larger context."[18] In other words, the messages often were sharpened.

Omissions and inaccuracies may increase the ambiguity of messages; however, since ambiguous messages are open to multiple interpretations, more agreeable meanings may be attached to them by the receiver. Thus, although ambiguity may result in slippage between the sender and receiver, such slippage may also promote consensus and agreement at least at one level of understanding. This consensus, in turn, may establish a working basis for further elaboration.

Basic Purposes of an MIS

With the development and maintenance of appropriate communication networks, the generation, storage, and retrieval of data should not be the main problem facing any organization. As Russell Ackoff has observed: "I do not deny that most managers lack a good deal of information that they should have, but I do deny that this is the most important informational deficiency from which they suffer. It seems to me that they suffer most from an *overabundance of irrelevant information*."[19] There is a very real danger that managers and decision makers will be literally covered up with hoards of data, much of which may be relatively meaningless or useless in solving problems or making decisions. "Without clear definition of decision points, their information needs, and the opportunities they present, data processing can drown the managers it is intended to serve."[20] In short, to be useful for management control purposes, data must be organized into some kind of system that can provide the proper kinds and quantities of information in an understandable format. The primary objective of such a system should be to aid the manager in making timely and informed decisions. Processing vast amounts of data is not itself helpful. Moreover, such data-processing activities can be an expense that is hard to justify if the problem-solving and decision-making ability of the manager is not substantially improved.

Designing an MIS

The design of an MIS should begin with an identification of the important types of managerial decisions required by the organization. This study should define relationships among decisions as well as determine the flow of decisions. Such a decision-flow analysis often reveals important decisions that are being made by default, for example, where past decisions that may no longer be applicable to current problems and procedures are still binding. This analysis may also uncover situations in which interdependent decisions are being made independently. The analysis of decision flows frequently identifies areas in which changes should be made in the responsibilities of management, in the organizational structure, or in measures of performance. Such changes are necessary to correct information deficiencies.

Decision analyses can be conducted in varying levels of detail, depending on the amount of time and resources available for such analyses. It may be preferable to undertake a fairly broad analysis of all the managerial functions of an organization rather than a detailed analysis of only one subset of functions. It often is easier to introduce more detailed information inputs into an integrated-information system than to combine relatively detailed, independent subsystems into one comprehensive MIS.

The next step in the design of an MIS involves an analysis of the information requirements of these major classes of managerial decisions. Ackoff has suggested that managerial decisions can be grouped into three types. (1) decisions for which adequate models exist or can be developed and from which optimal solutions can be derived; (2) decisions for which models can be constructed but from which optimal solutions cannot be readily extracted; and (3) decisions for which adequate models cannot be constructed.[21] In the first case, the decision model should have the capacity to identify what information is required and relevant, and the decision process should be incorporated into the MIS (thereby converting it, at least partially, to a control system). In the second case, the model may specify what information is required. However, a further search process may be necessary, including the examination of alternative approaches, to fully explicate the information requirements. In the final situation, further research is required to determine what information is relevant and how this information can be organized to address the decision situation. It may be possible to make implicit models used by decision makers more explicit and treat them as a type-2 decision situation. It is appropriate in each of these categories to provide feedback by comparing actual decision outcomes with those predicted by the models. It is important that the MIS have the capacity not only to answer questions that might be addressed to it but also to report any deviations from expectations (that is, actual decision outcomes that differ from those predicted). Each decision made, along with its predicted outcome, should become an input to a management-control system.[22]

Decision situations with similar or overlapping informational requirements should be aggregated into a single (or closely coordinated) management task. Such groupings should improve the performance of individual managers by reducing the information loaded on them. This approach should also increase the manager's understanding of his or her decision responsibilities. The aggregation of decision situations may result in some reorganization of assignments or redirection of communication/information flows.

Only when these initial steps have been completed should the procedures for collecting, storing, retrieving, and analyzing information be developed. The literature on computer systems and their application to managerial information makes a distinction between data base management systems, data management systems, and management information systems. A *data base management system* (DBMS) is: "A software system that provides for a means of representing data, procedures for making changes in these data (adding to, subtracting from, and modifying), a method for making inquiries of the data base and to process these raw data to produce information, and to provide all the necessary internal management functions to minimize the users effort to make the system responsive."[23] A data base has the following characteristics: (1) data are stored in a central place, (2) for one or several applications to serve information requirements, (3) such that current computer-hardware technology allows data for many applications to be shared by one storage device, and (4) the redundancy of data is thereby minimized.[24] According to Norman Enger, a *data management system* (DMS) is considerably broader in scope than a DBMS. It consists of a series of software programs that have the ability to create and update files; select, sort, and retrieve data; and generate various reports based on these data.[25] Data management systems differ in terms of the language utilized, the methods by which the files are organized and access is provided to the user, and the level of users for whom the system is designed to serve.

As these definitions suggest, the distinction between a DBMS and a DMS may be one of degree of organization and user access. A DBMS enables users "to search, probe, and query file contents in order to extract answers to nonrecurring and unplanned questions that are not available in regular reports . . . to 'browse' through the data base until they have the needed information."[26] A DMS provides the user with ready-made programs to structure and process information and "a report generating capability which can meet user specified parameters."[27] Figure 5–1 provides a schematic representation of a data base system. The alternative-communi-

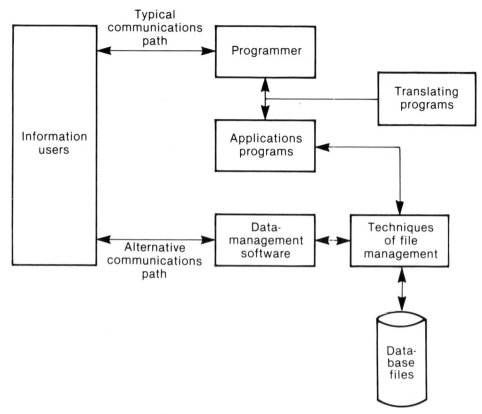

Figure 5-1. An Inquiry/Information-Flow Diagram for a DBMS/DMS

cation path would be strengthened significantly in a DMS.

An MIS may be built on a DBMS or DMS. However, an MIS goes beyond the objectives of centralized data collection and retrieval. As Walter Kennevan suggests, an MIS is "an organized method of providing past, present, and projection information relating to internal operations and external intelligence. It supports the planning, control and operational functions of an organization by furnishing information in the proper time frame to assist in the decision-making process."[28] An MIS must be flexible and adaptive. It must be assumed that there will be deficiencies to be accommodated as the system evolves. Procedures should be developed to detect these deficiencies and to correct the system to eliminate or reduce them. Managers, as well as information specialists and operations researchers, should participate in each phase of the design of an MIS.

Components of an MIS

The basic components of an MIS are further illustrated in figure 5-2. Three specific areas provide the data inputs for the formulation of decision information: (1) *environmental intelligence*—data about the broader environment of which the organization is a part, including assessments of client needs; (2) autointelligence—data about the component elements of the particular organization, including an evaluation of organizational resources and capacity (readiness) to respond to client needs; and (3) *historic data,* which bring together and analyze the lessons of past experience. Much of the environmental and internal data may not be applicable to immediate decision situations; these data are stored in the memory bank of the organization.

Forecasts of the probable outcome of events can be developed on these data foundations. Forecasting is the first and fundamental step in rational planning. Probable happenings are outlined by assuming the continuance of hypothetical futures. These probabilistic forecasts provide an important input into the determination of organizational objectives and serve as an initial impetus for strategic planning.

Once objectives have been identified (at least in preliminary fashion), and with further inputs from autointelligence, the strategic planning process can begin to suggest possible directions that the organization can take in response to client needs in the broader environment. Strategic planning can provide the initiatives for two important management components: (1) the search for possible new courses of action that will improve the overall performance of the organization; and (2) management planning and control. Tactical and technical innovations should be sought to improve the overall responsiveness of the organization (in the private sector, these innovations also improve the competitive position of the organization). Management plans are the mechanisms that translate the overall intent of strategic plans into more specific programs and activities.

Management planning and control activities draw on the memory bank of the organization in search for programmed decisions that have worked successfully in the past. Timely resource evaluations also provide an important input into the management planning process. These evaluations include information regarding the current fiscal status of the organization (accounting data) as well as the overall response capacity of other organizational resources (systems readiness). The management planning and control process should provide critical feedback to the further refinement of objectives, in some cases, requiring a recycling of the strategic planning process before proceeding to the next stage.

Program development involves the activities of task identification and budgeting. Specific operations are detailed within the framework of the

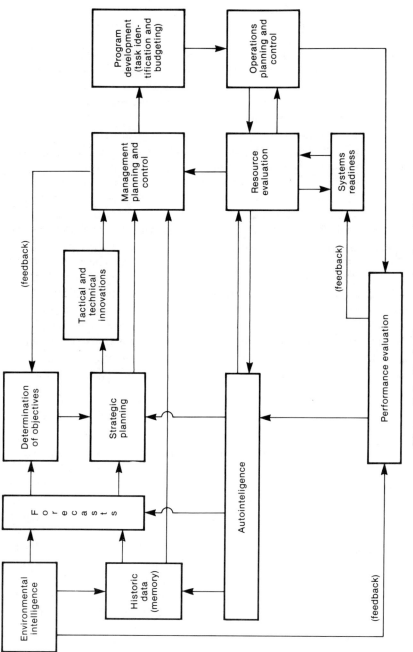

Figure 5-2. Basic Components of an MIS

management plan, and responsibilities are assigned for carrying out these operations. Resources also are assigned to these operations through the budget process. Specific operations may be further detailed through the procedures of operations planning and control [which include such programming techniques as Program Evaluation Review Technique (PERT) and Critical Path Method (CPM)]. These procedures may require further information regarding resource capabilities and may precipitate a recycling of the management-planning process.

The final component of the MIS involves the information derived from performance evaluation. Some writers view performance evaluation as a separate process outside the MIS; others recognize the importance of incorporating the data and information developed through such evaluations by referring to a management-information and program-evaluation system (MIPES).[29] Performance evaluation draws data from the broader environment regarding the efficiency and effectiveness with which client needs are met, problems are solved, opportunities are realized, and so forth.

Such evaluations provide new inputs into autointelligence and feedback in terms of systems readiness. A basic problem of managers today, whether in the public or private sectors, is to achieve a balance in the programs and decisions made to ensure a systems readiness, that is, response capacity, in the short-, mid-, and long-range futures. A posture of sufficient flexibility is required to meet a wide range of possible competitive actions. The development and maintenance of an MIS that includes the basic components outlined can contribute significantly to meeting this challenge.

Feedback and Feedforward

Feedback is a basic requirement of any MIS. Feedback must be obtained on the output of the organization in terms of quality (effectiveness), quantity (efficiency of service levels), cost, and so on. Programs (operating systems and subsystems) must be monitored to maintain process control. Evaluations of resources (inputs) provide feedback at the earliest stages of program implementation.

Feedback data must be collected and analyzed at various stages in the implementation of programs and the maintenance of ongoing operations. The analysis involves processing data, developing information, and comparing actual results with plans and expectations. Many decisions can be made within the control system itself, because routine adjustments may be preprogrammed in the set of procedures or instructions provided to those individuals who must carry out specific tasks. Within the management-control system, there is a flow of information to implement changes to the programs based on feedback from the operating systems. Thus, procedures are modified and files updated simultaneously with routine decision making and programmatic adjustments.

Summary and exception reports may be generated by the MIS and become part of higher-level processes of review and evaluation. These processes, in turn, may lead to adaptation or innovations of goals and objectives. Subsequent planning activities reflect such feedback, and the entire process is recycled. In time, an organization "learns" through the process of planning, implementation, and feedback.[30] Approaches to decision making and the propensity to select certain ends and means change as the value system of the organization evolves.

For the most part, existing management controls rely on feedback after deviations from desired performance have occurred and been detected. As a consequence, managers often are frustrated when they discover too late that actual accomplishments are missing the desired goals and objectives of the program or project. These frustrations are particularly evident if managers must depend on data and information that are largely historical in nature.

Managers must seek out data and information that will permit actions to be taken before problems reach crisis proportions. Historic data provided by conventional accounting systems (even when the time lag is only a few weeks) may be insufficient to meet these decision needs. Resource evaluations on the input side and resource monitoring as the program or project progresses can provide the more timely information required to anticipate rather than merely react to problems.

A modern management control system must use feedforward control, as well as control based on feedback. Feedforward anticipates the lags in feedback systems by monitoring inputs and predicting their effects on output variables. In so doing, action can be taken to change the input and, thereby, bring the output into equilibrium with desired results before the measurement of the output discloses an historical deviation from standards. The process of feedforward control involves the careful analysis of input variables and their relationship to the desired results (output). Inputs are monitored and changed to achieve the desired results before the deviation occurs. Such feedforward capabilities often are incorporated in contemporary applications of managerial accounting techniques.

Organizational Levels and Management
Information Needs

The types and sources of information required by managers varies by organizational level. John Burch and Felix Strater suggest a three-level classification: strategic, tactical, and technical.[31] At the strategic level, long-range plans and policies are very important; external data are of prime significance. Decisions at this level tend to be more intuitive and less subject to predetermined decision rules or programmed solutions. The art of management is more important at this level, with the manager relying on the best judgment he or she can muster.

Tactical decisions are those made by middle-level managers. These decisions involve the effectuation of plans of upper management and the control of first-line supervisors and program managers. Such decisions serve as an interface between strategic plans and operational activities. To perform most effectively, middle managers must rely more heavily on information generated within the organization—on historic data and autointelligence.

Technical decisions are those made by first-line supervisors and program managers. Their primary interest is in controlling the day-to-day operations of programs and projects. Internal information is most important to successful decision making at this level, and the process is generally much more structured than at either of the other two levels. This greater degree of structure often facilitates the solution of problems in a predetermined manner through the application of standard analytical techniques, such as those of operations research.

Public organizations in recent years have been faced with dynamic conditions, rapidly changing technology, changing client demands, and other similar phenomena that have required major adaptations. Adjustments have been made, but, in many cases, they have been made without recognition of the impact of organizational change on information systems. As a consequence, much of the information that may have been appropriate under previous organizational arrangements has become obsolete. Furthermore, additional types of information are urgently needed to plan and control current operations. As D. Ronald Daniel has observed: "Management often loses sight of the seemingly obvious and simple relationship between organization structure and information needs. Companies very seldom follow up on reorganizations with penetrating reappraisals of their information systems, and managers given new responsibilities and decision-making authority often do not receive all the information they require."[32]

Perhaps the most striking example in the public sector of this gap between information needs and decision-making responsibilities is found in those jurisdictions that have adopted more programmatic approaches to budgeting and fiscal management. Budgets built on a programmatic basis to reflect long-range goals and objectives may not be adequately served by the information flow provided by traditional financial-accounting systems. As a result, either secondary management information systems must be developed and maintained or other mechanisms that facilitate the "crosswalk" of data from one format to another must be adopted.

Management Information and Control: Summary

The traditional approach to management control is illustrated in figure 5-3. Such an approach has several shortcomings:

1. The control process often takes on a restrictive connotation, and the process becomes the overriding concern instead of the work that is to be controlled.

2. Control reports often are viewed as a tool to measure the compliance and/or specific performance of subordinates rather than as a means of improving operations.

3. Performance standards usually are related to short-run financial considerations (cost-efficiency), based on accounting data, and frequently overlook the measurement of progress toward overall objectives (effectiveness).

4. The time lag in variance reporting between a deviation from planned activities and its discovery often may preclude corrective action until it is too late to be undertaken effectively.

To overcome these shortcomings and thereby achieve a greater integration in the organization, a modern management control system should be constructed around four central ideas: (1) The control system should be designed for decision making and not post-facto reporting. The system should be defined by the information needs of the manager, rather than by file structures, retrieval techniques, computer hardware, or reporting frequency. (2) Timely information is essential—the ideal control system is one

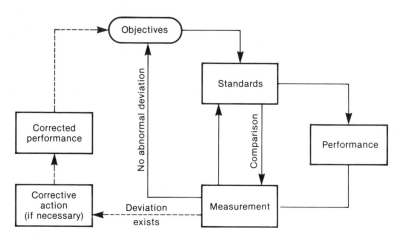

Figure 5-3. The Traditional Management Control Process

that provides information in sufficient time to correct a deviation before it actually occurs. Such systems rely on feedforward control as well as control mechanisms that are triggered by feedback. (3) The control system should be related to the current structure of the organization. The information system should be built around decision centers and not a financial chart of accounts. Moreover, the organization cannot achieve synergism unless the parts (functions or organizational elements) have been related to a set of unified objectives as well as to each of the other component parts. (4) Finally, each level within the organization should be provided with a planning framework that includes standards of performance (objectives) for the next lower level of operations. Thus, an essential ingredient in an effective management information/control system is the "means-ends chain" provided by strategic planning, management planning, and operations planning.

Notes

1. John Dearden, "MIS Is a Mirage," *Harvard Business Review* 50 (January–February 1972):90–99.

2. Herbert A. Simon, *Administrative Behavior* (New York: Free Press, 1957); John T. Dorsey, Jr., "A Communication Model for Administration," *Administrative Science Quarterly* 2 (1957):308–311; Chester I. Barnard, *The Functions of the Executive* (Cambridge, Mass.: Harvard University Press, 1938); Karl W. Deutsch, "Communication Theory and Political Integration," in *The Integration of Political Communities,* ed. Philip E. Jacob and James V. Toscano (Philadelphia: University of Pennsylvania Press, 1964); Eugene Jacobson and Stanley E. Seashore, "Communication Practices in Complex Organization," *Journal of Social Issues* 7 (1951):33; William V. Haney, *Communication and Organizational Behavior* (Homewood, Ill.: Richard D. Irwin, 1967); Lee O. Thayer, *Communication and Communication Systems* (Homewood, Ill.: Richard D. Irwin, 1968).

3. Alex Bavelas and Dermot Barrett, "An Experimental Approach to Organization Communication," *Personnel* 27 (1951):368.

4. E. Colin Cherry, *On Human Communication: A Review, A Survey, and A Criticism* (New York: Technical Press of MIT and John Wiley and Sons, 1957), p. 29.

5. Victor A. Thompson, *Modern Organization* (New York: Alfred A. Knopf, 1963).

6. T. Burns, "The Directions of Activity and Communication in a Department Executive Group," *Human Relations* (1954):92.

7. Ibid., p. 92. Several authors have documented the importance of the role of intermediaries or go-betweens in communicating things that no

one wants to assume responsibility for knowing, doing, or being associated with. See M. Dalton, "Unofficial Union-Management Relations," *American Sociological Review* 15 (1950):611–619; Theodore Caplow, "Rumor in War," *Social Forces* 25 (1946–1947):298–302; Norton E. Long, "The Local Community as an Ecology of Games," *The American Journal of Sociology* 64 (November 1958):251–261; and H. Menzel, "Innovation, Integration, and Marginality," *American Sociological Review,* 25 (1960): 704–713.

8. S. Habbe, "Communicating With Employees," *Studies in Personnel Policy,* National Industrial Conference Board Report no. 129 (New York: NICB, 1952).

9. K. Davis, "Management Communication and the Grapevine," *Harvard Business Review* 31 (1953):45.

10. D.C. Barnlund and C. Harland, "Propinquity and Prestige as Determinants of Communication Networks," *Sociometry* 26 (1963):468.

11. A study by Joseph Cooper and Gustav Jahoda ["The Evasion of Propaganda: How Prejudiced People Respond to Anti-Prejudiced Propaganda," *Journal of Psychology* 23 (1947):15–25] suggests that people who come in contact with communication that does not fit their own beliefs will psychologically evade the issue by unconsciously misunderstanding the message.

12. This discussion has been culled from the writings of Karl W. Deutsch, and, in particular, *The Nerves of Government* (New York: Free Press of Glencoe, 1963), pp. 85–86.

13. Freud has demonstrated this selective process most convincingly; see: *Psychopathology of Everyday Life* (New York: New American Library, 1960).

14. Jay Jackson, "Reference Group Processes in Formal Organization," *Sociometry* 22 (1959):323–324.

15. Dorsey, "Communication Model," p. 313.

16. Herbert A. Simon and James G. March, *Organizations* (New York: John Wiley and Sons, 1958), p. 166.

17. Richard M. Cyert and James G. March, *A Behavioral Theory of the Firm* (Englewood Cliffs, N.J.: Prentice-Hall, 1963), pp. 124–125.

18. Gordon W. Allport and L. Postman, "The Basic Psychology of Rumor," in *The Process and Effects of Mass Communication,* ed. W. Schramm (Urbana, Ill.: University of Illinois Press, 1954), pp. 146–148.

19. Russell L. Ackoff, "Management Misinformation Systems," *Management Science* (Application Series) 14 (December 1967), reprinted in Donald H. Sanders and Stanley J. Birkin, *Computers and Management in a Changing Society* (New York: McGraw-Hill, 1980), p. 37.

20. Richard B. Ensign, "Measuring the Flow of Management Information," *Journal of Systems Management* 21 (February 1972):2.

21. Ackoff, "Management Misinformation Systems," p. 44.

22. Ibid., p. 45.

23. Richard A. Bassler, "Data Bases, MIS and Data Base Management Systems," in *Computer Systems and Public Administration,* comp. Richard A. Bassler and Norman L. Enger (Alexandria, Virg.: College Readings, 1976), p. 203.

24. Richard F. Schubert, "Basic Concepts in Data Base Management," *Datamation* (July 1972):42-47; Richard L. Nolan, "Computer Data Bases: the Future Is Now," *Harvard Business Review* 51 (September-October 1973):98-114.

25. Norman L. Enger, "Data Management Systems," in Bassler and Enger, *Computer Systems,* p. 205.

26. Sanders and Birkin, *Computers and Management,* p. 80.

27. Enger, "Data Management Systems," p. 205.

28. Walter J. Kennevan, "Management Information Systems," in *Management of Information Handling Systems,* ed. Paul W. Howerton (Rochelle Park, N.J.: Hayden Book Company, 1974).

29. For a further discussion of the concept of MIPES, see Alan Walter Steiss, *Public Budgeting and Management* (Lexington, Mass.: Lexington Books, D.C. Heath, 1972), chap. 10.

30. Richard M. Cyert and James G. March, *A Behavioral Theory of the Firm* (Englewood Cliffs, N.J.: Prentice-Hall, 1963), p. 123.

31. John G. Burch and Felix Strater, "Tailoring the Information System," *Journal of Systems Management* 22 (February 1973):34-48.

32. Ronald Daniel, "Management Information Crisis," *Harvard Business Review* 39 (September-October 1961):112-113.

6 Productivity Improvement in the Public Sector

A basic objective of management control systems in the public sector is to improve the overall efficiency and productivity of governmental programs. As the National Commission of Productivity and Work Quality has observed: "Improving productivity means giving the taxpayers more services for their tax dollars, or giving them the same services for fewer tax dollars."[1] Increased emphasis on efficiency and accountability in the public sector has brought about renewed interest in productivity improvement.[2] Much confusion surrounds the topic, however, in large part because there seems to be little agreement on a definition of public-sector productivity, how to measure its growth or decline, or how it can be improved. As one local official has put it: "The public is now assailed by more irrelevant facts, half facts, and nonfacts on this subject than any issue in public affairs."[3]

Defining Public-Sector Productivity

A basic definition of productivity describes the relationship between the *inputs* (labor, capital, energy, and other resources) required to produce *outputs* (goods and services). Many analysts contend, however, that the narrow notion of productivity, as a simple relationship between inputs and outputs, is inadequate in defining governmental productivity. As Nancy Hayward observes: "Governmental productivity is the efficiency with which resources are consumed in the effective delivery of public services. The definition implies not only quantity but also quality."[4] To this observation, Steve Carter adds: "Cost efficiency which covers productivity in the traditional sense in the private sector is only one of several factors with which local governments must come to grips."[5] In response to court cases involving the equitable distribution of municipal services, others contend that "measures of social equity must increasingly accompany measures of productivity in order to assess the adequacy of public services."[6] Taking all these factors together, it would appear that *productivity* in the public sector must be defined in terms of efficiency, effectiveness, quality, and equity.

Broad Definitions versus Specific Applications

Popular definitions of public-sector productivity often are so inclusive that they do not really qualify as definitions at all. Osbin Ervin reminds productivity analysts to heed Aaron Wildavsky's warning to planners not to adopt an unmanageable definition ("If planning is everything, maybe it's nothing"). From his examination of improvement projects, Ervin concludes that: "There is clearly a gap between the exhortations to include effectiveness [in the definition of productivity] and the actual needs perceived and practices undertaken by local administrators."[7] The typical productivity-measurement effort in local government, he observes, is not concerned with the need to include quality or effectiveness indicators, but focuses instead on direct outputs such as "tons of waste collected" or "miles of streets paved."

Productivity is subject to political interpretations and is likely to be defined differently by management and labor. A call for increased productivity may simply be seen by government employees as a call for harder work. Victor Gotbaum of the American Federation of State, County, and Municipal Employees argues that public managers have no concept "of a true productivity approach in terms of management and labor working together. This concept of management is one part hostility and one part political opportunism."[8]

Differences between public- and private-sector definitions of productivity have been well documented. The relationship between inputs and outputs it more easily understood when it relates to the production of physical goods, such as automobiles, than with "soft" goods, such as social programs.

A fundamental difference between these productivity perspectives lies in the critical role played by the marketplace in arriving at the concepts of efficiency and effectiveness. Efficiency is concerned with the amount of work performed with a given level of resources, whereas effectiveness is concerned with the accomplishment of stated goals.[9] This distinction is illustrated in figure 6-1. In the private sector, the distinction between efficiency and effectiveness often is made—the most fundamental measure of the effectiveness of a business, after all, is its success in earning profits. To be effective means to be profitable; to be profitable means to use resources efficiently. The relationship between effectiveness and efficiency is thus solidified by the marketplace.

It is much more difficult in the public sector to determine the relationship between effectiveness and efficiency. No marketplace exists to inform service producers what to provide or to indicate acceptable quality and price levels. Only a weak competitive environment exists to ensure that the services are efficiently delivered.[10] Therefore, effectiveness is a much more ambiguous and subjective concept in the public sector. Without a natural linkage between efficiency and effectiveness, it is entirely possible, when evaluating a public service, to measure one while completely ignoring the other.

This problem lies at the root of the debate surrounding the definition of

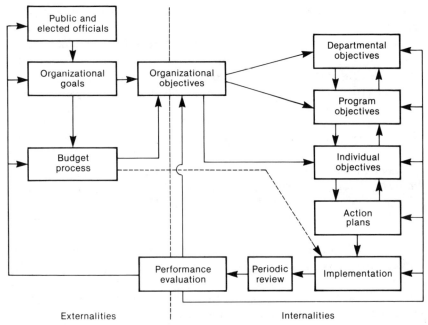

Source: Osbin L. Ervin, "A Conceptual Niche for Municipal Productivity," *Public Productivity Review* 3 (Summer/Fall 1978):15–24.

Figure 6–1. Efficiency- and Effectiveness-Measurement Schemes for Evaluation of Municipal Services

public-sector productivity. As Harry Hatry observes: "Improvements in unit costs or, conversely, output per unit of input, achieved at the expense of quality of service, can be said to represent an improvement in efficiency only by twisting the meaning of that term."[11] Such disregard for quality considerations is illustrated in the shift of solid-waste collection from backdoor to curbside service. Much of what is written on public-sector productivity rejects the notion that productivity improvements can be achieved through reductions in the quality of service. Consequently, a local government could not claim an improvement in the productivity of its solid-waste collection service by shifting the point of pickup from backdoor to curbside. Unders such circumstances, reductions in unit costs are made at the expense of service quality.

Technical Efficiency versus Allocative Efficiency

Economists actually recognize two different meanings of the term *efficiency*. Technical efficiency relates to the narrow, more mechanical concept of the relationship between inputs and outputs—in a strict sense, such efficiency is not related to the purpose or demand for the output. The discipline of economics, however, is based on the concept of maximum resource utilization, or the "maximization of consumer satisfaction (net benefits) within the constraints of limited means of production."[12] Thus, although technical efficiency relates only to the production process that provides benefits, the second interpretation of the economist—allocative efficiency— refers to the maximization of those benefits. This second interpretation of efficiency is directly related to the issue of effectiveness and quality.

Based on a review of hundreds of articles in his role as editor for *Public Productivity Review,* Robert Quinn has identified three dominant productivity orientations: those of (1) the economist, (2) the industrial engineer, and (3) the administrator. These divergent perspectives are summarized in table 6-1.

Economists are interested in such broad issues as the impact of productivity on the gross national product, the effect of rising wages, and the workings of the marketplace. Although they define productivity very precisely as the ratio of outputs to inputs, most economists writing about public-sector productivity recognize the need to supplement this definition with some consideration of output quality. In other words, they are concerned with both allocative and technical efficiency.

Industrial engineers are more likely to emphasize considerations of organizational throughput. Although their definition of productivity is similar to that of the economist, they narrow improvement efforts by focusing on increased efficiency through fine-tuning of the production process (technical efficiency).

Administrators have a broader perspective of productivity than those of economists or industrial engineers. They must operate in less abstract environments, often directing most of their attention to daily "brushfires." Administrators "do not lie awake at night worrying about the nation's competitive edge in the world market nor do they exclusively focus upon workflow, equipment, control, and measurement."[13] The administrator is likely to reject more rigid performance indicators in favor of determinations of how improvements might best be measured from situation to situation in resolving specific problems.

Productivity—Improvement Options

Although administrators may prefer broader definitions of productivity—which include such indicators as efficiency, effectiveness, political acceptability, employee morale, and client satisfaction—this is not to imply that such definitions are without form or direction. Assuming the service meets minimal effectiveness criteria, public administrators concerned with increasing productivity have a clear and overriding goal—the reduction of

Table 6–1
Dominant Productivity Orientations

	Economist	*Industrial Engineer*	*Administrator*
General orientation	Societal focus: national growth, world market, real income	Technical focus: workflow, measurement, equipment and control	Administrative focus: pressures for action, budgets, coordination, motivation
Need identified	More yield from the present workforce and equipment in society	Better measurement and control: more efficient throughput	Better overall performance of the organization
Definition of productivity	Precise: output over input with quality considered	Precise: output over input with quality considered	Ambiguous: better performance, with specific meaning varying from situation to situation

Source: Robert E. Quinn, "Productivity and the Process of Original Improvement: Why We Cannot Talk to Each Other," *Public Administration Reveiw* 38 (January/February 1978):42.

costs. The options available to improve productivity are as follows:

1. Input values can remain constant, while output values increase
2. input values can be reduced, while output values remain constant
3. input values can be reduced, while output values are increased to better reflect citizen demands
4. input values can be reduced, while quality levels are reduced
5. both input and output values can be increased if output values increase at a proportionally higher rate
6. both input and output values can be reduced if input values decline at a proportionately faster rate

Of these options, the second, fourth, and sixth will result in reduced costs as well as increased productivity, although some analysts would argue that the fourth option provides a "false improvement" if quality of service is reduced. The third option is obviously the ideal, although in times of high inflation, the first option may be the most pragmatic.

Pragmatic Reasons for Productivity Improvement

Voter-mandated limitations of the growth of revenue, coupled with high rates of inflation, make productivity-improvement efforts even more palatable. In an era of tax cuts and revenue-bond defeats, productivity improvements represent one of the few remaining options available to local officials in their attempts to balance the demands of citizens for more and better services against their demands for reduced taxes and greater efficiency in the use of public resources.

Proponents of formal measurement systems argue that well-designed productivity measures offer a source of vital information to the public manager. Good management decisions require good information, and without sufficient data, the public manager often must resort to making decisions based on intuition alone. A manager in the private sector could not survive without accurate productivity information on which to base day-to-day decisions. Why should the public manager expect to do otherwise?

Carefully designed productivity measures can provide an administrator with the means to identify critical problem areas. Such indices can serve as quantitative measures of goal accomplishment and can offer a practical means of performance comparison in both intraorganizational and interorganizational context. Finally, productivity measures provide valuable planning and budgeting information. Once unit costs are determined for a particular service, the consequences of changing service levels in response to changing demands can be assessed, and budget estimates can be calculated with far greater accuracy.

Productivity-improvement efforts also have real potential for affecting public attitudes as well as those of government employees. Whether justified or not, many citizens feel that public organizations and their employees are less productive than those in the private sector.[14] Productivity-improvement projects can improve the image of government, both to its own employees and the public at large. Research clearly indicates that the performance of any organization is actually improved by the measurement process itself.[15]

Measuring Productivity

As noted, the manager in the private sector has a distinct advantage over his public-sector counterpart in that input resources expended usually can be clearly linked to the production of measurable outputs. In using an indicator such as output per man-hour, the private-sector manager actually measures a much larger concept than simply the output of a single worker during a defined period of time. Very few services in the public sector involve such readily measured physical units of output, however. And it is often assumed that the use of traditional productivity measures in the public sector must be limited to private-sector-like functional areas, such as wastewater treatment or trash collection.[16] However, other approaches have been developed in recent years that hold the promise of more effective productivity measurement in areas of public service that are more difficult to assess.

Measurement Schemes: Single versus Multiple Measures

Two different approaches have been suggested to alleviate the measurement problem. One approach involves the development of new, comprehensive indicators that take into account both efficiency and effectiveness considerations and more clearly identify service-output units. For example, managers of social service programs in California during Governor Reagan's administration devised a system whereby a "contract" was established with service recipients. This contract outlined exactly what was to be accomplished during the time the service was rendered. Collectively, the service contracts were used as a basis for quantitative assessment of agency performance, client satisfaction, and overall productivity.[17]

A second broad approach to the measurement problem assumes that the relationship between inputs and outputs is far too complicated to allow for the use of a single indicator. Rather, a range of indices is advocated, involving the use of several traditional productivity indicators combined with measures of effectiveness into a multiple-measurement scheme. The key to this approach is the use of traditional measures only in conjunction with other types of performance measures.

A variation on the efforts to create a single, comprehensive measure can be seen in the development of indicators that quantify the relation among inputs, units of output, and quality. Drawing on the work of Jesse Burkhead and John Ross,[18] Robert Wallace has suggested that productivity can be measured by the following formula[19]:

$$\text{Productivity} = \frac{\text{Output}}{\text{Input}} = \frac{W \times Q}{I}$$

where W = workload (number of fires fought, acres mowed, and so on)

Q = quality measure

I = inputs (man-hours or cost)

Quality measures are further defined for each service element. In the case of firefighting, for example, after controlling for the number of men and units responding to an alarm, the average time "out of service" for alarms is used. A quality index is calculated by deriving a ratio of the average time out of service for the current year compared with the same measure for the previous year.

Everett Adam offers a similar formula to calculate a "quality production ratio" or QPR[20]:

$$QPR = \frac{\text{Number of good items processed}}{\begin{array}{c}\text{(Number of} \\ \text{items)}\end{array} \times \begin{array}{c}\text{(Processing} \\ \text{cost per} \\ \text{item)}\end{array} + \begin{array}{c}\text{(Number of} \\ \text{error items)}\end{array} \times \begin{array}{c}\text{(Error-processing} \\ \text{cost per item)}\end{array}}$$

The QPR can be increased either by improving quality or by decreasing the costs of delivering the service at the same level of quality. The difficulty involved in measuring error-processing costs, however, makes the application of this method somewhat difficult.

Hatry has warned that: "Simplistic notions of productivity measurement should be treated with great caution." He argues that, even as measurement techniques become more advanced, it is not likely that any one measure, no matter how "comprehensive," will ever be devised that can clearly encompass all aspects of productivity.[21] Thus, he advocates the multiple-measurement approach.

Workload and Unit-Cost Measures

A 1977 International City Management Association (ICMA) survey suggests that workload indicators are the most common productivity measure used in the public sector.[22] Workload measures relate the production of outputs to some unit of time. To an industrial engineer, workload measures are scientifically determined calculations of how much time is required for a trained employee to complete a unit of work at a prescribed quality level, while working at a normal pace in his regular job environment. Used in this context, work standards are determined through numerous time-study techniques, which can involve the use of time logs, stopwatches, historical data, motion picture films or video tapes, and various sampling procedures.[23] Information obtained through these techniques is used for a variety of purposes, ranging from evaluations of employee performance to the optimal use of space and equipment.

In a public agency, workload measures are more likely to be general indicators of output, such as acres of parkland maintained per year, miles of sidewalk constructed per month, or building inspections performed per day. Although workload measures by themselves do not indicate overall productivity rates, they are used by public managers to chart changes in agency output, to detect areas of general inefficiency, and to predict the effect of service-level changes on manpower requirements.

Unit costs, another traditional productivity measure, are defined as the total value of inputs consumed per unit of output. To reflect total input value, unit costs must include both direct expenses and indirect costs, such as fringe benefits, overhead costs, and management expenses. If all expenditures—direct and indirect—are included, unit costs can provide the public manager with valuable information concerning service costs and efficiency. Unfortunately, few local governments have accounting systems that can provide the required detail to operationalize such measures.

Indicators of service quality and effectiveness must also be available to integrate such measures into a broader evaluation system. As previously noted, this information is gathered only in rare instances. Such integration is not likely without a significant effort on the part of local-government officials.

Comprehensive-Measurement Approaches

Several attempts have been made to develop broader measurement systems to obtain more comprehensive productivity information. The Performance Monitoring System (PMS) as developed in 1972 in the District of Columbia, and with the technical assistance of the federal Office of Management and Budget, PMS was implemented in 1976 in sixty-three programs sponsored by thirteen different agencies in the District. More than 420 measures of program performance were devised for use in this project. In a report on the first year's accomplishments, administrators claim that PMS allows for "better utilization of available resources to meet public needs by measuring performance and service delivery and by taking improvement actions when needed."[24]

The Total Performance Management (TPM) approach was developed jointly by the Government Accounting Office (GAO), the National Center for Productivity and Quality of Working Life, and the U.S. Department of Housing and Urban Development. TPM consists of five basic components: an employee survey; a service-user survey; data on productivity, including measures of efficiency, effectiveness, and quality; information feedback to managers and employees; and action plans to correct deficiencies. The project report on TPM illustrates how broadly the concept of productivity has expanded since 1970:

> When an agency uses the TPM method, it not only measures its own productivity in traditional quantitative terms, but also finds out what employees think of their jobs, and how satisfied citizens are with the services the agency provides. The agency then goes on to show its workers the information it has gathered and to involve every employee in a bottom-up effort to solve problems and to eliminate shortcomings that have been identified.

The objective is a more effective work force that delivers better services to the community.[25]

The concept of performance auditing was first introduced by the General Accounting Office in its 1972 publication, *Standards for Audit of Government Organizations, Programs, Activities, and Functions*. Its intent is to expand the role of the audit from its traditional financial context to include considerations of efficiency and effectiveness. The performance-audit concept was field-tested in a joint GAO-ICMA project involving thirteen units of local government. Although the results have been decidedly mixed, the ICMA has judged the project a success.[26] The concept of performance auditing will be discussed further in a subsequent chapter.

Measurement Systems

A fundamental objective of productivity improvement is the development and implementation of measurement systems that can be fully integrated into the planning and management processes of government. A system denotes a continuous data-collection process, with periodic (monthly or quarterly) performance reports for management, rather than simply a one-time, special analytical effort.[27] The activity of information collection should be kept in proper perspective. Information should be timely and useful, and the collection system itself should be clearly understood by all participants. Measurement systems should not be too costly or require excessive maintenance. The overriding motive for making measurements, after all, is the improvement of productivity. It is important, therefore, that such performance information play an integral role in both day-to-day and long-range decision making.

The time requirements of all those involved in the process of data collection and analysis—from the mayor, city manager, and administrator to the field supervisors of the programs—should be considered in the design of the system. Measurement systems require accurate data, collected and reported on a timely basis, both as an historical record and as a basis for planning and programming. Such data are not likely to be gathered or processed unless sufficient importance is placed on the data-collection function by top management.

It is important, however, that a management system be designed with the realities of operational constraints in mind. As Samuel Finz has observed: "Agencies cannot be expected to drop everything whenever the periodic data-collection deadline arrives."[28] Local-government officials and managers are involved in more controversial and more pressing issues than collecting data and analyzing measurement reports. Productivity-measurement programs are not likely to survive unless such collection and reporting functions are fully integrated into the management information and management control systems.

Elements of a Productivity-Improvement Program

The primary objective of a public-productivity-improvement project should be to improve the quality of service, reduce cost, or some combination of the two. Local administrators implement productivity-improvement projects to obtain a better return on invested resources. It can be said that optimum productivity has been achieved when public-service demands are satisfied and public services are provided as efficiently as possible.

Although a variety of improvement techniques exist, the following five improvement categories offer the most promising potential in the public sector:

Adjustment of service and/or quality levels to more closely match citizen demands. Using this technique, input costs are adjusted by modifying the level or quality of services, when such alterations are in keeping with market demands. Reduction of service and/or quality levels may require that the citizen take on a greater role in the overall service-delivery system.

Reassignment of service-delivery responsibilities to achieve economies of scale. Such shifts usually are made through contractual arrangements between local governments and other jurisdictions or the private sector, but may also involve greater involvement on the part of citizens in the service delivery system.

Use of labor-saving equipment to achieve the most economical mix of labor, equipment, and capital inputs, and thus, to reduce total input costs. Less costly factors are substituted for more expensive labor-input costs.

Changes in procedures and methods to streamline the service-delivery system. Such techniques include the elimination of counterproductive regulations, improved allocation of labor, and better design of services to reduce input costs.

Improvement in the quality of labor input through training programs, attendance and/or performance incentives, improved employee motivation, and so on. This technique addresses the productivity problem on the level of the individual worker. It assumes that a better trained, more highly motivated employee performs more productively and that the overall productivity of an organization can be improved through maximum performance on the part of its individuals.

The appropriate mix of these five improvement categories is dependent on the type and scope of the public-service program involved. The first step in the implementation of a productivity-improvement project is to determine which approach or combination of approaches best fits the problems at hand.

Adjustment of Service Levels

The public manager plays a role similar to that of his or her counterpart in the private sector in the provision of services at levels acceptable to "customers" or "client groups." As James Heilbrun notes: "Local citizens want and are willing to pay for public goods and services such as parks, sanitation services, and police protection. One of the principal objectives of the local public sector is to provide such services in accordance with citizen preferences, just as the private sector provides bread and shoes and washing machines in accordance with customer preferences."[29] Matching service levels with demands, however, often is a difficult task. Although rough indicators of citizen demands may be available to local administrators, the ability to accurately gauge the level of demand in a particular community and to adjust service levels accordingly may depend on fairly sophisticated evaluation techniques.[30] The use of these techniques is further complicated by political considerations. It is generally difficult, for example, to reduce the level of any service once it is provided. Not surprisingly, a recent ICMA survey indicates that the adjustment of service levels is the least popular of the five methods for increasing productivity.[31]

Examples of Service-Level Adjustments

The level or quality of a public service often can be reduced in less dramatic ways and still result in improved productivity. Several instances can be cited.[32] In the City of Scottsdale, Arizona, for example, landscaped street medians, which previously required extensive maintenance and water resources, were replanted with semiarid, low-maintenance foliage. This change allowed the city to reduce manpower requirements for upkeep by 38 percent. In Honolulu, Hawaii, it was determined that approximately one thousand street lights could be turned off without adversely affecting safety conditions. Many of the remaining fixtures were replaced with mercury-vapor luminaries, resulting in a total annual savings of $85,000. Washoe

County, Nevada, reduced the annual expenditures of its consumer-health-services division as a result of several changes, including a reduction in the frequency of inspections from four to two per year for restaurants with good sanitation histories. This modification in workload allowed the county to eliminate two of its nine inspection positions. In each of these instances, the level of service was reduced within appropriate limits to improve productivity.

It is, of course, desirable to design service-delivery systems at the outset with minimization of maintenance and operating costs in mind. With the benefit of proper planning, for example, Scottsdale's traffic medians could have been landscaped with low-maintenance plantings in the first place. Design features in public schools that reduce the potential of damage from vandalism can directly contribute to lower maintenance costs. When such design considerations are taken into account, resources necessary to provide services can be maintained at much lower levels than would otherwise be the case. At times, a "penny-wise-pound-foolish" decision is made to forgo such design consideration or to skimp on initial construction costs, resulting in subsequent maintenance costs that are unnecessarily high. In constructing a school in a Virginia locality, only minimum roofing-material standards were met with the result that, after two years of operations, the entire roof had to be replaced because of water damage. Classes had to be rescheduled during the school year when classrooms were plagued by leaks.

Increased Participation by the Private Sector

As R. Scott Fosler notes, productivity can be improved through better cooperation between the public and private sectors in the coordination of overall service-delivery systems.[33] In the case of fire protection, for example, both sectors play distinctive roles—the public sector in terms of fire prevention and suppression and the private sector through the provision of fire insurance. In attempting to improve fire-service productivity through innovative staffing and equipment-deployment patterns, localities often are concerned that such innovations may lead to changes in their fire-insurance ratings. Fosler suggests that revisions in the Insurance Service Office rating standards, which in some areas are overly protective and/or obsolete, could contribute significantly to the potential for increasing fire-service productivity.[34]

Another example of improved public–private-sector coordination can be seen in the creative use of the regulatory authority of local government. Local governments recognize the productivity-improving nature of such regulations when land-use policies and building codes are developed with service-delivery requirements in mind. A local government frequently bears large service responsibilities when it accepts subdivision improvements initially provided by the developer. Subdivision regulations that set high standards for the construction of streets, sewers, sidewalks, and other public improvements can result in reduced maintenance requirements on the part of the local jurisdiction after a development is completed. Regulations governing the development of commercial areas, which take into account traffic flow, flood protection, crime control, fire protection (for example, sprinkler systems and smoke detectors), and other safety considerations, can directly affect the level of public productivity in providing services to these areas. Overregulation, on the other hand, can prove to be counterproductive. Economic conditions may require more flexible building codes and zoning regulations to encourage development.

Increased Participation by the Public

Whether made formally or informally, decisions regarding the most appropriate division of labor shape service-delivery policies. For example, service levels in residential solid-waste collections are determined by the frequency and point of pickup and the types of solid waste collected. Once-a-week, curbside pickup, limited to garbage, represents a much higher level of resident involvement than a system offering two backdoor pickups a week, with no restriction on the types of items collected.

The extent to which service-delivery responsibilities are shared between a local government and its citizens is sometimes the result of long-standing practices rather than the product of a precise decision process. "Sometimes citizens are adamant in their preference for one level of service over another. In other cases, citizens have simply grown accustomed to a given level of service, never stopping to question whether it could be changed, how much a change would cost, or how much would be saved by making the change."[35] A reduction in service levels and the assumption of service responsibilities by the citizens can result in improved productivity only when such reductions are in keeping with community demands and expectations.

Reassignment of Service-Delivery Responsibility

An increasing number of governmental entities are turning to other units of government or to the private sector for the provision of public services. According to one report, over 2,500 municipalities now contract with private firms for selected services in an attempt to reduce cost and improve staffing flexibility.[36]

Advantages and Disadvantages of Contracting

The decision whether to provide a public service directly or to purchase the service from a third party is similar to the "make-or-buy" decision often facing private-sector managers. The public-sector decision, however, frequently is more complex than a simple economic determination. The local manager must be concerned that the service will be provided in a responsive manner in accordance with citizen expectations. Therefore, the reduction of costs often must be balanced against other factors and priorities.

Advantages and disadvantages of contracting for services vary with the types of services involved. Advantages include: (1) avoidance of large start-up costs; (2) ability to acquire special talent that otherwise might not be available; and (3) flexibility in experimenting with new services or service-delivery methods. The potential disadvantages include: (1) high administrative and contract-maintenance costs; (2) possible loss of political and administrative accountability; (3) a decline in flexibility to respond to shifts in demands (especially during emergencies); and (4) possible adverse impacts on public employees.[37]

Reassignment to the Private Sector

Contracting with private-sector-service providers occurs more frequently in such areas as solid-waste collection, street maintenance, public transportation, and hospital administration. The most successfully contracted services are those that either are routine in nature, requiring little independent decision making (for example, tree trimming and mowing) or are so highly specialized that the service might be better provided outside the framework of local government (for example, day-care services, drug- and alcohol-abuse-prevention programs, assistance to rape victims).

Before exercising the contracting option, local administrators should consider several factors, including the capabilities of the suppliers (it may be desirable to have more than one qualified supplier available to ensure uninterrupted services); the nature of the service to be contracted; and the ability of government to administer the service contract.[38] Responsibilities for the administration of the contract should be clearly assigned, and procedures should be designed to monitor contractor performance and to enforce contract provisions.

Reassignments within the Public Sector

Municipalities commonly share service-delivery responsibilities with other jurisdictions in the areas of waste-water treatment, fire suppression, police protection, and library services. As Talley notes:

Intergovernmental-cooperation efforts can eliminate parallel services and duplicate costs. When cost savings occur, these moneys can be applied to increasing service quality. Intergovernmental cooperation has become more common in recent years. The geographic and fiscal limitations of most local governments often demand joint action. This trend toward intergovernmental arrangements is a recognition of the fact that interdependence is a way to achieve more yield from resources.[39]

Intergovernmental arrangements provide benefits additional to those that might be considered in contracting with private firms. Where services are duplicated (for example, by both the county and municipal governments), consolidation can provide an opportunity to reduce the total tax burden as well as to improve service effectiveness.

Intergovernmental cooperation, however, does not represent a foolproof means of productivity improvement. Many of the same disadvantages noted with regard to public–private-sector contracting also apply in the case of intergovernmental agreements. As Bruce Talley observes: "A popular axiom is that a single agency can provide a service cheaper than many agencies."[40] Whether this is actually the case depends on several factors, including: (1) the type of service; (2) the capability of other governmental units to provide the service; and (3) the likelihood that operating costs will be reduced through the transfer of service-delivery responsibilities. Sufficient administrative capability must exist to oversee formal contracting agreements between different jurisdictions.

Werner Hirsch contends that, with the exception of certain specialized activities, services for which unit costs can be reduced through economies of scale are limited.[41] He concludes that air-pollution control, sewage-disposal systems, power and water utilities, public transportation, hospitals and public-health services, and planning agencies are likely to enjoy major economies of scale. "Most of the other government units serving more than 50,000 inhabitants are unlikely to enjoy major economies of scale, if any."[42] As a general rule, Hirsch argues, the consolidation of vertically integrated services—such as electricity generation and distribution—are more likely to benefit from scale economies than the consolidation of horizontally integrated services.

Talley has cataloged five basic types of intergovernmental-service arrangements, ranging from informal discussions and "handshake" agreements to formal reorganization.[43]

Informal cooperation. This approach consists simply of discussions between local officials regarding common problems and issues. It may also encompass informal obligations, such as mutual-aid agreements for police and fire services, sharing of computer software, cooperative training of personnel, and so forth.

Voluntary associations of governments. Regional-planning commissions, councils of government, and other voluntary associations may be organized in an effort to improve coordination and to foster cooperation. Such associations are generally advisory bodies and do not directly impact local-government service-delivery problems.

Interlocal service agreements. Frequently associated with the so-called Lakewood Plan (after the arrangement implemented in 1954 between Los Angeles County and the City of Lakewood, California), this type of agreement can be most directly compared with the public-private contractual arrangement. Under this method, one governmental unit agrees to sell services to another public agency. The unit receiving the service maintains its authority and the provision of the service.

Service Transfers. Under this technique, one unit of government transfers not only service-delivery responsibility but also policy-making authority and financial obligations for the provision of the service. The creation of a special district or authority represents a common type of service transfer.

Reorganizations. The actual structure of local governments can be reorganized by means of consolidation, federation, or the creation of multijurisdictional councils to improve productivity through the consolidation of service-delivery activities.

Increased Use of Labor-Saving Equipment

Labor-saving equipment used in such industries as manufacturing and agriculture has dramatically improved the productivity of the average worker over the past century. In the public sector, labor-saving equipment is likely to be used in functional areas that are similar to private-sector industries. The use of labor- and cost-saving equipment is common, for example, in solid-waste collection and disposal, parks maintenance, gas and electricity distribution, water supply, and other public-works activities. In general, soft-service areas—such as personnel administration, planning, social services, inspections, code enforcement, and recreation—benefit less from the use of labor-saving equipment. Increased applications of word-processing techniques and other electronic equipment, however, hold the potential for significant changes in governmental administrative operations.

Research and Development Efforts

The lack of research and development (R&D) is one factor contributing to the limited availability of labor-saving equipment designed specifically for the public sector. The role of R&D in productivity improvement has long been recognized in the private sector. Certain public-sector activities have benefited from these efforts. Only 1 percent of the total industrial R&D effort, however, is directed to local- and state-government markets.[44]

The public sector generally represents a fragmented market, with little promise of standardization. This is a major factor contributing to the low level of R&D activity. A limited number of municipalities have developed their own products. William Donaldson, as city manager of Scottsdale, Arizona, is said to have ridden to fame on the specially designed garbage truck, "godzilla." When Donaldson moved to Tacoma, Washington, he was instrumental in the establishment of "Totem One," an urban laboratory for municipal R&D, which has produced a number of innovations.[45] Public Technology Incorporated (PTI) was founded as an idea exchange for R&D in local government and as a means of sharing the costs of new-product development.[46] These are but minor seeds planted in a fertile but as yet largely uncultivated field.

Prospects for Increased Automation

A relatively large inventory of labor-saving equipment currently is available to local government. The real challenges, however, are to determine how to finance the acquisition of expensive equipment; how to ensure its successful use and maintenance; and how to make adjustments in other production-resource levels (particularly labor costs). Bonafide productivity improvements associated with the introduction of equipment usually are of a long-term nature. Hardware is usually expensive; and therefore, extensive time often is required to break even. Labor costs may have to be reduced through personnel reassignments and attrition, and such shifts are not always easily accomplished.

Successful innovations may not necessarily be those that demonstrate at the outset relative advantages over existing practices. Such innovations are more successful, however, when they meet concrete objectives—preferably ones that affect the way in which clients use a service—rather than simply addressing internal administrative issues.[47]

Changes in Procedures and Methods

The analysis of work procedures and methods has been an accepted means of productivity improvement since the heyday of Frederick Taylor's efficiency experts in the 1920s. Public officials may be less inclined than their private-sector counterparts to hire management consultants or efficiency experts. There is a growing appreciation, however, for the potential of productivity improvement through changes in procedures and work methods. As Frederick Hayes observes: "The opportunity arises in part from the complexity of many work processes with numerous parallel and/or sequential actions necessary to deliver the product or service. . . . [W]ork arrangements tend to become obsolete with new developments."[48]

Techniques and revising procedures and work methods are directed at processes and input allocations. Attention is focused on maximizing the use of personnel and on streamlining the service-production process through workload planning, scheduling, and control and methods analysis. The functional areas most frequently benefited by the application of these techniques include law enforcement and public safety, public works, public utilities , inspections and code enforcement, parks and street maintenance, and financial functions such as tax collection and purchasing.

Several specific techniques are available within the broad area of change in procedures and methods. Patricia Haynes describes a variety of industrial-engineering tools that can be used in analyzing work methods in local government.[49] Work-distribution charts, for example, offer a means of determining whether work priorities are misdirected or job assignments and tasks are mismatched. Demand analysis involves an examination of the quantity and mix of resources required of a service-delivery system to meet citizen demands over time and in view of various geographic characteristics and administrative criteria.[50]

The redesign of work methods has been credited with significant local-government-productivity improvements.[51] Productivity gains of at least 15 percent were achieved in the inspection activities of several cities when these methods were applied. A 40-percent reduction in personnel costs and a doubling of the number of clients processed per day were reported in the San Diego County administration of the food stamp program through the use of these techniques. A revised staffing plan resulting from the redesign of work methods resulted in a net reduction of seven fire stations in Kansas City. Oak Ridge, Tennessee, realized an annual savings of 10 percent in its fire-department budget through another innovative staffing program.

Improvement in Input-Labor Quality

The importance of maximizing productivity on the part of individual employees is underscored by the fact that the public sector is largely a labor-intensive service industry. Many of the services provided involve direct interaction between the citizen or consumer and the local-government employee. Much attention, therefore, has been directed toward the individual employee's productivity level.

Many factors affect employee productivity. According to Robert Suter-meister, performance is largely a function of motivation, which, in turn, is determined by the individual's needs, organizational factors, and working conditions.[52]

Individual Needs

Public-sector employees are no less satisfied with their income and benefits than are their private-sector counterparts. A majority of employees in both sectors are dissatisfied with pay levels relative to what they feel is expected of them, and many in both sectors assume that they could earn higher salaries elsewhere.[53] Pay levels in themselves should not represent an impediment to productivity improvement, however.

Employee attitudes and perceptions are developed through a complex process that is not easily understood or controlled by the employer. The evidence indicates that employees who perceive themselves as part of an effective organization are more likely to be highly motivated than those who are less favorably impressed with the organization's performance.[54] Therefore, employee attitudes and perceptions impact collective behavior.

Individual-employee motivation is affected, to a large degree, by organizational and working conditions. *Working conditions* refer to environmental factors (lighting, temperature, ventilation, and so on), whereas *organizational conditions* are influenced by the quality of leadership, personnel practices, and, to a lesser degree, the formal and informal structure of the organization, management climate, communications, and the role played by unions.

The quality of supervisory leadership is important. Supervisors contribute to productivity-improvement efforts via their own individual performances as well as in terms of their subordinates' productivity levels. Public employees appear to be much less favorably impressed with the competence and effectiveness of supervisors and top managers than their private-sector counterparts. Perceived deficiencies include both inadequate technical and human-relation skills.[55]

Several local governments have developed personnel policies that seek to improve employee performance and maximize productivity levels. The determination of job content, the selection and placement of job applicants, the training of employees, and the evaluation of employee performance offer a variety of opportunities to establish organizational conditions conducive to productivity-improvement efforts. Certain of these initiatives can be implemented unilaterally by the employer. Other techniques require more extensive employee participation and cooperation.

Incentives

Productivity incentives can include the use of monetary rewards, expanded job responsibilities, more free time, or public recognition. An incentive is "anything offered to obtain desired performance or behavior from an employee."[56] Certain incentive programs are directed at the employee's relationship with his or her job. Other incentives focus on employee attendance. The incentives more directly related to increasing productivity are those aimed at the production of work—examples include output-oriented merit increases, work standards, performance targets, and productivity bargaining.

Job-content incentives include:

Educational incentives—official monetary or nonmonetary rewards given to encourage employees to continue their formal professional or technical education

career development—provision of well-defined promotional opportunities, such as career ladders, and their integration with training programs designed to qualify employees for the positions available

job enlargement—a variety of formal approaches designed to make the jobs of supervisory and nonsupervisory personnel more interesting and more responsible. Examples include: (1) job rotation through different work assignments; (2) team efforts—the grouping of employees to encourage cooperation and to provide a more varied view of the total work process; (3) increased participation in decision-making or problem-solving activities; and (4) job redesign—formal redefinition of work assignments.

When tied directly to modifications in input levels, such incentive programs have resulted in significant cost savings. Job-enlargement programs, especially when linked with other techniques, have permitted local governments to reduce input costs required to provide services. Administrators report that career development and job-enlargement programs improve morale, reduce turnover, improve communication, and generate better rapport among workers involved. Participating employees indicate their satisfaction with more stimulating job assignments. Insofar as productivity improvement is concerned, however, such programs have generally not resulted in immediately quantifiable rewards.

Absenteeism, especially in instances where each worker plays a key role as a crew or shift member, can have negative impacts on the productivity level of the working unit as a whole. Local governments have attempted to use the following incentives to maximize employee availability[57]:

Sick-leave incentives—monetary or nonmonetary inducements to encourage a reduction in sick-leave use

safety incentives—monetary and nonmonetary awards designed to minimize lost time tied to on-the-job injuries

task systems—paying a full day's wages to employees who are then allowed to leave work when they complete their assigned tasks, regardless of the actual time involved

variations in working hours—staggered hours, the four-day work week, gliding hours, flexible hours, and similar programs to better match work schedules to employee preferences

A popular form of attendance incentive involves the reimbursement of all or part of an employee's unused sick leave. Reward is usually given in the form of annual-leave credits, additional retirement benefits, or cash bonuses. Rewards for improved job-safety performance include public recognition and nominal cash awards. Task systems are among the most widely accepted incentive programs in effect.

Attendance-incentive programs have reportedly reduced absenteeism, decreased overtime, and improved morale. On the negative side, the extensive use of such incentives requires higher administrative costs. For example, in the case of the task system, special attention must be given to quality controls to assure that work is performed properly. Often, with many attendance-incentive programs, the enthusiasm generated at the time of implementation eventually subsides and attendance patterns return to normal. With the exception of output-oriented merit increases, incentive programs that most directly link rewards to improved productivity are among the most neglected of all techniques reported. "Public sector employees see a low opportunity for direct financial rewards based on superior performance. . . . The fact that less than one-third (30.2 percent) of the public sector employees believe that better performance will improve their chances for promotion suggests that the promotion system simply does not operate as an important incentive in more cases."[58] Various direct-performance and related incentives identified by the National Center for Productivity and Quality of Working Life include:

Output-oriented merit increase—permanent, nonpromotional increases in salary or wages given through merit system for specified performance levels

Performance bonuses—financial rewards paid to individuals for job performance that do not result in permanent salary or wage increases work standards—precise specifications of the work to be accomplished by employees or groups of employees (maintenance or repair time for a specific activity, minutes to take a welfare application, and so on)

performance targets—specific work-related objectives that are used as important criteria for determining pay levels

productivity bargaining—the use of labor-management negotiations to explicitly link added employee benefit to productivity increases

shared savings—financial rewards distributed among employees based on cost savings generated within a given period

piecework—a technique basing a worker's pay directly on the amount of output produced

competition and contests—rewards designed to encourage employees, individually or in groups, to improve performance in some facet of work

suggestion-award programs—employees are encouraged to contribute ideas on how to decrease costs, increase the quality of service, or otherwise improve the operations of their organization

Although programs directly linking pay to individual job performance seem to have significant potential for improving local-government productivity, there are several serious limitations to their use. Without the benefits of the private-sector's profit criterion and competitive-market environment, it is difficult to design adequate standards for making performance rewards. As a result, some of the jurisdictions using these techniques must rely on complex, often confusing formulas to select reward recipients. Public budgetary and legal constraints further restrict the applicability of certain incentive techniques, such as piecework, shared savings, and performance bonuses.

From Buzz Word to Tangible Applications

During the 1970s, productivity improvement became a "buzz word" among practitioners and a label loosely applied to almost any modification of operating procedures, introduction of labor-saving equipment, or initiation of new service-delivery programs. Despite this broad verbal support, genuine applications of productivity-improvement techniques have been relatively limited. The compulsory commitment of scarce resources, the inhospitable environment among public-agency employees, and the political risk taking required of the chief administrator are factors that have tended to discourage the initiation of broad productivity-improvement programs. Furthermore, although aggregate savings over the life of the improvement may be impressive in some cases, the annual savings are likely to be relatively modest, for example, less than 1 percent of a city's annual budget.[59] Such annual savings are quickly swallowed up by double-digit inflation, making these well-intended efforts relatively invisible.

Selection, Design, and Support

Hayes suggests that the initiation of productivity-improvement activities appears "to be an irrational act contrary to the realities of politics and government. Yet productivity programs are initiated. The obvious question is why."[60] Hayes concludes that, although productivity-improvement programs receive relatively little nourishment from the local-government environment, they are cultivated by innovative administrators, convinced that such endeavors are in the public's as well as their own best interest.

Much of the current productivity-improvement activity in state and local government is located in relatively respective environments and is sponsored by administrators who have successfully transformed the promise of improved productivity into tangible rewards. Successful programs suggest, however, that certain techniques are readily available for use in practically any government setting. Moreover, means are available to improve the receptiveness of local governments to improvement efforts. A prescription for initiating such efforts would include the following: (1) select improvement techniques that are appropriate for a given situation; (2) design improvement efforts with the realities of local government clearly in mind; and (3) build program support within the organization as well as the community at large.

There is still no cookbook for productivity improvement that can answer all the local administrator's questions.[61] Little of the existing information on productivity improvement is sufficiently detailed to be easily applied to specific situations. Furthermore, information frequently is limited to certain functional areas. At the risk of overgeneralization, however, some basic improvement techniques are transferable among local governments.

The adjustment of service and/or quality levels to more closely match citizen demands, often a difficult undertaking, has been applied in many functional areas, resulting in significant productivity improvements.[62] Input costs may be modified with only minimal impact on the services themselves. Changes made recently in the design of vehicles and facilities as a result of soaring fuel costs can be seen as examples. Existing services can be examined more closely in an effort to identify areas in which the level or quality of service exceeds actual needs. Such examinations have been successful in areas such as public transit, utility services, and solid-waste collection, where changes in service-demand levels are relatively easy to measure.

The reassignment of service-delivery responsibility is most likely to be applicable in areas where political sensitivity is not a primary concern, for example, street construction and maintenance and solid-waste collection. Intergovernmental-service arrangements have been especially successful in the provision of certain public-safety services (for example, dispatching, maintenance of jails, rescue-squad services), in the operation of libraries, and in special-service-agency functions, such as wastewater treatment, where a common service area is governed by more than one jurisdiction (for example, city-county cooperative service agreements).

Labor-saving equipment can be utilized most successfully in capital-intensive areas, such as park maintenance, street construction and maintenance, and solid-waste collection. When combined with staffing modifications, specialized equipment can also contribute to productivity-improvement efforts in public safety areas and in labor-intensive administrative operations (for instance, through the use of word-processing equipment).

Changes in procedures and methods to streamline service-delivery systems can be applied in all functional areas. These techniques are particularly useful in areas that are labor-intensive, where staffing reductions also can be achieved. This potential also exists with techniques aimed at improving the quality of labor inputs. Often such programs are dependent on the skills of the immediate supervisor, and, therefore, the probability of program success can be increased by including provisions to strengthen supervisory skills. The same can be said of programs addressing the individual employee's job content, attendance, and performance.

It is obvious from the documented success stories that care must be taken in the structuring of improvement programs. Those efforts most likely to succeed are designed with the needs of the particular government in mind, are of manageable size, and are pragmatic in nature. A productivity-improvement program characterized by complex and burdensome measurement or reporting requirements is not particularly well-suited to many local governments.[63]

A more selective approach may offer several advantages over comprehensive programs. Fewer management resources are required, and efforts can be concentrated on specific target areas. Improvement efforts implemented on a pilot-project basis often can provide an effective means of demonstrating to the organization and the community that productivity can be successfully improved. Programs can be directed to particular departments or to functional areas offering the highest potential for success—for example, areas generating the largest volume of citizen complaints, or where improvements have already been well documented in other jurisdictions.

Another approach is to take advantage of special opportunities as they arise. Attrition within a department, for example, can generate an opportunity to implement procedural revisions that permit manpower reductions. The termination of a service contract can provide an opportune time to modify service levels. Significant changes in the use of labor-saving equipment can be implemented at a time when large outlays for equipment replacement are required.

Successful productivity-improvement programs require a certain degree of organizational support. Special efforts should be made to acquire sufficient backing from department and agency heads, middle-management supervisors, employees, and the public in general. Such support is important not only during the design and initial implementation period but also during subsequent months to ensure that productivity efforts continue to their full fruition.

The exclusion of department heads and middle-management supervisors from the program-development process can prove to be a costly error.[64] Although such widespread involvement requires more extensive investment of time and manpower, the success or failure of a productivity-improvement program ultimately depends on the performance of individual employees. Resistance to change should be anticipated.[65] If improvement efforts in the private sector are to serve as a model, however, the inclusion of employees on every organizational level in the development and implementation of a program should be considered as vital to success.[66]

Consideration must be given to developing an organizational environment that is conducive to improvement efforts. One important factor is the tone set by top-management personnel; their visible involvement is crucial. They must recognize that productivity improvement cannot be viewed "as a crash program, or as a one-time effort, or as the exclusive responsibility of a specialized office or department.[67] Those responsible for program implementation must respond effectively and convincingly to those who feel they are doing all they can to improve their operations or who feel that improved productivity is "the other guy's job." Such misconceptions can only be corrected through an effective communications program. Top management, department heads, first-line supervisors, and employees all need to understand why productivity improvement is important to the organization as a whole and to them as individuals.

Assurances also must be communicated to address concerns that productivity improvements will have adverse impacts on individual employees. If a no-layoff policy can be incorporated into a productivity-improvement program, for example, this should be made clear to all employees. A stated commitment to thorough program design, development, and testing can help to demonstrate the probability of success to employees on all levels.

A pragmatic approach is necessary in generating support for productivity-improvement efforts from the public at large, groups outside of government, and local legislators. "Obviously, the public has to know about your program before it can support it. And it has to see some tangible results before it can get very excited. This suggests a careful laying of the foundation of public support."[68] It is important, however, to avoid overselling a program before it has any real substance. One way to increase the likelihood of support once the program is implemented is to involve city council or a committee composed of council members and other representatives in the initial-development stages. In some communities, city-council members are extensively involved in such programs and, in reality, are internal rather than external participants in the implementation process.

Local governing bodies must provide the resources and legislative mechanisms necessary to ensure the success of any improvement program. Legislative support is particularly important in instances where incentive programs are implemented, linking employee pay scales to performance standards. The local governing body also must take a certain amount of "heat" if the introduction of productivity-improvement activities generate opposition from outside groups or within the government itself. It is important that all parties understand that the responsibility for achieving a successful productivity-improvement program must be a shared one.

Prospects for Expansion

For a productivity-improvement program to succeed, the effort must be initiated with an appropriate blend of care and confidence. Adequate resources must also be available to design and implement the program. And sufficient internal and external support must be generated. A recent survey suggests that local administrators clearly appreciate the need for productivity improvement, whether or not they are actively involved in such programs.[69] The fiscal crisis facing many localities, the need for expanded economic development, requirements for improved capital facilities, and a general upgrading of the quality of community life are all priority issues that take precedence over public productivity-improvement programs. Productivity improvement, of course, can provide a major contribution to each of these priority areas.

Several factors could provide beneficial impetus to the future expansion of productivity-improvement programs. First a growing recognition of the fiscal crisis that confronts many localities can be expected to stimulate greater interest in the cost-saving potential of productivity improvements. Many local officials are now faced with a significant shift in orientation—from managing ever-increasing fiscal resources to the challenges of cutting back and curbing service expansions. Strong taxpayer opposition to continued tax increases, coupled with high inflation, may make productivity improvements more attractive to these officials.

Awareness of productivity improvements in other communities might result in increased public demands for improved efficiency and effectiveness. As techniques are successfully applied in a growing number of communities, the suspicions and misconceptions held by department heads and employees might also dissipate. Improved dissemination of productivity information could better ensure the successful application of such techniques.

Improved productivity remains one of the few means available to restore the public's sagging faith in the ability of government to perform. One local administrator has described productivity as "good management in disguise."[70] Carefully designed productivity measures enable managers to identify problem areas. Such indices potentially serve as quantitative measures of goal accomplishment. They also offer a means of performance comparison in both intra- and interorganizational contexts. Moreover, productivity information can be invaluable in the planning and budgeting processes of local government. Once workload and unit-cost measures are determined for a particular service, the consequences of adjusting service levels in response to changing demands can be identified, and budget estimates can be calculated with far greater accuracy.

Local administrators, determined to improve managerial effectiveness through the implementation of productivity-improvement programs, must be willing to commit resources to do so. The "fire-fighting override" prevalent in many local governments, however, makes is difficult at best to allocate the time and resources required to develop goals and objectives, measure progress, evaluate programs, and redirect efforts. These adjustments are not easily accomplished, even with the benefit of a well-designed measurement and evaluation system. However, in an era of increasingly tight fiscal resources, the improvement of productivity in the public sector may be the most viable avenue for survival.

Notes

1. National Commission on Productivity and Work Quality, *So, Mr. Mayor, You Want to Improve Productivity. . . .* (Washington, D.C.: U.S. Government Printing Office, 1974), p. 5.

2. The subject of public-sector productivity is not a new one. The annals of the *American Academy of Political and Social Science* in May 1912, featured twenty-eight articles on efficiency in municipal government, describing productivity improvements achieved at the turn of the century. The National Committee on Municipal Standards devised measures of

effectiveness for government services in 1928. The International City Managers' Association conducted studies of measurement of local-government services during the 1930s, resulting in one of the first handbooks on governmental productivity (which was revised and reissued in 1958). Interest in public-sector productivity on the federal level was first evidenced by the movement of the Bureau of the Budget into the Executive Office in 1939, and later, by the creation of the first Hoover Commission in 1949. In 1962, President Kennedy launched the first major productivity-measurement project, which resulted in the publication two years later of a measurement guide for federal-program managers. Reliance on quantitative measures also was expressed in contemporary budgetary techniques, such as PPBS (Planning-Programming-Budgeting-Systems), which were directed at more systematic evaluations of public programs.

3. Edward K. Hamilton, "Productivity: The New York City Approach," *Public Administration Review* (November/December 1972):785.

4. Nancy C. Hayward, "The Productivity Challenge," *Public Administration Review* (September/October 1976):544. As Katzell et al. note, private-sector definitions of productivity often include consideration of effectiveness: "By productivity, management and union policy makers refer essentially to the overall effectiveness and performance of individual organizations. In addition to quantity of output of goods and services they take into account various less tangible features . . . the term 'productivity' is not even used clearly or consistently in the professional literature. Sometimes it is used in its broad, all-inclusive sense to mean overall performance and sometimes in its narrower sense to mean output per unit of time or cost." See Raymond A. Katzell et al., *Work, Productivity, and Job Satisfaction: An Evaluation of Policy Related Research* (New York: Pyshological Corporation, 1975), p. 1.

5. Steve Carter, "Trends in Local Government Productivity," *The Municipal Yearbook—1975,* (Washington, D.C: International City Management Association, 1975), p. 99.

6. Stephen R. Chitwood, "Social Equity and Social Service Productivity," *Public Administration Review* 34 (January/February 1974):30.

7. Osbin L. Ervin, "A Conceptual Niche for Municipal Productivity," *Public Productivity Review* 3 (Summer/Fall 1978):20.

8. Victor Gotbaum and Edward Handman, "A Conversation with Victor Gotbaum," *Public Administration Review* (January/February 1978):20.

9. David Wilkins, "A Productivity Program for Local Government," *Public Productivity Review* 3 (Spring/Summer 1979):18.

10. Charles G. Leathers, "Language Barriers in Public Productivity Analysis: The Case of Efficiency and Effectiveness," Public Productivity Review 3 (Spring/Summer 1979):65.

11. Harry P. Hatry et al., *How Effective Are Your Community Services?* (Washington, D.C.: Urban Institute, 1977), p. 4.

12. Leathers, "Language Barriers," p. 63.

13. Robert E. Quinn, "Productivity and the Process of Organizational Improvement: Why We Cannot Talk to Each Other," *Public Administration Review* 1 (January/February 1978):41.

14. Responses to a Harris poll, conducted for the National Commission on Productivity and Work Quality, suggest that only 11 percent of those questioned felt that government workers demonstrate higher-than-average productivity, while 39 percent saw government-worker productivity falling somewhere below average. *So, Mr. Mayor,* p. 31, fig. 7.

15. U.S., Congress, Joint Economic Committee, *Measuring and Enhancing Productivity in the Federal Sector* (Washington, D.C.: U.S. Government Printing Office, 1972), p. 9.

16. Even if this limitation was imposed, there are many opportunities for the use of traditional productivity measures in the public sector. Many of the activities conducted by state and local governments, after all, are analogous to those conducted in the private sector. The treatment of wastewater is a municipal-service area in which traditional measures often are used. The end product of the treatment process can be measured in terms of quality and quantity. The objective is easily stated—to process a certain volume of sewage at an acceptable biochemical oxygen demand (BOD) level. The treatment operator, therefore, can take advantage of such measures as gallons processed per input dollar or output per man-hour to gauge his operation's productivity. A simple indicator, such as gallons of sewage processed per dollar at a specific BOD level, thus indicates several things—the total amount processed, the productivity of the sewage-processing functions, the quality of output, and the cost-effectiveness of the treatment plant.

17. Ralph C. Bledsoe et al., "Productivity Measurement in the California Social Service Program," *Public Administration Review* 32 (November/December 1972):80.

18. Jesse Burkhead and John P. Ross, *Productivity in the Local Government Sector* (Lexington, Mass.: Lexington Books, D.C. Heath, 1974).

19. Robert J. Wallace, "Productivity Measurement in the Fire Service," *Public Productivity Review* 2 (Fall/Winter 1978):21.

20. Everett E. Adam, Jr., "Quality and Productivity in Delivering and Administering Public Services," *Public Productivity Review* 3 (Spring/Summer, 1979):27.

21. Harry P. Hatry, "Issues in Productivity Measurement for Local

Governments," *Public Administration Review* 32 (November/December 1972):778.

22. Rackham S. Fukuhara, "Productivity Improvement in Cities," *The Municipal Yearbook, 1977* (Washington, D.C.: International City Management Association, 1977), p. 194.

23. Patrick Manion, *Work Measurements in Local Governments,* Management Information Service Report, vol. 6, no. 10 (Washington, D.C.: International City Management Association, 1974), p. 127.

24. District of Columbia Government, Executive Office of the Mayor, *Improving Program Performance: Report for Fiscal Year 1976* (Washington, D.C., 1976).

25. National Center for Productivity and Quality of Working Life, *Total Performance Management: Some Pointers for Action* (Washington, D.C.: U.S. Government Printing Office, 1978), p. 1.

26. *Performance Audits in Local Governments—Benefits, Problems and Challenges,* Management Information Service Report, vol. 8 (Washington, D.C.: International City Management Association, 1976).

27. Samuel A. Finz, "A Commentary on: 'The Enlarged Concept of Productivity Measurements in Government—A Review of Some Strategies,' " *Public Productivity Review* 2 (Winter 1976):59.

28. Samuel A. Finz, "Productivity—Measurement Systems and Their Implementation" in *Productivity Improvement Handbook,* ed. George J. Washnis (New York: John Wiley and Sons, 1980), p. 143.

29. James Heilbrun, *Urban Economics and Public Policy* (New York: St. Martin's Press, 1974), p. 320.

30. Werner Hirsch provides some useful examples of these techniques in *The Economics of State and Local Government* (New York: McGraw-Hill, 1970), chap. 2.

31. Rackham S. Fukuhara, "Productivity Improvement in Cities," *The Municipal Yearbook, 1977* (Washington, D.C.: International City Management Association, 1977), table 3/6.

32. International City Management Association, *Guide to Management Improvement Projects in Local Government,* vol. 2, no. 6 (November/December 1978) and vol. 3, no. 3 (May/June 1979).

33. R. Scott Fosler, "State and Local Government Productivity and the Private Sector," *Public Administration Review* 38 (January/February 1978):23.

34. Ibid., p. 418.

35. National Commission on Productivity, *Opportunities for Improving Productivity in Solid Waste Collection* (Washington, D.C.: U.S. Government Printing Office, 1973), p. 5.

36. Neal R. Pierce, "Cities Find Contracting out Efficient," *The Washington Post* (1979).

37. The American Federation of State, County and Municipal Employees has labeled the practice of contracting with private firms for the provision of public services a "new form of political patronage." See ibid.

38. Barbara J. Nelson, "Purchase of Services" in Washnis, *Productivity Improvement Handbook,* pp. 433–435.

39. Bruce B. Talley, "Intergovernmental Cooperation" in Washnis, *Productivity Improvement Handbook,* p. 450.

40. Ibid., p. 463.

41. Hirsch, *Economics of Government,* pp. 183–184.

42. Ibid., p. 184.

43. Talley, "Intergovernmental Cooperation," pp. 452–457.

44. National Center for Productivity and Quality of Working Life, *1977 Annual Report* (Washington, D.C.: U.S. Government Printing Office 1977), p. 26.

45. Frederick O'R. Hayes, *Productivity in Local Government* (Lexington, Mass.: Lexington Books, D.C. Heath, 1977), pp. 169–214. Among the innovations developed by Totem One under the cosponsorship of the National Science Foundation and the Boeing Corporation are a computerized model for the deployment of fire companies, an automated municipal-traffic-court scheduling system, a regional police-dispatching system, a quick-connect coupling for a fire hose, and a resource-recovery system with shredder/compactor equipment for the city's landfill.

46. Porter W. Homer, "Technology for Local and State Governments," *Public Management* 55 (August 1973):7.

47. Robert K. Yin et al., *Tinkering with the System* (Lexington, Mass.: Lexington Books, D.C. Heath, 1977).

48. Hayes, *Productivity in Local Government,* p. 7.

49. Patricia Haynes, "Industrial Engineering Techniques" in Washnis, *Productivity Improvement Handbook,* pp. 204–236.

50. John S. Thomas, "Operations Management: Planning, Scheduling, and Control" in Washnis, *Productivity Improvement Handbook,* pp. 177–198.

51. National Center for Productivity and Quality of Working Life, *Managing Inspections for Greater Productivity* (Washington, D.C.: U.S. Government Printing Office, 1977), p. 6; National Center for Productivity and Quality of Working Life, *Improving Governmental Productivity: Selected Case Studies* (Washington, D.C.: U.S. Government Printing Office, 1977), pp. 5–13; David N. Ammons, "Taking the Best of a Private Fire Service and Making It Public," *Municipal Management* 2 (Winter 1980):103–109; Thomas, "Operations Management," p. 182.

52. Robert A. Sutermeister, *People and Productivity* (New York: McGraw-Hill, 1976).

53. National Center for Productivity and Quality of Working Life, *Employee Attitudes and Productivity Differences between the Public and Private Sector* (Washington, D.C.: U.S. Government Printing Office, 1978).

54. Ibid., p. 4.

55. Ibid., p. 13.

56. Ibid., p. 3.

57. Ibid., p. 3.

58. Ibid., pp. 17–18.

59. Hayes, *Productivity in Local Government,* p. 255.

60. Ibid., p. 245.

61. A laudable effort to accomplish this objective is Washnis, *Productivity Improvement Handbook.*

62. One reason productivity-improvement efforts have been successful in solid-waste collection, for example, is that many refuse-collection practices were originally designed to provide services no longer required, for example, to accomplish such antiquated tasks as the removal of large quantities of coal ash from residences and businesses. The potential for improved productivity through the modification of service levels has existed for many years.

63. Samuel Finz is particularly critical of those who would overemphasize the role of measurement efforts. See Finz, "Commentary."

64. See Hayes, *Productivity in Local Government,* pp. 121–122, for a documented example of this problem in New York City during Mayor John Lindsay's administration.

65. See Robert Quinn, "Public Management Information Systems and Resistance: Towards a Better Understanding," *Public Productivity Review* 3 (Fall 1976):5–19 for further discussion on this point.

66. The advantages of maximizing the involvement of employees in all phases of program design and implementation are well documented in *Implementing a Productivity Program: Points to Consider* (Washington, D.C.: Joint Financial Management Improvement Program, 1977).

67. National Commission on Productivity and Work Quality, *So, Mr. Mayor,* p. 13.

68. Ibid., p. 32.

69. Survey of three hundred local administrators conducted by Joseph C. King and David N. Ammons of the Research and Budget Department, City of Oak Ridge, Tennessee.

70. *Public Management* 62 (May 1980).

7 Performance Evaluation

Performance evaluation has been a watchword in government for over two decades. Despite considerable fanfare, however, systematic assessments of public programs have remained more a promise than a practice. Public goals and objectives often are nebulous and ill defined. Consequently, the identification and measurement of program results is even more elusive. As Joseph Wholey has noted: "From the point of view of decision-makers, evaluation is a dangerous weapon. They don't want evaluation if it will yield the 'wrong' answers about programs in which they are interested."[1] In such situations, political pressures frequently override empirical evidence available from formal evaluations. Nevertheless, the evaluation of program results is a critical part of the management-control process. The conduct of such assessments is, in fact, what management control ultimately is all about.

Evaluation: A Many-Splendored Thing

The term *evaluation* has been applied to so many different activities that it has all but lost its functional meaning. D.N.T. Perkins, for example, identifies six basic types of evaluations:

1. Strategic evaluations are concerned with underlying causes of social problems, focusing on "implicit theories" as a basis for broad ameliorative programs.
2. Intervention effect assessments attempt to establish the relation between program interventions and outcomes or, in some cases, the processes involved in producing those outcomes.
3. Compliance evaluations examine the consistency of program objectives with broader legislative aims and attempt to ensure that public funds are allocated in accordance with policy guidelines.
4. Program design evaluations test the measurability of program assumptions, the overall logic of the program approach, and the assignment of responsibility and accountability for program results.
5. Management evaluations focus on the efficiency and effectiveness with

which managers deploy available resources to achieve program objectives.

6. Program impact evaluations deal with the program-delivery system and the relation between program results and the legislated goals and program objectives.[2]

The last three types of evaluations are perhaps most relevant in the context of management control.

A Working Definition of Evaluation

Some authors have suggested that the term evaluation be reserved for relatively high-order assessments of the effectiveness of policy decisions. This focus characterized many early efforts at systematic evaluation—what has been labeled evaluation research. "In its humble beginnings . . . evaluation research was much like the buzzard, attacking only dead programs. These postmortems were useful in developing a conceptual basis for evaluations but did little to improve policy formulation."[3] Such full-blown scholarly research sometimes evolved over five to seven years, making program improvements virtually impossible. Many of the federal programs chosen for such rigorous analyses were short-term pilot projects. Even when these programs continued, managers were unlikely to utilize the results of these evaluations because: (1) program evaluators were "out-siders"—academic types—often with different perceptions and opinions about the goals of the program; and (2) evaluators tended to focus on the negative aspects of a program and rarely offered constructive advice.[4]

The scale and time frame of performance evaluation must be such that management is assisted in formulating program improvements. Moreover, such evaluations must specify program problems in a way that provides clear indications of alternative courses of action to resolve these problems. As Robert Clark has observed, unless evaluation is keyed to specific information requirements and decision-making needs in a timely fashion ". . . it risks being irrelevant—a monument to what might have been."[5]

The interface/timing problem is particularly acute in those program areas that may have specific postaudit requirements but no formal mechanisms for translating the results into alternative plans. Evaluation research has turned up important information about second-order consequences and unintended impacts. Although knowledge of these impacts should result in improved program and project designs, at present the feedback loop, at best, is tenuous.

As David Nachmias has pointed out, evaluation can refer to both process and impact assessments.[6] Process evaluations are concerned with the extent to which programs are implemented according to predetermined guidelines. The thrust of a particular public program and its impact on the target population to be served may be substantially modified, elaborated, or even negated during its implementation. Impact evaluations examine the extent to which a program produces a change in the intended direction. Such evaluations depend on a clear definition of program goals and objectives and specification of criteria of success with which to measure progress toward these goals.

A distinction must also be made between programmatic and organizational evaluations. It is necessary to decide whether the program or the organization responsible for the program is to be evaluated. A program may be evaluated in terms of its effectiveness and costs, but an organizational structure should not be evaluated solely on the basis of its success (or failure) in operating a particular program. As E.S. Quade observes, an organization should be judged not by an initial program failure but by its capacity to learn from failure and to improve the operation of the program.[7]

Taking all these admonitions into account, a working definition of *evaluation* for the purposes of this discussion is an assessment of the effectiveness of ongoing and proposed programs in achieving agreed-on goals and objectives and an identification of areas needing improvement through program modification (including the possible termination of ineffective programs). Such evaluations must identify and take into account the possible influence of external as well as internal organizational factors on the overall effectiveness of the program.

Efficiency versus Effectiveness

The purpose of many performance evaluations has generally been to improve efficiency. Questions of efficiency often are defined an answered strictly in least-cost terms, with minimal consideration of priorities or of the relative worth of the programs pursued. It is possible to do things very efficiently, but if they are the wrong things to do they will have little positive impact on the problems at which a public program is directed. Improving efficiency may not require any drastic changes in program strategies. Increasing effectiveness, however, often entails radical program adjustments. This is one reason why evaluations that focus on effectiveness may not be fully utilized—there may be few opportunities to make the types of changes recommended. Nevertheless, increasing emphasis is being placed on effectiveness evaluations or assessments of program results.

Some authors argue that the distinction between efficiency and effectiveness is an artificial one and that, if properly applied, a criterion of efficiency is sufficient to measure both dimensions.[8] The notion of a criterion of efficiency was first formulated by Herbert Simon. It asserts that a choice among alternatives should be made in favor of the course of action that produces the largest result for a given application of resources.[9] To guide this choice, however, it is necessary to determine an appropriate level of goal attainment or level of program adequacy (for example, a minimum acceptable level of performance). In the absence of such definitive statements of goals and objectives, measures of efficiency cannot provide the insights necessary to make appropriate judgments about program achievements or benefits.

Formative and Summative Evaluation

A comprehensive evaluation system should be based on both formative and summative techniques (see figure 7-1). Formative evaluation provides information necessary to design and/or modify a service-delivery system. It includes: (1) an analysis of the needs to be met or the problems to be solved; (2) a determination of whether a public program should be initiated to meet such needs; and, if so, (3) how the program should be designed. Summative evaluation includes measures of performance and program impact. These types of evaluations are closely interrelated. Information derived from summative (impact) evaluations provides input for continuing formative evaluative efforts.

Three basic concerns should be addressed for each service area: (1) Should the service (or program) be provided? If so, what options are available and which should be selected? (2) Having implemented a program or service, how well is it being provided? (3) What benefits is the program or service providing and to whom? Are there measurable disbenefits? A sound evaluation system should be responsive to these basic issues, and the information obtained should be incorporated into the budget and other decision subsystems.

At first glance, the design of a measurement system capable of providing this information might appear to be an awesome undertaking. When seen in a historical context, however, practically all public services are provided as a result of decisions made over time, based directly on such formative and summative information. The mix of services provided by local government reflect a variety of commitments made by the governing body, regulations imposed by other levels of government, and administrative decisions made by appointed officials.

Formative decisions are expressed through local-budget documents, local ordinances, state statutes and regulations, federal laws, intergovernmental contracts and agreements, and so forth. Although administrators

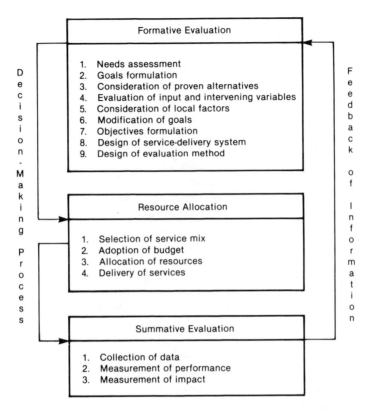

Figure 7-1. A Comprehensive Evaluation System

can make important contributions to these decisions, it is more likely that formative evaluations will be useful in developing better decisions concerning the improvement of service-delivery systems once these broader commitments are made. As Carol Weiss notes: "The analysis of program variables begins to explain why the program has the effect it does. When we know which aspects of the program are associated with more or less success, we have a basis for recommendations for future modifications."[10] In short, effective evaluation not only describes what is happening but also helps to determine which features of a program are successful and which are not.

To make such determinations, both input and intervening variables must be measured. Input variables include information that might be considered extraneous to the service program. However, analysis of input variables can provide the information necessary to identify more clearly why a program might or might not be successfully implemented in a particular jurisdiction. Data collection on input variables should be undertaken with the limitations of time and cost constraints in mind. As Weiss suggests, ". . . most evaluations have limited resources, and it is far more productive to focus on a few relevant variables than to go on a wide-ranging fishing expedition."[11]

There are two kinds of intervening variables: (1) program-operation variables; and (2) bridging variables, that is, the intermediate steps selected as a means to achieve program goals and objectives. In a local government's fire prevention program, examples of program-operation variables would include the allocation of personnel in the fire department to the prevention effort and the extent of coordination with other agencies (for example, code-enforcement department or planning office) in the development of an overall strategy for fire prevention. Bridging variables relate to the accomplishment of fire-prevention goals. Special and ongoing projects—such as home fire-safety inspections, smoke-detector-installation programs, and public education efforts—are assumed to contribute to the prevention of fires and thereby link program activities to desired results.

An understanding of intervening variables provides the most direct answer to the formative-evaluation question: "How can it be done?" A clear understanding of the causal relations between intermediate activities and their results have a direct impact on the ability of a government agency to meet its objectives. A poorly conceived program, no matter how effectively implemented, contributes relatively little to the overall effectiveness of an agency. In the context of pure-evaluation research, the relation between intervening variables and program results should be subjected to empirical analysis. This relation often is less formally deduced in the real world of local government.

Organizational constraints again will limit the time and resources that can be devoted to the analysis of intervening variables. One approach is to involve line managers, either through formal or informal procedures, in seeking answers to such questions. Whether or not the connections between program design and objectives are formally determined, "there are almost always some prevailing notions, however inexplicit, that certain intermediary actions or conditions will bring about the desired outcomes.[12]

Planning for Better Evaluations

Planning is necessary to develop a sound data base for empirical evaluations. It may be possible to initiate evaluation planning at approximately the same time as a program alternative is selected for implementation. The evaluation design may be an extension of the process applied in the analysis and selection of the program alternative. It may be reasonable to expect that program decisions will be affected by the evaluability of alternatives, since knowing that a program will be effective may be closely linked to showing that it is. This does not imply that program managers should do only that which promises to be most demonstrative. It does suggest, however, that an evaluation strategy is a vital consideration in program planning. As Peter Rossi has so aptly observed: ". . . the more formal aspects of systematic evaluations depends upon what transpires during planning and program development. As every sailor knows, the trick is not to navigate the seas but to get out of the harbor."[13]

Clarify Program Objectives

It is necessary to determine the exact character and intent of program goals and objectives before an evaluation is initiated. S.M. Shortell and W.C. Richardson have provided the following list of criteria for clarifying program objectives:

1. *Nature or content of the objective.* It is important to determine the intended changes to be brought about by the program.
2. *Ordering of objectives.* Objectives should be clearly presented at each level of abstraction, with corresponding operational indicators to determine if the objective has been met.
3. *Target group.* The specific group(s) to which the program is directed should be identifiable in terms of age, sex, ethnic catagories, geographic boundaries, etc.
4. *Short-term versus long-term effects.* It is important to document both the short-term and long-term effects of any program.
5. *Magnitude of effects.* It is necessary to determine how large (or small) an effect will be acceptable as a positive indicator of success.
6. *Stability of effects.* For many programs, the effects are meant to be lasting; but for others, particularly programs involving behavioral changes, additional exposure to the program may be necessary.
7. *Multiplicity of objectives.* It is important to clarify objectives to the point that possible conflicts among them can be identified and dealt with.
8. *Importance.* Objectives will differ in importance, and individuals often may disagree on the relative importance of each objective; however, some attempt should be made to place objectives in some general priority order.
9. *Interrelatedness of objectives.* Where a set of lower-order objectives may serve as an important component in the achievement of higher order objectives, such linkages should be identified in the statement of objectives.
10. *Unintended and unanticipated "second-order" consequences.* It is important to identify possible "side effects" of the program—

effects not intended but anticipated, or even unanticipated, by the
initiators of the program.[14]

Complete clarity seldom comes from an examination of the final statement
of a program planning process to determine what types of impacts are actually anticipated. The links between program planning and evaluation require mututal understanding of the tasks and procedures involved on both
sides.

The formulation of goals and objectives is important in answering the
last of the formative-evaluation questions: "How should it be done?"
Although an International City Management Association (IMCA) report
indicates that an impressive number of communities utilize goals and objectives in their policy and program planning, statements of goals and supporting objectives are not alwasy easy to develop.[15] As a result, evaluators often
must deal with goals that are vague or relatively noncommital (that is,
unmeasurable).

Although general or even subjective in nature, a goal statement should
clearly outline the intent of the public program in terms of altering, correct-
ing, or controlling an identified problem. "A program's goal, as the summation of its objectives, should reflect the program's relative ability to deal
with a problem. While the goal is subjective and less adaptive to measurement, it should not be so ambiguous or idealistic as to lose relevance to the
real intent of the program."[16] Goals are most effective in an evaluation
system when they are as specific as possible. For example, a broad goal such
as "to achieve a better health" is less useful than one that defines whose
health is to be improved (the elderly, the young, and so on); which aspects
of health are to be improved (nutrition, immunization, substance abuse,
and so on); and from whose perspective the improvement of health is to be
defined (public-health professionals, state health department, various
health-care providers, client groups, and so on).[17]

To contribute to an evaluation system, objectives should be more
precise, measurable, and time bound. This degree of specificity is not easily
achieved. The tendency is to state objectives that simply describe current activities. To avoid this pitfall, objectives should be expressed in "words of
change" (for example, to develop, to increase, to reduce, to eliminate, to
prevent, to maintain). Samuel Finz provides the following suggestions
regarding the formulation of objectives:

1. Objectives should provide quantitative levels to be achieved, for example, a rate of return on investment of a specific percentage per annum,
   or reductions of the average response time required on emergency calls
   to a maximum of five minutes.
2. Objectives that do not provide quantitative levels to be achieved should

at least provide a measure in terms of time and budget constraints, for example, to process all requests within twenty-four hours, or to reduce the cost of processing to a maximum of $10 per request.

3. Objectives can be expressed in terms of satisfaction or public acceptance on the part of those affected by the services provided, for example, the performance of a recreational facility as measured by the percentage of those persons using the facility who are satisfied with its use.

4. Objectives that cannot be expressed in the form of positive quantification nevertheless should be more specific than goals, for example, to maintain machinery to ensure continuous operation and efficient performance.[18]

The development of goals and objectives through formative evaluation techniques provides a foundation for the subsequent development of mechanisms with which to measure the actual performance of public programs and their impacts on citizens affected. The complexities inherent in the analysis of the relations that exist between government programs and desired results, and the difficulties surrounding the development of adequate goals and objectives, represent a significant challenge to the public manager.

It is not enough, however, to analyze causal relationships in establishing goals and objectives. It also is necessary to quantify, as accurately as possible, the exact level of service or achievement to be obtained. In certain instances, this requirement of specificity is relatively easy to meet. For example, the selection of a quantifiable objective relating to the city's return on investments can be readily set by a finance director who keeps abreast of changing interest rates and available investment options. On the other hand, the standard used by a fire chief to establish an objective concerning a reduction in the average response times for his fire company may be less clear. What level should be strived for—five minutes?—three? And how many library volumes per citizen should a local-library administrator set as an objective?

Community-Needs Assessment

To answer these questions, the local administrator must assess the needs of the community, just as his or her counterpart in the private sector must determine the demand for products. Peter Hunt, George Yearbower, and Paul Yingst note that: "Needs assessment is the process by which community needs are identified and priorities among them determined. It begins with a determination of what is an "acceptable state of affaris." A need may be defined as a condition in which there is a discrepancy between the acceptable state of affairs and an observed state of affairs."[19] Needs may be either objectively measured or subjectively estimated. Objective needs assessment relates to the comparison of the level of service provided with the level judged acceptable. In the case of subjective needs assessment, knowledgeable individuals must make judgments as to the extent to which a need exists. "A valued judgment is necessary in both procedures; in the first case in setting the level judged acceptable, in the second case in estimating the extent of need."[20] Objective criteria often are set by law, tradition, or administrative standards, or they may be supplied by professional organizations.

One effective means of assessing community needs is through a direct citizen survey. Such surveys, or course, are also an effective way to determine the impact achieved through the provision of public services. User surveys may be conducted to determine both the extent of service needs and the actual level of services provided. Trained field observers also have been used by some units of local government to measure service levels and conditions.[21]

The final products of the formative-evaluation process should be: (1) a service-delivery plan, based on an understanding of the causal relations between the activities to be performed and the desired results; (2) a set of goal statements, outlining a course of action in broad terms; and (3) supporting objectives, which provide for the quantification of progress toward goal achievement. Assuming that the techniques of formative evaluation have been utilized, the resulting goals and objectives should represent the best available solution for a particular community (within the constraints of available resources). Collectively, goals and objectives provide an answer to questions of whether a service should be provided, in what form, and at what level.

Measuring Program Effectiveness

Following the clarification of objectives a brief survey should be made of existing systems for measuring program effectiveness to determine how best to augment these systems. The General Accounting Office has described this activity as a four step process:

1. Identify and document existing systems for measuring effectiveness
2. assess the validity and sufficiency of the performance indicators, i.e., as quantifiable expressions of program objectives
3. assess the accuracy of performance indicator data; and
4. determine the appropriateness of the performance standards, i.e., desired levels of achievement for performance indicators[22]

Not all performance criteria (indicators and standards) will be expressed in quantitative terms. This is not as important, however, as other factors, such as: (1) Performance indicators should clearly reflect the intent of objectives. (2) They should permit the analyst to distinguish the impacts that obviously are attributable to other phenomena. (3) They should not be limited to workload and unit-cost measures.

It may be necessary in some cases to adopt temporary, ad hoc systems for measuring effectiveness. In general, the measurements obtained from an ad hoc system are not as refined or comprehensive as would be possible from a well-designed, "built-in" evaluation system. "Nonetheless, an ad hoc system provides the users . . . with more reliable effectiveness data than they had previously been provided and shifts the burden for fine-tuning the performance data back to program management."[23]

Traditional performance measures can provide meaningful management-control information when utilized within a broad evaluation framework that includes both formative and summative techniques. The following information on a local fire-prevention program, for example, might be developed through a carefully implemented evaluation process.[24]

A comparison of local fire data with state and national fire statistics reveals a large per-capita incident rate for a particular community. The predominant type of fire reported is structural, and the major causes are unattended cooking, defective wiring, and malfunctions of electrical appliances. Experience in other communities indicates that such fires are relatively preventable through home inspections and public-education programs. Further analysis of successful prevention programs provides some indication of the most effective methods of performing such prevention services. Data on local-housing conditions and land-use patterns provide the information necessary to modify these techniques to make them applicable to the target community. These data provide a basis for the design of specialized, tailor-made methods, best suited for use in the community.

From this evaluation, the fire-prevention goal of minimizing such preventable fires can be supported with specific objectives. Such objectives might include:

Conduct 2,500 home-safety inspections during the coming year.

Coordinate activities for a communitywide fire-safety program during Fire Prevention Week.

Make fifty fire-safety presentations to schools and civil groups during the coming year.

Supervise the installation of 1,000 smoke-detector devices in residential structures.

Identify residences with hazardous or defective wiring and coordinate the efforts of municipal departments to bring at least one-hundred of those structures up to building-code standards during the coming year.

Activities of the fire department must be coordinated and manpower carefully scheduled to accomplish these objectives. It is at this point that traditional performance indicators are particularly useful. The objective of conducting 2,500 home-safety inspections, for example, can be expressed in terms of an average rate of 7 per shift, or in the case of a small four-company fire department, 1.75 inspections per company per shift. The total productivity of each company obviously would depend on its ability to perform all its responsibilities, not just those relating to fire prevention. Each additional function, however, could be similarly measured.

Traditional Performance Measures

When a workload measure is related to a unit of input (for example, cost), it is transformed into an efficiency measure. Output can be related to input costs, to units of labor (such as man-hours), or to units of time. Thus, efficiency measures might include miles of street paved per unit of dollars expended, acres of park land mowed per man-hour, or number of buildings inspected per month.

Traditional performance measures also include work standards, that is, measures of the amount that specific tasks should require. In an evaluation system, performance is recorded relative to such standards. If the standard for reading electric meters is 200 per day, for example, a meter reader collecting data from 175 meters would have met 87.5 percent of the standard. The use of such measures requires service outputs that are characterized by fairly routine procedures, which themselves are standardized. Minimum quality standards also are required.

Another kind of performance measure relates to utilization statistics. Although such measures do not involve traditional output-to-input calculations, they do offer useful performance information. Examples include the percentage of total capacity utilized, equipment downtime, and nonproductive staff time (for example, the time spent by case workers in carrying out recordkeeping activities which takes away from their time available to work with clients). Utilization statistics should be integrated into the performance-evaluation system in a manner similar to other indicators, that is, they should be linked directly to goals and objectives.

Finally, traditional performance measures can include some effectiveness criteria. For example, rather than stating police-patrol performance in terms of arrests made per officer, the number of arrests can be qualified by indicating only those successfully clearing the initial judicial screening. Instead of measuring the number of households provided with a given service, an assessment can be made of those households satisfied with the service. Such information can be related to unit costs as well—for example, the number of households satisfied per input dollar.

Impact Evaluation

Ultimately, the most important information provided through an evaluation system is that which relates to the impact of public programs. Impact evaluation answers questions concerning the accuracy of assumptions made in the formative-evaluation stage, the ability of the governmental-service unit to achieve stated goals and objectives, and the results achieved—intended or unintended, positive or negative. "Impact evaluation recognizes the necessity of dealing empirically with the inter-relatedness of economic, environmental, social and psychological factors, all of which affect service program effectiveness. In contrast to performance evaluation, it provides information relating to the impact of a service program rather than its inputs or outputs."[25] Several techniques are available with which to measure the impact of services provided. The use of surveys, as noted, has become increasingly popular. Other information can be obtained through standard reporting procedures employed by many agencies of local government. The site-inspection technique, involving trained observers, can also serve as a means of impact evaluation. For example, the physical appearance of public thoroughfares might be observed before and after the implementation of a cleanup campaign to measure the effectiveness of the campaign.

Basic Approaches to Evaluation

Ideally, evaluation seeks to compare what actually happened to what would have happened or what conditions would have prevailed if the program had not been initiated.[26] Since it is difficult, if not impossible, to determine exactly what would have happened, the problem is to develop and apply evaluative procedures that can approximate this state. Several standard approaches are available to conduct an evaluation, including: (1) before-and-after comparisons; (2) time-trend-data projections; (3) with-and-without comparisons; (4) comparisons of planned versus actual performance; and (5) controlled experimentation.

The First and Final Steps

Each of these approaches begins and ends with the same procedural steps. The first step is to identify the relevant objectives of the program under evaluation and the corresponding evaluative criteria or effectiveness measures. The final step should include an explicit and thorough search for other plausible explanations for the observed changes and, if any exist, an estimate of their effects on the data.

The major purpose of evaluation is to identify changes in those criteria that reasonably can be attributed to the program or activities under study. A major problem, however, is that other factors, such as external events or the simultaneous introduction of other related programs, may have occurred during the time covered by the evaluation. One of these other factors, and not the program under evaluation, may have been the significant cause of the observed changes. Explicit provisions for controlling at least some of these exogenous factors are included in the second, third, and fifth approaches previously listed.

Rossi and his colleagues offer the following list of competing processes that may influence the outcome or program effects:

1. *Endogenous change:* The condition for which the program is seen as a remedy or enhancement may change of its own accord. In medical research, the phenomenon is known as "spontaneous remission."
2. *Secular drift:* Relatively long-term trends in the target population or in the broader community may produce changes that enhance or mask the effects of a program.
3. *Interfering events:* Short-term events also may produce enhancing or masking changes.
4. *Program-related effects:* The actual evaluation effort may contribute to a bias in the program results; this is the problem of the "uninvolved observer."
5. *Stochastic effects:* Chance or random fluctuations in any measurement effort may make it difficult to judge whether a given outcome is, in fact, large enough to warrant attention. Sampling theory identifies how much variation can be expected by chance.
6. *Unreliability:* Data collection procedures are subject to a certain degree of unreliability, a major source of which may be the measurement instrument itself.
7. *Self-selection:* Segments of the target population easiest to reach are those most likely to change in the desired direction for other reasons. Similar processes in the opposite direction may lead to differential attrition. Dropout rates vary from project to project, but are always troublesome in evaluation.
8. *Maturation trends:* Programs directed toward changing persons at various stages in their life cycle must cope with the fact that considerable changes also are associated with the process of maturation.[27]

The outcome of a program is a function of net program effects and these confounding elements. The isolation of these competing processes must be undertaken in each of the evaluation approaches described in the following sections.

Before-and-After Comparisons

Perhaps the simplest and least costly approach, as well as the most common, involves an examination of conditions in a given jurisdiction or target population at two points in time—immediately before a program is introduced and at some appropriate time after its implementation. The assumption is that any changes in the "after" data, as measured by appropriate evaluation criteria, have occurred as a consequence of the new program. This approach is least capable of separating other influences from the effect of the program activities. Therefore, it is valid only in situations where program comparisons are not likely to reflect short-term fluctuations and where program-related changes are clearly measurable.

The effectiveness of this approach can be increased if the evaluation is carefully planned prior to program implementation. In this way, appropriate data can be collected as a basis for the evaluation criteria. Reliance on data available in established collection procedures seldom provides an adequate basis for such an evaluation. Special data-collection procedures will increase the cost of the evaluation, but this approach is still the least expensive of the methods outlined.

Time-Trend-Data Projections

A second approach draws comparisons between actual postprogram data generated by the evaluation criteria and extrapolated data suggestive of conditions that would have prevailed without the program. Data on each evaluative criterion should be obtained at several intervals before and after the initiation of the program activities. By means of standard statistical methods, preprogram data are projected to the end of the period covered by the evaluation. Actual and projected estimates are then compared to determine the amount of change resulting from the introduction of the program.

This approach is most appropriate when there appears to have been an underlying trend over a period of time that would have been likely to continue if the new program had not been introduced. The program objective is to change the direction of this trend—to amplify some desirable change or to dampen some undesirable condition. Such statistical projections may be relatively meaningless, however, if data for prior years are too unstable. Likewise, if there is strong evidence that underlying conditions have changed in very recent times, data for prior years probably should not be used.

The time-trend approach adds two cost elements to the first method: (1)

the cost of technical expertise to undertake the statistical projections, and (2) the added data collection for prior years. This latter requirement may become problematic in ensuring that preprogram data are compatible with postprogram or current data.

With-and-Without Comparisons

A third approach seeks to draw comparisons between a jurisdiction with a particular program and one or more communities without comparable programs. This approach also can be used if some segment of the population within a community is to be served by a given program but others are not, as is the case when a pilot program is tested. Changes in the values of the evaluative criteria (rates of changes as well as amounts) for the "with" and the "without" groups form the basis for this comparison. The characteristics determining the choice of comparative groups will vary with the types of programs under evaluation. The choice ultimately is based on the judgment of the evaluator as to what nonprogram-related factors might influence the effectiveness of the program under study. Although this approach controls for some important external factors, it is generally not a fully reliable measure of program effects. It is best applied in conjunction with other evaluative methods.

The identification of comparable communities or populations within communities may require considerable effort. The cost may be reasonable if standard data categories are adequate (such as similar population size, proximity, and so forth). The costs may rise significantly, however, if communities are selected for particular combinations of characteristics or to ensure that a similar program effort does not exist in the "without" communities. Since the type of data collection and the precision of these data are likely to vary from community to community, the availability of comparable data may be severely limited. Thus, the cost of this approach will be considerably higher if special data-collection efforts are required.

Comparisons of Planned versus Actual Performance

Despite rather straightforward procedures, after-the-fact comparisons are still surprisingly rare. This approach requires the establishment of specific measurable objectives or targets prior to the initiation of the program. Targets should be established for specific achievement within specific periods (for example, reductions in the incidence of juvenile delinquency by 15 percent in two years, rather than: the elimination of juvenile delinquency). Such evaluations can be readily undertaken if program targets are expressed in terms of effectiveness measures.

Like the before-and-after approach, this method provides no direct means of indicating the extent to which the changes in values of the effectiveness criteria can be attributed solely to the new program. As with other techniques, an explicit search should be made for other plausible explanations as to why the targets have been met, exceeded, or not met.

Appropriate, realistic objectives must be established as the basis for evaluation criteria. The setting of such objectives may not be taken seriously if the evaluations are not used seriously—a problem with all evaluation techniques. Targets may be overstated and, therefore, unattainable, or they may be understated to make the program achievements look better. If the evaluation findings are used seriously by decision makers, however, a valuable spinoff of this approach is that the establishment of targets is likely to become an important issue. Higher-level officials, as well as program managers, should participate in this process, and the targets should explicitly encompass all key program effects.

The after-the-fact approach can be applied more widely once provision is made for the regular collection of necessary data for measuring effectiveness. Targets can be set each year for one or more future years. This approach is particularly useful for annual program evaluations. Much can be learned from a careful, systematic examination of the immediate, short-term consequences of a program, even if a more elaborate evaluation method is not applied.

This evaluative technique is relatively inexpensive compared to other methods. Costs depend primarily on the expenditures necessary to gather additional data for the evaluation criteria selected. The setting of appropriate (measurable) objectives is likely to entail relatively small costs, at least in dollar terms.

Controlled Experimentation

Controlled experimentation is by far the most potent approach to program evaluation. Unfortunately, it also is the most difficult and costly to undertake. The procedures of this approach may involve many technical steps of experimental design techniques, which can become very complex with respect to a particular program evaluation. The basic steps, however, are as follows:

1. Identify relevant objectives and corresponding evaluation criteria (effectiveness measures)
2. select members of the target population that have similar characteristics with respect to their likelihood of being treated effectively by the program

3. assign members of the target population (or a probability sample of that population) in a scientifically random manner to control and experimental groups
4. measure the preprogram performance of each group using the selected evaluation criteria
5. apply the program to the experimental group but not to the control group
6. continuously monitor the operation of the experiment to determine if any actions occur that might distort the findings
7. adjust any such deviant behavior, if appropriate and possible; if not, at least identify and estimate its impact on the eventual findings
8. measure postprogram performance of each group using the selected evaluation criteria
9. compare pre- and postprogram changes in the evaluation criteria of the groups
10. search for plausible alternative explanations for observed changes and, if any exist, estimate their effects on the data[28]

The controlled experiment is most appropriate for the evaluation of programs directed toward specific individuals, such as health programs, manpower training, and so forth, and for a variety of treatment programs such as those for drug and alcohol abuse, correction and rehabilitation, or work-release. It is not likely to be appropriate, however, for programs requiring large capital investments in equipment or facilities.

An important variation on this approach involves the comparison of different geographical areas. Many programs can be split geographically—introduced initially in some localities and not in others. For example, new crime-prevention programs, solid-waste-collection procedures, programs of traffic control, and so forth often are tried out and evaluated in a few areas before receiving widespread application. Areas with similar characteristics with respect to the program being tested could be identified, and some of these areas then randomly designated as program recipients. If trends in the evaluation data before and after the new program was in operation show significant improvements in those areas with the program, then a basis would be provided for attributing the change to the introduction of the program.

This approach is not without its special problems—problems that can bring the observed results into question. Some of these are as follows:

1. Members of an experimental group may respond differently to a program if they realize that they are part of an experiment. This problem is known as the "Hawthorne effect," after studies by Dickson and Roethlisberger in the late 1920s at the Western Electric Company's Hawthorne Works in Chicago. In these studies, the productivity of the test group

increased even under adverse conditions as a consequence of their selection for evaluation. To help reduce this problem it may be necessary to inform members of the control group that they too are part of an experiment.

2. If the experimental groups is only one part of a community, the program results may differ significantly from what would occur if all parts of the community were to receive the benefits. For example, a new crime-prevention program introduced on a pilot basis may merely cause a shift in the incidence of crime to other parts of the community without any overall reduction in the crime rate.

3. In some situations, political pressures may make it impractical to provide services to one group while withholding them from others. Such problems may be lessened by testing variations of a program in several locations rather than allocating program resources on an all-or-nothing basis.

4. It may be considered morally wrong to provide a government service temporarily if the service might cause dependency among clients and leave them worse off after the program is withdrawn.

5. If persons are permitted to volunteer to participate in the experimental group, the two groups are not likely to be comparable. A self-selected group will probably be more receptive to the program and thus may not be typical of the whole target population.

6. Problems may arise in the administration of the service, for example, a trained research group may not be familiar with service-delivery problems and, therefore, may introduce a bias into the program results. A specially trained staff also may be able to deliver the pilot program at a level that cannot be met by those agency personnel who will be called on to administer the full-scale program.

The use of the controlled-experiment approach generally costs considerably more than the other evaluation techniques because of: (1) the greater time required to plan and conduct the experiment and to analyze the data; and (2) the higher level of analytical and managerial skills required. This approach also implies certain indirect costs arising from the temporary changes made in the way the program operates to achieve differential benefits. Innovative projects can be evaluated more readily because pools of unexposed potential targets usually are available. Established projects, on the other hand, may require statistical methods that measure the effects in degrees of exposure as well as by reflexive controls that utilize time-series analysis.[29]

Combined Approaches

The selection of an appropriate approach will depend on the timing of the evaluation, the costs and resources available, and the desired accuracy. It should be evident that these approaches are not either/or choices, however. Some of or all the first three methods often are used together. The before-and-after method is relatively weak when applied alone, but becomes much more useful in combination with other approaches. The after-the-fact approach, involving comparisons of planned versus actual performance, is likely to be used more extensively once management information systems become more widely accepted and implemented in the public sector. Although the experimental approach provides the most precise evaluation, its costs and special characteristics result in its being applied on a very selective basis.

Decisions about public programs inevitably are made under conditions of considerable uncertainty. Evaluations can reduce this uncertainty but cannot eliminate it totally. Even though it may not be possible to isolate the effects of a program from other concurrent events, it may be unnecessary to be overly concerned if the evaluation indicates significant benefits to the community or target population.

Applications of Evaluation Findings

The most comprehensive evaluations are little more than academic exercises if their findings have no impact on the processes by which policies are made and programs are developed. Evaluation research has had only modest implications for the policies and programs to which these scholarly studies have been directed. As Rossi et al. have observed: "Evaluations cannot influence decision-making processes unless those undertaking them recognize the need to orient their efforts toward maximizing the policy utility of their evaluation activities."[30] At the same time, the need for evaluation must be recognized and accepted by those public officials responsible for the development and implementation of programs and policies.

Sunset Legislation

Added impetus for more systematic evaluation procedures has emerged with the adoption of sunset laws by various states and localities. This mechanism of legislative oversight requires periodic evaluations of programs and the termination of those for which continuance cannot be justified. Differing from state to state, most sunset legislation provides for the following:

1. Agencies and/or programs are assigned a mandatory termination date, and if the legislative body takes no formal action, the enterprise is concluded (that is, the sun sets) on this date.

2. The agency is given an opportunity to justify its continued existence

(or the continuance of certain programs) prior to termination. This justification may entail any number of evaluation indices (and may involve a performance audit or may be undertaken in conjunction with zero-base budgeting).

3. The legislative body has the option to reinstate or reconstruct the agency or program, or to terminate it. Reinstatement may leave the agency relatively unchanged, whereas reconstruction may lead to significant modifications in the mandate and responsibilities of the agency.

4. If reauthorized or reconstructed, the agency or program will again be subject to review and possible termination at the end of the next cycle.[31]

As initially conceived (in Colorado and Florida), sunset laws were to be relatively selective in application, focusing for the most part on state regulatory agencies. In instances where the sunset process has been expanded to include a broader set of activities (for example, Alabama), it has proven difficult and cumbersome. Bruce Adams has suggested that in one state so many agencies were covered, it was reminiscent of the Coliseum in ancient Rome: "people were asked to put 'thumbs up' or 'thumbs down' on one agency after another."[32] Without a firm basis of analysis, legislators took the safe route by allowing the agencies to continue. This approach, of course, defeats the purpose of sunset laws. While sunset laws can be a much more pervasive tool than experience to date has evidenced, their application remains highly dependent on previously constituted management decisions.

Performance Auditing

The role of audit procedures in a management control system will be outlined in further detail in a subsequent chapter. However, a relatively new audit focus, promulgated by the General Accounting Office (GAO), has particular relevance to this discussion.

The traditional emphasis of the postaudit has been on an assessment of financial transactions for accuracy, legality, and fidelity—on the question of financial compliance. Gradually, more emphasis has been placed on *management audits* that ask: Did you achieve your milestones in the most efficient and economical way possible? Management audits involve an assessment of resource-utilization practices, including an examination of the adequacy of management-information systems, administrative procedures, and organizational structure. More recently, however, the emphasis has expanded further to include an assessment of *program results,* addressing the question: What difference did the program make? An examination of program results seeks to determine whether the desired benefits were achieved, whether program objectives were met, and whether alternatives were considered that might yield the desired results in the future at a lower cost.

Taken together, these three audit components constitute what the GAO has labeled a "performance audit."[33] Such an audit is generally undertaken when a program or project has been completed or has reached a major milestone in its funding.

Program Reconstruction

The scale and time frame of performance evaluations must be such that the findings can assist in formulating program improvements. Moreover, evaluations must specify program problems in a way that alternative courses of action are clearly indicated.

The real art of program improvement is not the bold guillotining of unpromising programs but rather is the reconstruction or renegotiation of the program-developing process. The concept of program reconstruction is based on the feedback stage of the systems model, wherein initial program outputs are modified in response to the reactions of affected groups and sources of support. Reconstruction suggests a refining and retargeting of programs (and policies) rather than setting totally new directions.

Program terminations are rare; curtailment is likely to be a more common approach. There are a number of problems associated with the actual termination of a program. Some of these problems of organizational and sociopolitical inertia can be outlined as follows:

1. Institutional performance: policies and agencies are designed to endure; complex organizations have an uncanny survival instinct
2. Situational dynamics: programs are constantly adapted to emerging situations to avoid termination
3. Intellectual reluctance: given the hard-fought battles necessary to obtain a policy or program in the first instance, public officials have a natural reluctance to consider the issue of termination
4. Antitermination coalitions: significant political and/or clientele groups often support programs beyond their span of effectiveness
5. Legal obstacles: programs have certain rights of "due process"
6. High startup costs: mounting campaigns for termination often is costly, both monetarily and politically[34]

Strategic reconstruction often is possible with public programs, particularly if such adjustments are amenable to entrenched interests. Peter de Leon provides the following "guidelines" for program modification:

1. Modification and/or termination should not be viewed as the end of the world; rather, it is an opportunity for policy/program improvement.

2. Modification and/or termination should coincide with systematic evaluation.
3. Policies and programs have certain "natural points"—times and places in their life spans—where reconsiderations are more likely and more appropriate.
4. The time horizon for gradual change is a significant factor.
5. The structure of incentives might be changed to promote modification; for example, agencies might be permitted to retain a portion of the program funding that they voluntarily cut.
6. Agencies might employ a staff of "salvage specialists," trained in reallocating resources.

Increasingly, governmental activities are constrained by impending fiscal crises, and thus, terminations or at least serious reconstructions are becoming more viable.

Although evaluations may not have realized their full potential in the past, new techniques, coupled with sunset provisions and the concept of performance auditing, provide additional incentives for administrators to heed evaluations and to use them as management tools for improving program performance.

Notes

1. Joseph S. Wholey, "What Can We Actually Get from Program Evaluation?" *Policy Science* 3 (1972):361–369.

2. D.N.T. Perkins, "Evaluating Social Intervention: A Conceptual Schema," *Evaluation Quarterly* 1 (November 1977):642–645.

3. Alan Walter Steiss and Gregory A. Daneke, *Performance Administration* (Lexington, Mass.: Lexington Books, D.C. Heath, 1980), p. 226.

4. See Rehka Agawala-Rogers, "Why Is Evaluation Research Not Utilized?" *Evaluation Studies,* vol. 2 (Beverly Hills, Calif.: Sage Publications, 1979); Carol Weiss and Michael J. Bucuvalas, "The Challenge of Social Research to Decision-Making," in *Using Social Research in Public Policy Making,* ed. Carol Weiss (Lexington, Mass.: Lexington Books, D.C. Heath, 1977), pp. 213–234.

5. Robert Clark, "Policy Implementation: Problems and Potentials" (Paper presented at a meeting of the Southern Political Science Association, October 1976), p. 2; available from the U.S. Community Services Agency.

6. David Nachmias, *Public Policy Evaluation* (New York: St. Martin's Press, 1979), p. 5.

7. E.S. Quade, *Analysis for Public Decisions* (New York: American Elsevier Publishing, 1975), p. 235.

8. Lennox L. Moak and Albert M. Hillhouse, *Concepts and Practices in Local Government Finance* (Chicago: Municipal Finance Officers Association, 1975), pp. 380–391.

9. This concept was first proposed in Herbert A. Simon and C.E. Ridley, *Measuring Municipal Activities* (Chicago: International City Managers' Association, 1938) and further expanded in Herbert A. Simon, *Administrative Behavior* (New York: Macmillan, 1957), chap. 9.

10. Carol H. Weiss, *Evaluation Research* (Englewood Cliffs, N.J.: Prentice-Hall, 1972), p. 46.

11. Ibid., p. 47.

12. Ibid., p. 50.

13. Peter H. Rossi, Howard E. Freeman, and Sonia Wright, *Evaluation: A Systematic Approach* (Beverly Hills, Calif.: Sage Publications, 1979), p. 120.

14. S.M. Shortell and W.C. Richardson, *Health Program Evaluation* (St. Louis, Mo.: Mosby, 1978), pp. 18–20.

15. Rackham S. Fukuhara, "Productivity Improvement in Cities," *The Municipal Yearbook, 1977* (Washington, D.C.: International City Management Association, 1977), p. 194.

16. *Multnomah County POPS Field Manual: A Handbook for the Implementation of the Multnomah County Program Objective Productivity System,* Management Information System Clearinghouse (Washington, D.C.: International City Management Association, 1974), p. 10.

17. Donald A. Krueckeberg and Arthur L. Silvers, *Urban Planning Analysis: Methods and Models* (New York: John Wiley and Sons, 1974), p. 8.

18. Samuel A. Finz, "A Commentary on: 'The Enlarged Concept of Productivity Measurements in Government—A Review of Some Strategies,' " *Public Productivity Review* 2 (Winter 1976):59–61.

19. Peter J. Hunt, George T. Yearbower, and Paul V. Yingst, *Evaluation Process Handbook for Local Government Services: A Program Evaluation Guide* Management Improvement Department, City of St. Petersburg, Florida (Washington, D.C.: ICMA Report Clearinghouse, 1975), p. 16.

20. Ibid., p. 16.

21. Harry P. Hatry et al., *How Effective Are Your Community Services?* (Washington, D.C.: Urban Institute, 1977), pp. 207–213.

22. General Accounting Office, *Comprehensive Approach for Planning and Conducting a Program Results Review* (Washington, D.C., 1978), p. 31.

23. Ibid., p. 46.

24. The following scenario is based on the actual experiences of Joseph C. King while serving as a productivity-improvement analyst in the City of Oak Ridge, Tennessee.

25. Hunt, Yearbower, and Yingst, *Evaluation Process Handbook,* p. 14.

26. Harry P. Hatry, Richard E. Winnie, and Donald M. Fisk, *Practical Program Evaluation for State and Local Governments* (Washington, D.C.: Urban Institute, 1973).

27. Rossi, Freeman, and Wright, *Evaluation: A Systematic Approach,* pp. 172–175.

28. Adopted from Hatry et al., *How Effective?*

29. Rossi, Freeman, and Wright, *Evaluation: A Systematic Approach,* p. 224.

30. Ibid., p. 283.

31. See Bruce Adams, "Guidelines for Sunset," *State Government* 49 (Summer 1976):139.

32. Quoted in Peter J. Ognibene, "Do We Need Sunset?" *Parade Magazine* 2 (October 1977), p. 9.

33. U.S. General Accounting Office, *Standards for the Audit of Government Organizations, Programs, Activities, and Functions* (Washington, D.C.: 1972), p. 2.

34. These programs were distilled from: Peter de Leon, "A Theory of Termination" (Paper presented at the American Political Science conference, September 1977); available as a publication of the Rand Corporation, Santa Monica, California.

35. Ibid.

8 Attitudes of Management

The attitudes of management toward the problems that an integrated management control system is designed to address inextricably influence the overall success of such a system. It is a tendency of human nature to resist change, particularly when the effects of change are uncertain. Even if operating managers acknowledge that current procedures are inadequate, they have worked with and are likely to be more or less comfortable with them. New procedures may require major changes in management styles. Middle management may be expected to accept greater responsibility and accountability (or a shift of power from operating levels to top management may result). The desired qualifications of managers may be altered; often professionally educated managers are hired over those qualified principally by experience. These tendencies, if perceived by members of an organization, can create resistance to change, especially in a mature organization, where managers may be primarily interested in job security. There is no way to completely remove uncertainty, for there is no way to communicate accurately what will happen when new procedures become operational or major modifications are made in existing procedures. These effects must be experienced to be fully understood.[1]

Types of Management Styles

Management occurs at all levels in every public organization. It may operate systematically or haphazardly, formally or informally. It may involve a team effort or individuals acting independently. It may have a short- or long-term focus. And it may be highly responsive to perceived needs, or it may be carried out in a perfunctory fashion. It follows that management styles often are situational and, at times, highly disjointed. Each situation is a little different, and the management approach that works best in one case may be relatively ineffective in another. It would be impractical, however, to approach every situation as if it were totally unique. In practice, most managers seek common dimensions among the problems with which they must deal and, in this way, develop procedural responses to accommodate most areas of responsibility.

The Management Grid: Variations on a Basic Theme

The work of Robert R. Blake and Jane Mouton is perhaps the best-known approach to the question of management styles. Their Managerial Grid built on two universal dimensions of human behavior: a horizontal axis represents "concern for production," and a vertical axis denotes "concern for people."[2] Each axis is divided into 9 degrees of intensity (1 is low and 9 is high), thus producing eighty-one different cells, representing varying mixes of concern for production and for people. Blake and Mouton draw five major characteristic management styles from this grid:

1. A 1,1 manager exhibits a low concern for both production and people and exerts a minimum effort to get the required work done. This approach, Blake and Mouton assert, leads to an abdication of responsibility, supervisory bankruptcy, and alienation among workers.

2. The 1,9 manager devotes considerable attention to the needs of people, producing a comfortable, friendly organizational atmosphere at the expense of productive results. This approach is highly permissive in its dealings with people.

3. A produce-or-perish attitude (9,1) emphasizes efficiency in operations by arranging work conditions in such a way as to minimize interference from human elements. This management style, however, motivates people to beat the system and reduces their contributions to the organization.

4. The 9,9 style is identified by Blake and Mouton as "solution-seeking" and seeks to emphasize work accomplishment through a "common stake" in organizational purpose. High standards are used to achieve rigorous goals through involvement, commitment, and the readiness to confront issues needing resolution.

5. In the middle of the grid is the 5,5 management style, which emphasizes accommodation and compromise. Adequate organizational performance is sought by balancing the necessities of production with the maintenance of a satisfactory work morale.

Blake and Mouton indicate a strong preference for the 9,9 style of management. The 1,1 style appears as the least desirable, with the other three styles considered less than perfect.

The Dilemma of Public Service

James Q. Wilson has suggested that the American public has built an inherently schizophrenic system of public service.[3] On the one hand, the public expects government agencies to be responsive—to adapt to unique situations in meeting the needs of the various publics. On the other hand, the public demands that agencies be highly responsible, that is follow strict rules and procedures in dealing with problems on a fair and equitable basis. This is a complex dilemma. Responsiveness implies that government can redress social inequities and remedy social ills. In pursuit of these objectives, however, there often are perceived winners and losers—temporal as well as long-term inequities may result that are in conflict with the expectations of fairness and even-handed administration. An appropriate mix of responsibility and responsiveness is a critical ingredient in any management control system.

Michael Harmon has adopted the two-dimensional grid to describe styles of administration appropriate to this public-service dilemma. In his Policy Formulation Grid, policy responsiveness is depicted on the vertical axis, and the horizontal axis indicates the extent to which administrators are willing to become advocates for policy change. The terms responsiveness and advocacy, according to Harmon, are intentionally broad to accommodate the varying intepretations implicit in the five styles of his model. In general, *responsive behavior* is that which is accountable in some way to the democratic process by which public demands are (or might be) translated into policy. *Advocative behavior* refers to the degree of active support by administrators for the adoption of policies. The five styles of administration defined by Harmon can be summarized as follows:

1. In the survival style (1,1), to ensure survival of their agencies, public administrators limit access of political authorities and interest groups to promote the efficient continuation of existing programs. The 1,1 style describes administrative activity that is both nonadvocative and unresponsive.

2. The rationalist style (1,9) focuses on public demands as legitimately expressed through elected representatives and thus avoids direct involvement in the determination of agency policies and programs. The administrator is seen as an agent of political authorities, building on the assumption that all legitimate values relevant to policy formulation are expressed through voting or elected representatives.

3. The prescriptive style (9,1) builds on the presumption of professional expertise. Administrators are closest to and most knowledgeable of the problems confronting their agencies and, therefore, should be the key formulators of agency programs and policies. This style predominates in organizations where there is wide latitude for statutory interpretation by administrators or where technical complexity requires particular expertise.

4. In the proactive style (9,9), administrators participate in policy formulation both by acting as advocates of new policy and by facilitating access of interest groups to the political and administrative systems to maximize their opportunities to influence public policy. In determining policy, proactive behavior implies reciprocal influence between the administrator and those to whom he is responsible.

5. In the reactive style (5,5), the difficulty in drawing clear distinctions between policy formulation and implementation requires administrative reactivists to operate in both areas, although they may regard separation of the two as an ethically desirable, although unattainable, norm. Their advocacy and responsive behavior varies according to the context within which policy questions emerge.[4]

Like Blake and Mouton, Harmon favors the 9,9 or proactive style of administration, suggesting that, although the proactive administrator is not assured correct answers, he or she will be aided in asking more of the right questions. In practice, however, it would seem that a majority of managers and administrators would prefer to think of themselves as 5,5 types (as described by both Harmon and Blake and Mouton) with tendencies toward (but not total commitment to) the 9,9 style.

The Third Dimension

W.J. Reddin has added a third axis to the typology to form a cube, which he calls the Tri-Dimensional Grid."[5] In so doing, he has added the dimension of effectiveness to the two axes of concern for people (relationships) and concern for production (tasks), as developed by Blake and Mouton.

Reddin's approach produces four pairs of management styles, sharing common characteristics in terms of concern for people and production but differing according to level of effectiveness. The Bureaucrat, for example, is effective because he follows procedures, maintains the appearance of interest, and does not have dysfunctonal impacts on morale. The Deserter is ineffective not only because of his lack of interest in production, but also because of the impact that he may have on organizational morale. The Developer is effective (where the Missionary is not) because he seeks to create a conducive work environment and encourages subordinates to develop commitments to both himself and the job. The Benevolent Autocrat succeeds by overcoming the coercive nature of the Autocrat and thereby, is able to get people to carry out their specific job assignments without creating resentment that might cause a decline in production. The Executive is effective both as a motivator and as a production coordinator, whereas the Compromiser is ineffective in achieving an integration of factors and concerns. Reddin suggests that managers adopt different styles according to their responsibilities and that organizations with particular missions have discernible characteristic-style profiles. As with the other paradigms, however, he implicitly favors one style—the Executive.

The Fourth Dimension

F. Gerald Brown has added a fourth criterion to the basic formulations to create what he calls the "Managerial Field of Vision."[6] Brown suggests that management styles can be characterized by how much active involvement an administrator typically chooses to have regarding four basic factors involved in achieving work objectives: (1) concern for tasks, (2) concern for people, (3) concern for interfaces, and (4) concern for things. Brown derives six pure management styles from these four factors, as follows:

1. Concern for Tasks: the task-oriented management style has two major subvariations:

a. The Master Craftsman leads by example; keeps up with the field; serves as a professional model for employees; and seeks interaction with the work group at a quasi-peer level.

b.The Boss, is good at making work assignments and setting production expectations; carefully plans activities on a short- and medium-term basis; and places importance on schedules and performance standards.

2. Concern for People: the human-relations style of management emphasizes good relationships with employees and the delegation of responsibility. Such a manager supervises rather than controls and depends on a reward system that features recognition as a means of stimulating performance.

3. Concern for Things: this style assumes that employees know what they are doing and what must be done and that the organization will operate effectively as long as the work group has what is needed to get the job done. Such an administrator sees his role primarily as providing the best setting possible in which to accomplish the organization's objectives, including an appropriate physical environment, materials and supplies, budgets, and other resources.

4. Concern for Ideas: this approach is characterized by a relatively low concern for task and for people. Delegation is highly desirable; and this management style emphasizes the principle of management by exception. The focus is on planning, the identification of goals and objectives, and on innovations.

5. Concern for Interfaces: this manager is oriented to individuals and groups outside the immediate work situation. He strives for good relations with other groups and the maintenance of two-way communications between the work group and the outside world.

6. Integration of Factors: The All-Together Manager has learned to shift focus between thinking and doing, between technological process and the social system of the organization. The approach is "objective-centered"—the manager assesses the objectives and what needs to be done at any given time and directs his energies accordingly. In short, this style embodies all of the positive attributes of the other five styles.

Brown suggests that each of these management styles has its place and is an appropriate response in its kind of situation. As with each of the previous paradigms, however, there is a compositive style that incorporates most of the best features of the other approaches in the typology. Thus, according to these conceptual frameworks, public administrators should strive to be solution-seeking, proactive, executive, all-together managers.

Managerial Attitudes and Concerns

The quality of management, in large measure, depends on how people influence each other in solving problems and making decisions, how they handle disagreements, and how they seek out facts, share information, and communicate with one another. These activities, in turn, are often a function of the basic attitudes that management personnel bring to these tasks. Therefore, an important issue is what basic attitudes might public managers adopt as they attempt to sort out information, identify goals and objectives, and in general carry out their principal responsibilities?

In most situations, there is an inherent desire to put things into some kind of order, to establish priorities, to relate specific activities to broader purposes, and to provide some mechanisms for measuring success. Three key ingredients lie at the core of these concerns:

1. Purpose: an awareness of and concern for the relevance of specific occurrences in terms of overall goals, objectives, and orientation. An attempt is made to place new events and objectives into some kind of future-oriented priority system.

2. Stability: the desire to reduce the effects of chance or randomness in the operations of the organization. Every organization seeks to develop some set of expectations—norms, standards, rules, policies, and procedures—for determining courses of action appropriate to objectives or for dealing with specific problems and issues. The desire for stability is reflected in the need to establish order, sequence, and predictability (to reduce uncertainty), to anticipate events, and to establish procedures to deal with problems as they arise.

3. Comprehensiveness: concern with an organizational (or community) as a total entity. A community, institution, or organization can be thought of as a complex system with many related and interdependent subsystems (that is, smaller units within the total entity). In maintaining direction (achieve purpose) and stability, information from one part of the system must be linked with information obtained from all other parts to create a comprehensive whole.

These three ingredients are closely linked. The more management personnel are aware of the total system, the more they can plan and work in terms of the system's purpose and stability. Conversely, if personnel do not have an appreciation for the overall purpose and goals of the system, it is difficult—if not impossible—for them to carry out their responsibilities in a way that will maximize their contributions to the total system.

Decisions continually must be made that involve opportunities, risks, and innovations. Sometimes the risks are personal; at other times, they relate to the entire organization. From the standpoint of the organization, when something new is attempted the risks involved generally include higher costs, reduced effectiveness, negative public reaction, or program failure. Innovation and risk taking are inevitable bedfellows. A risk is taken no matter what the decision; for even if the decision is to do nothing, there is the risk of lost opportunity. One quality of effective managers—whether in the public or private sector—is that they are aware of how opportunity, innovation, and risk are interrelated and are willing to take risks appropriate to their level of responsibility. The ultimate decision as to what risks to take should be based on a weighing of available information, the exercise of logic, the assessment of uncertainty, and an estimate of alternative payoffs or gains.

The attitudes that managers hold toward *risk* can be arrayed on a continuum. At one end of the scale, risk is synonymous with challenge or the opportunity to develop situations in the best interest of the organization. At the opposite end of the continuum, there is strong resistance to risk. Between these end-points are various degrees of acceptance or avoidance of risk. Since the possibility of windfall returns are rather slight in the public sector, the acceptance of risk has been relatively limited. However, as accelerated change makes the future increasingly uncertain, public officials will find significant degrees of risk in even simple management functions (for example, garbage pickup).

Public management personnel must be cognizant of various *time dimensions* associated with public decisions and the commitment of fiscal resources arising from these decisions. Some problems demand immediate solutions and have a relatively short-range time concern in that they focus on elements that can be altered at will if the initial decision proves incorrect. Although long-range approaches may be necessary to identify the causes and implications of such problems (and to develop strategies to prevent the reoccurrence of these situations), the urgency of the problems may demand more immediate responses. Other problems, particularly those involving capital investments in public improvements, have relatively long-term time dimensions. Decisions associated with such projects can be modified only at considerable public expense. Thus, the time demands raised by problems and issues may provoke different approaches along a continuum, with short-range, day-to-day time dimensions at one extreme and the longer-range time dimensions associated with forecasting and planning at the other. Between these points are a number of levels of time concerns.

A Paradigm of Managerial Attitudes

A descriptive paradigm or model can be organized around these three basic sets of concerns.[7] Such a model, in essence, reflects the following key issues:

1. The extent to which managers should be concerned with the total system (that is, organization or community).
2. The level of risk, innovation, and opportunity that managers are willing to accept.
3. The extent to which managers take the long-range point of view in formulating policies and implementing programs.
4. How managers relate these basic concerns to their use of facts and information.

Combining these continua of concerns results in four basic "attitude sets" or approaches to management, each of which has two subsets:

1. Traditional approach: High concern for the system and its stability, coupled with a desire to avoid risk and innovation. In this attitude set, the concern is primarily with systems maintenance, the status quo, supporting and extending traditions and precedents, and minimizing risk and uncertainty.

    a. Procedural approach: Reflects a continual desire to apply established policies and practices to current problems. The focus is on short-range, immediate problems; long-term commitments are avoided. Decisions are processed incrementally along the carefully laid tracks of the past, within the safe boundaries of established policies, rules, and regulations.

    b. Bureaucratic approach: Seeks to avoid any kind of risk or innovation, while maintaining the long-term consistency and continuity of the organization. The bureaucratic response results in tighter control and rigidity based on strict adherence to traditions (a long-range time perspective that is backward looking).

2. Crisis-oriented approach: Low or negative concern for the system, coupled with a strong desire to avoid risk. Every problem—regardless of its magnitude or relevance to organizational purpose—appears at the moment the most important task facing the manager.

    a. Fire-fighting approach: Each event is seen as a distinct, short-range problem that must be contained or controlled. Each problem is without precedent or antecedent and is handled without reference to long-term purpose. Problems must be solved as quickly as possible, with minimal cost and risk.

    b. Impulsive approach: Reflects a very short-range concern for time; no attempt is made to limit risk or to weigh it against potential gains. Such behavior tends to be erratic and unpredictable, with few internal ground rules; and tends to ignore established precedent and policy.

3. Opportunistic approach: Low to negative concern with the system and its stability, coupled with a desire to take advantage of opportunities

and a willingness to accept risk. Organizational personnel become preoccupied with growth, exploration, and speculation.

    a. Entrepreneurial approach: Exhibits an affinity for risk—for new opportunities—often at the expense of long-term direction and purpose. The primary orientation is: "How can we make a quick deal and exploit an opportunity?"

    b. Speculative approach: Little concern for the system in terms of the impact of risk or experimentation; as one moves further and further from any systemic considerations of goals, one moves from calculated risk, to risky exploitation, to pure speculation. The speculative manager may attempt to create opportunities where none actually exist.

4. Synergistic approach: High concern for the system (purpose, stability, and comprehensiveness), coupled with a willingness to accept risk and a desire to take advantage of opportunities. A sense of the total system is integrated with a desire for experimentation, innovation, and increased interaction with the public.

    a. Experimental approach: Maintenance of an analytical attitude in attempts to deal with risk and to exploit opportunities in the achievement of long-term goals. The pitfalls of both compulsive and overly rigid behavior are avoided by maintaining a long-range, purposeful outlook.

    b. Systemic approach: Reflects a concern for the total organization, the relationship between the parts and the whole, and with long-range direction as well as short-term purposes within this longer time dimension. Information is gathered and analyzed in an effort to reduce uncertainty. The systemic manager may tend to move too cautiously to meet more immediate demands.

Although the notion of management control often evokes images of the procedural/bureaucratic approach management control as envisioned in this presentation operates most effectively under the synergistic/systemic approach to management responsibilities. Management control mechanisms should be developed in response to a concern for the total organization—its purpose, stability, and comprehensiveness. Such controls should clearly delineate—but not unduly inhibit—the range within which risk and opportunity should be accepted as part of the total organizational response to changing conditions in the broader environment.

Any organization is constantly influenced by a series of small decisions that accumulate to produce a decision-making climate. This climate, in turn, is a reflection of the management styles and attitudes adopted by the leadership of the organization. It may be a false and dangerous assumption that, because things are going well within an organization, wise decisions are being made. In reality, the organization may be living off good decisions made several years ago. The statement frequently is made that corporate profits are not possible without change and innovation. The same understatement can be made in nonprofit organizations, except the term "effectiveness" must be substituted for the word profit—effectiveness in terms of the capacity of a public agency to handle problems, motivate its workers, and resolve potential conflict situations in an efficient and effective manner.

Motivating Staff Members

Successful implementation of any program or project, in large measure, will depend on a manager's ability to motivate staff members to carry out day-to-day activities. Psychologists and behavioral scientists have made a number of significant contributions to our understanding of what motivates people. Among the best-known and most widely accepted motivational theories are those of Douglas McGregor, Abraham Maslow, Clare Graves, Frederick Herberg, David McClelland, John Atkinson, and Prescott Lecky; discussion of some of their work follows.

Theory X and Theory Y

In his book, *The Human Side of Enterprise,* McGregor distinguishes between two commonly held views of the relationship between supervisors and subordinates. He refers to these two types of attitudes about work relationships as Theory X and Theory Y.[8] Theory X is based on the assumption that some people do not like to work; the only reason they work is because they have to. Thus, a Theory-X manager assumes that people have to be coerced or threatened to work. By the same token, people do not like to think or plan for themselves; they prefer to be told explicitly what to do. This view leads a Theory-X manager to believe that an authoritarian approach to management will be most effective in accomplishing specific program goals and objectives. According to Theory X, the threat of unemployment, on the one hand, and the reward of various fringe benefits on the other, can be used to enforce the rules of employment and ensure productivity.

Theory Y, on the other hand, holds that people develop their attitudes toward work (likes and dislikes) based on their own personal experiences. The Theory-Y manager believes that employees will actively seek additional responsibilities, will set personal goals, and will accept challenges if they believe rewards for such behavior will be forthcoming.

In the ideal situation, of course, all employees should be self-motivated and self-disciplined. In reality, however, each manager must create an environment that encourages a commitment to self-direction, creativity, and self-discipline on the part of subordinates at all levels. An effective manager should view his or her job as one of helping staff members to set and achieve objectives that are mutually desirable to them as individuals and to the organization as a whole. Periodic performance evaluations or ratings that use a standard checklist seldom accomplish this mutually supportive approach. It may be much more appropriate to have a frank and open discussion on a one-to-one basis with staff members (perhaps followed by a written evaluation) in which both the strengths and weaknesses of the employee can be identified. The basis for grievance procedures often is the employee's assertion: "Nobody told me what I was doing wrong."

Maslow's Hierarchy of Needs

Although some people disagree with the details of Maslow's work, as described in his book *Motivation and Personality,* his basic theory of human behavior is widely accepted and can be quite useful to managers at all levels.[9] All our actions, according to Maslow, are derived from some motives—the forces that drive us to do what we do. Some of our motives are conflicting and some reinforce each other. Maslow's theory asserts that our motives are actually needs and that our needs can be classified according to their level of degree of importance to us. Maslow's hierarchy of needs is shown in figure 8-1.

The most basic human need are psychological—food, shelter, warmth, and so forth—and these needs are the strongest motivators. Needs of safety and security constitute the next level of needs (and in modern society, include such things as job tenure, health insurance, and savings). Social needs take over as strong motivators for most people once safety and physiological needs have been satisfied.

Next above social needs on the hierarchy are the egotistic needs—self-esteem, recognition, respect, status, achievement, self-confidence, independence, and freedom. For some people, egotistic needs will be even stronger motivators than safety needs, because these individuals come from a segment of the society that places a very high value on egotistic needs. Their importance is also related to the ease with which the other more basic needs are fulfilled. If someone has never had to worry about basic physiological needs, then social and egotistic needs will assume greater importance.

The highest level on Maslow's hierarchy is the need for self-fulfillment or self-actualization. The desire to realize their fullest potential and to become all that they are capable of becoming is a strong motivating factor

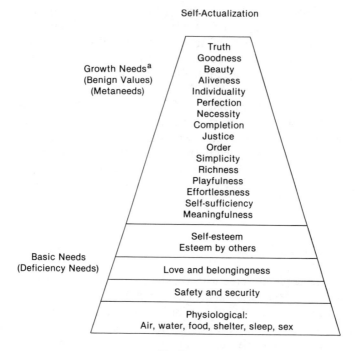

Self-Actualization

Growth Needs[a]
(Benign Values)
(Metaneeds)

Truth
Goodness
Beauty
Aliveness
Individuality
Perfection
Necessity
Completion
Justice
Order
Simplicity
Richness
Playfulness
Effortlessness
Self-sufficiency
Meaningfulness

Self-esteem
Esteem by others

Basic Needs
(Deficiency Needs)

Love and belongingness

Safety and security

Physiological:
Air, water, food, shelter, sleep, sex

The External Environment

Preconditions for Need Satisfaction
Freedom, Justice, Orderliness

Challenge (Stimulation)

Source: Abraham H. Maslow, *Motivation and Personality* (New York: Harper, 1954).
[a]Growth needs are all of equal importance (not hierarchical)

Figure 8-1. Abraham Maslow's Hierarchy of Needs

among many people. The need to be creative may be latent in some, but most people have the desire to excel in something.

In reality, human needs are not readily separable into neat compartments as described in Maslow's hierarchy. One need is not independent from all others—human needs overlap, as is quickly demonstrated when one tries to determine the single most important need that is motivating an individual's behavior. Needs may work to reinforce one another, or they may be in conflict. Maslow's theory says that when there is conflict among needs, the lower-level needs usually will motivate behavior most strongly.

Managers often may wonder why staff members are not motivated to put forth more than a minimum effort when they have an excellent compensation plan, a generous fringe-benefit package, and good working conditions. When the hierarchy of needs is examined, it is obvious that only the lower-level needs of the employees have been satisfied. Little has been done to satisfy the higher-level needs that are actually motivating employee behavior.

Employees may be looking for self-esteem, recognition, appreciation, or self-fulfillment. Unfortunately, traditional incentives provided in compensation plans often fail to recognize many of these forces that motivate human behavior. Needs that are conducive to effective program implementation and a high level of productivity go far beyond an adequate income and a pleasant working environment. Although this relationship has been demonstrated in production line jobs, it is no less important to agency personnel in the public sector. Provisions must be made for individuals to satisfy their higher-level needs—to improve, to grow, to feel a part of the organization, to receive recognition for their efforts, and to be respected.

In summary, employees will worry primarily about basic (lower-level) needs until they are satisfied. Once this is achieved, employees will look to higher level needs as motivators. Research has confirmed that high productivity and low turnover are found where employees have a high level of job security and good opportunities for self-fulfillment. If the need for self-fulfillment is satisfied, all other needs have probably been satisfied, and performance is likely to be good.

Levels of Human Existence

First receiving widespread recognition as an application of personality theory to explain the deterioration of work standards in industry, the Graves's theory represents a freely acknowledged extension of Maslow's conceptual framework. When first published in the *Harvard Business Review,* Graves's concepts generated requests for over 15,000 reprints. During the late sixties, his seven levels of human existence became the basis for a favorite cocktail party game in some circles. Graves's Levels of Human Behavior are characterized in table 8-1. In more recent writings, Graves has added still another level to the base, resulting in an eight-level hierarchy, with some explicit hints that there may be more levels to come.[10]

Although his theory began as a descriptive-predictive tool for the analysis of individual personalities, in his more recent writings Graves has expanded his formulations to suggest an open-systems theory of values for society as a whole. According to Graves, values change in a regressive-progressive fashion when each set of existential problems is solved, and these changes foretell the movement to higher-level psychological systems. When old values no longer appear appropriate to some segment of the society as it

Table 8-1
Graves's Levels of Human Behavior

Level	Characteristics
First level (autistic)	Consumed in the process of staying alive, in maintaining a balance between catabolic and anabolic processes; aware of little more than the problems of sustenance, illness, reproduction, and primative disputes; fantasy confused with reality; a state of psychological nonexistence
Second level (animistic)	Concerned primarily with survival; governed by superstition, totem and taboo; beginning of self-awareness; consciousness but not comprehension; egocentric behavior; productive only within extremely narrow limits; responsive to naked force
Third level (ordered)	Motivated by strong sense of order; things seen in terms of absolutes; follow traditional religions; rigid, absolute, dogmatic, theologically based position in life predetermined by extrahuman power; comfortable with autocratic rather than participative relationships
Fourth level (materialistic)	Motivated by a mastery of the physical world; value system built around a search for power and material gains; dogmatic but pragmatic; domination over others; respond to contrived incentive systems
Fifth level (sociocentric)	Team player and group thinker; junior executive type, determined not to rock the boat; seek self-esteem and social status; has achieved basic personal and economic security; concerned with social rather than basic personal or material matters.
Sixth level (aggressive individualistic)	Motivated by self-esteem, by a feeling that one's potential must be realized; driven to right the evils of a disordered world; ends-oriented not means-oriented; does not accept authority well.
Seventh level (pacifistic individualism)	Driven by a desire to acquire and disseminate information; seeks scholarship; resists coercion and restrictions, but not in an exhibitionistic manner

Adopted from: Clare W. Graves, "Deterioration of Work Standards," *Harvard Business Review* 44 (September–October 1966):117–128.

Note: In Graves subsequent writings an eighth level—Tribalistic—is inserted between the autistic and animistic levels.

deals with manifest problems, these values break down, and the group searches regressively for a different value system that is more congruent with their new state of being. Behavioral crisis, such as confrontations, social unrest, and riots, may develop as groups strive to go beyond the established value system. They fight "the establishment," which in turn resists the new, embryonic ways of thinking. As time passes, past values may eventually be replaced by new values, and the movement consummates in a new steady state.

There is evidence in contemporary society to support Graves's formulations. Regressive-progressive sequence of change can also be observed in many organizations. The need to adjust values and attitudes may be encountered in the implementation of a new program or project. Resistance to change may come from within the agency or from the larger community. Groups may fall back on more traditional values when faced with the need to adopt new values. Techniques for overcoming such resistance to change and for managing conflict will be discussed in a subsequent section.

Extrinsic versus Intrinsic Motivators

Managers often seek to improve job satisfaction by eliminating dissatisfaction. However, according to Herzberg, job satisfaction and dissatisfaction are not opposites. Rather job satisfaction usually comes from actual achievement of the tasks at hand, whereas dissatisfaction is more likely to arise from the work environment itself. It is not enough simply to remove the causes of worker dissatisfaction by improving the work environment; the work itself must offer the opportunity for job satisfaction. Employees need to have a sense of achievement.[11]

Thus, Herzberg makes the distinction between extrinsic motivators—such things as company-paid insurance plans, an annual dinner dance, a company softball team, improved fringe benefits—and instrinsic motivators—those that come from performing the actual work and not from the surrounding conditions. Extrinsic motivators, given to all employees in equal measure, are not enough; it is necessary to provide intrinsic motivators, geared to the particular and unique needs of each employee. Intrinsic motivators are literally a management tool that money cannot buy.

The Need for Achievement, Affiliation, and Power

McClelland and Atkinson offer a further articulation of the higher-order needs suggested by Maslow's hierarchy.[12] In addition to the need for achievement—the need to excel or to accomplish something in relation to a specific set of standards—McClelland and Atkinson suggest that the need for affiliation (to have close, friendly interpersonal relationships) and the need for power (to influence other people) are important motivational factors in some segments of any organization. These motivations are strongest in those situations where the lower-level needs cited in Maslow's hierarchy are fully satisfied.

The McClelland/Atkinson theory of motivation stresses the importance of situational clues. An individual who is situationally motivated will welcome an opportunity to satisfy his or her needs for achievement, affiliation, and power and, as a consequence, will likely be a more productive employee.

Theory of Self-Consistency

Prescott Lecky has suggested that, however illogical a person's behavior may seem to others, it may be logical and consistent with that person's own view of his or her personality.[13] This theory of self-consistency is especially useful in explaining what appears to be self-defeating behavior.

Our beliefs about ourselves—as rational, consistent, and whole personalities—often are impacted by feedback from the outside environment. We react to feedback that contradicts our beliefs in ourselves in one of two ways: (1) we change our self-appraisal so that it is consistent with the new feedback; or (2) we reject the feedback as wrong, inappropriate, or as a misjudgment. Rejection of feedback is the most common reaction; otherwise, our self-image would shift so often that serious anxiety would result. This is one reason why people try to shift the blame to others when they have made a poor decision—to avoid admitting that their judgment was poor. Likewise, we tend to view those people who are praising our judgment as having excellent judgment themselves.

Mature, well-adjusted individuals who have confidence in their overall personality find it less anxiety producing to modify some segment of their behavior as a result of feedback. For most people, it is very difficult to ignore continued and consistent feedback that conflicts with their self-evaluation. Sooner or later, they must admit that the feedback must be right and their self-evaluation wrong.

Instead of shaking his head at the illogical behavior of an employee, a manager should ask: "Does that behavior seem consistent from the perspective of the employee and does it reflect a reaction of feedback which he or she may have received to previous actions?" Instead of attacking the behavior which may be judged to be illogical—and thereby, heighten the negative reaction to such criticism—it may be more appropriate to modify expectations regarding the individual's behavior to more fully match up with his or her own self-concept.

The Need for More Dynamic Perspectives

The differences among personalities are far greater than these theoretical constructs would imply, of course. What may appeal to one person in a particular job situation may be extremely frustrating to another person. One of the most common mistakes made by a manager is to assume that the needs and wants of subordinates are the same as his or her own. Most managers are strongly motivated by a need to achieve. The failure of subordinates to demonstrate similar motivations may be attributed to laziness or indifference. It is one thing to recognize that our social needs may be different from those of your subordinates, but it often is quite a different thing to manage to allow for these differences.

It is not possible to design every job so that every employee will be satisfied. The important thing is to recognize that each situation involves a dynamic human process with a variety of human motives at work.

Overcoming Resistance and Managing Conflict

A major pitfall in management is the assumption that a new program or project will be conflict-free and that all participants will support the objectives of the program plan. The presence of conflict in any organization is inevitable. As an organization increases in size and diversity and as new program activities are initiated, the likelihood of increased interpersonal and intergroup conflict will challenge the ability of management to carry out its coordinative tasks. Reducing conflict—or increasing cooperation—is one of management's most persistent objectives. Increased organizational cooperation leads to more productive and effective programs.

Conflict Theory

Organizational theories about conflict have changed markedly over the years. Under the scientific-management approach, for example, conflict was seen as a temporary imperfection, resulting from a failure to establish sound management-worker relations. Administrative-management theory and theories of bureaucracy emphasize the power of rational problem solving. In such theories, therefore, there was no need for any special consideration of the role of conflict and its resolution. The human-relations approach also views conflict as a temporary phenomenon—as something to be resolved through a better understanding of the organization's formal-informal social system. The origins of conflict in this view is the improper attitudes and values of the work group.

Even Chester Barnard, who provided insights into so many aspects of organization theory, assigns no special place to conflict. Barnard's coopera-tive-system approach is the antithesis of the notion that conflict is an inevit-able feature of all organizations.

In these traditional approaches, management tends to remain as the final arbitrator in the resolution of conflict. The notion of management and workers "working through" problems that may give rise to conflict simply does not emerge from these theories. Contemporary theories about orga-nizations, however, give much more explicit attention to the phenomenon of conflict. Such theories acknowledge the functional as well as dysfunc-tional aspects of conflict and suggest mechanisms for the partial resolution of conflict.

Sources of Conflict

Before conflict can be reduced or managed, it is necessary to recognize some of the principal sources or conditions that may give rise to conflict. Conflict may be personal (often referred to as "role conflict"), interpersonal (or intragroup), and/or intergroup. Although the latter two categories may be the more overt forms of conflict in any organization, role conflict may be the source of much of the friction that you perceive as a program manager. Therefore, before attempting to deal with group conflict, it is important to understand the four basic types of role conflict: (1) person-role, (2) inter-role, (3) multiple expectations, and (4) counterexpectations.[14]

Person-role conflicts occur when the requirements of a role (a set of job responsibilities) violate or clash with an individual's needs, values, atti-tudes, and capacities. A first-line supervisor, for example, often has close ties with the people in his or her work group—former peers in many cases. Such supervisors may be called on to discipline workers or may be expected to carry out orders in a "hard-nose" fashion. In such cases, the responsibil-ities of the position may clash with the expectations of friendship, resulting in personal conflict (which may also result in interpersonal conflict when the expectations of either the supervisor's superiors or subordinates are not met). To resolve the personal conflict, the supervisor may "pass the buck" upward by suggesting that he or she has no choice but to carry out orders. This response, in turn, may result in the workers labeling the supervisor as a lacky of management.

Interrole conflict results when an individual must respond to multiple goals arising from his or her involvement in several groups. The expecta-tions of one role come into conflict with those of another. The most famil-iar example is when job expectations conflict with an individual's family role. Managers may have to spend many evenings away from home in meet-ings, perhaps missing key events in the lives of their children. Dance recitals, football games, cub-scout meetings, father-son dinners, and so forth may vie with job responsibilities. To resolve such role conflicts, an individual must rank the various demands and develop a system of trade-offs that allows him or her to decide, on balance, how to respond to particular situations that have the potential of conflict. Here again, such personal conflict can erupt into interpersonal conflict when the expectations of any potentially conflicting situations are unmet.

Role conflict arising from *multiple expectations* is quite common in project-management situations. Such conflict stems from the pressures on an individual to respond to similar expectations coming from many directions within the organization. Any office that provides services to many other organizational units experiences such conflict. Everyone presents their requirements under the guise of highest priority. Obviously, it is impossible to respond to all requests simultaneously, and, therefore, some sort of queuing system must be invoked. In trying to satisfy everyone, the service unit may satisfy no one. If one group is perceived to be getting preferential treatment, intragroup or even intergroup conflicts may result.

Counterexpectation conflict develops when conflicting instructions or expectations are transmitted to an individual. A typical example is the supervisor's expectation that a subordinate should improve efficiency, when the supervisor has explicitly denied the subordinate the necessary authority to accomplish this objective. Such conflicts also can occur in the transmission of messages that have conflicting parts or from contradictory messages sent at different times.

A related cause of role conflict is *expectation overload*—multiple expectations may not necessarily be in conflict, but their sheer volume makes it impossible for one individual to fulfill the requirements. Thus, a conflict is created between the role expectations and the capacity of the individual to perform. If overload role conflict persists for an extended period, more than ad hoc adjustments may be required in the realm of an individual's responsibilities.

Although role conflict is evident in all organizations, the degree of conflict can vary significantly. The more complex the job is, the more likely the existence of role conflict. Task specialization provides a means for defining job descriptions more narrowly, with explicit instructions for a particular task. This helps to forestall role conflict. Many people prefer such task specificity—to know what they are supposed to do—and feel uncomfortable when called on to exercise their own initiative and judgment in job-related situations.

A manager with coordinative responsibilities typically must serve as a mediator and compromiser. As a result, much conflicting information will be received, designed to influence decisions that must be made and the roles that must be played. Many managers are called on to operate on the boundary of their organization—serving in various capacities in other organizations and groups. Therefore, a manager may be subject to considerable multiple expectations and interrole conflict.

As Vance Packard has observed, two general strains of organizational "folklore" may lead to role conflict for the manager. "The ambitious, zestful young manager who is eager to make a mark may at first find pyramidclimbing an exasperating experience. For one thing, he will find himself working in a conflicting value system. He must appear a hot competitor, in keeping with the folklore, yet at the same time—and more importantly—he must prove himself a hot cooperator."[15] The conflict between aggressive competitiveness and unaggressive cooperation has important implications, not only for the individual but for whole units within an organization. Some organizations are structured to promote competition among units and thus, to foster potential conflict.

Group Conflict

Conflict is most often viewed in terms of its negative, disruptive impacts on organizations, but it can have positive as well as negative effects. As Lewis Coser has observed: ". . . no group can be entirely harmonious, for it would then be devoid of process and structure. Groups require disharmony as well as harmony; dissociation as well as association; and conflicts within them are by no means altogether disruptive factors."[16] Thus, Coser and others have concluded that a certain degree of conflict is an essential element in group formation and persistence. Out of conflict situations often arise increased group solidarity, clarification of goals and objectives, and the momentum to capitalize on new opportunities.

Intragroup conflict can arise in a variety of ways. In the early stages of development of a group or organization, there is likely to be disagreements over goals, plans, and the roles of various members. Such differences have to be resolved sufficiently for the group to proceed. On the other hand, if conflict is suppressed completely, it may eventually erupt into open hostility. Conflict that results in mutual distrust among members of the group is unlikely to be a useful contributor to the overall effectiveness of the organization. A conflict-free group, however, may be static and may operate at considerably less than capacity. Some friction should exist as a condition for the generation of fresh ideas. Conflict that arises out of genuine differences in the needs and values of group members can be an important vehicle for achieving a workable consensus.

A manager's ability to recognize stress, tension, or anxiety among staff members is an important attribute. The ability to deal effectively with conflict-producing situations and to channel them toward more positive ends is even more important.

Just as conflict is inevitable in social relationships, it is inevitable between subgroups within an organization. Such conflicts can develop between groups on the same level (particularly if they are competing for the same scarce resources) or between groups on different levels of the organization. Such intergroup conflicts may foster increased loyalty and cohesiveness within the conflicting groups (and often may suppress intragroup conflict).

Communications

Improved communication and the exercise of appropriate leadership often are the most relevant means available to the manager to reduce the potential of conflict. Full and honest communication can improve relationships within any group or organization; in fact, without such communication, it is unlikely that any improvements can be achieved. Communication can also make a group or an individual more aware of an unfavorable position. Thus, conflict can increase if actions are taken based on this new awareness. After the new awareness has been gained, however, further positively oriented communication often can lead to a resolution of the conflict.

Important advances have been made in recent years in understanding the mechanics of communication flow. This work—pioneered by Claude E. Shannon of Bell Laboratories and Norbert Weiner, the father of modern cybernetic theory—provides important insights into the responsibilities that program managers have to communicate clearly the intent of a program and the specific assignments that must be carried out to minimize subsequent misunderstanding and conflict.[17]

Noise is an important concept in communication theory; it is any form of interference that reduces the effectiveness of communication by introducing errors into the flow of information. Noise may reduce a message to obvious nonsense. Often worse, however, is when noise results in the conversion of a message into another meaningful but entirely misleading message. For example, suppose the message was as follows: "As a follow-up to our meeting yesterday, don't forget about . . ." Obviously, changing (or not receiving) one word in that message—*don't*—completely changes its meaning. On the other hand, if the message was: "As a follow-up to our meeting yesterday, forget about . . . ," the inflection given to certain words in the message (or not received because of noise) might alter the receiver's interpretation of the true intent.

Communication channels are never without some noise. In addition to interference that may arise from outside the information flow—static in electronic channels, typing errors in written messages, and so forth—there are two other important sources of noise in any communication system: (1)

semantic noise, which occurs between the information source and the encoding of messages (for example, the particular words chosen by the sender); and (2) *semantic-reception noise,* which occurs between the encoded message and its actual destination (for example, the mental set of the receiver when he or she gets the message). These latter sources of noise are related to the human factor of information distortion and misinterpretation. Inherent in the communication system of any organization is the factor of selective filtering, that is, the conscious or unconscious reduction of message content to facilitate transmission.

The only effective weapon against noise is some form of *redundance.* Redundance involves the tailoring of a message with respect to the capacity of a communication channel so that the channel will be exploited effectively without overcrowding. The average message, transmitted in the English language, contains over 50 percent redundancy. A shorthand or coded message (for example, one that contains certain professional or organizational jargon) may reduce this "natural" redundancy rather significantly. However, unless the receiver fully understands the jargon, considerable message content and/or intent can be lost. Although redundance always lowers the amount of information that can be conveyed, this inconvenience often is tolerated to overcome the masking effects of noise.

The request to: "Put it in writing," for example, when a staff member approaches a manager verbally with an idea, may have the effect of: (1) improving and refining the idea by having the staff member think it through as he or she puts it down on paper; and (2) facilitating the manager's review of the idea since he or she can consider it more fully when it is in written form.

On the other hand, written communications usually contain considerably more redundance than verbal communications. And if the receiver is overloaded with written materials, he or she may find it more difficult to absorb the message. This redundance-overload problem is one reason why it is good practice in written communication to: (1) state the message succinctly; (2) elaborate on the message; and (3) restate the message, perhaps with fuller emphasis on those points raised through the elaboration. In short, state it; elaborate it; and restate it.

The particular characteristic of a message that distinguishes it from nonsense and from other messages is termed its "content of information." One practical problem in all communication is to maintain the same content of information from source (sender) to destination (receiver). Again, semantic noise is greater in oral communication, especially if the sender and receiver are not operating "on the same wave length." The preservation of information content is improved—although not fully guaranteed—by written communications.

Conflict Resolution

A successful manager is skilled in the creative use of conflict when it is potentially beneficial in generating alternative solutions in problem-solving situations. Managers must also seek to understand the differences among their staff that can give rise to potential conflicts. In so doing, however, the task of consensus formation may become increasingly difficult.

Many measures to combat the problem of conflict have been proposed by social scientists and management specialists, including the use of legal sanctions, the creation of social contracts between conflicting members or groups, and the dissemination of information to break down false stereotypes and prejudices. Perhaps the most significant mechanism, however, is the leadership provided by the manager in potential-conflict situations.

Mary Follett wrote in 1933 that there are three leadership approaches to settling differences: by domination, by compromise, or by integration.[18] Fremont Kast and James Rosenzweig have suggested five approaches to conflict resolution: (1) withdrawal, (2) smoothing, (3) compromise, (4) confrontation, and (5) forcing.[19] Other authors have used such terms as isolation, bargaining, and suppression to describe various points on a continuum.

At one end of this continuum are approaches to conflict resolution that lead to withdrawal or isolation of the conflicting groups or individuals. To reduce the potential of conflict or to resolve existing conflicts, a manager may have to carefully schedule the interaction among groups or individuals to minimize their contacts. Such approaches may offer a temporary solution, but they seldom can be pursued on an extended basis or in all cases. Continued withdrawal from the group—whether voluntary or mandatory—may eventually so weaken the group that it can no longer function satisfactorily.

Smoothing involves more of a working-through-the-problem approach. It also has the connotation of "glossing over" real problems by getting agreement on relatively minor, superficial issues. Smoothing may offer a temporary solution, but it may result in even more disruptive conflict when the real issues resurface. Withdrawal, isolation, and smoothing tend to perpetuate the status quo.

Bargaining or compromise suggest more active approaches to working out problems of conflict. Bargaining and compromise involve trade-offs on both sides—something is given up to gain something. Both sides are likely to be less than totally satisfied with the resolution of the problem. Compromise often is used to determine how to divide a given "pie." The problem is, however, that relatively little attention is given in a compromise to making a bigger or better pie.[20]

Integration seeks a solution that each side will find completely accept-able—where no sacrifice is made by anyone. The basic goal is a win-win approach rather than a win-lose situation. Integration seeks to rise above the somewhat static condition of compromise. Instead of both sides focus-ing on "my way instead of yours," a third approach is sought that will be satisfactory to all parties. Integrative resolutions frequently represent breakthroughs to totally new solutions. However, it takes creative conflict management to find such integrative solutions. By anticipating situations that hold the potential of conflict, a manager may be able to achieve a more integrative solution by bringing together the involved parties before the fact to "brainstorm" the situation. In this way, different opinions can be aired before opposing positions are solidified.

A confrontation approach may or may not facilitate the achievement of integrative results. Confrontation means getting all the cards on the table, actively seeking solutions that satisfy all protagonists, and developing an empathy for alternative viewpoints. Open confrontation may be therapeu-tic, even if the temporary or long-term solution is to decide not to agree. All parties should feel that at least they got a fair hearing on their position. Ten-sions and antagonisms that smolder below the surface drain off con-siderable physical and psychic energy. Getting these feelings out into the open can afford a necessary release to all parties and may help to clarify underlying differences. Often it is discovered that these differences are not as great as first presumed. Confrontation as a means of resolving conflict must be used with care, however, because "going to the mat" on every issue can only result in a lot of mat burns.

Domination, suppression, or forcing occurs when one party in a con-flict situation is able to force its solution on the others, usually as a result of a greater position of authority or power. We are all familiar with the car-toon showing the chairman of the board stating: "All in favor say 'aye'; all opposed say "I resign."' A forced solution is likely to be unsatisfactory for the losing side. Frequently domination results in the manipulation and ex-ploitation of individuals or groups. Such manipulation may result in deep-seated resentment and, therefore, holds the potential for further conflict, particularly if the power or authority that is exercised is temporal and even-tually shifts to others.

In a landmark study of intergroup conflict, Muzafer Sherif and Carolyn Sherif have demonstrated the effectiveness of superordinate goals in reducing group friction and conflict.[21] Superordinate goals are those that can only be attained by group cooperation. Politicians, educators, and managers frequently put this notion into practice by providing such goals for their organizations. The establishment of superordinate goals is usually the most effective way to reduce intragroup conflicts—efforts to attain such goals usually increase group cohesion. This approach also can be applied to reduce intergroup conflict (as external force is identified that poses a threat to all groups).

Stability/Continuity versus Adaptation/Innovation

A manager must seek to maintain a dynamic equilibrium between stability/ continuity and adaptation/innovation in the program and projects under his or her responsibility. Both cooperative and competitive relationships are typical to any group. Although the advantages of cooperation are generally well understood, the positive attributes of competition and conflict often are not so well appreciated. Effective communication is the key to cooperation. Yet, communication can increase conflict if it makes a group more aware of its grievances. Such awareness, in turn, may offer an opportunity to resolve the conflict. The existence of superordinate goals is an effective way of reducing intragroup conflict. Recognition of this principle is an underlying factor in the techniques of management by objectives (MBO), whereby members of the group or organization participate in the identification of such superordinate goals and relate their individual objectives to these goals.

MBO

Various methods have been devised to contribute to the overall efficiency of management. Many of these techniques also have been successfully evaluated against the broader criteria of creativity, innovation, effectiveness, and flexibility. MBO scores well according to these criteria. MBO can facilitate more effective performance, given competent administrators who are willing to make the necessary adjustments in their own attitudes and approaches to organizational responsibilities.

MBO in the Public Sector

Although recognized as a valuable tool in the private sector for over fifty years, MBO only recently has been explored by public agencies. MBO gained attention and application at the federal level in the wake of planning-programming-budgeting systems (PPBS). It is highly compatible with such results-oriented budgetary systems. Interest at the state and local levels has followed in response to citizen demands for greater accountability of program results.

Given the history of use in the private sector, there is no shortage of literature concerning MBO. However, for the most part, these materials are unresponsive to the different needs and purposes of the public sector. As a consequence, some interpretation is required to fit the techniques and procedures of MBO to the unique characteristics of public management.

By its very simplicity, MBO is a management approach that provides organizations with a framework for identifying, integrating, monitoring, and evaluating organizational, programmatic, and personal objectives. MBO requires that objectives be measured in either quantifiable or descriptive terms. Such verification is a significant endeavor in the public sector, where objectives frequently and deliberately are obscured to achieve political consensus, or where objectives often must undergo significant redefinition when made operational.

In the application of MBO, the identification of goals, the specification of their derived objectives, and the evaluation of performance are carried out through a cyclical process (see figure 8-2). Accountability is more clearly delineated in the MBO process, which assumes a commitment of individuals to objective and includes a self-evaluation process. Failure or success in meeting objectives, therefore, can serve as a powerful stimulus for MBO participants.

Commitments and Productivity

Management by objectives foregoes more rigid and formal processes of traditional administration for a more open, fluid, and democratic approach. Employees at each level of the organization participate in the formulation of objectives, which then are integrated with broader organizational objectives. The basic purpose of the MBO cycle is to make personnel aware not only of what they do, but why they do it; of how their activity relates to organizational goals and objectives; of what their individual performance targets are, and how they are progressing toward these targets.

The technique of participative management predates the concept of MBO. As Peter Drucker, one of the earliest writers on the subject, has observed, the objective of MBO is not merely employee participation but employee commitment.[22] Under MBO it is assumed that those employees who are involved in the formulation of objectives will exhibit a commitment to these objectives and that a committed employee—more fully aware of his or her role within the organization—will display top performance and productivity. MBO builds on the notion that the traditional incentives of money, job security, promotion, and other status symbols often are insufficient responses to the many needs of the individual employee. Thus, it is assumed under MBO that work can provide a source of commitment and satisfaction to the individual, thereby, motivate employees to meet needs at a higher level than those of more immediate economic gratification.

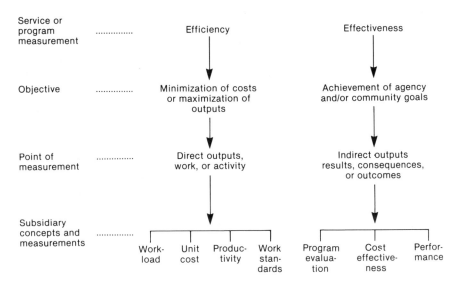

Figure 8-2. Management by Objectives in the Public Sector

A major feature of MBO is the mechanism provided for review and evaluation of performance. Based on Drucker's concept of self-control, employees have responsibility for evaluating the results of their own performance in meeting objectives that they previously established. They also have the corresponding responsibility for making the necessary adjustments suggested by this evaluation. Thus, management must delegate the authority as well as the responsibility to achieve individual objectives. An often-heard complaint in the public sector is that authority is not commensurate with responsibility. Although MBO does not address this complaint explicitly, its assumptions necessarily strive to correct this situation.

This approach to evaluation departs significantly from other methods of performance evaluation, such as those that involve checklists of work habits or subjective comments on work incidents. When evaluation is based on individual performance relative to objectives that the employee has shared in formulating, the responsibility for results is more clearly identified and understood.

From the outset of any MBO program, areas of responsibility and corresponding objectives must be clear and specific. Employees may be provided with job descriptions, but these may not be adequate to meet the needs of MBO. More importantly, application of MBO requires that understanding of the job be achieved through a dialogue between the manager and the employee. The emphasis on defining jobs and responsibilities may give rise to the need for further clarification as to how a given job or assignment relates to the larger organizational effort. Having achieved this understanding, it is assumed that the individual employee is capable of recognizing personal areas of responsibility and proceeding with the critical task of formulating objectives related to the job and its performance. Conflicts between individual and organizational objectives are brought to the attention of the manager through this process, rather than remaining a potentially debilitating factor at a subsurface level. Individual weaknesses and strengths also are examined to produce the most efficient use of resources and the most effective administration and operation of the organization.

Establishing Program Objectives for MBO

As Harry Havens has observed: ". . . a major difficulty in evaluating the accomplishment of goals stems from the inadequate information and communication for setting program objectives."[23] MBO attacks this problem at several points. Open communication is a keystone to the whole concept of MBO. Specific techniques, such as milestone charts and network diagrams, enable both the supervisor and the subordinates to assess progress toward the achievement of objectives for performance-evaluation purposes. Obviously, clear definition and quantified and descriptive measures are required for MBO to effectively span the cycle of objective formation to performance evaluation to the realization or reassessment of objectives.

Although primarily an internal-management mechanism, MBO can provide important information to the governing body and can serve as a tool for public-information dissemination and accountability. MBO has the "potential for reassuring legislators and the polity that government units actually are committed to specifying objectives and to reporting progress toward them."[24]

A common problem of public programs is that objectives not only are difficult to define, but often are not amenable to empirical measurement. The nature of public-sector activities tends to be ambiguous, and the interrelationship of public administration with the political environment introduces further ambiguity. In the first instance, it is difficult to manage programs effectively in accord with objectives that are virtually meaningless. Specificity is necessary—such objectives as "to improve living environments," "to provide children with a decent education," or "to maintain law and order" declare little more than broad intentions. Performance and its measurement are arbitrary when operating procedures must be based on such broad, generic objectives. Often a series of more specific subobjectives must be identified to define fully the scope of a public program. The MBO cycle should begin with full staff participation at the level of such subobjectives.

Public programs and organizations are dependent on the continuing goodwill and fiscal support of the governing body. This dependency contributes to the ambiguity in objectives, however, as attempts are made to evolve some consensus among widely polarized factions. Political compromise can be a major deterrent to the identification of explicit program objectives. At the federal level, for example, so-called objectives have withstood decades of debate and numerous presidential administrations without ever being finally delineated.

On the other hand, delimiting objectives increases the participants awareness of the critical linkages that exist between and within organizational activities. As Drucker has observed, management by objectives forces the administrator to realize that, notwithstanding the language of policy statements, there cannot be one single objective.[25] When attempts are made to identify more specific objectives, it is likely that conflicting as well as multiple objectives will be discovered: ". . . the identification of conflict on objectives is one of the benefits of MBO."[26] Awareness of these conflicting objectives is essential, whether they can be reconciled or merely are recorded as constraints within which the program must operate.

Decision Focus of MBO

MBO creates a framework that is strongly antithetical to crisis-oriented, ad hoc management. MBO operates most efficiently and effectively under a synergistic, systemic approach to management (that is, where concern is for the total organization). As Drucker suggests: "The ultimate result of management by objectives is decision. . . . Unless MBO leads to decision, it has no result at all; it has been a waste of time and effort. The test of MBO is not knowledge, but effective action. This means, above all, risk-taking decisions."[27] When decisions are made in the context of goals and of clearly defined objectives, the utility and relevance of such decisions for the total organization can be more carefully appraised. An effective manager must be willing to take risks when such risk-taking decisions contribute to the achievement of organizational, programmatic, and personal objectives. Valid risk-taking decisions are distinguished from mere opportunism by a concern for risk relative to the objectives of the system. Organizations depend on such decisions for innovation and change. Thus, a balance must be maintained between decisions of a stability-maintenance nature and those of a risk-innovation nature.

In its basic formulation, MBO does assume that ". . . organizations are 'closed' and participants in the decision process are easily identified."[28] This assumption can be a problem in the application of MBO in the public sector. No public organization is a closed system. The formulation of programs and policies often involves numerous interest groups and lobbying concerns. This interaction with the broader environment adds to the complexity and ambiguity of public objectives. Where the official organization ends and interest groups begin often is difficult to discern. This open situation can certainly confuse the identification of participants in the objective-setting and decision-making processes.

MBO is only one procedure that can contribute to more effective decision making and performance. It cannot eliminate the ambiguity in public decisions that arise from the open system, nor can it guarantee effective performance or changes in leadership style. Applied in conjunction with other management techniques, however, MBO is a potentially valuable tool for decision making in the public sector.

Management Commitment to MBO

A commitmet by management is essential to the successful implementation of MBO. Rodney Brady has observed from his experience at the federal level that: "the primary constraint to the success of MBO at HEW has been an attitude on the part of some managers that the regular attention required of them by such a system is either (a) not consistent with their roles or (b) not as effective a way to manage as some other approach."[29] Although some advocates argue that MBO is more successful when the manager operates with participative-management techniques, other methods may work equally well (for example, the initiation of MBO procedures from the top-down by chief administrative or elective officials). The important point is that the manager should assess the organizational climate before making a decision to use any method or combination of methods. Various organizations and programs will have their own unique characterstics to which the manager must be sensitive in introducing MBO. Certainly one method will be more natural than others, depending on the personalities and personal theories of management.

The implementation of MBO does have significant implications for the role of the manager, especially for the manager who, in the classical sense, sees himself in an authoritative role. Changing these views often is difficult, if not impossible. Resistance from such managers can be a serious obstacle to the implementation and utilization of MBO. Care must be taken not to introduce MBO as a threat to functions of the managers but as a tool for their use. Managers must be given sufficient background information to understand both the merits and shortcomings of MBO. If MBO is not to result in frustration and be discarded prematurely, managers must anticipate problems in the initial phases. Knowledge of concepts and techniques is not sufficient; practical experience in application of this knowledge is always necessary.

One of the features of MBO that may lead to problems in its application is that "MBO encompasses little formal administrative machinery."[30] Unlike many techniques, MBO does not necessarily generate a great amount of forms and paperwork. On the other hand, MBO is based on the assumption that an adequate management information system (MIS) exists. Although it is doubtful that MBO can be operative without an MIS, an MIS can operate quite independently and effectively without MBO. An agency seeking to implement MBO should have an MIS but must be careful not to confuse one with the other.

Although MBO has been subjected to recent criticism, these challenges have focused on specific features and not on the merits of MBO as a basic concept. On the other hand, MBO should not be oversold. Perhaps the greatest danger in establishing MBO is to expect too much in terms of accomplishments and/or to expect results too soon. MBO cannot solve all the problems of government accountability; it cannot increase employee satisfaction 100 percent; it cannot end the problems of measuring government productivity. It is unrealistic to anticipate that a single technique can transform all objectives into clearly specified, rational statements accepted by committed personnel. As Havens cautions, in using MBO: "In the final analysis, . . . the process of setting objectives and managing toward their achievement is but one element in a complex analytical/political/managerial decision making process."[31] Thus, if MBO is to be more than just another management fad, its limitations must be recognized, and the manager must not anticipate results in excess of what the process is capable of producing.

Notes

1. Robert N. Anthony and Regina Herzlinger, *Management Control in Nonprofit Organizations* (Homewood, Ill.: Richard D. Irwin, 1975), p. 322.

2. Robert R. Blake and Jane S. Mouton, *The Managerial Grid* (Houston, Texas.: Gulf Publishing, 1964).

3. James Q. Wilson, "The Bureaucratic Problem," *The Public Interest* 3 (Winter 1967):3–9.

4. Michael Mont Harmon, "Administrative Policy Formulaton and the Public Interest," *Public Administration Review* 29 (September–October 1969):483–491.

5. W.J. Reddin, "The Tri-Dimensional Grid," *Training Directors Journal* 18 (July 1964):9–18.

6. F. Gerald Brown, "Management Styles and Working with People," in *Developing the Municipal Organization,* ed. Stanley P. Powers et al. (Washington, D.C.: International City Management Association, 1974), pp. 69–83.

7. For a further elaboration of this paradigm, see: Alan Walter Steiss and Gregory A. Daneke, *Performance Administration* (Lexington, Mass.: Lexington Books, D.C. Heath, 1980), chap. 3.

8. Douglas McGregor, *The Human Side of Enterprise* (New York: McGraw-Hill, 1960).

9. Abraham H. Maslow, *Motivation and Personality* (New York: Harper, 1954).

10. Clare W. Graves, "Levels of Existence: An Open System Theory of Values," *Journal of Humanistic Psychology* 10 (Fall 1970):131–154.

11. Frederick Herzberg, *The Managerial Choice* (Homewood, Ill.: Dow Jones-Irwin, 1976).

12. David C. McClelland et al., *The Achievement Motive* (New York: Irvington Publishers, 1976); David C. McClelland, *Motivation* (New York: Van Nostrand, 1978).

13. Prescott Lecky, *Self-Consistency; A Theory of Personality* ed. by John F.A. Taylor and Frederick C. Thorne (Garden City, N.Y.: Doubleday, 1969).

14. A similar set of role-conflict categories is offered by Fremont E. Kast and James E. Rosenzweig, *Organization and Management: A Systems and Contingency Approach* (New York: McGraw-Hill, 1979), pp. 276–278.

15. Vance Packard, *Pyramid Climbers* (New York: McGraw-Hill, 1962), p. 21.

16. Lewis Coser, *The Functions of Social Conflict* (New York: Free Press of Glencoe, 1956), p. 20.

17. See Claude E. Shannon and Warren Weaver, *The Mathematical Theory of Communication* (Urbania, Ill.: University of Illinois Press, 1949) and Norbert Wiener, *Cynerbetics: Or Control and Communication in the Animal and Machine* (New York: John Wiley & Sons, 1948).

18. Mary Parker Follett, "Coordination," in *Classics in Management,* ed. Harold F. Merrill (New York: American Management Association, 1960), p. 341.

19. Kast and Rosenzweig, *Organization and Management,* p. 584.

20. Herbert G. Hicks and C. Ray Gullett, *The Management of Organizations* (New York: McGraw-Hill, 1976), p. 117.

21. Muzafer Sherif and Carolyn W. Sherif, *Groups in Harmony and Tension* (New York: Harper & Brothers, 1953).

22. Peter Drucker, "What Results Should You Expect? A Users'

Guide to MBO," *Public Administration Review* 36 (January–February 1976):19.

23. Harry S. Havens, "MBO and Program Evaluation, Or Whatever Happened to PPBS," *Public Administration Review* 36 (January–February 1976):5.

24. Frank P. Sherwood and William J. Page, "MBO and Public Management," *Public Administration Review* 36 (January–February 1976):11.

25. Drucker, "What Results?" p. 14.

26. Bruce H. Woolfson, "Public Sector MBO and PPB: Cross Fertilization in Management Systems," *Public Administration Review* 35 (July–August 1975):388.

27. Drucker, "What Results?" p. 19.

28. Sherwood and Page, "MBO and Public Management," p. 8.

29. Rodney H. Brady, "MBO Goes to Work in the Public Sector," *Harvard Business Review* 51 (March–April 1973):66.

30. Woolfson, "Public Sector MBO," p. 389.

31. Havens, "MBO and Program Evaluation," p. 45.

9

Budgeting as a Mechanism for Management Control

A budget should be much more than a formal document presented annually for review and approval by the governing body. A budget should represent the culmination of a complex decision process whereby: (1) public policy is formulated, (2) action programs are identified and implemented, and (3) both legislative expectations and management controls are established. The annual cyclical nature of the budget process should not be misinterpreted as an inflexible routine. Budgets seldom can be "set in concrete"; they must have the capacity to accommodate changes in public needs, interests, and available technology for the delivery of public services.

Alternative Budget Formats

Several alternative budget formats have been developed to meet these broad objectives. Four of these basic formats are: (1) the line-item/object-of-expenditure budget, (2) the performance budget, (3) the program budget, and (4) the zero-base budget. Each of these budget formats arose from the financial-management needs of state and local government at a particular time, and each reflects various decision-making capacities. The management information needs of each of these formats also vary, and the accounting and management control systems that support each of these approaches have certain distinctive characteristics. A mismatch among the accounting, budgeting, and management control systems is one of the fundamental sources of problems in public financial management.

Purposes of Budgeting

A budget can be thought of as a control mechanism, a management tool, and an important component of long-range planning. It is a control mechanism to ensure financial integrity, accountability, and legal compliance—this is the traditional role of the budget. The budget is a management tool used to ascertain operating economies and performance efficiencies. As a component of planning, the budget must reflect public goals and objectives

229

and the overall effectiveness of governmental programs in meeting public-service needs.

A *budget* can be defined as "the financial articulation of the activities of a governmental unit . . . which recognizes anticipated revenues, authorizes activities, and appropriates expenditures" for a specific period.[1] A budget provides the legal basis for public spending and fiscal accountability. Through the budget process, financial authority and responsibility can be delegated and appropriate central control can be maintained. Budgeting is integrally linked to an accounting process, whereby revenue and expenditure information is structured to facilitate continuous monitoring, evaluation, and control. These aspects of budgeting were discussed in detail in chapter 2.

One of the most pervasive elements in determining the content of any budget is its relation to the preceding budget. This practice of "building on the budget base" results in a form of *incrementalism* that has been the subject of much criticism in the annals of public budgeting. More recent procedures and techniques for public budgeting have been developed, in large part, in response to the incremental nature of traditional public budgeting.

Budgeting also involves decision making under conditions of uncertainty, where such decisions may have significant future consequences. Before a budget can be prepared, goals and objectives should be formulated, policies analyzed, and plans and programs delineated. The purposes of the public budget are both policy and administration.[2] Budgeting is the public substitute for mechanisms of the economic-market system—the process by which decisions are made regarding the allocation of public resources—that is, the politics of who gets what.

Objectives of the Annual Budget

In most state and local governments, a distinction is made between the annual operating budget and the capital budget. The basic function of the *operating budget* is to rationalize the projected allocation of resources over the coming fiscal year in such areas of expenditures as salaries and wages, contractual services, materials and supplies, and other consumables. The annual operating budget provides the basis on which the governing body may adopt an ordinance or resolution that authorizes agencies to incur obligations and to make payments with respect to these commitments. It also provides the basis for such accompanying revenue measures and adjustments to fiscal policy as may be required. Although the budget provides the limits to spending, the adoption of the budget ordinance or resolution by the governing body should be viewed as a positive act. The tendency to emphasize the control aspects of the budget can result in a negative psychology surrounding the process, with significant adverse effects in the execution of the budget.[3]

The operating budget can provide a system for measuring the public objectives to be attained within a given fiscal period. It also facilitates the scheduling of work and the coordination of personnel and nonpersonnel service requirements. Thus, the budget process can enhance the understanding of the governing body and the general public as to the proposed plans of operations for the ensuing fiscal year. The process also permits the revision of proposed plans prior to legislative approval.

Once the budget is approved, activities planned for the upcoming year can be adjusted by the agencies to conform to their fiscal appropriations. Finally, the budget provides a basis for a fiscal audit and, as appropriate, a performance evaluation both during and after the close of the fiscal year.

The *capital budget,* on the other hand, represents a statement of capital expenditures to be incurred over a period of years to meet public-improvement needs (capital facilities) and the means of financing these commitments for the current fiscal period. A capital budget often is supported by a capital improvement program, which documents improvement priorities over a longer period (usually five to six years). The capital budget is the first year of this program statement. In some jurisdictions, a capital facilities plan also is developed, encompassing an even longer time horizon (fifteen to twenty years), to provide an analysis of the financial resources available to support debt commitments that might be incurred through the issuance of municipal bonds to finance public improvements.

The operating budget and the capital budget usually are incorporated into one budget document and are approved by the governing body at the same time. In some jurisdictions, however, the capital budget is presented separately and on a different time cycle from the annual operating budget. Different accounting principles and procedures are associated with the financial transactions generated by each of these budgets, as discussed in chapter 2.

The Budget Cycle

Budget making requires careful scheduling if public officials are to be given adequate time and information for sound budget decisions. Regardless of the format adopted, the budget process commonly involves four major steps: (1) executive preparation, (2) legislative review, modification, and enactment, (3) budget execution, and (4) post audit and evaluation. The steps in this process must be undertaken in a logical sequence if the mass of detail required is to be coordinated and important deadlines are to be met. Responsibility for performing each specific step must be clearly assigned.

It is essential that well-designed forms be provided to the agencies to ensure that their requests are submitted in as uniform and complete a manner as possible. It also is desirable that policies and special instructions for the guidance of agency-budget preparation be set forth in writing (that is, as a budget manual).

Budget Calendar

A budget calendar should be established, setting forth key dates and assignments of responsibility for carrying out the preparation of the budget. At the local level, controlling dates often are established by state law, city charter, or ordinance and serve as important deadlines for submitting the budget to city council and for setting the annual levy and rate for property taxes. The total time for annual budget preparation will vary from four to six months in larger cities and from two to three months in smaller municipalities. The time intervals allowed for each step will vary somewhat in accordance with the size of the jurisdiction, established legal requirements, and the type of budget format applied.

The Executive Budget

The chief executive—mayor or manager—has primary responsibility for preparing budget estimates and for developing a preliminary budget document. Decisions made in connection with an annual budget often have implications far beyond the next fiscal year. Projections of demographic and economic characteristics (for example, income and employment) are important to the development of estimates of both revenue supply and service demand. Fiscal analysis provides assessments of the probable consequences of current public policies, identifies specific fiscal issues, and establishes a foundation for decisions regarding new or modified policies. Long-range financial planning attempts to place the current budget into perspective in terms of future revenues and expenditure commitments.

A budget guidance memorandum should be issued to all agencies, along with a detailed set of instructions or manual for completing the requisite forms and supporting information and justifications. This memorandum should outline: (1) anticipated fiscal policies, (2) established goals and objectives, and (3) performance expectations. Statements of total public needs and demands should be presented to establish levels of program activity or services to be further structured in the agency submissions. Budget targets may be set forth, reflecting preliminary estimates of revenue potentials.

Each agency should complete the required budget forms to reflect a best estimate as to the most appropriate assignment of resources for personnel, equipment, materials and supplies, and so forth to carry out the programs and activities within its legislative mandate. Agencies may be called on to further refine the broad goals and objectives identified in the guidance memorandum to place their specific programs into perspective. Budget justifications may include various performance measures and measures of effectiveness. A priority listing of all programs and an identification of the current or proposed status of each program may also be required. Major policy issues or administrative problems, if any, should be identified, and the requirements for new legislation should be outlined, as appropriate.

The initial function of the central budget agency is to check agency submissions for completeness and accuracy. Agency requests are then compiled into a preliminary document to provide an overall summary of total dollar needs. The central agency staff may also prepare preliminary projections of changes in employee compensation and benefits, develop estimates of the amounts required for such items as debt service and interfund transfers, and identify any policy changes inherent in agency-budget requests.

The chief executive must work closely with department heads and other officials to make the necessary adjustments that will bring the total budget into line with overall fiscal constraints. State laws usually prohibit jurisdictions from making expenditure commitments that exceed expected revenues. New or modified fiscal policies may have to be examined to provide increased resources to meet justified program needs. All too often, preliminary revenue estimates are taken as an absolute constraint, with the result that documented program needs in response to identified goals and objectives are adjusted downward, often with detrimental consequences for the community. It is important that the incidence and effect of new revenue proposals be examined to ensure reasonable equity in terms of the tax burden that will result.

The Budget Document

When budget data have been analyzed and major allocation decisions have been made, the executive-budget document can be prepared for legislative review. This document should provide a clear picture of both the programs to be carried out and the financial basis to support these activities. The budget must be designed so that it can be readily understood by members of the governing body, administrators, reporters, and citizens, as well as financial experts. Particular attention should be given to important policy decisions that must be made. The enthusiasm of budget technicians for complete detail often must be curbed in the interest of clarity and simplicity. Clarity can be achieved, however, without omitting important facts, by a well-constructed budget message, by choosing summaries carefully, and through the use of tables and charts to explain service programs and the interrelationship among various elements of proposed expenditures.

Legislative Action on the Budget

The first step in the legislative review of the budget is for the governing body to consult with the chief executive and his or her staff for detailed explanations of the proposed programs and means of financing them. The governing body should receive more than a thick document, with page after page of tables, providing little or no explanation of the services to be provided or the intent of the administration. Under such circumstances, members of the governing body may nit-pick over details, and important policy decisions involved in setting public-service levels may never be faced directly. The governing body should not concern itself with minor details except as they may relate to major policies and programs.

Public hearings on the budget generally are required by law at the local level, and a summary of the tentative budget may be published, together with a notice of the time and place of the hearing. Even if not required by law, a brief budget summary should be prepared for wider distribution than the complete document will receive. Public hearings on budgets often have proven dismal failures. Relatively few citizens attend unless they are irate over some aspect of the budget. Officials should be prepared for surprises, however. Citizens may decide to attend the hearings, and public officials must be ready to answer any questions.

On the basis of these hearings and subsequent executive-session discussions, the governing body makes amendments to the expenditure portion of the budget and to the proposed revenue measures. The final product is reported in public session and is likely to be adopted in the form thus presented. The governing body may approve the budget by resolution, or it may adopt a separate appropriation ordinance that lists specific amounts for specific agencies by specific categories of expense. An appropriation ordinance provides a more effective benchmark for administration and postauditing. However, care must be taken not to limit the ability of agencies to make adjustments during the fiscal year to meet changing conditions in the implementation of their program activities.

Budget Execution

When the appropriation and tax-levy measures have been adopted, the budget is returned to the chief executive for execution—the second half of the budget cycle. Budget execution is both a substantive operational process and a financial process. It involves the initiation of authorized projects and programs within an established time schedule, within monetary limits, and ideally, within standard cost limits. This stage covers the full fiscal year and overlaps both the formulation and legislative-review stages of the succeeding year's budget.

Patterns of budget administration vary considerably among local jurisdictions. In some cases, budget administration consists of little more than the establishment of appropriate accounts and the recording of expenditures as processed for payment, that is, a cash-flow bookkeeping system to track the outflow of funds in accordance with predetermined item accounts. In more advanced budgetary control systems, however, the steps in administration include: (1) allocation, (2) allotment, (3) expenditure control, (4) performance monitoring, and (5) adjustment.

The process of *allocation* subdivides the appropriation according to minor organizational units, classes of expenditures, and/or programs. Often allocations are made for personal services (salaries and wages) and for operations, with further subdivisions of the operating allocations by programs, projects, or organizational units. Thus, the appropriation of the health department, for example, might be subdivided to show a stipulated amount for an outpatient clinic in the children's hospital, for a community mental-health unit, for public-health nursing services, and so forth.

In some cases, specific allocations are encumbered from the outset of the fiscal year and are then liquidated on an as-billed basis (legal services or other consultant's fees, indirect support payments for employee benefits, and so forth). The purpose of this encumbrance is to ensure that these funds will be available at the time needed, that is, that they will not be spent for other purposes.

Following the process of allocation, it may be determined that provisions should be made for an *allotment system* under which allocations are further subdivided into time elements (for example, monthly or quarterly allotments for personal services or for some group of items in the nonpersonal-service categories). Such an allotment system is particularly appropriate in such circumstances where expenditures are contingent on some future events, such as the availability of grants from other levels of goverment or the projected opening of a new capital facility. Under such an approach, the portion of the appropriation in question may be retained in the unallocated or unallotted category until required for actual commitment.

The accounting system plays a major role in the implementation of *expenditure controls,* as detailed in previous chapters. Budgetary accounting supplies the control mechanisms for enforcing allotment and appropriation limits through periodic internal-budget reports. Cost accounting (or other adaptations of financial accounting that produce cost figures) and statistical reporting provide a basis for developing unit costs for various workload levels and comparisons with performance and cost standards. Project budgets for construction, work schedules, and other related performance reports can be incorporated into an accounting system serving the needs of management control (see chapter 3). Although much of this accounting is highly centralized, partial decentralization has taken place in some larger jurisdictions to keep financial and cost accounting close to the operating centers of expenditures.

Mechanisms to control specific expenditures are provided to the governing body through such devices as line-item appropriations, periodic budgetary reports, and the independent audit at the close of the fiscal year. In addition, the governing body may insert control conditions on the use of specific funds and/or may require that proposed transfers between appropriation items have legislative approval (usually over some predetermined percentage change). In some jurisdictions, the state legislature imposes mandatory expenditures on local governments (for example, for education), and a state supervisory authority must be satisfied that the legal aspects of budgeting have been met.

In addition to these expenditure controls, certain supplemental management controls often are established:

1. Position controls—such as restrictions on the filling of vacancies, moratoria on promotions, formula allocations of various classified (clerical) positions—may be exercised by the personnel director or chief executive; such controls may also require coordination with the budget director (often with sign-off approval).
2. Property-management procedures may reduce the need for new capital outlays by improving equipment care through a preventative-maintenance program.
3. Central-purchasing procedures involve quantity and quality controls, competitive bidding for nonroutine purchases, and blanket ordering.
4. Efficiency or administrative audits can provide valuable information regarding future operational controls that should be incorporated into ongoing procedures.
5. Performance-monitoring procedures give specific recognition to the work actually performed in relation to that which was planned; if projected performance levels do not materialize, it may be necessary to determine alternative patterns of funding for the balance of the fiscal year.

Many departmental officials, with some justification, may consider these controls an unnecessary intrusion on their responsibilities. Obviously, competent agency head wants his or her operational decisions second-guessed by central budget officials who may only see the fiscal implications of such decisions. On the other hand, without the discipline of central review, expenditures may be made contrary to their fund justifications, thereby producing short- and long-term commitments that might prove politically or administratively embarrassing.

Budgetary Adjustments

Most operating budgets require some adjustments during the fiscal year. Frequent assessments of current performance and of changing environmental conditions can point up the need for such adjustments to ensure adequate flexibility in operations. Departmental officials should take the initiative when problems come to their attention. However, the central budget agency has the ultimate responsibility for recommending any necessary actions to avoid fiscal crises, such as missed paydays or the lack of funds to buy critical materials or equipment. The central budget office should maintain sufficient information—through the accounting process and contacts with individual agencies and programs—to anticipate requirements for formal amendments during the fiscal year. Some amendments may require immediate attention. Many can be handled more efficiently through a single omnibus amendment, usually made during the last two to three months of the fiscal year.

During the final quarter, revised estimates also must be made of the anticipated closing status of any unappropriated surplus accounts. Some accounts may be limited as to their fiscal-year carry-over, that is, unspent funds revert back to the general accounts at the end of the fiscal year. Many departments will attempt to zero-out such accounts as the end of the fiscal year approaches. Caution must be exercised, however, that the expenditures will stand the test of a post audit, that is, are eligible items of expense for the agency to incur. Year-end reversion of funds often is cited as a major shortcoming of traditional budgeting procedures. Such reversions promote year-end spending and offer no incentives for conserving resources.

Auditing the Budget

Procedures for auditing the budget at the close of the fiscal year will be discussed in further detail in a subsequent chapter. Suffice it to say here that there are two basic types of audits: internal and external. *Internal audits* are conducted on a periodic basis (for example, quarterly or semiannually) by government staff and produce reports for internal management control purposes. The *external audit* is conducted by certified public accountants after the fiscal year has been completed. This audit normally is required by state law and is submitted to the regulating state agency as well as to the local governing body. The governing body, in turn, reviews the audit to be sure that revenue and expenditure activities were conducted in accordance with the intentions of the budget and appropriation ordinance.

The Planning and Control Continuum

The role of budgeting in the public financial management system tradition- ally has been that of fiscal control. More recent developments, however, have emphasized the planning aspects of this resource-allocation process. Unfortunately, some of these applications of budget reforms have all been abandoned or have significantly altered the control features of more tradi- tional budget approaches. In part, this counterswing is a reaction to per- ceived shortcomings of the line-item/object-of-expenditure budget. It also is a consequence of a more centralized, top-down approach to budgeting that seeks to improve the rationality of public decision making through both structural and procedural changes. Techniques and procedures to increase the efficiency and effectiveness of resource-allocation decisions must be incorporated in any financial management system that is responsive to the demands of contemporary society. By the same token, the mecha- nisms of accountability and control must be retained in a balanced approach to budgeting. Various major efforts to achieve this balance will be examined in the following sections.

Management Emphasis on Performance

In the late 1930s, the budget began to be recognized as an important tool of management—providing a focus on operating economies and performance efficiencies. These efforts culminated in the concept of *performance bud- geting*, which had its heyday in the late 1940s and early 1950s. This budget format seldom is discussed in any detail in contemporary texts on public budgeting, relegated for the most part to a historical footnote. Neverthe- less, many of the attributes of performance budgeting have survived to become important, integral parts of modern balanced-budgeting systems.

The budget objective of efficiency and economy derives much of its conceptual and technical basis from cost accounting and the precepts of scientific management. The following procedural steps are suggested by Jesse Burkhead for the development and operation of a performance budget[4]:

1. Joint undertaking by central budget office and department administrators to identify work programs that are meaningful for management purposes.
2. Examination of work programs in relation to organizational structure to determine if some realignments are necessary.
3. Identification of performance units within each work program, either in terms of activities or by specific end-products.
4. Full measurement of performance costs—it may be desirable to introduce cost-accounting procedures to accomplish such measurements.
5. Establishment of internal-reporting systems through which accomplishments can be continuously compared with work plans.
6. Preparation of legislative appropriations in work program terms.
7. Establishment of a system of accounts to control and record disbursements on a work-program basis, subdivided by performance units.

Two key components distinguish performance budgeting from other approaches: (1) the identification of performance units within work programs, and (2) the effort to provide full measurement of performance costs. Although these two components represent particular strengths of performance budgeting, in another sense they also reflect the basic shortcomings of this approach in terms of its implementation. Work programs relate to particular functions or processes carried out by public agencies. Very few functions of government, however, are conducted by only one agency or department. Although functions may cut across organizational lines, in application, work programs were usually identified within the established agency structure. Programmatic gaps and potential conflicts and inconsistencies in this approach limited its application as an aid to decision making at the policy level. Many local governments encountered difficulties in developing a uniform and consistent basis for identifying performance units. This problem, coupled with a reluctance to adopt cost-accounting procedures to assist in measuring performance costs, resulted in significant obstacles to implementation for many local jurisdictions. As a consequence, many applications of performance budgeting focused only on selected components, such as activity-classification systems and work-cost measurements for fairly routine activities.

Performance measures are most relevant to the problems of lower- and middle-management levels of an organization. Unit costs and workload data are useful to operating managers in assessing the efficiency of their programs and organizational units. These data, however, are too detailed and provide relatively few insights into the overall effectiveness of organizational activities, that is, whether program objectives relevant to public policies are being attained.

Although performance budgeting seldom is practiced in its pure form in government today, many of its characteristic attributes have survived. Performance measures—workload and unit-cost measures—and the concept of performance levels or levels of service have been incorporated into many contemporary applications that seek greater efficiency and economy in the allocation of fiscal resources. Thus, the focus on cost-efficiency, which was a hallmark of performance budgeting, has parallel emphases in current budget formats. Cost accounting systems—a stumbling block in the 1950s—are beginning to receive wider application in local and state governments, particularly in support of the techniques of cost-benefit and cost-effectiveness analysis.

Some jurisdictions have adopted what perhaps can best be described as a "performance/program budget." Performance measures often are retrospective, whereas program budgeting is prospective. Performance measures are concerned with the processes of work, whereas program budgeting is more concerned with the purposes of work. In proper combination, however, these two formats offer a great deal of complementarity.

Performance measures and the evaluation of levels of service also have found considerable application in what has come to be known as zero-base budgeting (ZBB). The objectives of ZBB are quite similar to those of performance budgeting—increased efficiency and economy in the allocation of fiscal resources. In addition, ZBB seeks to overcome one of the principal sources of inefficiency and diseconomy in government operations—the practice of incrementalism.

The Problem of Incrementalism

For over sixty years, budget reformers have criticized the incremental aspects of the budget process as arbitrary and irrational. They have pointed to a lack of coordination and the neglect of important values in traditional budget-building procedures, suggesting that they produce only small changes in the status quo. The results from previous allocation decisions are accepted as the primary decision criteria in incremental budgeting. Therefore, existing programs are continued into the future, often without intensive reexamination. A comprehensive analysis of previously allocated resources—the *budget base*—seldom is undertaken under the incremental approach. Therefore, incremental budgeting is suspect as to its ability to limit the growth of governmental appropriations or to allocate scarce fiscal resources in the most economical, efficient, and effective manner. As E. Hilton Young observed in 1924: "It must be a temptation to one drawing up an estimate to save himself trouble by taking last year's estimate for granted, adding something to any item for which an increased expenditure is foreseen. Nothing could be easier or more wasteful and extravagant."[5]

The objective of fiscal control is adequately served through the use of the line-item/object-of-expenditure format in current public-budgeting practices. In an era of increasing demand for public accountability in the delivery of services, however, there is growing recognition among public officials of the shortcomings of these conventional practices, including:

1. Insufficient information—conventional budgeting practices provide relatively little useful information about: (a) the type and level of services provided, (b) the objectives and beneficiaries of the service, or (c) the special resources required in the provision of specific levels of service.

2. Lack of choice mechanisms—with increasing frequency, governments do not have sufficient financial resources to fund all services at the requested levels. Conventional budget practices provide few mechanisms to help make choices or to identify the trade-offs among different services on a cost-benefit basis.

3. Impact of change unclear—no meaningful processes exist to: (a) predict how significant changes in funding will affect service delivery, (b) determine the benefits in services afforded by increases in funding, or (c) identify the absolute minimum level of service that a jurisdiction can provide.

Although they have received the greatest publicity at the federal and state levels, zero-base-analysis techniques may have even more significant potential in application at the local level. Programmatic decision packages are more readily identified and managed at this level. The basic objective remains the same—to circumvent the shortcomings of incremental budgeting. However, current applications of ZBB have taken a somewhat more modest (and more realistic approach as compared to earlier efforts in the mid-1960s). The detailed analysis of programs "to the zero base" has been replaced by the concept of *levels of effort*. ZBB requires agencies "to examine their budgets below the base; the base being their current level of expenditure. . . . Zero-base budgeting requires each agency to specify—on paper—as part of its regular policy submission—possibilities for spending less money than the current year."[6] Programmatic aspects have been adopted from other contemporary budget formats—in fact, a number of budgeting systems currently in operation under the labels of program budgeting or ZBB are really amalgamations of these two basic formats.

The complexity of the ZBB process, as perceived by many public officials and administrators, has served as a deterrent to the adoption of this budget format. Many have argued that ZBB is a budgetary fad and have predicted its demise in the near future. Growing public concern for greater accountability in the delivery of services, however, is not a passing thing. Just as with performance budgeting and PPBS, there are worthwhile components of ZBB that are likely to outlast the full-blown approach. Local government offers a good proving ground for the application of *service-level analysis,* for example. The relative "completeness" of units of local government reduces the analytical task to more manageable dimensions. Service level analysis has particular relevance to the objectives of an integrated management-control system.

Objectives of Service Level Analysis

The primary mission of local government is service. Therefore, public activities at the local level can be readily identified and often can be measured in service-delivery terms. This is the first step in establishing the framework for service-level analysis. The basic objective is to justify budget requests "from the bottom up" in terms of public-service needs and program objectives. Various levels of funding both above and below current expenditure levels (the established budget base) can be assigned to component levels of service to determine the potential impacts of such changes in appropriations. Budget requests for alternative service levels can then be ranked according to funding priorities established on a municipalwide basis. Rather than involving any radical departure from established budget methods, service level analysis embodies the long-accepted principal of building the budget on the basis of a sound appraisal of needs matched against the limitations of resources.

A number of organizational or budgetary improvements can be achieved through the use of service level analysis, depending on the objectives and commitments of public officials.[7] Objectives in employing this analytical approach may include: (1) more effective allocation of limited fiscal resources; (2) greater equity in service delivery and resource utilization; (3) greater control of expenditures and reductions in costs; (4) improved managerial insights into the activities of line agencies; (5) closer linkage between budgeting and operational-planning processes; (6) increased involvement of operating managers and staff in budget-formulation procedures; (7) increased credibility of program justifications; (8) better evaluation of management capabilities; and (9) fuller diagnoses of community-service needs to refine policies and establish long-range objectives.

Service level analysis is applicable to all actionable programs or activities, that is, those in which agencies have some discretion in the courses of action pursued. The process must allow the definition and evaluation of a range of program choices (decision packages), including alternative ways of providing services and alternative levels of funding. Service level analysis requires information concerning output or performance, as well as cost, to broaden the basis on which to analyze allocation alternatives.

Service level analysis can have only limited application to programs where the level of expenditures are imposed by laws or statutes, intergovernmental commitments, or other constraints. It can assist, however, in identifying the public costs of such constraints. Although so-called action-able or discretionary programs (that is, those for which expenditure levels are not fixed) make up only a portion of the total budget, they often represent activities that are more difficult to analyze and plan.[8] Thus, more effective management control of these components through service level analysis can greatly affect the entire budget.

Unfortunately, there may be some confusion between fixed expenditures and essential levels of service. Local governments may have relatively little choice about the funding of essential service levels, and such service levels may comprise a major portion of the budget. However, one of the basic objectives of service-level analysis is the identification of these essential service levels so that a jurisdiction can maintain and deliver—and be held accountable for—such programs in a more efficient and effective manner. Labeling a public service as "essential" is not the same thing as defining its supporting expenditures as "fixed." Essential services can be provided more efficiently (at less cost) or more effectively (with greater benefits). With experience, expenditure categories excluded from service level analysis should be significantly reduced relative to the total budget.

Procedural Steps of Service Level Analysis

There are three basic components to a service level analysis (terminology may vary from application to application), as follows:

1. Identification of budget units—an examination of goals and objectives, current purposes and method of operation, ways of measuring performance and effectiveness, and the relationship with other budget units
2. decision package analysis—the identification of alternatives and the justification of various levels of service at which each budget unit might operate
3. priority ranking and evaluation—the arrangement of all levels of service in descending order of importance and the determination of a funding cut-off point

Linkages between these analytical components are shown in figure 9-1.

The first step in a service level analysis is to establish what units will submit budgets. Graeme Taylor offers the following criteria for identification of such units: (1) Budget units should correspond to the responsibility structure for budgetary decision making in government agencies. (2) They must be of reasonable size so that they are not constrained by the capacity of available data and accounting systems. (3) They should permit the clear

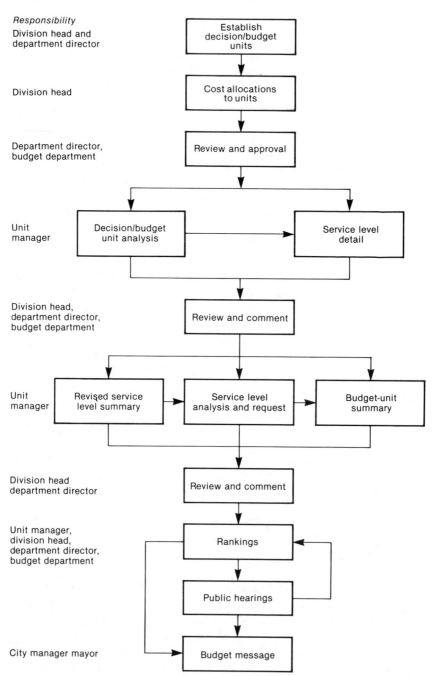

Figure 9-1. Flow Chart for Service Level Analysis

assignment of responsibility (accountability) not only for budget information but also for the execution of the approved budget.[9]

Identification of appropriate budget units may be a time-consuming
effort, requiring considerable thought and organizational analysis. It is
unlikely, however, that budget units will change significantly from one
year's budget to the next. Consequently, the identification of budget units
generally is a one-time task, requiring only minor adjustments in subsequent years as new program responsibilities are assigned.

After budget units have been identified, the current appropriations for
each department or agency should be apportioned to the respective budget
units. Each authorized position (and its cost) should be assigned to one of
the budget units, and nonpersonnel costs should be examined to determine
the appropriate share to be distributed to each unit. Since these estimates
cannot be accurate to the dollar, excessive time need not be devoted to this
"crosswalk." The primary purpose of this cost assignment is to provide a
data baseline from which subsequent comparisons can be made.

The next step is to describe the current methods of operation, including
the resource used. A good description would briefly trace the flow of work
and identify the outcome from that work. Alternative methods of operation
should also be identified and evaluated. Managers of individual budget
units should describe *critical linkages* between their operations and other
units. A typical example would involve one budget unit that provides services to clients referred from another unit and, in turn, provides information on these services and clients to a third unit. To ensure maximum coordination, critically linked budget units should exchange their respective
analyses of service levels. In some cases, it may be desireable to plan service
levels on a joint basis.

Budget units are subdivisions of the larger organization, but *decision
packages* are discrete sets of services, activities, and resources required by
these units to carry out program responsibilities. Each budget unit may be
responsible for several decision packages. The key to developing appropriate decision packages rests with the formulation of alternative methods of
accomplishing program objectives or performing assigned operations.
Decision packages may be variations on a basic theme, that is, alternative
approaches that make use of different mixes of resource inputs. Or they
may involve alternative methods for achieving agreed-on service objectives
(for example, contracting for certain activities involved in service delivery).
For many essential services, there may be only one readily evident package.
The level of investment from prior years may be such that a continuation of
the current approach is the only feasible decision. However, such prior program investments, whether in dollar terms or in terms of other administrative (or psychological) commitments, should not preclude a search for alternative decision packages. Maintaining existing programs simply because

they represent the way business has always been done is one of the under-lying sources of waste and inefficiency in governmental operations.

Once appropriate decision packages have been selected, several levels of service should be identified for each package. A minimum service level represents the level of funding below which it would not be feasible to con-tinue an existing program or initiate a new program (in ZBB this is some-times labeled the "survival level"). Often it is hard to get agency personnel to think in such terms, and in such cases, a percentage of the current level (for instance, 65 to 80 percent) may be set as the minimum level. The budget unit manager would then be asked to identify the level of service that could be provided at this reduced funding level.

Each succeeding service level above the minimum level should expand the services available, step-by-step, until the level is back to, and even above, current service standards. Each level must be analyzed in terms of the specific quantities and qualities of work of to be performed (services to be provided), and each level should be assigned appropriate costs. The po-tential impacts of each level should be described and its importance justified.

Those aspects of a service level that can be quantified should be identi-fied through the use of program measures or descriptors. Program mea-sures can be used to clarify: (1) the amount of work to be done (demand for services, needs, population served, and so on); (2) the targeted accomplish-ments and the impact or effectiveness of the services to be performed; and (3) the responsiveness of services (response times, waiting times, and so on). Some measures relate to the expected efficiency to be attained at various levels of service and funding, and other measures attempt to describe the effectiveness (benefits) associated with different service levels.

Such measures cannot characterize every important aspect of a pro-gram. However, they can help to clarify words frequently used to justify levels of service, such as "more," "better," "increased," and so forth. Measures add precision, and, together with written justifications, they give some idea of what the public can expect to obtain at different levels of fund-ing within a program area. Several iterations may be required before suit-able measures are devised for each budget unit. Some measures will be sug-gested by the process of clarifying objectives, and others can be developed from established accounting and reporting procedures.

It might be argued that time and effort could be saved if only the best or optimal alternative service level were presented in one neat package. This approach is less desirable, as it may create problems in subsequent reviews. Agency heads may not like the recommended alternative and thus might spend additional time generating other alternatives in an attempt to improve the program. Members of the governing body might not agree with the pro-posed service level or simply may not have enough funds to support it. Therefore, top management might be forced to deny the request or to try to break down the package to a more affordable level. Although all alternatives and related service levels can be identified, to reduce the workload and resulting paperwork only one or two that initially appear to be most feasible need to be analyzed in depth.

The following information should be developed by the budget-unit manager for each service level:

1. Nature of the operation and work to be performed at the service level—only the highest priority activities at the lowest feasible level of performance should be identified at the minimum-service level. At each successive level, improvements to operations and services delivered should be described over and above the preceding level.

2. Description of how services provided in a given level will differ from the current level of service—this information underscores what the unit is not able to do (or what can be accomplished at a higher than current level of funding) and brackets what services are to be provided.

3. The impact on services that funding a particular level will have—this type of statement is designed to justify why a service level should be funded (how conditions in the community will improve if it is funded) and to point up changes in community-service delivery if funding is below current appropriations.

The budget summary for each unit should reflect the resources required to deliver each level of service, including detailed costs from all funding sources and a summary of positions by type.

It is at this point that the mechanisms of the object-of-expenditure budget format are reintroduced. In effect, once the detailed cost data have been established for the minimum level of service, these costs are then built on in cumulative fashion for each successive level. It is not necessary to prepare a separate and distinct object-of-expenditure budget for each level of service. In exceptional cases, where the decision packages present distinct alternative approaches to the delivery of a particular service (as, for example, a labor-intensive versus a capital-intensive approach), separate budget summaries may be necessary.

The final step in service level analysis involves the *ranking* of all service levels, in turn, by the unit managers, the division or department heads, the central budget staff, and the city manager and/or city council (to provide a communitywide perspective). The difference between formulating levels of service and ranking them is similar to the distinction between efficiency and effectiveness. Peter Drucker has defined efficiency as "doing things right" and effectiveness as "doing the right things." The formulation of levels of service, in essence, involves a determination of how to do things right. Deciding to do the right things is the objective of the ranking process.

In each successive review, ranking establishes an order of priority for each service level. Highest-priority (most important) service levels are procedures for capital improvements programming (CIP). It is merely the CIP priority system applied to the operating budget as well.

To reduce the complexity of ranking, the various decision packages might be divided into five or six major groups. The first or highest-priority grouping would consist of those service levels that are essential to the maintenance of public health, safety, and/or welfare. The second grouping would include service activities required to maintain minimum standards in a continuing agency program or to make major public improvements fully useful. The remaining service levels would be distributed among other priority categories, with specific rankings becoming critical only as the lower-priority categories are reached.

It is likely that more service levels will be presented than can be funded from available revenues. Three alternative strategies can be employed, either separately or in combination, to bring the budget in balance: (1) funds can be withheld from the lowest-priority service levels; (2) efforts can be made to further reduce the cost of providing a given level of service; and/or (3) taxes can be raised to increase revenues. The final priority list can be used to fund service levels in rank order until anticipated revenues are exhausted. At this point, a funding-cut-off line is drawn, and those service levels below this line are not funded. Unfunded service levels should be reexamined, and if deemed necessary to the well-being of the municipality, the other two alternatives can be explored.

Management Control Implications

An examination of the consequences of various funding levels can be an important tool for management control, especially when budget requests must be balanced within available financial resources. Without a ranking process, budgeting is little more than a juggling act—trying to find the proper pieces in a hit-and-miss fashion that will add up to an acceptable whole. Unable to discern which programs or activities are of lower priority and therefore can be deferred or eliminated, budget makers often are forced to make across-the-board cuts. Service level analysis minimizes this need by establishing a priority listing.

Service level analysis also can be helpful in driving *accountability* for budget execution deeper into the organization. These analytical techniques require the involvement of operating managers from the outset, thus tapping a larger reservoir of program knowledge and analytical skills. Direct involvement of program managers in policy and budget making often increases their concern for the proper implementation of these policies. Thus, service level analysis facilitates the transformation of policies into plans and plans into action.

Operating managers may be reluctant to participate in service-level analyses for several reasons. Realizing that the objective is to reduce inefficiency, the manager may be apprehensive of intensive scrutiny of past activities in his or her agency or program. Managers may also be reluctant to recommend innovative alternatives over current practices. Rather than expecting to be praised for such innovations, they often are concerned about possible reprimands for not suggesting such improvements sooner. Thus, service level analysis may be perceived as a threat to program survival and, therefore, a threat to job security.

It is natural for operating managers to be dedicated to existing programs and to seek ways to expand activities by building on this established base. This type of program loyalty, however, often can interfere with the formulation and ranking of decision packages. A manager may rank a pet project at a higher priority than more basic projects in the hope that essential projects with lower priorities will be funded, thus ensuring the funding of the pet project.

The introduction of service level analysis will create additional work for managers and budget staff. Time and workload requirements are dependent on the design of the analytical system. The more objectives pursued, the greater is the involvement of operating managers, and the more types of measures involved, the greater is the workload and the longer the budget-building process. Although a major benefit of service-level analysis is the involvement of numerous operating managers, the diversity of people involved may create some communication and administrative problems. A good deal of work may be required to design the system and to educate those who will be working with it. Workloads should decrease significantly as the process evolves and ages and as management directives become more precise and planning assumptions become clearer.

First and foremost, service level analysis, like ZBB in which it is frequently applied, is an attack on budgetary incrementalism. Service-level analysis goes beyond an examination of new programs and incremental changes in existing programs to include a closer scrutiny of all activities, old and new. In this sense, service level analysis serves as a control mechanism —a mechanism for increased accountability—to eliminate unnecessary spending that may be the result of obsolete, inefficient programs or program duplication. Funds are thus channeled to more important demands, thereby increasing overall efficiency.

Budgeting for Program Effectiveness

The search for more efficacious methods of financial management—tools and techniques that will increase efficiency, accountability and effectiveness in the allocation of limited financial resources—has led to a further examination of the functions of planning and control. It has been recognized in recent years that, to be truly effective and responsive to public needs, budgeting procedures should reflect a longer-range perspective—a planning perspective. As David Page has observed: "A budget should be a financial expression of a program plan. Setting goals, defining objectives, and developing planned programs for achieving those objectives are important integral parts of preparing and justifying a budget submission."[10] In short, a budget should be interwoven with and a product of the entire public policy-making process.

Planning Objectives of Public Budgeting

It has long been recognized that the budget process offers the potential for periodic reevaluation of broad governmental goals and objectives and comparisons of public programs and their costs in light of these longer-range objectives. The budget document can provide a common terminology for describing the plans and programs covering diverse public operations. However, the fiscal-control focus of traditional budgeting procedures largely overshadowed this planning potential.

An emphasis on planning in the budget process was first brought to full public attention in August 1965, when President Lyndon B. Johnson proclaimed that by fiscal year 1968 all federal departments would adopt the budgeting system that had been followed for some years in the Department of Defense. As with many innovations introduced by dictum, however, inadequate groundwork was laid for the establishment of a Planning-Programming-Budgeting System (PPBS) at the federal level and even less so in state and local governments. PPBS was received with enthusiasm by the proponents of a more rational and comprehensive approach to financial management and with great skepticism by many who had survived earlier experiments with performance and program budgeting. What had been a fairly successful technique for the evaluation of weaponry systems in the Defense Department proved to have only limited immediate application in other public agencies. Soon, proponents of PPBS were faced with strong arguments concerning its "failures," even in the Defense Department. As one wag put it, there was too little planning at the beginning of PPBS and too much BS at the end.

The objective of PPBS was to provide a basis for policy analysis and decision making within the context of a central review by the chief executive and legislative body. As Schick has observed:

> PPB reverses the informational and decisional flow. Before the call for estimates is issued, top policy has to be made, and this policy constrains the

estimates prepared below. For each lower level, the relevant policy instructions are issued by the superior level prior to the preparation of estimates. Accordingly, the critical decisional process—that of deciding on purpose and plans—has a downward and disaggregative flow.[11]

Unfortunately, PPBS was never fully integrated with the bottom-up information flow that characterizes more traditional budget formats, and, as a consequence, operating agencies often were left on the periphery of the process. Operating agencies were required to provide new responses to policy directives (for example, measures of effectiveness), but they had little understanding or appreciation of how these responses would impact their resource allocations. As a result, agency personnel, operating in a realm of uncertainty, tended to be suspicious of the consequences of PPBS. These suspicions were further reinforced by the emphasis of PPBS on across-the-board program structures, which carried the threat of agency reorganization. The pendulum had swung to the opposite extreme from the focus of traditional budgeting practices, and many agencies were totally unprepared for (or unwilling to participate in) the transition.

By the early 1970s, even the proponents of PPBS were eulogizing its demise. PPBS had attempted to go too far, too fast in reforming the budget process. The emphasis on planning to the near exclusion of management-control functions proved disorienting to both operating agencies and policy makers. Out of the PPBS ashes of the 1960s, however, like the proverbial phoenix, have emerged such concepts as program budgeting, mission budgeting, ZBB, and related management-control techniques, such as management by objectives, productivity assessment, and performance auditing.

The successor to PPBS—program budgeting—is actually its predecessor, as the roots of program budgeting can be traced back to turn-of-the-century budget-reform efforts. Program budgeting offers considerably more latitude to combine a more systematic and comprehensive approach to budgeting—the planning orientation—with the basic functions of management control. Therefore, program budgeting holds the potential of a more appropriate interface between long-range planning and the day-to-day operations of public programs. It provides a foundation for a *dual budgetary system* that is more fully attuned to the basic objectives of greater accountability, efficiency, and effectiveness.

Implementation of a Program Budget Format

Although the term "program budgeting" is used fairly consistently throughout the country, applications of the techniques and methodologies of this concept differ significantly. Few program budgeting systems in operation at the state and local levels of government are identical. Many are actually performance budgets—presenting information strictly in work-efficiency terms by activities or projects. Other programmatic formats have been tailored to the point that they are not easily recognizable as program budgets in the pure, conceptual form. This tailoring process usually is the result of the perceived needs of local governing bodies and should not be considered as a violation of the basic conceptual framework of budgeting for increased effectiveness.[12]

A major component of all these approaches is the use of programs as the pivotal ingredients around which to organize budget information. A *program* can be defined as a group of interdependent, closely related activities or services that possess or contribute to a common objective or set of allied objectives. A program is a distinct organization of resources directed toward a specific objective of (1) eliminating, containing, or preventing a public problem; (2) creating, improving, or maintaining a condition affecting the public; (3) supporting or controlling other identifiable public programs. Each program should permit at least partial quantification and should bring together all costs associated with its execution. In designating a cluster of activities or series of operations as a program, the following aspects must be taken into account:

1. A program should permit the comparison of alternative methods of pursuing imperfectly determined policy objectives.
2. Even if the objectives are clearly defined, a program should seek alternative means of achieving these ends.
3. Programs may consist of a number of complementary components, some of which may be effective without the others and some of which are highly interdependent on the whole.
4. A program defines a series of activities (program elements) within a larger process, and usually these activities are linked to other program elements.
5. Programs may have overlapping structures, where these overlaps are used as means to meet certain common objectives.
6. A program is concerned with a time-span of expenditures; it extends beyond the current fiscal period in its operation.

Programs often are formulated in response to broad public goals. Detailed analysis at this level often is not feasible because of the lack of specificity of these goals. It may be difficult to identify and measure accurately cause-and-effect relationships, since the linkages between specific program inputs (costs) and immeasurable outputs (accomplishments) may remain rather vague. Therefore, programs may be "factored" or subdivided into component parts—for example, subprograms and program elements—with more specific, measurable objectives, activities, and outputs associated with these components. Resources provided for subprograms often are interchangeable for the maximum accomplishment of program objectives. That is to say, given a budget target at the program level, an agency must determine how to distribute the resources available among the component subprograms to achieve the most optimal output.

Programming and budgeting are different but complementary processes and should be consistent with one another. As Frederick Mosher points out: "Budgeting is tied in with programming in a number of ways, but the processes are fundamentally distinct: the organization and individuals concerned differ in part; and the procedures, the timing, the philosophy, and the classifications differ."[13] Good program preparation depends on the programming and budgeting systems used. When the techniques of budgeting and programming develop at different rates and achieve different levels of sophistication, particular care must be exercised to ensure consistency in the total effort.

Programming involves the ordering of proposed activities and projects based on some schedule of priorities and the assignment of price tags to their implementation over a reasonable period of time. Planning points up needs; programming provides a basis for determining the sequence in which these needs can be met most effectively. This process seeks ever-increasing precision in the identification of relationships between inputs (resources) and outputs (accomplishments).

To accomplish this delineation, agencies must seek answers to questions of (1) why—statements of long-range agency goals; (2) what and when—statements of agency (or program objectives in priority terms; and (3) how—identification of strategies or actions to be undertaken to achieve identified objectives. Agencies must also identify measures of output (in service units, clients, or products) that will be used to determine performance effectiveness throughout the operation of the program. Responses to these questions assist in the definition of the hierarchy of programmatic activities that will be pursued in the accomplishment of public goals and objectives.

The formulation of precise, nonquantitative goal statements is not an easy task. A common tendency is to describe what the agency does instead of addressing why these activities are appropriate within the agency's mandate. Thus, the goal of a public-employment-assistance agency is not: to interview, test, counsel, and place unemployed persons in jobs. This statement focuses on a *process*—on what the agency does—rather than on a *mission*. A more appropriate goal statement for this agency might be to assist the unemployed and underemployed in securing satisfactory jobs appropriate to their abilities to contribute to an increased standard of living. Subgoals or objectives might be concerned with accomplishing the principal goal for specific target groups, such as the disadvantaged, handicapped, youths, residents of urban ghettos, the rural unemployed, and so forth.

Perhaps the most critical step in program budgeting involves the setting of objectives. Objectives bring specificity to program goals by identifying key results to be accomplished within a specific period of time. Since objectives form the basis for program strategies and measures, they should be quantifiable or verifiable to the extent possible. Although objectives should be realistic and attainable, they also should present a challenge to improve conditions consistent with existing governmental policies, practices and procedures. A program objective also must be consistent with the resources available (or anticipated) and should assign singular responsibility and accountability even in joint efforts.

Program objectives specify the what and the when of anticipated agency activities. There is a tendency, however, to focus on the how. Thus, an appropriate program objective of a municipal fire department might be to reduce current response time to all fire and emergency-vehicle calls by 25 percent during the next two years. A statement such as: to build, equip, and staff a third fire station tells how the program objective might be accomplished and should be reserved for the next level in the delineation.

Strategy statements describe how and where specific resources (personnel, equipment, materials, capital expenditures, and so on) will be used in accomplishing stated objectives. A strategy should specify the means for achieving a key result based on the resources (fiscal and personnel) available or anticipated. These statements, in turn, should be related to *performance measures* and *measures of effectiveness* that identify the products, service units, and/or clients associated with the activities of the agency in carrying out the operations of a program.

Strategy statements also can be used to determine the adequacy of current or proposed funding levels by asking such questions as:

What combination of inputs can most appropriately be applied to achieve the desired level of outputs?

How much additional resources will be needed to attain this level?

If the limitation of available resources prohibit the attainment of this tentative level, what estimated level could be achieved within the budget constraints?

Without a systematic effort to define appropriate strategies and measures, there is no base line against which to test the notion of adequacy. As a consequence, the traditional least-cost compromise is likely to prevail.

Performance and effectiveness measures provide the mechanisms for determining the success (or lack thereof) of a program (or subprogram) in achieving agreed on objectives. Although some measures may be equated to inputs, efforts must be made to go beyond the more common workload measures that tend to measure efficiency rather than effectiveness. Measures such as number of man-days spent, number of requests received, or number of cases per worker may be appropriate in measuring agency efficiency, but they do not provide a measurable base for assessing the effectiveness of programs or activities in relation to their costs.

The output of many public activities may be difficult to define and measure in direct terms. As a consequence, secondary measures of effectiveness (surrogates) often must be used to test alternative approaches and to evaluate costs. The problem frequently centers on the data-gathering and recordkeeping procedures of public agencies—the management-information system, of which accounting and management control data are a major part.

It frequently is argued that the cost of generating the necessary information required for an effective program analysis or evaluation is too great in light of the consequent limited improvements in program performance. This argument may be valid in some situations, but all too often it is merely a smokescreen to hide organized resistance to change or general ineptness among agency personnel. In some cases, however, defensive behavior regarding the application of more sophisticated budgeting techniques is well-founded. Overzealous attempts to impose inflexible and often arbitrarily defined formats for the analysis of agency activities, for which the analysis may not have a full understanding or appreciation, can prove very detrimental to the program objectives of an agency. Costly data-collection efforts may yield vast quantities of computer printouts, resulting in an institutionalization of the very bureaucratic inflexibilities that gave rise to the need for improved decision-making in the first place. In seeking more rational and "scientific" procedures for program analysis and evaluation, safeguards must be exercised to avoid the substitution of one inflexible, ineffective structure for another.

Although the procedural steps leading to an effectiveness-oriented program budget may be initiated sequentially, more often they are carried out through a series of iterations (see figure 9-2). In identifying goals and objectives, for example, further clarification may be achieved as to the appropriate programs and subprograms of the agency. This application, in turn, may assist in determining which activities should be placed within each subprogram. Sometimes it will not be possible, however, to formulate precise statements of goals and objectives until the activity schedule of the agency has been examined in some detail. The establishment of such schedules, in turn, may require careful examination of alternative strategies and associated measures of performance and effectiveness. Thus, the budget must be viewed from the top-down in terms of goals and objectives and from the bottom-up in terms of agency activities designed to carry out these goals and objectives.

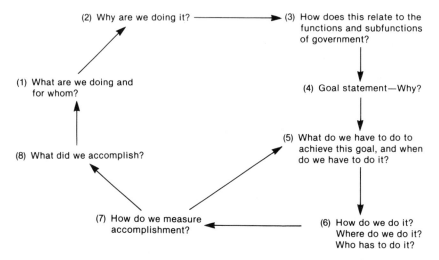

Figure 9-2. Iterative Process for Setting Goals and Objectives

As a general rule, it is neither practical nor desirable for a locality to adopt overnight all features of an effectiveness-oriented budget. Initially, emphasis should be placed on making necessary revisions in the budget document so that explanations and justifications of expenditures are presented in terms of public-service programs. Longer-range goals and objectives should be identified in programmatic terms. In the early stages of conversion, such presentations may be based on the more traditional object-of-expenditure approach. Detailed expenditure data may be aggregated to provide the initial basis for the necessary conversion (crosswalk) to a pro-grammatic format. Within the limitations of time and data availability, attention should be focused during budget preparation and review on the development of appropriate indices—performance measures and measures of effectiveness—to support all fiscal requests in terms of the agreed-on goals and objectives. The experience of several budget cycles operating under these procedures may be required before the essential features of a program budget are fully installed.

A Dual Budgetary System

As Martin Gannon has observed, " . . . planning and control are intimately related and, in fact, represent opposite sides of the same coin. Without planning, there can be no control."[14] As suggested at the outset of this discussion of alternative budget formats, a budget can serve as both a control mechanism and an important component of long-range planning. Unfortunately, no one of these basic formats, taken separately, can serve these dual objectives of management.

The traditional object-of-expenditure budget (discussed in chapter 2) serves the purpose of *administrative analysis* and *control.* It offers two distinct advantages over other budgetary approaches: (1) *accountability*—a detailed set of accounts is established through which expenditures can be recorded, controlled, and audited; and (2) *personnel management information*—because of the close linkage between personnel and other budgetary requirements, the control of positions can be used to control the entire budget.

The primary purpose of program budgeting is *policy analysis* and *planning.* The extended time horizon of the program budget seeks to shift the decision focus from the traditional one-year budget cycle to a multiyear time frame. Most public programs extend for periods beyond the annual budget cycle, and decisions regarding the allocation of resources in any fiscal year can have significant implications well beyond the budget under consideration. Multiyear program plans provide a more comprehensive basis for annual budget deliberations.

The object-of-expenditure approach focuses on inputs, such as expenditures for personnel, materials and supplies, equipment, and so forth. The programmatic approach emphasizes outputs—the commitment of resources to achieve program goals and objectives. Program budgeting provides a better basis for the comparison of program outputs to resource inputs in terms of costs and benefits or effectiveness.

Performance budgeting sought to strengthen the management aspects of the budget process by providing a focus on operating economies and performance efficiencies. Two key components distinguish performance budgeting from other approaches: (1) the identification of *performance units* within *work programs,* and (2) the effort to provide full measurement of *performance costs* through the use of cost accounting techniques. Workload and unit-cost measures provide a level of detailed management information useful to operating managers in assessing the efficiency of their programs and organizational units. These data, however, provide relatively few insights into the overall effectiveness of organizational activities, that is, whether program objectives are being attained relevant to public policies.

Service level analysis, as a core component of ZBB, seeks to overcome the problem of incrementalism that characterizes traditional budget formats. The identification of *budget units* is analogous to the specification of cost and responsibility centers under managerial accounting procedures. *Decision packages* provide a rough parallel to subprograms and program elements in the program-budget format. By arranging all levels of service in descending order of importance and determining a funding-cut-off point, alternative program approaches can be ranked with respect to their capacity to meet objectives. Therefore, more rational expenditure decisions can be made (with greater accountability).

Each of these budget formats has obvious strengths and weaknesses. By combining the strong points of each format in a hybrid approach, however, it is possible to establish a budget system that more nearly achieves the dual objectives of planning and control. The framework for such a dual budgetary system is outlined in tables 9-1, 9-2, and 9-3. These tables provide only a basic skeleton framework; many variations are possible, depending on the informational needs of decision makers and managers.

As shown in table 9-1, various types of costs (inputs) can be distributed to subprograms or decision packages on an object-of-expenditure or line-item basis. These subprograms/decision packages have been labeled V, W, X, Y and Z, but they could have been designated as any type of program activities the jurisdiction may have established (health, public safety, housing, transportation, recreation, sewer and water supply, and so on). Although the costs of a particular subprogram/decision package may be found totally within one agency, many program activities cross departmental lines. Therefore, to determine where the costs originate, it is necessary to know the amount of costs from each departmental cost center (or budget unit) that goes into each program. This type of cost allocation is illustrated in table 9-2.

Perhaps the most valuable type of program analysis from a management control standpoint is that which brings together the types of costs by cost center (budget unit) for each program (or subprogram). These data are illustrated in table 9-3. If multiple service levels are to be analyzed, this account matrix would be repeated for each service level. Finally, all these

Table 9-1
Type of Costs by Subprogram

Subprogram	Total Costs	Personal Services	Materials and Supplies	Travel	Equipment	Debt Costs
V	300	170	25		85	20
W	200	90	25		80	5
X	150	75	10		60	5
Y	100	50	35	15		
Z	47	25	10	12		
Totals	797	410	105	27	225	30

Table 9-2
Program Costs by Cost Centers

Subprogram	Total Costs	Cost Centers				
		A	B	C	D	E
V	300	120	45	35	55	45
W	200	80	30	30	30	30
X	150	60	20	20	30	20
Y	100	40	15	6	19	20
Z	47	30	5	5	7	
Totals	797	330	115	96	141	115

Table 9-3
Subprogram-Z Costs by Types and Centers

Cost Centers	Total Costs	Personal Services	Materials and Supplies	Travel	Equipment	Debt Costs
A	30	15	7	8		
B	5	3	1	1		
C	5	3	1	1		
D	7	4	1	2		
E						
Totals	47	25	10	12		

costs data can be brought together in an integrated comparison of program costs to the budget, as illustrated in the three-dimensional chart shown in figure 9-3. The budget must be based on costs rather than expenditures to compare program costs with the appropriations for the various activities.

This dual or complementary budget system is designed to provide different information formats, reflecting the range of decisions that must be made at various points in the budget process. The basic premise is that program analysis (service level analysis) and planning decisions must precede budget commitments and that administrative analysis and control decisions must be made during the execution of the budget. Control mechanisms can also be maintained through such cost-accounting devices as workload measures and unit-cost data. Although these functions overlap, such that no clear-cut distinction can be made, the informational needs of each function

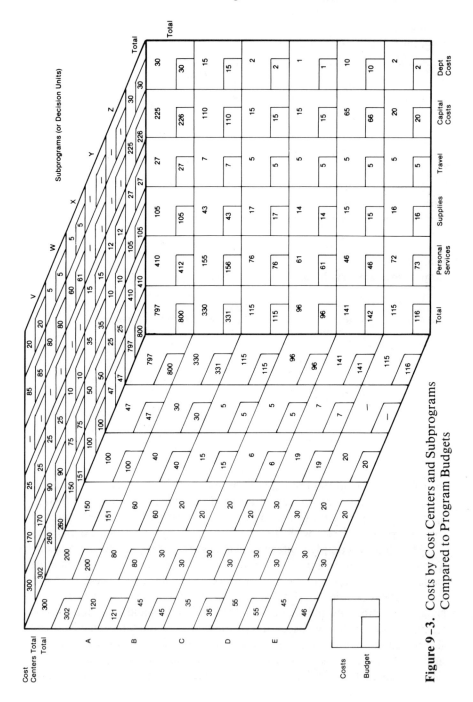

Figure 9–3. Costs by Cost Centers and Subprograms Compared to Program Budgets

can be facilitated by the format of this dual budgetary approach—which combines features from each of the budget formats described in this chapter.

Notes

1. James C. Snyder, *Financial Planning and Management in Local Government* (Lexington, Mass.: Lexington Books, D.C. Heath, 1977), p. 99.

2. Frederick C. Mosher, *Program Budgeting: Theory and Practice* (Chicago, Ill.: Public Administration Service, 1954), p. 5.

3. Lennox L. Moak and Albert M. Hillhouse, *Concepts and Practices in Local Government Finance* (Chicago, Ill.: Municipal Finance Officers Association, 1975), p. 81.

4. Jesse Burkhead, *Government Budgeting* (New York: John Wiley & Sons, 1956), pp. 153–155.

5. Cited in Aaron Wildavsky and Arthur Hammann, "Comprehensive versus Incremental Budgeting in the Department of Agriculture," *Administrative Science Quarterly* 7 (December 1965):321.

6. Allan Schick, "Putting It All Together," *Sunset, Zero-Base Budgeting and Program Evaluation,* Proceedings of a Conference on Legislative Oversight (Richmond, Virg.: Joint Legislative Audit and Review Commission, 1977), p. 41.

7. Graeme M. Taylor, "Introducing Zero-Base Budgeting," ibid., p. 54.

8. Schick, "Putting It All Together," p. 17, suggests that actionable or discretionary programs account for less than 25 percent of most public budgets.

9. Taylor, "Introducing Zero-Base Budgeting," pp. 47–48. Taylor and others refer to these basic building blocks as "decision units," whereas other writers have used the term "budget units," as adopted here, to avoid possible confusion with the concept of "decision packages."

10. David A. Page, "The Federal PPBS," *Journal of the American Institute of Planners* 33 (July 1967):257.

11. Allen Schick, "The Road to PPB: The Stages of Budget Reform," in *Planning Programming Budgeting: A Systems Approach to Management,* ed. Fremont J. Lyden and Ernest G. Miller (Chicago: Markham Publishers, 1968), p. 42.

12. David Novick, *Current Practices in Program Budgeting (PPBS): Analysis and Case Studies Covering Government and Business* (New York: Crane, Russak, 1973), p. 13.

13. Mosher, *Program Budgeting,* p. 59.

14. Martin, J. Gannon, *Management: An Organizational Perspective* (Boston: Little Brown), p. 140.

10 Planning and Management Control

Decision making is one of the most pervasive functions of management. If a public agency is to carry out its mandate, decisions must be made and action programs arising from these decisions must be implemented. Rational decision making, however, is dependent on effective problem analysis and a long-range planning framework. Through planning and analysis, goals and objectives can be identified and policies and programs can be systematically evaluated.

Public Management and Planning

Management science in recent years has provided managers with vastly improved techniques for problem analysis, goal identification, and decision making. As management scientists have noted, some decisions—particularly those concerning tactical considerations—can be made with a high degree of certainty as to the outcome of subsequent actions. There are many situations, however, in which the manager must deal with an uncertain future and where decisions involve a certain amount of risk. In general, a responsibility of management is to reduce uncertainty and to bring risk within tolerable limits and, thereby, improve the rational basis on which decisions can be made. Quite obviously, planning should be a vital aspect of public management. Traditional concepts of public planning, however, have frequently been an appendage to, rather than an integral part of, the process of public management.

Strategic versus Operations Planning

In attempting to identify an appropriate role of planning in public management, a distinction must be made between *strategic planning* and *operations planning.* Strategic planning involves the identification of overall goals and objectives and the development of strategies (including policies and procedural guidelines) for achieving those objectives. Operations planning

263

focuses on the tactics of performance and the use of specific resources to achieve overall objectives that are integral parts of strategic plans. Operations planning is concerned primarily with programming, scheduling, and control of various individual-program activities. Effective and efficient operations planning always means the difference between "on time" and "late." Effective and comprehensive strategic planning can mean the difference between success and failure in the delivery of vital public services.

Many practitioners in the field of public administration espouse a planning posture. Frequently, however, their approach is limited to a form of operations planning. Although it is a critical aspect of the public-management process, operations planning without strategic planning can do little to reduce the uncertainty that surrounds many of the activities of government. As a consequence, public programs may be carried out more efficiently, but the more important issue of their effectiveness—their ability to achieve long-range and comprehensive objectives—will be left unresolved.

From a One-Shot Optimization to a Planning Process

A common approach to public planning involves the formulation of a plan for some specific target date, ten to twenty years in the future. Under this approach, various demographic and economic factors are projected for a defined period of time, suggesting that by 1990 or the year 2000, the population of a particular jurisdiction will be of such-and-such a magnitude (often expressed as a range). Based on these projections, it is then suggested that public services and facilities will have to be expanded accordingly, employment opportunities will have to be provided in a given quantity, land consumption will be of a given magnitude, and so forth. As a rule, considerable attention is also devoted to an identification of the more immediate problems of growth (or the lack of it) and to suggested solutions to those problems.

Under such an approach, problem-solving often takes precedence over the establishment of long-range goals and objectives. Program proposals frequently are based on anticipated demographic and economic conditions—a simple extrapolation of the status quo. When the overriding focus is on solutions to more immediate problems, the cumulative process becomes short-range planning, albeit applied to a long time period. The results, benefits, and profits to be gained from such short-range plans cannot be assured in the long run and, in fact, may be lost in the crisis of disjointed problem solving. A plan is of relatively little value if it does not look far enough into the future to provide a basis on which change can be logically anticipated and rationally accommodated.

Charles Lindblom has described public decision making as a process with little concern for goals and objectives; because public objectives are so difficult to define, and consensus can rarely be achieved, the best course of action is incrementalism.[1] Incrementalism results from competition among interest groups and produces short-range programs rather than long-range policies. Democracies are composed of widely different factions that compete for the public's interests. Even if these interests were not contradictory, our ability to foresee the full consequences of our actions is so limited that, according to Lindblom, objectives must be approached in small, manageable steps. Thus, he dismisses categorically any attempt to develop more synoptic or comprehensive approaches to decision making on the grounds that they do not conform to reality. Some writers have argued that "disjointed incrementalism" is a necessary—and desirable—consequence of the democratic process.[2] As an extension of this assertion, some would argue that planning is contrary to, or at least inappropriate and difficult to achieve within, a democracy.

The most significant flaw in the concept of disjointed incrementalism is that it fails to consider all the incremental alternatives between the existing system and the strawman extreme of synoptic planning. Lindblom and his followers have oversimplified the alternatives and, thus, have stacked the argument in their favor. A planning approach that recognizes the need for inputs "from the bottom up"—which conforms to or adapts to the ideals of the democratic process—and that, at the same time, secures a more rational basis for decision making, is also an option on this continuum. The "pragmatic incrementalists" seem to ignore this alternative.

Many traditional planning efforts tend to be one-shot optimizations, drawn together periodically, often under conditions of stress. Once "the best plans" are laid, there is little attempt to test their continued efficacy against the realities of current conditions. It has been said that: "Few plans survive contact with the enemy." And indeed, rarely are policies and programs executed exactly as initially conceived. Random events, environmental disturbances, competitive tactics, and unforseen circumstances may all conspire to thwart the smooth implementation of plans, policies, and programs. In short, the traditional planning process does not provide an adequate framework for more rational decision making. Fixed targets, static plans, and repetitive programs are of relatively little value in a dynamic society.

What is required is a planning framework within which decisions can be subjected to continuous testing, correction, and refinement. Through such an approach, alternative courses of action can be identified and analyzed, and a desirable range can be established within which choices can and should be made. The concept of strategic planning, as it has evolved over the past fifteen years, offers one important response to this need for a more dynamic planning process.

The Origins of Strategic Planning

The concept of strategic planning first found application in the private sector in the late 1950s and early 1960s. As B.W. Scott observed in a 1965 publication of the American Management Association:

> Strategic planning is a systematic approach by a given organization to make decisions about issues which are of a fundamental and crucial importance to its continuous long term health and vitality. These issues provide an underlying and unifying basis for all the other plans to be developed within the organization over a determinate period of time. Thus a long-range strategy is designed to provide information about an organization's basic direction and purpose, information which will guide all its operational activities.[3]

The term "strategic" was applied to these planning activities to denote the linkage with the goal-setting process, the formulation of more immediate objectives to move the organization toward its goals, and the specific actions (or strategies) required in the deployment of organizational resources to assist in achieving these objectives. The term also was adopted to distinguish the scope of this process from the so-called planning that characterized much of the forecasting and other piecemeal efforts undertaken by industry and business concerns. The use of strategic planning in the military, of course, can be traced back to ancient times, where strategy—as the art and science of conducting military campaigns on a broad scale—was distinguished from tactics—the maneuvering of troups to gain more immediate objectives.

Efforts to apply strategic planning in the public sector began to surface in the late 1960s and early 1970s, in part as a response to criticisms of comprehensive planning that had been advocated (but seldom achieved) in government for over three decades. In a series of articles that culminated in a 1970 book entitled, *Systemic Planning: Theory and Application,* Anthony Catanese and Alan Steiss describe an alternative to the traditional planning process; this alternative combines elements of operations research and systems analysis in a long-range decision-making system that focuses on probabilistic futures. This "hybrid model," they suggest, presents a challenge to a new generation of planners to combine the best features of more sophisticated analytical techniques with "humanistic traditions" of public planning; to avoid "technocratic determinism" while attaining a more systematic approach to public decision making.[4]

The initial *P* in PPBS (Planning-Programming-Budgeting System) was a reflection of the same general concern for a longer-range perspective to the formulation of goals and objectives. It was assumed that such planning could provide a broader framework within the more detailed functions of programming and budgeting could be undertaken. Unfortunately, the PPBS approach was a top-down model in which goals and objectives were formulated in the upper echelons of the organization, filtering down through a series of what Herbert Simon has called "means-ends chains." At the end of a lengthy process, specific programs were to be developed and implemented to achieve these goals and objectives. In the absence of a well-developed strategic-planning process, however, the central direction from the top often was poorly coordinated, contradictory, often counterproductive, or nonexistent. As a consequence, many agencies operating under a PPBS mandate went through the motions of fulfilling the procedural requirements, using the appropriate buzz words, but with little change in their traditional incremental approach to programming and budgeting of activities.

Program budgeting—a forerunner of PPBS—and management by objectives (MBO) emerged in the seventies as alternative responses that were more bottom-up in their orientation. These approaches seek broader involvement within an organization or agency in the goal-setting and objective-formulating processes that are precursory to the commitment of resources to specific-program activities.

Another important component in the development of strategic planning was the recognition of a management or planning hierarchy that more clearly articulates the respective responsibilities at various levels within an organization. Robert Anthony describes this hierarchy in private-sector applications in terms of a management-control system consisting of: (1) strategic planning, (2) management planning, and (3) operational control.[5] *Management planning* is a pivotal ingredient in this approach, involving: "(1) the programming of approved goals into specific projects, programs, and activities; (2) the design of organizational units to carry out approved programs; and (3) the staffing of those units and the procurement of necessary revenues."[6] In the absence of a strategic-planning framework, however, management planning can become disjointed and counterproductive. At the same time, without the consistent follow-through of management planning (programming and budgeting) and operations planning (scheduling and control), strategic planning may be little more than a set of good intentions with little hope of realization. Thus, the linkages among these three basic components of this hierarchy are as important as the components themselves.

A Strategic Planning Model

From a total-systems perspective, strategic planning should be a continuous process that includes performance evaluation and feedback. It should involve a continuous examination of alternative courses of action and estimations of the impacts and consequences that are likely to result from their implementation. Explicit provisions should be made for dealing with the uncertainties of probabilistic futures. As has been suggested, the art of management is to reduce uncertainty and to bring risk within the bounds of tolerance. In this context, strategic planning can play an important role by assisting managers in organizing goals and objectives and developing feasible action plans to achieve them. In so doing, the major priorities can be ordered, the impacts of resource decisions can be assessed, and the activities and functions of the organization can be integrated into a more cohesive whole.

Basic Components of the Model

The strategic planning model advocated herein to support the management control system consists of five basic components[7]:

1. Basic research and analysis
    a. basic data collection, inventories, and broad needs assessments
    b. external and internal environmental analyses to determine system readiness
    c. identification of planning horizon and levels of clientele groups to be served
2. Diagnosis of trends and needs
    a. macrolevel trends and related considerations
    b. microlevel technical and applied studies, including facilities analyses and specific needs assessments
3. Statements of goals and objectives
    a. formulation of hypotheses concerning conceptual aspects of the organization's mission
    b. delineation of significant structural changes required to realize the mission statement
    c. definition of the desired state of the system (goal statements)
4. Formulation and analysis of alternatives
    a. development of an objectives matrix
    b. redefinition of the desired state of the system in light of more detailed objectives
5. Policy alternatives and resource recommendations
    a. translation of goals and objectives into general policies
    b. formulation of explicit policy sets
    c. delineation of effectiveness and performance measures
    d. establishment of decision guidelines for the allocation of financial resources

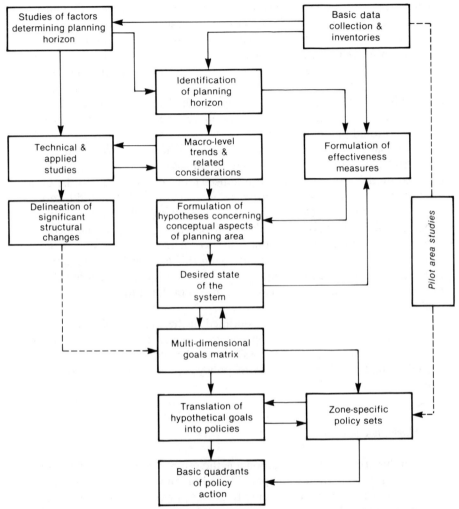

Source: Alan Walter Steiss, *Public Budgeting and Management* (Lexington, Mass.: Lexington Books, D.C. Heath and Company, Copyright 1972, D.C. Heath and Company), p. 205. Reprinted by permission of the publisher.

Figure 10-1. Schematic Diagram of the Strategic Planning Process

The linkages among these basic components are shown schematically in figure 10-1.

Fundamental to this model of strategic planning is the assumption that theoretical constructs—derived from a concentration of data concerning the organization under study—can lead to the formulation of preliminary goals and objectives concerning the desired future state of the system. The development of this mission statement is a pivotal step in the process. Statements of goals and objectives, in turn, serve as a basis for the development of appropriate policies and decisions. This emphasis on orderly evolution—from a broad mission statement, to statements of goals and objectives consistent with the mission statement, to more explicit policies and implementing decisions—seeks to establish or reinforce linkages that are missing in the disjointed incremental approach. The absence of consistency from the general to the specific is also one of the major shortcomings of most traditional planning efforts.

The goal-formulation process also serves as a vehicle for avoiding the basic tendency to posit future plans on existing conditions. Through a goal-oriented model, policies—factual premises representing what can be done are tested against goals—value premises representing what should be done. Thus, statements of goals and objectives play a vital role in the day-to-day process of decision making. The danger of sacrificing the basic merits of the strategic plan to technical or politically expedient considerations, in large measure, can be circumvented by applying this approach. When compromises must be made, as they always will, the decisions can be more clearly based on the optimal or normative conditions outlined in the statements of goals and objectives.

Although several of the steps outlined in the strategic planning model are common to most planning approaches, others are unique to this model and therefore merit further discussion: (1) the planning horizon, (2) the objectives matrix, (3) formulation of policy sets, and (4) the use of effectiveness measures.

The Horizon Concept

Basic to this strategic planning model is the use of a planning horizon—the farthest point that can be anticipated based on an interpretation of what is known about existing and emerging trends. Applying this concept, a series of plans can be developed for a given level of service at the planning horizon. Each plan represents an alternative mix of clientele groups and programs. Just as with the natural horizon, as the specific service level is approached, the planning horizon continues to recede, making adjustments in long-range goals and objectives both necessary and possible. Therefore, the horizon concept provides a more dynamic approach to strategic planning. The planning horizon can be changed, revised, or even dismissed as the body of information of which it is based is enlarged.

It is possible to establish both objective (measurable) and subjective criteria for determining the planning horizon of any organization. For example, the service capacity of various public facilities may serve as one criterion in establishing a planning horizon; optimal staff-client ratios might provide another criterion. Some criteria are products of the level of technology at any given time. Other criteria are established on a somewhat subjective basis, which may be altered (and should be reevaluated) from time to time as, for example, client profiles change.

A plan formulated on the horizon concept is not a comprehensive plan or general plan in the traditional sense. Rather, it yields a series of policy alternatives to guide future development toward some desired state. As such, strategic planning deviates from the traditional cumulative approach to planning. The horizon concept offers the basis for a *thesis* rather than merely a *synthesis*.

This thesis emerges from a series of hypotheses or what-if studies, whereby various mixes of clientele groups and programs are explored within the overall parameters of the planning horizon. Each alternative has different implications for the distribution of resource requirements. Further, there are likely to be a number of combinations and permutations based on a relatively well defined set of pure alternatives. From these hypotheses, the mix that best fits the mission statement of the organization can be identified and set forth as the thesis of what should be (that is, the desired future state of the organization). Policies and programs should then be developed to implement this chosen alternative.

An Objective Matrix

In the strategic planning model, a deductive approach replaces the more typical inductive techniques of planning. The task becomes one of forming tentative goal sets and testing them in the context of specific horizon alternatives, allowing new factors to emerge and be considered. Thus, the goal-formulation process can serve as an educational device as well as a planning tool. It increases the awareness of the participants with respect to the changes that may be taking place within the organization, but it also allows them to react to these changes in accordance with their own values, norms, and expectations.

In the strategic planning model, explicit recognition is given to the fact that value inputs (personal biases) are likely to occur at critical points, namely, in connection with the formulation of more explicit objectives. This tendency can never be completely eliminated. Therefore, statements of objectives must be formulated within a concise framework that provides an opportunity to clearly identify conflict positions, that is, statements of existing or potential value conflicts. The basis for this identification of conflict situations is a multidimensional objectives matrix.

Conflicts can emerge on several different levels. The first conflict dimension is between objectives of the organization and those of individuals or groups within the organization. A second level of possible conflict arises from territorial consideration, that is, the prerogatives of various units within the organization. A third level of conflict emerges with regard to explicit issues and the various viewpoints that can be brought to bear on their resolution. The purpose of this analysis is to more clearly identify both the potential conflicts and the areas of agreement or congruence. The objectives matrix merely provides a convenient scorecard for recording these points, so as to avoid the tendency to assume that objectives are mutually exclusive.

The matrix is built through a series of iterations, involving a broad cross-section of participants. First, an objective statement is posited for each identified issue area. These objectives are then categorized according to territorial considerations and the organization—the individual dimension. At the end of this first iteration, a number of cells in the matrix should be filled and others should remain empty. The next iteration should focus on filling the empty cells by identifying objectives that parallel (complement or are in conflict with) the previously identified objective in that particular dimension. This iteration may reveal additional issue areas, which produces yet another cycle. The end product of this phase of the analysis should be a fully articulated matrix, with each cell containing one or more objectives. Finally, those objectives should be identified that (1) are clearly in conflict with one another, (2) evidence potential conflict or consensus, and (3) are mutually reinforcing.

This approach has been successfully applied in small groups through the use of a modified Delphi technique and on a communitywide basis using a series of questionnaires and public meetings.[8] The matrix can reveal different levels of understanding regarding the broader goals of the institution. Respondent conflict must be expected and analyzed. The general premise underlying this matrix approach is that information regarding conflicts among respondents will be valuable in identifying levels of comprehension with respect to complex organizational issues.

Explicit Policy Sets

In the context of the strategic plan, policy statements are intended to cover the entire range of actions required for the identification of a goal to the point at which that goal is attained. The formulation of policy, therefore, embraces various points on a continuum of means—ranging from long-range, general, and educational objectives to more immediate, specific, and action-oriented programs. The number of policy steps along this continuum, of course, will vary from situation to situation. In his analysis of policy planning, Franklyn Beal suggests three distinct categories of policy, focusing on: (1) what is to be accomplished (objectives); (2) where it is to be accomplished (locus); and (3) how it is to be accomplished (means).[9] In addition to these three categories, it also may be suggested that policy must address questions of: (4) priority, and (5) standards of accomplishment, evaluation, and control.

These five policy categories span a range of statements from norms and values, on the one hand, to explicit guidelines on the other. Taken as a set, however, they do not provide a complete categorization of policy concerns. An important element not included is the degree of generality or specificity of action required to implement each policy. Such action may fall within the realm of general policies at one end of the spectrum and control policies at the other. Between these extremes might be arrayed plan policies, program policies, and implementation policies. Taken together, the five categories of policy and the five divisions on the generality-specificity continuum provide the X and Y coordinates of a policy matrix, as shown in figure 10-2.

Policy content may require strategic, management, or operational-planning inputs. Objectives and priorities generally require strategic planning, whereas means and standards express the inputs of operational planning. Locus—the place where implementation is accomplished, be it a physical locale or an administrative unit—provides a tactical bridge between strategy and operations. Management planning, however, also must be attentive to questions of priority and means of implementation.

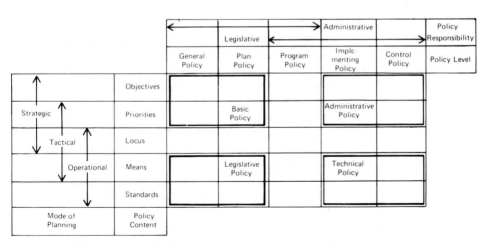

Source: Alan Walter Steiss, *Public Budgeting and Management* (Lexington, Mass.: Lexington Books, D.C. Heath and Company, Copyright 1972, D.C. Heath and Company), p. 221. Reprinted by permission of the publisher.

Figure 10-2. Multiple-Policy Matrix

As shown in figure 10-2, there are four quadrants in the policy matrix that require the attention of various participants in the policy-making process. Basic policy is primarily of a strategic nature and focuses on objectives and priorities within a general-planning context. Legislative policy is required to establish operational means and standards within the framework of the general-planning context. The objectives and priorities of implementation and control are part of the strategy of administrative action, whereas the means and standards of implementation and control are, in most instances, technical in nature. Each of these quadrants suggests a particular realm of policy formulation responsibility and, further, delimits the focus and emphasis appropriate to each of these realms. The notion of specific policy sets, therefore, underlines the importance of maintaining these parameters—to ensure that one policy quadrant does not encroach unduly on the responsibilities of another quadrant.

The cross-shaped area formed by the demarcation between these four quadrants represents, on the vertical plane, the trade-offs that must be made between legislative and administrative policy and, on the horizontal plane, the overlap between strategical, managerial, and operational considerations. This area corresponds to what Beal calls "the intermediate level of policy planning" and is the most critical area of policy formulation because ". . . at the middle level conflict between policies is, practically speaking, inevitable."[10]

Effectiveness Measures

Effectiveness measures must be formulated and applied to measure goal achievement. Effectiveness measures involve a scoring technique for determining the state of a given system at a certain point. They are indicators that measure direct and indirect impacts of specific resources in the pursuit of certain goals and objectives.

Effectiveness measures can be defined by: (1) establishing current levels and types of performance in discrete categories; (2) estimating the current impacts of resources on this performance; and (3) then defining desired levels and types of performance. The development of positive statements of performance provides a base from which change may be defined and evaluated. This approach is based on the concept of marginal change from the current state of the system.

Performance must be defined in output-oriented terms based on a vocabulary of understandable program and policy variables. Policy and program variables, in turn, must identify administrative and legislative policy and those interests that make up the patterns of performance to be affected. An important assumption in the development of effectiveness measures is that they can be derived or inferred from current conditions (but are not limited to those conditions). This means that current operations and their effects must be continually monitored (that is, the basic data-collection component of the strategic planning model). This continuous evaluation is probably the most effective means available for initiating a goal-oriented-planning and decision-making system within an existing organizational structure.

A Continuous Process, Not a Panacea

This overview of strategic planning is intended to acquaint the reader with the rudiments of the process and its possible applications in conjunction with an integrated management control system. Such a cursory presentation runs the risk of generating an impression that the process is simple and relatively easy to implement. This is not the case, however. Organizations that have adopted this approach are well aware it is not a panacea. Strategic planning will not immediately resolve all problems confronting an organization, nor is its implementation easy to administer. A firm commitment by those who will be involved to see the process through is essential to its success—it should not be merely another form of one-shot optimization.

Strategic planning must be a continuous process performed in annual cycles and coupled with continuing involvement of administrative personnel and other participants in different phases of the process. The cyclical nature of this process, however, does offer an opportunity to introduce the various components in a series of refinements rather than on a whole-cloth basis. Formalization of the process, however, is at the very root of successful strategic planning, as distinguished from the forecasting and rather piece-meal analytical efforts that have characterized public planning in the past.

Operations Planning and Scheduling

If a program or project is to be implemented successfully, three diverse and often contradictory elements must be coordinated into an operations plan and schedule:

1. Operations: the things that must be done (activities or jobs), each with a sequential relation to other operations and each requiring resources for some period

2. resources: the things utilized in a program or project, normally reduced to a common standard of cost, but including personnel, equipment, materials, and time
3. constraints: conditions imposed by outside factors, such as budgetary limits, completion deadlines, availability of resources, inputs from other units, and so forth

The argument that the techniques of operations planning, developed in the private sector, are not directly applicable to nonproduct-oriented activities is fallacious. The two basic requirements for the application of these techniques are: (1) an ability to clearly state a work program (including a delineation of operations into specific activities); and (2) the skill to attach cost and other resource requirements/constraints to each activity in the program. Although many government activities are process oriented, that is, do not result in an end product as such, most public processes have some objective analogous to a project completion. Further a range of cost and time constraints can be associated with most government activities. Given this fundamental management information, several operations planning and scheduling techniques are available to determine maximum time allotments, as well as costs involved, for each job.

The Operations Plan

The primary purpose in applying these techniques is to develop both a plan and a schedule that will provide managers with mechanisms for continuous control over program activities. In this context, an *operations plan* is a delineation of the order or sequence in which activities must be performed to implement successfully a given program or project. Such a plan should permit the program to be completed (or maintained) in the best time, at the least cost, and with the smallest degree of risk. An operations plan must be dynamic—it should provide managers with the capacity to: (1) consider the costs, in dollars and time, of pursuing several alternative sequences of activities; (2) establish criteria for resource allocation and scheduling; (3) evaluate the accuracy of cost and resource estimates and assist in refining these estimates; (4) identify and assess the effect of change with minimum delay: (5) revise and update the plan within an acceptable period; and (6) communicate and assimilate data regarding the program's progress. Any operations plan, of necessity, will have certain practical restraints. Deviations between predicted and actual results, for instance, must be identified quickly so that managers can take the necessary action to correct such situations. Available data, however inaccurate, must be made to produce better results.

The Operations Schedule

The scheduling function can be properly performed only after operations planning is completed. *Scheduling* involves a determination of the times or dates for resource utilization. A schedule must reflect the total resource capacity assigned to the program or project. It must take into account the availability of resources, the sequence of activities or jobs, the resource requirements, and possible starting times for each activity.

The basic requirement in producing an efficient operations schedule is to level the use of resources, that is, to avoid dramatic shifts in resource requirements (particularly personnel). This objective is accomplished by using the total "float" available within the program or project to select the best or optimal starting time for each activity. Float is merely the discretion that a manager has in scheduling the various activities that make up the project or program. Thus, in developing a schedule, the critical path (that is, the longest sequence of activities) is determined not so much by the duration of the various activities as by the segment of resources out of the total resource capacity that can (and should) be assigned to complete each activity.

It is possible to assume the minimum duration for each activity, with a resultant maximum use of resource, and to perform the critical-path calculations. This approach will give a minimum duration for the total program or project. However, it may very well result in personnel and equipment requirements that exceed the capabilities of available resources. The requirement of scheduling, therefore, is to establish a duration for each activity with varying levels of resources to be utilized so that the schedule still remains within the limits of peak efficiency. This approach to scheduling yields a minimum cost for each activity and, presumably, for the total program or project.

Although many factors combine to provide this kind of control, none is more important than communications. Operations planning and scheduling techniques are excellent tools of communication because they show graphically the interrelationships of activities in a program or project. They also indicate clearly where responsibilities for supervision and management lie. When a change in the plan or schedule is required, the work program should show clearly which activities will be affected by any changes. This focus, by itself, can relieve program supervisors (for example, field staff) of much unnecessary paperwork that only serves to keep them from their more valuable function—the continuous oversight of program activities.

Operational Objectives and Performance Requirements

Operations planning begins with a clear definition of operational objectives and performance requirements. Operational objectives should include a reason for the existence of the project, a brief description of the desired results, and the management approach to be adopted. Performance requirements should further define the end product of the project. If it is a construction project, general specifications may define an appropriate product. If a study or research effort is involved, a definition of the area to be examined and the subject matter of the final conclusions or recommendations often will suffice. If it is a task that must be performed, such as a move to a new facility, a description of the conditions to be attained and the measures of accomplishment is needed.

Performance requirements should also define any constraints on how the project is to be carried out. Imposed schedule deadlines and budgetary limitations are in this category. Any requirements for doing work in-house or by subcontract should be stated. Appropriate management philosophies and strategies should also be identified. The amount of verification of the project's end product performance also may be defined.

Criteria for decision making should reflect the relative importance of project performance, development costs, production cost, and ultimate operational costs. These criteria may be both quantitative and qualitative and may eventually be translated into more sophisticated decision criteria, such as used in cost-benefit or cost-effectiveness analyses. It is not necessary in this initial stage for management to forecast every contingency. General decision guidelines will suffice.

Any basic incompatibilities in or disagreements about the operational objectives should be exposed early and not left to cause inevitable misunderstanding and trouble later. Detailed examination of the tasks required to complete the project can expose overly optimistic assumptions and can lead to more realistic project schedules. Inconsistencies may be discovered between the desired performance of the program or project and the funds and time available to develop it. It may become apparent that the objectives cannot be met, either because they are too ambitious or because they have not been thought through sufficiently to ensure that the necessary resources will be available when and where they are needed.

No amount of operations planning can guarantee that problems will not occur during the project implementation, however. In fact, too much planning may inhibit effective project execution. The right amount of operations planning, however, can prevent unnecessary problems from arising, leaving the project staff to devote its efforts to solving the really unforeseen problems.

Activity Identification

Operations planning should provide a basis for action. Its primary purpose should be specific identification of activities and techniques that can and should be carried out in the implementation of a program or project. An operations plan represents the best current statement of the most appropriate way to get the job done. If such a plan is not intended to serve as a basis for implementation, it is a waste of time. Many projects and programs contain nonrepetitive tasks and elements of risk that may require change. Therefore, an operations plan must be flexible enough to undergo revisions as the activities evolve.

Organized brainstorming sessions often can be of considerable assistance in identifying activities appropriate to a given project. Such sessions should be fairly unstructured, free-wheeling, and unconstrained. All ideas should be recorded no matter how "far out" they may seem at first. Each individual associated with the project should be involved. It may be desirable for the project manager to maintain a relatively low profile in these sessions to prevent premature closure of discussion. A member of the project team may be appointed to serve as the session facilitator; in this way, the manager can adopt an observer's role and not unduly influence the flow of ideas by his or her own responses. Efforts to refine, combine, and assign priorities to the ideas derived from brainstorming should follow only after the project has been thoroughly discussed and all participants have had an opportunity to express themselves.

Along similar lines, an *opportunity analysis* may be used to raise the enthusiasm and morale of those involved and to implant more positive attitudes toward the project among the staff. Periodic sessions are held to discuss the current status of the project and to explore opportunities that may be presented. Although many of the ideas generated in such sessions may not be relevant to the more pressing requirements of the project, an effective program manager cannot afford to overlook any possibilities in a preoccupation with mere status quo procedures.

Ideas about project activities also can be elicited and refined through the use of the *Delphi technique*. This technique involves an iterative process whereby a series of interrogations is conducted (usually through the use of questionnaires) using a panel of knowledgeable individuals. The Delphi approach is characterized by three fairly elementary concepts: anonymity, controlled feedback, and statistical-group response. The free exchange of brainstorming is replaced by a formal exchange of information under the control of a steering group or exercise manager. Responses are not matched with respondents, and the identity of the participants often is not revealed until the end of the exercise. After each iteration, the information is fed back to the participants so that they may revise their earlier responses (and often, modify their attitudes concerning the project). After several iterations, opinions tend to converge with feedback. Rather than forcing unanimity, a statistical index is used to represent the group response. In this way, the pressures of conformity are reduced, and the opinion of every participant can play a greater role in the final determination of the group response.

Decision Loops

The preceding process implies a linear progression from defining project objectives, to examining performance requirements, to identifying the specific activities of the project. Although the logic of such a process is sound, seldom is it followed in a straightforward manner. Many decision loops are required during operations planning—some are relatively minor and some compel major changes in the whole project concept.

After the initial performance requirements have been stated, a series of broad trade-offs must be made, resulting in a decision on how much is to be spent (cost) for how good a product (effectiveness). During this process, it may be found that assumptions about one part of the project tend to place unreasonable requirements on some other parts. Assumptions may have to be changed, perhaps several times, to achieve an optimal design. It may be found that certain features of the project add significantly to the time duration; activities or even whole tasks may have to be modified to conform with schedule deadlines. Schedule risks may be reduced by spending extra money. Performance may be improved by increasing project costs by a few percent to take advantage of an emerging technology. It may be possible to accomplish project tasks partly in parallel, rather than totally in series, thereby permitting sufficient cost reductions to offset the costs associated with the additional resource requirements resulting from the overlap.

Work-Breakdown Schedule (WBS)

Project objectives must be linked together so that the manager can see the project in its true perspective—so that the relationships are clear between and among all the procedural steps. A WBS provides a preliminary outline or schematic of the way in which the supporting objectives can mesh together to ensure the attainment of the major objectives and goals. WBS has been used successfully in the private sector for a number of years. Most of us learned the fundamentals of this technique, albeit under a different name, when we were struggling with English composition in junior high school.

Divide and Subdivide

The basic idea of the WBS is to divide the total project into major tasks, then to subdivide these tasks into subtasks, the subtasks into activities, and so on. The project may be subdivided through as many levels as necessary to provide final work units of the desired size, that is, small enough to permit adequate visibility and control without creating an unwieldy administrative burden. The WBS should be detailed enough to allow the eventual construction of a project schedule that will reflect the significant relationships among events and activities. Excessive zeal in pushing the WBS into too many subdivisions, however, may create an unproductive management structure. Further, it is not necessary to extend the WBS to the same number of levels for all tasks. The structure should be flexible so that it can be expanded over time, in both depth and scope. Managers with different levels of responsibility may seek varying degrees of detail in the WBS.

A WBS can be used for a variety of purposes in addition to describing the tasks necessary to realize the operational objectives of a project or program. It can be used as a common framework for several project-management activities, such as budgeting and control of project costs; issuance of work authorizations; scheduling of work; reporting and monitoring the status of work activities; and tracking technical performance. In essence, a WBS can provide the manager with an important tool for the integration of planning and control functions at various responsibility and authority levels within an organization. It also serves as an important mechanism for the communication of project-management information.

The WBS Format

A WBS should be structured in a consistent manner, according to some orderly identification scheme. This structure should allow for expansion, if necessary, during the time required to complete the project. Such a structural approach is provided through a so-called indented-decimal system. The decimal format makes it easy to build the WBS into a management information system and to develop inputs into a managerial accounting system. For example, account codes can be expanded to include the numerics of a project's WBS so that the project manager can monitor costs at various levels of activity.

The first division (1.0, 2.0, 3.0, and so on) represents the major tasks of the project associated with the major operational objectives. The second level (1.1, 1.2, 2.1, 2.2, and so on) represents the further breakdown of tasks into subtasks. The third level (1.1.1, 1.1.2, 1.1.3, and so on) begins to identify specific-activity clusters or job assignments that are required to successfully carry out the subtasks. Subtasks and activities are logical divisions of larger tasks and should be distinct from each other. No task should be divided into a single activity—just as Ms. Finch, our eighth-grade English composition teacher, used to drill into our heads, if there is a 1.1.1, there must be a 1.1.2. It also is important to maintain the integrity of the task hierarchy—to guard against the misplacement of activities under an inappropriate subtask or to repeat the same activity under more than one subtask. Each entry in the WBS should have its own unique descriptive title or brief identifier to distinguish it from other work units.

Since there is no need to provide the same level of subtask division for each task, flexibility of the schedule can be maintained. This is especially important in the early stages of a project. In fact, the WBS can be sent out to various personnel with the work divided into major tasks only. As project planning is refined, the major tasks can be subdivided. In addition, by issuing a first, gross draft of a WBS, the project manager allows for the fuller participation of affected personnel. Such a process may result in a better WBS and more successful project. At a minimum, however, such a process allows relevant personnel to participate in the planning of program scheduling, monitoring, and control. Through the allowance of opportunities for such participation on the part of potential project personnel, greater cooperation and understanding of the project may be anticipated as well as a higher potential for realizing a successful project.

Gantt and Milestone Charts

Contemporary scheduling techniques can be traced back to the work of pioneers in the field of scientific management, such as Frederick Taylor and Henry Laurence Gantt. Taylor's time-and-motion studies are familiar to students of industrial engineering and administration. Gantt charts form the basis for many modern production-scheduling systems. The relative simplicity of the Gantt chart is one reason why this technique continues to receive widespread application. The so-called time-line diagram is one of the more common forms of Gantt charts used today.

The Momentum of Facts

Gantt reasoned that management decisions that affect the future must be based on information as to what has happened in the past. Knowing that a certain amount of work has been completed is useful in making such decisions. Gantt concluded, however, that the manager must also know when the work took place and the rate at which it was done. In other words, the manager must understand the relationship of facts to time, that is, the importance of the momentum of those facts. The Gantt chart compares what was done with what has to be done. It records the actual progress made in the implementation of the program. If that progress is not satisfactory, it can help uncover the why.

The Gantt chart was the first tool of management that permitted application of the principle of management by exception. Rather than monitor each and every activity, the manager can focus attention on the deviations from the operations plan and take the necessary actions to bring the operations back in line with the projected program. The Gantt chart also provides a basis for fixing responsibility for success or failure. Cause-and-effect relationships and their time dimensions are brought out more clearly. As a consequence, the manager is able to foresee future happenings with greater accuracy.

The Gantt Chart in Application

Each division of space in the Gantt chart represents an amount of work to be done in a specified amount of time. Lines drawn horizontally through that space show the relation of the amount of work actually done to the amount scheduled in that period. Equal divisions of space on a single horizontal line represent: (1) equal time divisions, (2) varying amounts of work scheduled, and (3) varying amounts of work completed. Thus, the Gantt chart shows the relation of time spent to work accomplished.

Assume that a work schedule, as shown in table 10-1 is adopted. The variations in the numbers may be the result of differences in the availability of staff or equipment, other project assignments, or any number of other reasons. The work schedule is converted to a Gantt chart, as shown in figure 10-3. The numbers under each day represent: (1) daily production on the left, and (2) total production scheduled to date on the right. To record the work completed, a line is drawn through the daily space to show a comparison between the scheduled and actual accomplishment. On Monday, for example, the space represents 100 work units, but only 75 units were done, so a light line is drawn through 75 percent of the space. On Tuesday, 125 units were planned; 100 were completed, so a line is drawn through 80 percent of the space; note that the daily space is always relative to the number

Table 10-1
Weekly Work-Unit Schedule

Days of the Week	*Work Units*
Monday	100
Tuesday	125
Wednesday	150
Thursday	150
Friday	150

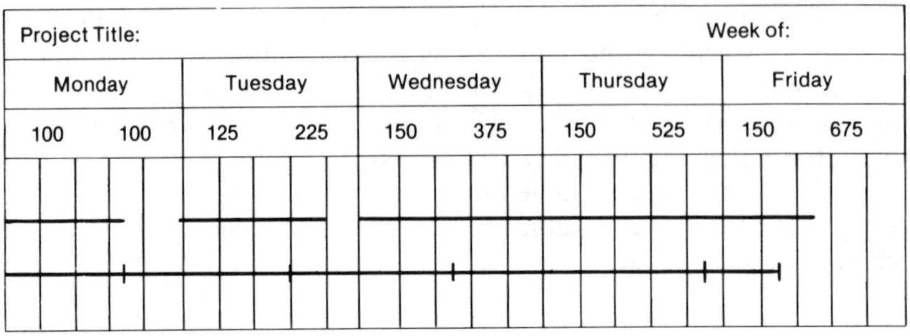

Project Title:				Week of:
Monday	Tuesday	Wednesday	Thursday	Friday
100 100	125 225	150 375	150 525	150 675

Figure 10–3. Gantt Chart

of work units scheduled. Since the subdivisions of the daily space represent percentages, it is common practice to divide the space into 5 to 10 subunits.

It also is desirable to know how the whole week's work compares with the schedule; a heavier line is added to the chart to show this comparison. On Monday, the heavy line is the same length as the light line. Of the 100 work units completed on Tuesday, 25 must go to make up the shortage for Monday. The remaining units are applied to Tuesday's schedule and the heavy line is drawn through 60 percent of the Tuesday space (that is, 100 minus 25 equals 75; 75 divided by 125 equals 60 percent). Of the 150 work units completed on Wednesday, 50 are required to meet the schedule through Tuesday night, and the remaining 100 units are applied to Wednesday's schedule of 150, the heavy line being drawn through 67 percent of the daily space. The cumulative line shows that by Friday night, the work is approximately two-thirds of a day behind the week's schedule.

The completed Gantt chart shows: (1) the relation of the schedule to time, (2) the work completed in relation to both time and the schedule, and (3) the cumulative work done and its relation to time and the schedule. An important feature of the Gantt chart is its compactness. It has been estimated that the information concentrated on a single Gantt chart would require as many as thirty-five charts if shown on more traditional production charts.

Shortcomings of Original Charting Techniques

The application of Gantt charts to relatively large-scale engineering projects soon revealed some fundamental weaknesses in this approach, including:

1. An inability to show interdependencies that exist among the tasks or activities represented by the bars

2. the inflexibility of a bar chart plotted against a calendar scale, which prevents it from easily reflecting slippage or changes in plans
3. an inability to reflect uncertainty or tolerances in the duration estimates for the various activities

The inability to show interdependencies is a serious deficiency when attempting to schedule a program or project in which various activities involve a large degree of concurrency, that is, overlapping of interrelated project activities. Using only a bar chart as reference, a manager often may overlook critical linkages between two or more activities, because conventional Gantt charts cannot display such relationships. The inability to reflect uncertainty in estimated durations can be critical in contemporary management.

Milestones Charts: An Important Step Forward

One relatively successful attempt to extend the capability of the Gantt chart to meet more contemporary project-management needs forms an important link in the evolution to current network-analysis techniques. This innovation is the milestone chart, used extensively in industry and the military prior to the development of Program Evaluation and Review Techniques (PERT). Milestones are key elements or points in time that can be identified in the progress of a program or project. A Milestone chart provides a sequential list of the various tasks to be accomplished in the program or project (tasks, in turn, can be broken down into specific activities if this level of detail is warranted). The milestone approach also increased awareness (if not effective display) of the interdependencies between tasks. The list of tasks and milestones are displayed on charts adjacent to a time scale. Symbols on the time scale identify the dates (or times) that each milestone is scheduled, when it is completed, if it has slipped, and so forth. The milestone approach also makes it possible to accumulate this information in machine-readable form and to code the data for various sorts or arrangements using electronic data-processing equipment. Thus, data can be presented in various ways: by organizational unit, by project and subproject, by performance status, and so forth.

Figure 10–4 illustrates a milestone chart for a simple project involving seven related tasks. The duration of each task is indicated by an elongated U-shaped symbol. To show how work is actually progressing, a line or bar can be drawn within the uprights of this symbol, the length of which represents the amount of work actually completed to date. Bars to the left of any observation point (for example, the end of the seventh week as indicated by the arrow) represent underaccomplishment, and those to the right represent overaccomplishment.

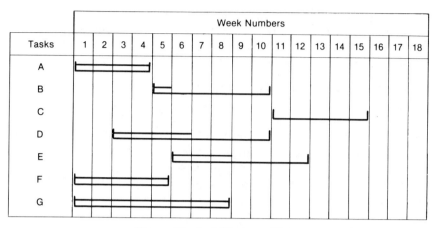

Figure 10–4. Milestone Chart

If the milestone chart in figure 10–4 has been filled in correctly and is examined at the end of the seventh week, the following information should be readily apparent:

Task B is dependent on the completion of task A, and task C cannot begin until tasks B and D have been completed.

Task E cannot begin until task F is completed, but all other tasks appear to be independent, that is, their durations tend to overlap.

Task A should be completed by the end of the seventh week and, in fact, is (although from this representation of the chart, we cannot tell if task A was done by the end of week four as scheduled).

Task B should be 50-percent completed but is only 17-percent finished.

Task C should not be started and, in fact, has not been.

Task D should be approximately 62-percent complete but is only 50-cent finished.

Task E should be 30-percent complete but, in fact, is approximately 43-percent complete.

Task F should be and is completed.

Task G should be 87-percent complete and, in fact, is totally complete.

Reasons for any delays can be noted on the chart by the use of codes or symbols. Thus, the milestone chart combines both the planning and recording of progress functions. For many tasks, the milestone chart is unsurpassed, and its use has been highly developed.

The milestone approach is not without limitations, however. Relationships among milestones are still not fully established. Although milestones are listed in chronological sequence, they are not necessarily related in a logical sequence, that is, not all the important interrelationships are displayed. Further, the milestone chart does not allow for measuring the effect of changes and slippages; it merely improves the reporting of them. Although the use of data-processing equipment provides a greatly improved sorting and listing capability, the full use of the computer is not achieved in milestone charting.

Network Analysis and the Critical-Path Method

The techniques of network analysis provide the most straight-forward way to "map" the various steps required to successfully implement a projector program. Network analysis produces a visual display of the tasks and activities to be performed in carrying out the program. More importantly, networking provides a basis for determining the order in which activities should be undertaken—their sequence and priority—and the critical linkages among activities. Even the most detailed and apparently complex networks are merely composites of a number of relatively simple networks. Therefore, by understanding the basic techniques of network analysis, the manager should be able to build as comprehensive an analysis as necessary to convey specific assignments to those responsible for carrying out activities.

The Origins of Network Analysis

The use of network analysis is not new; these techniques have been used by industrial managers in production planning since the turn of the century. Industrial engineers developed process-flow charts and programming techniques prior to World War II that are quite similar to methods of network analysis, which form the basis for PERT. Similarly, business analysts for many years have used a work-programming approach that parallels the network algorithms used in both PERT and the critical-path method (CPM).

An investigation was launched at E.I. DuPont de Nemours in 1956 to determine the extent to which the emerging capacity of high-speed computers might be applied to improve the planning, scheduling, and progress reporting of the company's engineering projects. Morgan R. Walker, a DuPont engineer, and James E. Kelley, Jr., a Remington-Rand computer specialist, worked on the problem, and, late in 1957, they ran a pilot test of a unique arrow diagram or network method. This network approach came to be known as the critical-path method.

Concurrently, the U.S. Navy Special Projects Office (SPO), Bureau of Ordinance, established a research team to work on a similar strategy. The assignment of the SPO team was a project called PERT, which was aimed at formulating techniques for the efficient management of huge, complicated weapons-systems-development projects (in this case, the polaris submarine). What emerged was an approach to solve some of the fast multiplying problems of large-scale projects in which technical innovation, complex logistics, and concurrent activities must be integrated. PERT is credited (along with a dedicated, project-oriented management) with making it possible for the Navy to produce an operational ballistic-missile-firing nuclear submarine years ahead of schedule. The actual benefits of PERT in the polaris project are subject to question; a great deal of press agentry surrounded the effort at the time. Subsequently, PERT was adapted and extended to hundreds of management situations, setting a pattern for management information and management control systems of the future.

Similarities between CPM and PERT

Pert is more sophisticated than the CPM approach, since it is designed to deal with large-scale projects characterized by (1) unclear objectives, (2) multiple and/or overlapping management responsibilities, (3) relatively high levels of uncertainty as to time requirements and costs, (4) complex problems of logistics, and (5) problems of sufficient complexity to justify the use of the computer. CPM, on the other hand, has been described as a "back-of-an-envelope" or "in-the-field" approach, with much less dependence on data-processing and computer-programming experience. CPM techniques are particularly applicable to well-defined projects under the direction of a single management with relatively limited levels of uncertainty.

As both of these methods have been revised and improved, attractive features of one approach have been incorporated into the other. The arrow diagram or network is common to both methods. It is necessary to identify a critical path in the development of a PERT network, and the "three time estimates" used in PERT (as a means of dealing with uncertainty) can also be applied in CPM. In current applications, the differences are found in the format of the diagrams rather than in the underlying conceptual framework.

The CPM has proven useful in guiding elemental as well as complex public projects and programs. CPM is relatively easy to understand and apply and, further, can be used as a convenient tool to communicate program-activity assignments. For these reasons, the techniques of CPM will serve as the major focus in the balance of this chapter.

Application of CPM

A CPM network essentially is a graphic plan of action, it provides a visual depiction of operational objectives and linkages among related program activities. CPM facilitates the selection of a best route to be followed to reach these objectives and also identifies potential obstacles and delays that might be encountered along the way. CPM can assist program managers in recognizing the relationship of the parts to the whole and in determining which activities actually control significant completion times.

To illustrate these procedures, assume that the operational objective is to establish a new prenatal-health-care clinic. Three component tasks must be initiated to accomplish this objective: (1) adequate space must be secured and equipped for the clinic, (2) a clinic staff must be recruited, trained, and certified, and (3) the programs of the clinic must be publicized and eligible applicants must be screened and enrolled. The following subtasks and activities might be identified as part of this project (shown in a WBS format):

1.0 Secure and equip space for the clinic
   1.1 locate appropriate space for the clinic
   1.2 negotiate rental contract on clinic space
   1.3 equip office and clinic space
      1.3.1 make physical modifications to rented space, as necessary, to accomodate clinic layout
      1.3.2 order office equipment for the clinic
      1.3.3 order medical supplies, drugs, and other materials
      1.3.4 order office supplies and materials
   1.4 open clinic to eligible applicants

2.0 Train and certify clinic staff
   2.1 hire/assign clinic staff
   2.2 orient staff to agency procedures
   2.3 train staff in clinic operations
   2.4 certify professional and volunteer staff members

3.0 Publicize programs and screen applicants
   3.1 develop informational materials on clinic programs
   3.2 publicize the availability of the clinic and its programs
   3.3 screen initial applicants for eligibility and complete their enrollment in the program

Often in brainstorming a project, ideas will flow in a somewhat unstructured fashion, and this approach should be encouraged to ensure that all ideas get out on the table. The WBS format helps to organize these subtasks and activities into logically related clusters.

To further establish the links between various activities, three basic questions must be asked about each activity: (1) What must be done before this activity can begin? (2) What must immediately follow this activity? (3) What activities can be undertaken concurrently? The answers to these three questions identify the predecessor-successor relationships among the activities and subtasks.

The following statements might be assumed to reflect the initial perceptions as to the linkages among the fourteen activities and subtasks that comprise the operations plan for the establishment of this prenatal-health-care clinic.

1. Locating the clinic space (1.1) and hiring and/or assigning staff to work in the clinic (2.1) are the initial subtasks of the project and can be performed concurrently.
2. Ordering office equipment (1.3.2) must follow after the rental contract for the clinic space has been negotiated (1.2).
3. Developing the appropriate layout of the space (1.3.1) is dependent, in part, on the receipt of office equipment (1.3.2) and securing office supplies and materials (1.3.4).
4. Staff members cannot be certified (2.4) until they have been hired and/or assigned (2.1), oriented (2.2), and trained (2.3).
5. The orientation and training of the staff can be carried out concurrently.
6. Publicity on the clinic programs (3.2) must precede the screening and enrollment of eligible applicants (3.3).
7. Program publicity cannot begin until space has been secured (1.2) and program information has been developed (3.1).
8. The new clinic can be opened only after all other activities have been completed.

Table 10-2 illustrates these relationships in a somewhat more formal and ordered manner than available from the initial perceptions. These relationships can easily be converted into an arrow diagram, the initial portrayal of a CPM network. If an activity is donated as a direct link between two nodes (events) in a network, an arrow (symbolizing the activity) indicates the direction of dependency and time flow from one node to another. A dependency relationship is assumed to mean that, before the dependent activity

Table 10-2
**Linkages and Predecessor-Successor Relationships for the Establishment
of a Prenatal-Health-Care Clinic**

Activity	Linked to:	Preceded by:	Followed by:
1.1	(1.2), (1.3.4)	None	(1.2), (1.3.4)
1.2	(1.1), (1.3.2), (3.1)	(1.1)	(1.3.2), (3.1)
1.3.1	(1.4), (1.3.2), (1.3.2)	(1.3.2), (1.3.4)	(1.4)
1.3.2	(1.2), (1.3.1)	(1.2)	(1.3.1)
1.3.3	(1.3.4), (1.4)	(1.3.4)	(1.4)
1.3.4	(1.1), (1.3.1), (1.3.3)	(1.1)	(1.3.1), (1.3.3)
1.4	(1.3.1), (1.3.3), (3.3)	(1.3.1), (1.3.3), (3.3)	None
2.1	(2.2), (2.3)	None	(2.2), (2.3)
2.2	(2.1), (2.4)	(2.1)	(2.4)
2.3	(2.1), (2.4)	(2.1)	(2.4)
2.4	(2.2), (2.3), (3.3)	(2.2), (2.3)	(3.3)
3.1	(1.2), (3.2)	(1.2)	(3.2)
3.2	(3.1), (3.3)	(3.1)	(3.3)
3.3	(1.4), (2.4), (3.2)	(2.4), (3.2)	(1.4)

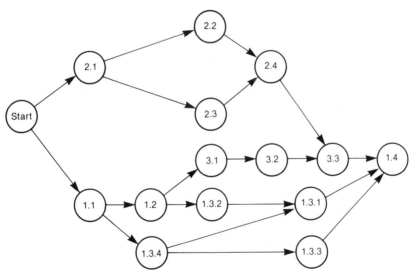

Figure 10-5. Arrow Diagram for Prenatal-Health-Care Clinic

can be initiated, the other related activity must be completed. Table 10-2
can be translated into an arrow diagram as shown in figure 10-5.

Since the nodes in the arrow diagram represent the completion of an
activity (that is, an event), the term *start* is used to anchor the initiation of

the network. Each arrow represents a linkage between events; more than one arrow can designate the same activity. For example, the two arrows that terminate at node 2.4 represent the activity of staff certification. This approach has certain advantages in determining time durations and in delimiting the critical path, as will be illustrated subsequently.

The arrow diagram is composed of a series of sequential relationships or paths. Each path should be completed in the indicated sequence in order for the various activities to be carried out in proper relation one to another and for the overall project to be successfully implemented. Once the various connections have been drawn, a critical route can be determined and progress can be more easily followed and measured against key check points or milestones.

Calculations on the Network

Each activity (arrow) in the diagram/network requires a specific amount of time to complete, called its *duration*. The next step in the CPM process, therefore, is to assign time estimates to each of the paths.

Suggested durations for each of the fourteen activities in the prenatal-health-care project have been loaded on to the arrows in the network in figure 10–6. Each arrow (activity) leading to a given node (event or activity completion) is assigned the duration for the designated activity. In this way, all the possible paths to that node can be easily traced. No effort has been made at this point to draw the diagram to a time scale.

Beginning at start, the time durations for each path should be summed to determine: (1) the earliest possible time that an activity that terminates at a given node can be completed—this is known as the earliest possible occurrence (EPO); (2) how long it will take to complete the entire project (project duration); (3) which activities establish and control the project duration (the critical path); (4) how much leeway (float) there is in the activities that do not control the project duration. In figure 10–6, for example, the path from start to 2.1 (assign/hire staff) to 2.2 (orient staff) to 2.4 (certify staff) would take 8 time units, whereas the path from start to 2.1 to 2.3 (train staff) to 2.4 would take 11 time units. Therefore, the EPO for the completion of activity 2.4 is 11 time units. Other activities dependent on the completion of staff certification (for example, screening of applicants) cannot begin until 11 time units into the project.

The EPO of the final activity node has added significance—it is the earliest possible completion time for the entire project. Thus, activity 1.4 (opening of the clinic) cannot begin until 15 time units into the project and has a duration of 1 time unit. Therefore, the project duration for establishing a new prenatal-health-care clinic is 16 time units.

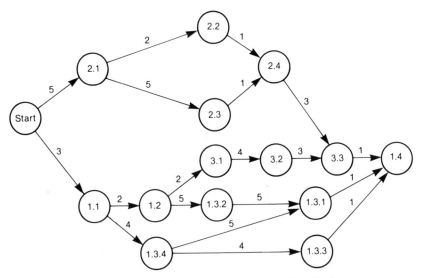

Figure 10-6. Arrow Diagram with Duration Estimates

Operational Leeway—Float

The amount of time that an activity can be delayed or its duration extended without affecting the EPO of any other activity is its *float*. To determine this operational leeway, calculations must be made by taking the EPO of the final node and subtracting the time durations back to the nodes that lead to this final activity. This process is repeated for each node, in turn, back to start. These calculations determine the latest possible occurrence (LPO), that is, the latest time that the activities terminating at a given node can finish without causing the project duration to exceed the originally determined project duration.

Whereas, the EPO is the longest path from start to a given node, the LPO is the shortest path from the termination of the project back to a given node. The EPO and LPO for each given node is given in figure 10-7; float is the difference between the EPO and LPO.

The Critical Path

It should be clear that no activity with a positive float can control the duration of the entire project. The durations of these activities can be shortened as much as is physically possible or extended by an amount equal to the

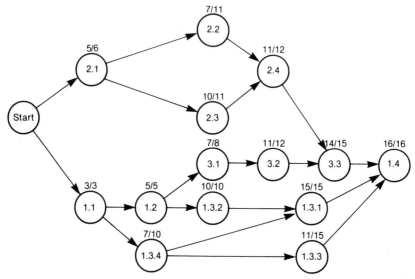

Figure 10-7. Arrow Diagram Showing EPO/LPO for Each Activity Node

float that they possess without affecting the EPO of any other activity. This means that the EPO of the last activity node will not be affected and, thus, that the project duration will not be altered. This characteristic of float limits the search for critical activities to those that have a float of zero.

Not all activities with zero floats control the project duration, however. The activities that do control are the ones that have zero float and form a continuous path, starting at the first activity and ending at the last one. In figure 10-7, this path is made up of the links between 1.1, 1.2, 1.3.2, 1.3.1, and 1.4. If any of these activities are delayed, the project-completion time will increase by the amount of that delay. It is this sequence of activities that defines the critical path.

Summary of CPM Procedures

The preceding discussion can best be summarized by listing the steps involved in applying the CPM to a project or program:

1. Define all the activities that make up the project or program
2. define the linkages and sequence of performance for each activity

3. draw an arrow diagram that defines the sequence of performing the various activities
4. estimate the duration of each activity
5. calculate the EPO and LPO for each activity node
6. determine the float for each activity (LPO minus EPO)
7. locate the critical path, that is, those activities with zero float that form a continuous sequence from the beginning to the end of the diagram

Once the actual program or project is implemented, the critical path can be monitored continually so that any potential delays can be determined before they occur. Such delays can be avoided by shifting personnel, materials, or other resource inputs to the critical path from those paths that have float. Therefore, the identification of the critical path also provides the manager with a dynamic-control mechanism.

In addition, the CPM network offers a convenient form of shorthand to express a complex set of relations. It offers a medium of communication and prediction. And it facilitates the subdivision of work so that each person involved can proceed with the more detailed planning of his or her own part of the project or program.

The CPM approach provides a basis for an analysis of the costs involved when utilizing float time to reduce overall project costs. Or in many instances, where the critical path time is to be reduced, CPM can assist in the determination of the cost of a crash program. In general, the CPM approach determines (1) the sequential ordering of activities, (2) the maximum time required to complete the project or program, (3) the costs involved, and (4) the ramifications in time and costs for altering the critical path.

Crash Scheduling

There may be a temptation to schedule activities on the critical path on a "crash" basis, that is, to use all available staff resources to complete the critical activities as they occur in the operations plan. Depending on the nature of the project, however, such crash scheduling may merely result in a shift in the critical path to other activities having minimal float. It also may produce a staffing overload, whereby too many resources are assigned over too short a period. The result may be increased inefficiency as staff members get in each other's way. Crash scheduling at the outset of a project may use up a management option that may become important later on when the project is operational. The ability to crash on a critical-path activity when it falls behind schedule is an important aspect of dynamic program management.

Estimating Durations: The Problem of Uncertainty

Often a manager is unable to predict the exact duration of any given activity in a program or project. The time estimate chosen may reflect the most probable value of an unknown distribution function. If the variance of this distribution is relatively small, the most likely duration may provide a reasonably close approximation of the actual time required to complete the activity. If the variance is large, however, the duration is said to be "uncertain."

The problem of uncertainty is frequently cited as a justification for not applying network-analysis techniques in the public sector. Public programs, this argument holds, are often too uncertain to apply the rigor of network analysis. This argument is fallacious, however, since these techniques were first developed and applied in industry and in the military because of uncertainty in time estimates.

It often is difficult to determine the exact distribution function and variance of activities in any program or project. Therefore, two possibilities exist: to use a single time estimate, or to assume some form of probability-distribution function and proceed to establish a range of confidence for the resulting time estimates. The original PERT team took the latter approach—to estimate time requirements to achieve a given event, together with a measure of uncertainty regarding these estimates. These efforts led to the adoption of the so-called beta distribution formula, as shown here:

$$t_e = 1/6(t_a + 4t_b + t_c)$$

where: t_a = the most optimistic time estimate

t_b = the most likely time estimate

t_c = the most pessimistic time estimate

The beta distribution or expected time formula is based on the assumption that the duration of any activity or project is unimodal, that is, only one mode exists—b) and that the variance of the distribution is the square of the standard deviation, which, in turn, can be estimated as roughly one-sixth of the range (that is, the difference between t_a and t_c.

The application of the beta distribution formula is relatively simple. When some doubt exists as to the appropriate duration to assign to any activity, the manager should ask those who will be responsible for carrying out the activity: "If everything goes right with this job, what is the shortest time you will require to complete this activity?" Then the manager should ask: "If everything goes wrong—if the absolute worst happens—what is the longest time required to complete this activity?" Finally, assuming the range established by the answers to the first two questions, the manager should ask: "What is the most likely time required to complete this activity?"

To gain a clear understanding of how the beta distribution formula can be applied under conditions of uncertainty, consider the following three examples.

Example 1. Assume that the most optimistic time for the completion of some activity is 10 days; the most likely time in the judgment of the staff is 15 days; and the most pessimistic time is 20 days. Applying the formula for t_e, the estimated time for completion would be:

$$t_e = 1/6(10 + 4 \times 15 + 20) = 15$$

Thus the most likely time and the computed time estimate are the same, which follows from the fact that the distribution of variance approximates a normal curve. The standard deviation in this example is 1.67 days (that is, the most pessimistic time minus the most optimistic time, divided by 6).

Example 2. Assume that the most optimistic and most likely time estimates remain the same (10 and 15 days respectively) but that the most pessimistic time estimate is extended to 26 days due to the uncertainty surrounding the completion of various tasks. These conditions result in a distribution that is skewed to the left. Therefore the computed time estimate lies to the right of the most likely time (that is, t_e is larger than the most likely time). Applying the beta-distribution formula, t_e equals 16 days (that is, 10 + 4(15) + 26, divided by 6), and the standard deviation in this example is 2.67 days.

Example 3. In the final example, the most likely and pessimistic time estimates are the same as in the first example (15 and 20 days respectively), and the most optimistic time estimate is reduced to 5 days. This results in a distribution that is skewed to the right, with t_e at 14.17 days smaller than the most likely time. The standard deviation in this example is 2.5 days (that is, 20 minus 5, divided by 6).

Relationship between Expected Time and Variance

As may be seen from these three examples, expected time and variance—although statistically related—act somewhat independently in real-world situations. Expected time corresponds to "average" or "mean" in common language—there is a 50 percent probability that the estimated time will be exceeded by the actual duration. Variance, on the other hand, is a measure of uncertainty. If the variance is large, there is greater uncertainty as to the time in which the activity will be completed. If the variance is small, it follows that the uncertainty will be small. Thus, although the estimated time in the third example is less than in the first (14.17 days as compared to 15 days), there is greater uncertainty in the third example, as illustrated by the larger variance (that is, the square of the standard deviation or 6.25 days).

The concept of variance can be used to evaluate the risk or probability of meeting a specific time schedule. An F value can be determined by subtracting the earliest possible occurrence from any given activity completion from some imposed schedule-completion time (S) and dividing the result by the standard deviation for that activity. By consulting a table of values for the normal curve, this F value can then be interpreted in terms of the probability of meeting the imposed schedule.

To illustrate these procedures, assume that the project duration of the 16 weeks in the prenatal-health-care-clinic project had a standard deviation of 2 weeks. What is the probability of completing this project in, say, 15 weeks? The calculations to determine the F value are as follows:

$$F = \frac{\text{Imposed schedule deadline minus expected duration}}{\text{Standard deviation of expected duration}}$$

$$= \frac{14 - 15}{2} = -0.5.$$

From the table of values for the standard normal-distribution function, it can be determined that the value for an entry of -0.5 is 0.3085. In other words, there is approximately a 31 percent chance of the project being completed in 15 weeks.

Assume that with an estimated duration of 16 weeks, the manager of the project is given 17 weeks in which to carry out the assignment (again with a 2-week standard deviation). What is the probability of completing the project within this extended time allocation? The F value of $+0.5$ in this is 0.6915; in other words, increasing the duration of the project to 17 weeks raises the probability of success from 50 percent to 69 percent.

This method of assessing risk can be applied in reverse to determine an appropriate duration for any activity in a project (or for the total-project duration), given some acceptable level of risk (as determined by the project manager or decision maker). Again using the expected duration in the prenatal-health-care-clinic project, assume that a 20 percent level of risk is chosen. What time duration should be allowed for the completion of the project? The appropriate formula is as follows:

$$\text{Imposed schedule deadline} = F(\text{standard deviation of } t_e) + t_e$$

The F value for a 20-percent level of risk (that is, an 80-percent probability of success) is approximately 0.843. Therefore, the project duration to achieve this projected level of success would be: 0.843(2) plus 16 or approximately 17.7 weeks. To raise the probability of success to a 90-percent level (10-percent level of risk) would require approximately 2.5 additional weeks (or a total of 18.5 weeks), whereas to approach a success level of 100 percent would require nearly 7.75 weeks beyond the 16-week duration. The F values for various probabilities of success are provided in table 10–3.

This brief discussion provides an important insight into the concept of risk based on the normal distribution function. It may be possible to reduce the level of risk (increase the probability of success) from the 50-percent level assumed by the beta distribution by adding a relatively small amount of time to the estimated project duration (t_e). However, the increments of time required become increasingly larger beyond the 90-percent level of success, often beyond any realistic expectations. Changes in the standard deviation of the expected duration will have a significant impact on the additional time required to increase the probability of success. Reducing the standard deviation (reducing the uncertainty) will reduce the additional duration required for any chosen level of success.

In most situations, the three-time-estimate approach of the beta distribution gives a more pessimistic outlook than would be obtained by using only the most likely duration. Staff members have a tendency to "hedge their bets" when asked to provide three time estimates, that is, to be more conservative. In many projects, the manager should use the best time estimate possible and then control the project in a dynamic fashion. In short, regardless of how the estimate of time is obtained, a major responsibility of management is to control the project or program once it is implemented.

Table 10–3
F Values for Various Levels of Risk/Probability of Success

Probability of Success (percent)	F Value
55	0.1208543
60	0.2516285
65	0.3821697
70	0.5225311
75	0.6727744
80	0.8429417
85	1.0428190
90	1.2825607
95	1.6417270
100	3.8700000

The Bridge between Planning Processes

At the outset of this discussion, a planning continuum, which spans strategic planning, management planning, and operations planning, was identified. Although the focus of this chapter has been on strategic and operations planning, management planning is the bridge between these two processes. In the strategic-planning process, management must determine the goals and objectives of the organization and the main strategies (policies and programs) for achieving these goals. Operations planning takes these goals, objectives, and strategies as givens and seeks to plan and schedule activities that will lead to their effective and efficient achievement. A basic responsibility of management planning is to identify and budget the wherewithal of financial resources and personnel to implement agreed-on program objectives and to provide the framework for an integrated management system to control and evaluate the use of these resources. In short, management planning is the inherent focus of this entire book.

In practice, operations planning, scheduling, and control activities tend to become institutionalized, and this tendency can place a damper on the more creative activities required in strategic planning.[11] Although private organizations are turning increasingly to the concept of strategic planning as a framework for decision making, public organizations need strategy far more than do profit-making entities.

> Their goals are more complex, their sources of support are more complex, and the interaction between their support and performance is more complex. Consequently, the problem of identifying optimal policies and potential strategies must be inherently more complex. In fact, most institutions would find their planning and policy formulation much easier if they were profit-making organizations. Then at least they would have a common denominator for their objectives and strategies.[12]

Notes

1. Charles E. Lindblom, "The Science of 'Muddling Through,'" *Public Administration Review* 19 (1959):79–88; Charles E. Lindblom and David Braybrooke, *A Strategy of Decision* (New York: Free Press of Glencoe, 1964); Charles E. Lindblom, *The Intelligence of Democracy: Decision Making through Mutual Adjustment* (New York: Free Press, 1965).

2. Lindblom, *Intelligence of Democracy;* Aaron Wildavsky, *The Politics of the Budgetary Process* (Boston: Little, Brown, 1964).

3. B.W. Scott, *Long-Range Planning in American Industry* (New York: American Management Association, 1965), p. 63.

4. Anthony J. Catanese and Alan Walter Steiss, *Systemic Planning:*

Theory and Application (Lexington, Mass.: Lexington Books, D.C. Heath, 1970), chap. 16. Also see "The 'Next Generation' of Planners," *Journal of Housing* 23 (December 1966):633–635; "An Action Programmes Model for Governmental Comprehensive Planning," *Annals of Collective Economy* 38 (July–September 1967):237–250; "Systemic Planning for Very Complex Systems," *Planning Outlook* 5 (August 1968):7–27; "Systemic Planning," *Ekistics: 1968* 26 (August 1968):179–184; and "The Search for a Systems Approach to the Planning of Complex Urban Systems," *PLAN, The Journal of the Town Planning Institute of Canada* 10 (1969):39–51.

5. Robert N. Anthony and Glenn A. Welsch, *Fundamentals of Management Accounting* (Homewood, Ill.: Richard D. Irwin, 1974), p. 303.

6. Alan Walter Steiss, *Public Budgeting and Management* (Lexington, Mass.: Lexington Books, D.C. Heath and Co., 1972), p. 148.

7. Adapted from ibid., chap 9.

8. For a further discussion of these procedures, see: N.B. Mutunayagam, " Cooperative Management: An Alternative Approach to Multijurisdictional Management of Resources" (Ph.D. diss., Virginia Polytechnic Institute and State University, 1981).

9. Franklyn H. Beal, "Defining Development Objectives," in *Principles and Practices of Urban Planning,* ed. William I. Goodman and Eric C. Freund (Washington, D.C.: International City Management Association, 1968), pp. 327–348.

10. Ibid., p. 338.

11. Robert N. Anthony and Regina Herzlinger, *Management Control in Nonprofit Organizations* (Homewood, Ill.: Richard D. Irwin, 1975), p. 183.

12. *Strategy for Institutions* (Boston, Mass.: Boston Consulting Group, 1970).

11 Auditing and Management Control

The audit function has been an integral part of the process of financial management for many years. More recently, however, the financial and compliance emphasis, which has been the traditional focus of auditing, has been greatly expanded, and new audit functions have been recognized. The impetus for this broader approach emerged from the 1973 publication by the U.S. Comptroller General entitled: *Standards for Audit of Governmental Organizations, Programs, Activities, and Functions.* In this publication, the objectives of the financial and compliance type of audit have been extended to include what has come to be known as *operational* or *performance auditing.* To more fully understand the procedures of performance auditing, it is first necessary to comprehend the basic objectives of more traditional auditing practices.

Auditing Objectives: Accountability or Management Control?

Peter McMickle and Gene Elrod offer the following comprehensive definition of auditing:

> Auditing is an analytical *process* consisting of preparation, conduct (examination and evaluation), reporting (communication), and settlement. The basic *elements* of this process are: an independent, competent, and professional auditor who executes the process upon an auditee for an audit recipient. The *scope* or area of concern can involve matters of the following nature: financial (accounting, error, fraud, financial controls, fairness of financial statements, etc.), and/or compliance (faithful adherence to administrative and legal requirements, policies, regulations, etc.), and/or performance (economy, efficiency, and/or effectiveness of operational controls, management information systems, programs, etc.). The *objective* or purpose of auditing can be some combination of accountability and management control.[1]

This conceptual framework identifies two objectives of auditing: accountability and management control. These two terms frequently appear in the literature of public management and auditing. Their exact relation, however, is somewhat unsettled.

Accountability and Responsibility

Most dictionaries define *accountability* as synonymous with *responsibility*. Observation of current usage, however, would suggest that accountability generally implies a higher or stronger degree of obligation than does responsibility. There also is the implication that a person may be responsible for many things, but formally accountable only for certain things. In other words, accountability, in some instances, may be more restricted in scope than responsibility, even though the degree of obligation is greater. Hence, one may be responsible for doing a satisfactory job but formally accountable only for safeguarding certain assets.

Some authorities go a step further, stating that, to also be accountability, responsibility must be "specified and measurable." This appears to be a logical requirement, for it seems unfair to hold a person accountable for vague, unclear, or implied responsibilities. Yet, in reality, managers are sometimes held accountable for certain responsibilities that are only implied and/or are difficult to measure. Therefore, for purposes of this discussion, *accountability* will be defined as: the state of being held answerable or formally responsible for certain specified or implied performance.

The most basic accountability relation involves two parties—a higher authority and a subordinate. This basic relation is quite common and can arise for various reasons. It may evolve naturally, as when one person needs assistance to accomplish certain objectives that are beyond his or her physical ability, for example, beyond the "span of control." Such relations are most often intentionally created and form the foundation for organization theory and management hierarchies in both public and private sectors. This relation can also exist between groups of individuals and organizations. For example, state agencies may be accountable to federal agencies relative to the management of federal grant-in-aid programs.

Thus, the concept of accountability implies the existence of authority, responsibility, and control. There is the further implication that: (1) a person or organization is answerable or formally responsible for certain specified or implied performance, (2) the actual performance will be reviewed, and (3) as a result, appropriate action (controls or sanctions) may be taken by the higher authority.

Auditing as an Accountability Device

Historically, auditing has referred to those reviews conducted by an independent auditor for the primary objective of accountability. Usually, auditing is not the only accountability device in such situations. Production reports, information from other managers, and general observations, for example, also contribute to the flow of accountability. Audit techniques enhance the objective of accountability for two reasons: (1) the independence and competence of the auditor add credence to the audit (accountability) report, and (2) auditing can provide an added dimension of information—advice and recommendations.

The objective of the traditional financial audit is to verify that all transactions have been properly processed and recorded in compliance with legal restrictions. The financial audit involves a systematic examination of source documents, records, and procedures relating to financial transactions. For example, a number of interlocking checks are examined with regard to the assessment and collection of property taxes. Assessment procedures are examined; for example, a sample of properties are compared with the tax rolls to determine if any taxable property has been omitted. Tax payments on a sample of individual properties are traced to bank deposits. Outstanding property-taxes receivable are tested to verify that, in fact, they are uncollected. Any adjustments or write-offs of taxes receivable are checked for proper authorization. These and similar procedures covering other types of transactions and related balance-sheet items enable the auditor to form an opinion regarding the statement as a whole. The ultimate objective is to ensure that the financial statement produced from the accounting records accurately reflects the financial stewardship of public officials entrusted with these fiscal responsibilities.[2]

Although the independent audit function is most often carried out "after the fact," (the so-called postaudit after the close of the fiscal year), *internal audit controls* are being mandated for public agencies with increasing frequency. The objectives of such internal controls are described in the following statement, which appears in reports by independent auditors engaged in an examination of the adequacy of an agency's internal controls:

> The objective of internal accounting control is to provide reasonable, but not absolute, assurance as to the safeguarding of assets against loss from unauthorized use or disposition, and the reliability of financial records for preparing financial statements and maintaining accountability for assets. The concept of reasonable assurance recognizes that the cost of a system of internal control should not exceed the benefits derived and also recognizes that the evaluation of these factors necessarily requires estimates and judgements by management.[3]

There are inherent limitations in such internal controls, however: (1) Errors can result from misunderstanding of instructions, judgmental mistakes, carelessness, or other "human frailties." (2) Control procedures that depend on segregation of duties can be circumvented by collusion. (3) Procedures may become inadequate because of changing conditions and/or deterioration of the degree of compliance with such procedures.[4]

The scope of auditing has expanded in recent years to encompass such matters of a performance nature. This extension of auditing, in many instances, has been a direct result of an expansion of the scope of accountability—both specified and implied. The force behind this extension is an increased awareness on the part of the public, the press, and governmental officials of the need—in fact, the necessity—for greater economy, efficiency, and effectiveness of governmental organizations and programs. What once were implied responsibilities are now being clearly specified.

By spelling out acceptable performance in legislation, regulations, or guidelines, governmental authorities, in turn, have extended the scope of auditing of these programs to include evaluations of such performance. Hence, the auditor, in some instances, must review performance matters, because acceptable minimum standards of performance accountability are spelled out in the law. Thus, the scope of auditing as an accountability device has been expanding because accountability has been expanding. However, auditing has also received pressure to expand because of its potential as a managment-control technique.

Auditing as a Management Control Technique

Management control, like accountability, also implies a review; the main difference is a matter of emphasis. Accountability implies a review for purposes of supervising or evaluating the subordinate manager. Management control, on the other hand, implies a review for purposes of aiding or assisting both the higher authority (audit recipient) and the subordinate manager (auditee).

Auditors traditionally have made suggestions to management as a by-product of the usual accountability audit. In recent years, however, the potential of auditing as a management-control technique has been increasingly recognized. As a result, a number of auditors have been encouraged, both by management and through their own professional activities, to extend the scope of their audits and, at the same time, to deemphasize accountability and to accentuate management control.

There has also been a movement to make auditing in the government environment more oriented to the objectives of management control. Both through appropriately worded audit reports and in their own internal-audit guides, some state and federal auditors have emphasized the positive aspect of aiding management and improving future operations rather than criticizing past actions. Thus, auditing is increasingly used as a management control technique because of a growing acceptance of and desire for this kind of auditing on the part of both management and the auditing profession.

Auditing as an Instrument to Promote Better Management

Although the scope of auditing in many areas encompasses matters of a management or performance nature, a crucial question remains: Can improved management be better accomplished through coercion (accountability) or cooperation (management control)? It would seem that auditing would be more effective as an instrument for the improvement of management if the objectives of auditing were oriented more toward management control instead of accountability.

However, accountability must and will continue to be a cornerstone of organizational systems—particularly those of government, where public trust is paramount. Also, by its very nature, auditing is irrevocably linked to accountability. Even when an audit report is used primarily for management control at the auditee level, there still exists an environment of accountability—that is, an environment of authority and responsibility. In other words, the auditor reports primarily to the higher authority to whom the agency or individual under audit is responsible. When an independent examination is (1) for the exclusive benefit of the subordinate manager, (2) solely for management control at the subordinate levels, and (3) not associated with accountability, then it is more properly considered a management review of service rather than an audit.

It would appear that the very nature of auditing inhibits the attainment of optimum cooperation from the agency or individual under review. However, even though auditing is basically an accountability device, it has been demonstrated that the fiscal aspects of auditing often can be deemphasized in favor of more positive aspects of management control. Thus, the modern objectives of auditing can be viewed as a balance between accountability and management assistance/control.

Types and Characteristics of Audits

The U.S. Comptroller General has classified and described audits under the following categories[5]:

1. Financial and compliance—determines (a) whether financial operations are properly conducted, (b) whether the financial reports of an audited entity are presented fairly, and (c) whether the entity has complied with applicable laws and regulations.

   Examinations of financial transactions, accounts, and reports and the compliance with applicable laws and regulations shall include sufficient audit work to determine whether:

    a. The audited entity is maintaining effective control over revenues, expenditures, assets and liabilities.

    b. The audited entity is properly accounting for resource liabilities, and operations.

    c. The financial reports contain accurate, reliable, and useful financial data and are fairly presented.

    d. The entity is complying with the requirements of applicable laws and regulations.

2. *Economy and efficiency*—determines whether the entity is managing or utilizing its resources (personnel, property, space, and so forth) in an economical and efficient manner and the causes of any inefficiencies or uneconomical practices, including inadequacies in management information systems, administrative procedures, or organizational structure.

A review of efficiency and economy shall include inquiry into whether, in carrying out its responsibilities, the audited entity is giving due consideration to conservation of its resources and minimum expenditures of effort. Examples of uneconomical practices or inefficiencies the auditor should be alert to include:

    a. Procedures, whether officially prescribed or merely followed, which are ineffective or more costly than justified.

    b. Duplication of effort by employees or between organizational units.

    c. Performance of work which serves little or no useful purpose.

    d. Inefficient or uneconomical use of equipment.

    e. Overstaffing in relation to work to be done.

    f. Faulty buying practices and accumulation of unneeded or excess quantities of property, materials, or supplies.

    g. Wasteful use of resources.

Efficiency and economy are both relative terms and it is virtually impossible to give an opinion as to whether an organization has reached the maximum practicable level of either. Therefore, it is not contemplated in these standards that the auditor will be called upon to give such an opinion.

3. *Program results*—determines whether the desired results or benefits are being achieved, whether the objectives established by the legislature or other authorizing body are being met, and whether the agency has considered alternatives which might yield desired results at a lower cost.

A review of the results of programs or activities shall include inquiry into the results or benefits achieved and whether the programs or activities are meeting established objectives. The auditor should consider:

    a. The relevance and validity of the criteria used by the audited entity to judge effectiveness in achieving program results.

b. The appropriateness of the methods followed by the entity to eval-
    uate effectiveness in achieving program results.

c. The accuracy of the data accumulated.

d. The reliability of the results obtained.

Another classification more directly related to performance auditing is
the following: (1) All efficiency and economy audits and all compliance
audits that result in more efficient and economical operations are called
"management audits." (2) All audits that review the results of programs or
activities are called "program audits." (3) Both management and program
audits are "performance audits." All other types of audits are called
"financial" and "fiscal-compliance audits," and although they deal with
the financial performance of management and employees of an organization, these audits do not meet the criteria and/or objectives of performance
audits. Anthony and Herzlinger refer to the second and third types of audits
listed in the Comptroller General's report as operational audits, suggesting
that:

> Operational auditing, if properly conducted, can be a valuable tool in the
> management of a nonprofit organization. If not properly conducted, how-
> ever, it can be a source of friction and frustration, with no constructive
> results. . . . Operational auditing serves as a useful purpose if, and only if,
> it shows how *future* decisions can be made in a better way, that is, if it dem-
> onstrates that changes in policies and procedures should be made.[6]

The Elements of an Audit

The following definition of auditing identifies the distinct elements that the
auditor must consider.

> Auditing is the planning for, the obtaining of, and the evaluating of suf-
> ficient relevant, material and competent evidence by an independent
> auditor on the audit objective of whether an entity's management or em-
> ployees have or have not accepted and carried out efficiently, effectively, or
> economically appropriate accounting, management, or operational prin-
> ciples, policies, or standards. From this evidence, the auditor comes to an
> opinion or conclusion on the objective. He then reports his opinion or con-
> clusion to a third party.[7]

Thus, the auditor must: (1) identify an appropriate standard (appropriate
accounting, management, or operational principles, policies, or standards),
(2) review the action of management or its employees (whether an entity's
management or employees have or have not accepted and carried out appropriate responsibilities), and (3) assess the results of the actions as measured
against the standards (efficiently, effectively, or economically).

Three Basic Elements

The elements of an audit have been defined as follows:

1. *Criteria*—any appropriate standards or group of standards that can be used to measure the actions of management, employees, or their delegated agents in any audit situation.
2. *Causes*—actions of management, employees, or their delegated agents that took place or action that should have taken place in carrying out their assigned resposibilities.
3. *Effects*—results achieved as determined by comparing actions taken (causes) with the appropriate standard (criteria).[8]

These three elements are the foundation for whatever the auditor finds in his review of agency/individual activities. They are not necessarily everything reported to the higher authority, for the auditor often provides background data and scope of audit information to let the reader know more about the conditions pertaining to the conclusion of the audit. The auditor also may recommend certain actions to be taken. The basic audit conclusion, however, always is composed of these three essential elements.

The auditor cannot reach a conclusion from evidence unless fairly specific guidelines are available as to the nature of what is to be audited, for evidence should only be gathered relating to the specific objectives of the audit. Therefore, the audit objective is a question or a statement at the start of the detailed examination concerning the results expected. The evidence gathered will allow the auditor to reach a conclusion on the statement or to answer the question. This statement of the audit objective should include the same three elements as found in the audit conclusion—criteria, causes, and effects.

Audit Evidence

Audit evidence represents facts and information used by the auditor as a basis to come to a conclusion on the audit objective. The information must be relevant, material, and competent. There also must be enough evidence to significantly influence the mind of the auditor, or any other person who may use the information from the audit, to come to the appropriate conclusion on the audit objective.

All information found in an audit is not evidence. Background data often are used to set the scene for the report or to provide information that would lead to the evidence. Recommendations and conclusions are extensions of the audit for management's possible use; they are not evidence but are based on evidence. Opinions are not evidence and should not be used as evidence. Assertions, implications, or innuendoes are not evidence and should not be used as a basis for the auditor to come to a conclusion on the audit objective.

Evidence must be gathered on all three elements of the audit objective to come to an appropriate conclusion on that objective. The evidence must be relevant, material, and competent. *Relevancy* means that the information is related to the criteria of the audit objective. *Materiality* means that the information is significant. *Competency* means that the information comes from a competent source.

Sufficient evidence must be obtained to come to the appropriate conclusion. Sufficiency varies with the type of information obtained. Some information, such as direct evidence, may influence an auditor to come to a conclusion on his audit objective with only a small amount of information. Other types of information, such as circumstantial evidence, require a great deal more information to influence the auditor toward a conclusion than does direct evidence.

The auditor often obtains data to make certain analyses. This analysis in turn provides information that is good evidence—analytical evidence. Other sources of information used as evidence are from records, from interviews or written requests, or from observations by the auditor. The auditor should always use the best evidence available. For example, a copy of a document should never be used if the original can be obtained. Second-hand information should never be used if information can be obtained directly.

With a statement of the audit objective and with sufficient relevant, material, and competent evidence, the auditor should be able to come up with a report to an appropriate third party or use it as a basis for the second party to improve his management control.

The Phases of the Audit

There are four basic phases of an audit: (1) preliminary survey, (2) review and testing of management control, (3) detailed examination, and (4) audit report. Table 11-1 provides a conceptual model of the four basic phases of an audit.

The discussion to this point has focused on the latter two stages. The point has been made that the audit report—the final product of an audit—has three essential elements: the criteria, the causes, and the effects. The audit objective also is based on these same three elements. Information developed to support a conclusion on the audit objective is *evidence*. These two steps in the developing of an audit comprise the report development and detailed examination phases of an audit.

Table 11-1
A Conceptual Model for Auditing and Communicating Information about and to Management

	The Audit		The Communication	
	Phase I: *Define Possible Objective,* *Consider Alternative Objectives*	*Phase II:* *Delimit Objective*	*Phase III:* *Come to Conclusion on* *Objective*	*Phase IV:* *Report Conclusion*

	Auditors:
	1. Should obtain background information on the area being considered
	2. Should obtain evidence on one or more of the elements—criteria, causes, or effects—of a possible audit objective in the management process being audited:
	  a. by analyzing background data
	  b. by interviews, records examinations, or observations
		Auditors
		1. Should obtain additional background information on the management area being reviewed
		2. Should obtain sufficient evidence on audit objective to determine:
		  a. that there could be a reasonable and firm criteria
		  b. that action or lack of action at one or more levels of responsibility could cause an effect
			Auditors
			1. Should obtain additional background information
			2. Should obtain additional evidence on the audit objective to determine:
			  a. the acceptability and appropriateness of criteria and that any arguments against acceptability and appropriateness of criteria can be rebutted
			  b. the specific action or lack of action at levels involved that caused the effects
				Auditors
				1. Should obtain additional background information needed to communicate conclusion on audit objective examined in Phases I, II, and III
				2. Should communicate the conclusion to the audit objective:
				  a. should set the scene through the use of background data and statement of the audit objective

3. Should assert the other element or elements to have a possible audit objective

4. Should assert alternative criteria and other elements to establish possible alternative objectives

5. If possible alternative objectives are to be considered, should obtain evidence on one or more elements of the possible alternative audit objective when no evidence has previously been obtained

6. Should summarize evidence and assertions

7. Should conclude from evidence and assertions that they:
   a. should go to Phase II on the audit objective or
   b. should stop

c. that the possible effects could be significant

d. that evidence could not be obtained on the three elements of the audit objective

3. Should summarize the evidence obtained

4. Should conclude whether the evidence warrants that they
   a. should go to Phase III, or
   b. should stop

c. the significance of the effects

d. that for the audit objective, no appropriate criteria, no determinable causes, or no significant effects can be determined

3. Should summarize evidence in terms of criteria, causes, and effects

4. Should conclude from the summarized evidence that the effects are significant when the results of the actions are evaluated against the criteria

5. If the evidence supports the conclusion, should report finding, Phase IV

6. If the evidence is not sufficient to support conclusion:
   a. should obtain additional evidence to support conclusion, and report finding
   b. should stop

b. should provide reader sufficient evidence on criteria, causes, and effects to let him come to the same conclusion on the audit objective as the auditors

3. Should provide recommendations to the proper levels of management to carry out criteria as standard for future management actions

Source: Adapted from Leo Herbert, *Auditing the Performance of Management* (Belmont, Calif.: Lifetime Learning Publications, 1979) pp. 38, 39, 44, and 45, and original manuscript. Reprinted with permission.

Certain other information, other than evidence, is needed during these two phases of the examination—background data and recommendations, for example. Recommendations come about as a result of the audit, but background data should be obtained during the early phases of the audit. The preliminary survey is used to develop background data sufficient to determine the type of audit to be made and to identify possible audit objectives. The auditor only needs enough information on each element of the audit objective to be convinced that it is worthwhile to continue the examination. If so, the auditor would then continue to gather information from actual operating conditions (that is, management control). The process of reviewing management control is to follow a transaction through the system or organization, that is, to start with a determination of requirements, examine procedures for acquiring and distributing resources, determine the performance of these resources, and observe the impacts or consequences of the use of these resources.

Notes

1. Peter L. McMickle and Gene Elrod, *Auditing to Improve Departments of Education—The AIDE Project* (Montgomery, Ala.: Alabama Department of Education, 1974), chap. 3.

2. J. Richard Aronson and Eli Schwartz, eds., *Management Policies in Local Government Finance* (Washington, D.C.: International City Management Association, 1975), p. 297.

3. American Institute of Certified Public Accountants, *Codification of Statements on Auditing Standards* (New York: AICPA, 1977), p. 243.

4. Ibid.

5. The Comptroller General of the United States, *Standards for Audit of Governmental Organizations, Programs, Activities, and Functions* (Washington, D.C.: General Accounting Office, 1974), pp. 2, 11, 12.

6. Robert N. Anthony and Regina Herzlinger, *Management Control in Nonprofit Organizations* (Homewood, Ill.: Richard D. Irwin, 1975), pp. 311–312.

7. Leo Herbert, *Auditing the Performance of Management* (Belmont, Calif.: Lifetime Learning Publications, 1979), p. 6. Reprinted with permission from the original manuscript.

8. Ibid.

12 Implementation of a Management Control System

The implementation of a new management control system or the subsequent revision of an existing system can be a traumatic experience. As a minimum, changes in management control procedures will impact the way in which plans are made and programs are developed. Such changes will alter the procedures for evaluating performance, both by program activities and from the standpoint of individuals. New patterns of communications will emerge as a consequence of changes in management control systems. And new information—presumably better information—will be available to assist managers in carrying out their decisions-making and administrative responsibilities. All these changes will take some getting use to. In addition, studies leading to the development of improved management controls may uncover needed changes in organizational relations—in the established structure and functional interfaces within the organization. And these organizational changes may be even more upsetting than the procedural changes that may be necessary to implement the management-control system.

Implementation in the Public Sector

Management control is more difficult in public agencies than in private, profit-oriented organizations. The measure of profit provides a semiautomatic "red flag" in day-to-day management decisions and can serve as an important criterion for assessing alternative courses of action, as well as a measure of performance. The absence of this objective in the public sector, however, makes the development and application of planning and control even more important.

Benefits and Costs of Management Control

An organization can gain two major benefits from a good management control system: (1) better plans related to organizational objectives, which, in many cases, can be based on analyses of the relative costs and benefits of alternative courses of action; and (2) better control, that is, greater assur-

315

ance that activities will be carried out as efficiently and effectively as possible in accomplishing organizational objectives. Although control is not as glamorous as planning, and often is viewed as an unpleasant task, it is vital that top management recognize that both functions are essential. Planning and control are complementary responsibilities of management; one cannot operate effectively without the other. Regardless of how well it may be designed, a management-control system will be ineffective unless top management adopts the attitude that ensuring the efficient and effective use of resources is vital in public organizations.

Implementation often is more difficult in the public sector than in a profit-oriented organization, because system changes are likely to represent a greater departure from past practices. Many of the basic concepts of management control are taken for granted in the private sector—accrual-accounting procedures, cost and responsibility centers, the relationship between the assignments of individuals and performance results, and so forth. In the environment of most profit-oriented organizations, a formal management-control system may be viewed as a refinement of existing concepts and procedures and not the introduction of a fundamentally new process. Many public organizations do not have even the rudiments of satisfactory management controls. At the same time, the climate that is essential for the functioning of such a system may not be readily available. Thus, the introduction of a new system can represent substantial change in the established way of doing business, which can be viewed with considerable alarm (and generate significant resistance) by those within the organization.

Such problems are not nearly so severe in the implementation of an operating control system, as distinguished from a management control system. New procedures for processing payroll, or for maintaining inventory information, or for handling new state or federal regulations regarding the accountability of intergovernmental transfer funds (for example, grants and contracts) may encounter various technical problems. With some perseverance, however, these technical problems can be worked out with minimum negative impact in terms of serious organizational problems.

Often the major impediment to the implementation of such operating control procedures is the uncertainty that may surround the "ripple effects," that is, the further implications for subsequent organizational changes. If these operational procedures are technically sound, and if appropriate assurances are communicated early to eliminate the uncertainty of these ripple effects, it is less likely that resistance will develop among members of the organization. As soon as they are convinced that such changes will help them do their jobs better, they will support their implementation.

Essential Prerequisite—Top-Management Commitment

Different viewpoints are evident in the literature regarding the essential prerequisites for the successful implementation of improved management control procedures. One view is that the major impetus for such changes must come from within the organization—that managers at the operating level must request, welcome, and support such changes from the very outset. Rensis Likert labels this view as the "participative approach" and clearly supports such a bottom-up process.[1]

On the other hand, there are those who suggest that the impetus for change must come from top management—that support from operating managers would be desirable but is not essential. Robert Anthony and Regina Herzlinger support this view, suggesting that ". . . the driving force behind a new system must come from top management, . . . it is unlikely that a majority of operating managers will voluntarily embrace a new system in advance of its installation, let alone be enthusiastic advocates of it."[2] Although Likert and others believe that efforts to develop new systems must await the full support of operating managers, Anthony and Herzlinger assert that ". . . if systems designers wait until that day arrives, they will be quite old."[3]

Regardless of which approach is advocated, the active support and involvement of top management is a prime prerequisite to the successful implementation of a new or improved management control system. Without this support, the effort probably should not be undertaken, even with enthusiastic support from various operating managers within the organizational hierarchy.

Top-management support means more than acquiescence. Responsible managers must be willing to devote sufficient time and effort to fully understand the general concepts and objectives of such management control systems. They must explain to principal subordinates how these procedures will help them and the organization as a whole. If problems arise during the design and implementation of these procedures, top management must listen to opposing viewpoints and then make decisions that will resolve such problems and remove impediments. The top manager may also have to "do battle" with outside interest groups, which might otherwise seek to prevent the adoption of such systems. It often is tempting for top management to fall back on the old saw: "We have no choice but to implement these procedures to meet externally imposed requirements." However, in so doing, the basis has been laid for less-than-enthusiastic support (and perhaps organized resistance) from within the organization.

If systems designers are not convinced that an appropriate degree of support will be forthcoming from top management, then they may be well advised not to attempt to implement any major system changes. It may be possible, however, under such circumstance to implement parts of a management-control system (for example, various operating controls) or to install a more integrated system in a segment of the total organization (for example, in areas where external requirements for accountability are most evident) in the hopes that the more comprehensive system can be built incrementally on the success of this foundation.

Successful Implementation—A Political Process

If the implementation of a management control system is successful, the organization will be managed in a different way—this is, after all, the basic objective of such a system. This success may present a significant challenge to the systems designers, however, because the human element is involved—attitudes, perceptions, misconceptions, and biases regarding the manifest and latent intent of management control.

Efforts to involve operating managers in the development of the management control system and to educate them to the benefits that they will derive from such a system can help to reduce negative attitudes. However, education alone probably cannot eliminate totally these problems. They will disappear only after the system has been in full operation for a substantial time. It is important for systems designers to recognize these potential sources of resistance and to accommodate to them as best as possible. As Anthony and Herzlinger observe, systems designers

> . . . can expect less than full cooperation in obtaining the information needed for systems design, and they can expect that efforts will be made to delay the introduction of the system in the hope that if it is delayed, it may never materialize. . . . They should understand that the installation of a new system is a political process. It involves pressure, persuasion, and compromise in proper proportions as in the case with any important political action.[4]

It is always easier to implement a new management-control system when operations are expanding and budgets are increasing. Whether warranted or not, operating managers will associate such control measures as the consequence of growth—a "necessary evil" that accompanies boom times. It is much more difficult to implement a new management control system in periods of program contraction and funding reduction. Under such circumstances, the system is likely to be associated with a "tightening of the screws." Unfortunately, all too often more systematic management controls are not deemed necessary in periods of growth and only are called on in periods of tight fiscal resources.

The concept of *responsibility centers* should be emphasized in the development and implementation of management control systems. As defined in chapter 3, a responsibility center is that subunit of the larger organization where the purpose or objectives are clearly defined and the resource inputs required to carry out these objectives are under the direct control of the center's manager. The relationship of program activities to management responsibility for these activities must be clearly identified. Operating managers should be held accountable for program performance only to the extent that the wherewithal has been provided to carry out agreed on objectives. In the absence of such a clear delineation of responsibility, the management control system will be viewed, at best, as merely a mechanism for reporting performance to top management and, at worst, as an unjustified and unwarranted "spy system."

Operating managers will likely support the new system if they are convinced that, on balance, it will benefit them in carrying out their assigned responsibilities. The new system will provide operating managers with better information about the activities and performance of those staff members for whom they are responsible. With this information the operating managers should have a better basis for directing and controlling these efforts of subordinates. By the same token, however, operating managers can readily perceive that the new system will also provide better information to those individuals in the management hierarchy to whom they are responsible. For operating managers, management control is a two-way street. If the proposed system provides information that reduces the uncertainty about the tasks of others on the staff, the manager will likely support it. If, on the other hand, the uncertainty of superiors about the manager's performance is reduced, he or she may resist the system (depending on personal interpretations of how such information will be received by "higher ups").

As has been suggested, the successful implementation of a more comprehensive management control system may be dependent, in part, on the acquiescence, if not direct support, of agencies outside the unit targeted for such procedures. For example, the initiation of new budgetary procedures (for example, program budgeting or zero-base budgeting) within a given agency may have significant implications for other agencies in terms of the compatibility of information or procedures. As noted in previous chapters, the accounting systems appropriate to these budget formats are quite different from the more traditional line-item/object-of-expenditure format. Failure to provide appropriate crosswalk mechanisms to ensure compatibility with accounting data from prior years may result in a significant information gap, which, in turn, could adversely affect the implementation of these new budget procedures. Thus, a dual system may be needed to minimize the impact of the new procedures on supporting agencies.

task. On the one hand, the job requires someone who not only can deal effectively with managers at all levels, including top management, but also has a fairly broad understanding of management controls. It also requires someone who is willing to devote careful attention to detail—a large part of the time must be spent on rather tedious matters.

Systems designers operate in a staff relationship in carrying out their technical responsibilities and need ready access to top management, either in person or through not more than one intermediary. The management control system must reflect the style of management that the top leadership of the organization wants. The only way to ensure that this character is reflected in the proposed system design is to discuss these matters directly with top management. Top management must set the example in terms of the importance of the system-design effort by their willingness to take time away from other pressing problems to discuss their management-information needs and expectations. Few, if any, staff specialists require a corresponding amount of an operating manager's time. Therefore, top management's participation in these efforts will help to convince operating managers to devote the necessary and appropriate time and effort to the task.

Professional systems-design organizations have existed for several decades. Such consulting groups have the general expertise and specific knowledge of appropriate management control techniques to assist many organizations in the design of appropriate systems. Outside consultants often are perceived by operating managers as unbiased—they have no particular "ax to grind" and can take a more detached view of organizational problems. This objective perspective, coupled with their expertise, can add prestige and respectability to the systems-design effort.

It is important to recognize, however, that a control system ultimately must be an integral part of the management process. Therefore, although an outside firm may be engaged to assist in the development of such systems, in-house personnel must also be involved. All good systems-design firms insist on such involvement. They recognize that, when they depart, there must be a continuing staff effort on the part of those within the organization who regard the system as "their" system. A system designed by consultants, described in an impressive report, and turned over to the organization for implementation is usually soon forgotten.

The Element of Time

In retrospect, it seems evident that one of the principal reasons for the failure of planning-programming-budgeting systems (PPBS) in the federal government was that not enough time was allowed for the design and implementation of the system. In August 1965, to the chagrin of some of the strongest advocates for PPBS, President Johnson announced publicly that nearly all federal agencies would have a PPB system in place by July 1967, less than eighteen months later. In the absence of an adequate foundation for a satisfactory system and as a consequence of the time lost at the outset in "window-dressing" efforts by many agencies, the fate of PPBS was quickly sealed. By the late 1960s, its demise was being eulogized by even its strongest supporters.

Although it is difficult to be specific about an appropriate period required to successfully design and implement management controls, in a large organization two to three years may elapse between the time a decision is made to initiate systems development and the date that the change over to the new system is made. The time available is never quite enough, because there are always refinements that could be made that would be worthwhile. However, if enough time were allowed for all these fine-tuning efforts, the system might never go into operation.

Developing the Information Base

Some operating managers may resist the implementation of a management control system in which information is collected and furnished to them by a presumably impartial source outside their own agency or program. Direct access and control of data is both a matter of prestige—others must come to "the source" for information—and of security—data can be screened and interpreted to provide information that will cast favorable light on the agency's programs. Even when the data are presented in their raw form, subject to little interpretation, there is still greater security in providing these data directly rather than having them gathered and presented to superiors by a third party, no matter how impartial that group may strive to be.

Ask the User

An obvious starting point in designing a management control system is to ask managers what information they need to carry out their responsibilities more effectively and efficiently. However, this approach seldom is sufficient to ensure an adequate information base, because operating managers often do not know what information they need and/or are not aware of available information that would be of use to them. Therefore, the informational needs of operating managers often must be uncovered by indirect methods. Operating managers may be interviewed, for example, to determine their perceptions of the various program tasks that they have been assigned, the procedures necessary to carry out these assignments, and the objectives to which these activities should be directed. Relations between assigned, the procedures necessary to carry out these assignments, and the objectives to which these activities should be directed. Relations between responsibility center also should be identified. Based on this information, a management-control system can be designed to provide the information that managers should need.

Discussions with operating managers can point up the feasibility of implementing certain aspects of a system. Top management may want certain kinds of information that managers on the firing line may be able to demonstrate would be impractical to collect. Operating managers can also uncover mistaken assumptions about the availability or exact nature of data. Proposed reporting formats should be tested out with operating managers to determine if the information is appropriate for their intended use and accurate in terms of information that they generate.

It is much less costly to develop management information from raw data that has been gathered for other puposes than to develop new data specifically for purposes of management control. It may be necessary to sacrifice some "ideal" type of management information if slightly less desirable data can be obtained from existing sources.

Information Content of the System

The control system should contain two principal account classifications, structured by (1) programs and (2) organizational responsibility. At the lowest level, the building blocks of these accounts should relate both to *program elements* and to *responsibility centers.* Summaries are obtained by aggregating these building blocks by program elements, subprograms, and programs and by various levels of responsibility within the organizational hierarchy. The program structure should be designed to provide a basis for (1)making program decisions, (2) comparing costs and outputs of similar programs, and (3) setting appropriate user rates for those services that are provided on a full-cost-recovery basis. If each program is assigned to a separate responsibility center then the program structure and the organization structure can be one and the same. No further effort is required to invent program labels for the work done by these centers. In any case, program elements and, if feasible, subprograms should be defined in such a way that quantitative output measures can be associated with each.

The system should contain both historical data (for example, records of financial transactions) and data on estimated future costs and outputs. To be most effective, the historical data should be defined and structured in the same way as the estimated future data. A program budget that is not supported by an accounting system that collects historical data in the exact same terms as the programmatic data does not provide an adequate basis for control. As noted at the outset, a principal weakness of many newly adopted program-budget systems is the failure to provide appropriate accounting support.

Inputs are measured in terms of costs, that is, monetary measures of the amount of resources used for some purpose. Operating cost incurred in a specific period are the expenses for that period. Expenses should be measured on an accrual basis. Failure to use accrual accounting is a fundamental weakness in some management-control systems, for without it other important control techniques are not possible. Even if accounts are kept on a cash and/or obligation basis, as is required with many governmental agencies, expenses should be measured on an accrual basis, and expense data should be used as a basis for control.

Cost comparisons should be made in terms of full cost, that is, direct cost plus a fair share of indirect costs. The accounts associated with the program structure may only reflect direct costs, however, with the indirect costs required for program decisions obtained from estimates made outside the formal accounts. All items of direct cost should be reported by responsibility center, whether or not these costs are controllable by the center manager.

To the extent possible, the principal objectives of the organization (and its programs) should be stated in quantitative terms, and performance should be measured in these terms. If objectives cannot be measured directly, valid surrogate measures should be developed. Measures should reflect effectiveness (accomplishment of objectives) as well as performance (measures of the quantity of effort).

A management control system is predicated on the notion that some measure of output is better than none. At the same time, however, the limitations of existing output measures should be recognized, and there should be continuous search for new, more valid measures. Only those output measures that are actually used in the management control system should be collected. Since many people dislike the idea of accountability, the collection of output measures that have no forseeable application only further aggrevates this basis for resistance to further management control.

Information Crosswalk

In implementing a new management control system, it is important to ensure information continuity, in terms of both the existing data base and other data users. Often a new system may be implemented in one segment of the larger organization on a trial basis or is designed to serve the specific needs of a particular functional area within the organization (for example, to provide further accountability for contracts and grants or other forms of external funding). In such instances, explicit provision must be made to cross walk data from the new system's format to other established formats within the organization. It also may be necessary to develop crosswalks for outside agencies that have grown accustomed to receiving information in a certain format.

The crosswalking process requires that information in management control records (for example, accounts) be reclassified into the file formats required by agencies outside the system. In some cases, this reclassification can be exact; that is, detailed data exist in such a form that they can be rearranged in the prescribed format. More often, however, the reclassification can only be approximate—some records must be subdivided, combined, and/or reclassified, more or less arbitrarily, to obtain the summaries required. To the extent possible, however, every effort should be made to hold such crosswalks to a minimum, since from the standpoint of the organization this is a relatively nonproductive activity.

In some cases, it may be necessary to operate a dual system. This requirement arises when the control expectations of one group are fundamentally incompatible with the system adopted for management-control purposes. For example, a dual system may be required when general-fund accounts are maintained on a modified cash basis but federally funded projects require accounting information on a modified accrual basis (Federal Management Circular 74-7, on federal grants, contracts, or other agreements with state and local governments, stipulates that when a federal sponsoring agency requires reporting on an accrual basis, the recipient shall not be required to establish an accrual accounting system but shall develop such accrual data for its reports on the basis of an analysis of the documentation on hand). The existence of a dual system can result in mixed signals to the operating managers. And when these signals conflict, which can happen quite frequently, managers must decide which signal is stronger.

In designing a new system, it is necessary to determine what features of the existing system, if any, should be retained and how the transition from the old to the new system should be accomplished. It usually is neither feasible nor desirable to abandon entirely the old system. Operating managers will have much to learn about the new system, and to the extent that it incorporates familiar practices—particularly familiar terminology—from the existing system, the new system will seem less strange to them. There are obvious advantages to running the new system in parallel with the existing system until the bugs have been worked out. This approach avoids the possibility that bugs in the new system may result in the permanent loss of vital data.

It is important, however, that top management use information from the new system as soon as it becomes available. Operating managers are not likely to take the plunge in using the new systems format until top management breaks the ice. The utilization by top management is particularly important when a dual system is in place.

If the new and old systems are run in parallel, the old system should be discarded slightly before managers become completely comfortable with the new system. Thus, "holdouts" will have no choice but to use the new system when the old data are no longer available.

Education through Participation

The importance of a thorough educational program as a part of the installation of a new management-control system cannot be overemphasized. All too often, insufficient time and attention are given to this effort, often with dire consequences. In the rush to solve the many technical problems that surround the implementation of the system, not enough time is left to mount the educational program.

The preparation of manuals, sample reports, and other explanatory materials is a necessary part of the educational process. These materials are not the most important part of the process, however. Operating managers must be convinced that the new system, in fact, is going to be used and that it will help them do a better job. Although those individuals who have developed the system and have a detailed familiarity with the technical aspects of its operations must play a major role in these educational efforts, managers must also be involved. In fact, the best way to "pass the word" is to have managers teach managers; that is, top management should discuss the new system with its immediate subordinates, who then carry the message to their subordinates, and so on. Systems designers can provide technical support at such educational meetings, but it is preferable that these sessions be conducted by managers. Since the teachers must themselves become more fully indoctrinated, this process aids in the education of all those involved. At a major northeastern university, for example, the president initiated a new management-information system by installing terminals in the offices of all the vice-presidents, substituting electronic-mail messages for the more traditional written memoranda. The vice-presidents quickly adapted to this system (as a matter of survival) and began communicating with academic deans and other administrators through the same process. In short order, the system was activated throughout the campus. Once a system goes into operation, even on a trial basis, the use of the information that it generates is the best educational device available.

In promoting the use of a new system, however, it is important not to oversell its potential. A management control system is an aid to management—it is not a substitute for good management practices. Even with the best system, data must be analyzed and interpreted by managers, and judgment must be exercised in decision making based on this information. Allowance must be made for the inadequacies or unavailability of data. Although the system can provide certain decisions parameters, it cannot make decisions—managers must continue to exercise judgment regarding the exceptions that prove the rules. Such caveats must be empasized during educational processes, otherwise managers who are skeptical or are aware of such limitations will regard the whole effort as the work of impractical theorists.

Steps to Implementation

Anthony and Herzlinger suggest eight major steps for the design and installation of a management control system, as follows[5]:

1. Planning—an operations plan should be developed for the design and installation of the system, including a detailed schedule or timetable of activities to be undertaken and a careful delineation of responsibilities.

2. Analysis of objectives and organization—the objective and existing structure of the organization should be analyzed in an effort to identify any shortcomings in existing systems, as well as any gaps between real and perceived objectives.

3. Inventory of current information—existing sources of information should be carefully examined; much of this information is collected for operational needs (for example, payroll, inventory transactions, and so on) and can be included in the management-control system at little additional cost.

4. Develop control structure—the control structure usually is developed from the general to the specific, starting with major program categories and working down to program elements and activities; appropriate output measures should be formulated for each level within the structure.[6]

5. Develop procedures—once a tentative control structure has been delineated the specific procedures for data gathering, analysis, and reporting must be developed; some iteration between steps 4 and 5 may be necessary.

6. Test proposed structure and procedures—this test may be initiated in one part of the organization or for one functional area of responsibility; such testing of structure and procedures should provide concrete examples of the essential materials to be included in the broader educational program.

7. Education—after initial pilot tests, a broader educational program should be developed and implemented.

8. Implementation—to the extent possible, the new system should be

operated concurrently with the existing system, and, as soon as feasible, obsolete elements of the existing system should then be phased out.

It often is desirable to implement a new system in stages. In this way, managers can become accustomed to the techniques required at one stage before proceeding to the next. A possible staging sequence is as follows:

1. Develop budgets for direct costs by programs (or decision packages) and responsibility centers (or budget units), requiring rough output measures (performance measures and measures of effectiveness); retain existing accounting system; identify most critical service centers for full costing.

2. Improve output measures and expand service-center coverage.

3. Develop new accounting structure and begin to collect information in accordance with this new structure, educating managers to the use of this information through timely management reports.

4. Refine output measures and begin program-evaluation process through performance-auditing and productivity-monitoring procedures.

5. Expand the system by extending the service-center concept, initiating cost-allocation procedures, and depreciate capital facilities and equipment.

As has been suggested, it may not be feasible to install a new management control system in the whole organization all at one time. Initial efforts may have to be limited to one part of the organization where the results of such improvements would be most visible. Demonstrated success in one area can lead to more general acceptance of the system throughout the organization. It may also be appropriate to first implement a reporting system for management information and then to build on this base to a full-blown management control system.

Aaron Wildavsky offers ten "rules" to guide public officials in the implementation of management information and control systems. These guidelines are presented in a somewhat tongue-in-cheek fashion, but they provide a very pragmatic basis for avoiding the major pitfalls in the implementation of new management systems.

1. The rule of skepticism—when presented with the initial concept of an improved management system, public officials should exercise a good deal of skepticism (as Wildavsky suggests, consultants have a capacity for self-deception by listening to their own sales pitch).

2. The rule of delay—officials must be prepared to give the system adequate time to develop and to face periodic setbacks in its implementation. As Wildavsky observes: "if it works at all, it won't work soon."

3. The rule of complexity—"When a new information system contains more variables than, shall we say, the average age of the officials who are to use it, or more data bits than anyone can count in a year, the chances of failure are very high.

4. The rule of thumb—the volume of data output from the system

must be of manageable proportions—not any thicker than the analyst's thumb—if it is to be useful and comprehensible to the manager.

5. The rule of childlike questions—the public official should ask many questions regarding the usefulness of data, their acquisition costs, and their relevance to decisions.

6. The rule of length and width—the length of the data flow over time should not involve more than three or four links (that is, the points through which it must pass); otherwise it is likely that data will be lost, diverted, or misinterpreted. The usefulness and appropriateness of data will be significantly reduced if information must go through more than one level in the organization (the width of the band of clientele).

7. The rule of anticipated anguish—public officials must be prepared to invest personnel, time, and money to overcome system breakdowns as they occur. Essentially a restatement of Murphy's Law—"most of the things that can go wrong, will."

8. The rule of known evil—people are used to working with the existing system; they know the "fudge factors" necessary to overcome its shortcomings. In a new system, these relationships must be reestablished in areas of some uncertainty and risk.

9. The rule of the mounting mirage—the possible benefits of better information are readily apparent in the present—everybody could use better information. However, the costs involved in developing better information must be incurred before the benefits are achieved. Therefore, there is a tendency to inflate the future benefits to compensate for the increased commitment of present resources.

10. The rule of discounting—anticipated benefits should significantly outweigh estimated costs.[7]

The Information Demon—Genius or Devil?

Around the turn of the century, Clerk Maxwell, an English physicist, suggested a very clever way to overcome the Second Law of Thermodynamics. The Second Law has to do with the phenomenon of *entropy*—a measure of the unavailability of useful energy in a system. According to the Second Law, the general trend of all physical events is toward a state of maximum disorder, with a leveling down of differences among component elements. At this final state, all energy is degraded into evenly distributed heat of low temperature (maximum entropy), and the world process comes to a stop— the so-called heat death of the universe.

Maxwell envisioned a small, but very intelligent creature—a demon— who could see molecules and could serve as a gatekeeper between two containers of gas at equal temperature and pressure. By carefully opening and closing the gate, the demon could permit faster-moving molecules to move to one container, while slower molecules moved to the other. Over time, one container would get hotter and the other cooler and, thus, the available energy in the system—as measured by the temperature differential between the two containers—would be increased without adding any new energy to the system (other than Maxwell's smart demon). Thus, the Second Law of Thermodynamics would be circumvented.

Maxwell's demon, of course, is an allegory for anything that contributes *organization* to a disorganized or chaotic situation. Contemporary systems theory suggests that, in open systems, the process of entropy can be reversed and order can be restored to random arrangements of elements. The counterforces thus developed are referred to as *negentropy,* defined as "a measure of order or organization."[8] Two points concerning the concept of negentropy are noteworthy. First, even though negentropy can be evidenced as matter and/or energy, it is primarily considered to be synonymous with information. Second, there is a general tendency in open systems to create a contingency surplus of negentropy to "live on borrowed time during periods of crisis" and where possible, to "develop toward states of increased order and organization."[9]

The information demon can be a positive genius, designed to address a host of problems, "while reducing administrative costs as a percentage of total costs, through satisfaction of this increasingly voracious appetite for decision-influencing management information and information-related . . . administrative support services."[10] Or it can become a resource-demanding devil—an organizational black hole that can absorb considerable energy with little apparent payoff. The careful design and implementation of a management control system—to include the various elements discussed in this book—can contribute significantly toward the demon-genius—or at least can help avoid the demon-devil.

Notes

1. Rensis Likert, *New Patterns of Management* (New York: McGraw-Hill, 1961).

2. Robert N. Anthony and Regina Herzlinger, *Management Control in Nonprofit Organizations* (Homewood, Ill.: Richard D. Irwin, 1975), p. 316.

3. Ibid., p. 316.

4. Ibid., p. 323.

5. Ibid., pp. 330–331.

6. Initially, output measures may be rather crude in many cases and may have to be further refined with subsequent iterations of the system.

The design and implementation of the system should not be held up unduly because of such inadequacies, however.

7. Aaron Wildavsky, "Review of *Politicians, Bureaucrats and the Consultant,*" *Science* 28 (December 1973):1335-1338.

8. Ludwig von Bertalanffy, *General Systems Theory* (New York: George Braziller, 1968), p. 42.

9. Ibid., p. 41. For a further discussion of the application of these concepts to public management and planning, see Alan Walter Steiss, *Models for the Analysis and Planning of Urban Systems* (Lexington, Mass.: Lexington Books, D.C. Heath, 1974), chap. 7.

10. Robert C. Heterick, "Administrative Support Services," *Cause/Effect* 4 (November 1981):29.

Index of Names

Index of Subjects

About the Author

Alan Walter Steiss is associate dean for research administration at Virginia Polytechnic Institute and State University. He received the A.B. in psychology and sociology from Bucknell University and the M.A. and Ph.D. in urban and regional planning from the University of Wisconsin. Dr. Steiss has served at Virginia Tech as director of the Center for Urban and Regional Studies, chairman of the Urban and Regional Planning Program and Urban Affairs Program, chairman of the Division of Environmental and Urban Systems, and associate dean for research and graduate studies of the College of Architechture and Urban Studies. He has been a guest lecturer at several universities, including Rider College, New York University, the University of Wisconsin, Georgia Institute of Technology, Virginia Commonwealth University, the University of British Columbia, and the University of Virginia. He was formerly the head of statewide planning for the state of New Jersey and has served as consultant to the states of Wisconsin, New Jersey, Maryland, Virginia, South Carolina, New York, and Hawaii, the Trust Territory of the Pacific, and the Federal-State Land Use Planning Commission for Alaska. Dr. Steiss is the author of several books, including *Planning Administration: A Framework for Planning in State Government; Systemic Planning: Theory and Application* (with Anthony J. Catanese); *A Public Service Option for Architectural Curricula; Public Budgeting and Management; Models for the Analysis and Planning of Urban Systems; Urban Systems Dynamics; Dynamic Change and the Urban Ghetto* (with Michael Harvey, John Dickey, and Bruce Phelps); *Local Government Finance; Capital Facilities Planning and Debt Administration; Performance Administration* (with Gregory A. Daneke); and *Accounting, Budgeting and Control for Government Organizations* (with Leo Herbert and Larry N. Killough). He has contributed to numerous professional journals in the United States and abroad.

DATE DUE